Defining the nonprofit sector

Though the growth of the nonprofit, voluntary or third sector has been widely recognized throughout the world, considerable confusion persists about how to define this sector or what it contains. The present book fills this major gap, at both the global level through a comparative analysis and at the national level.

In the book's first part, Lester Salamon and Helmut Anheier provide the building blocks for a common definition and a common classification of this sector internationally whilst still recognizing the incredible diversity of voluntarism around the world. The main body of the book is a rich panorama of the nature of the nonprofit sector in thirteen nations from the developed, developing and post-socialist worlds. Included are the US, the UK, France, Germany, Italy, Sweden, Japan, India, Brazil, Egypt, Thailand, Ghana and Hungary.

Defining the nonprofit sector demonstrates beyond doubt that the division of societies into public and private sectors is much too simplistic. A third sector with its own characteristic features and dynamics has already emerged as a powerful force in the global economy.

Students, social scientists and policymakers interested in the nonprofit sector, social welfare policy, economics, public management and democratic practice will find this book of considerable interest.

Lester M. Salamon is Director of the Johns Hopkins Institute for Policy Studies and the Johns Hopkins Comparative Nonprofit Sector Project and Professor at the Johns Hopkins University. Helmut K. Anheier is Associate Director of the Project, a Senior Research Associate at the Johns Hopkins Instutute for Policy Studies, and Associate Professor of Sociology at Rutgers University.

Johns Hopkins Nonprofit Sector Series

edited by Lester M. Salamon and Helmut K. Anheier
Institute for Policy Studies, The Johns Hopkins University

Manchester University Press is proud to be publishing this
important new series, the product of the most comprehensive
comparative analysis of the global nonprofit sector ever
undertaken. The growth of the sector between the public and
the private, known variously as the nonprofit, voluntary or
third sector, is one of the most significant contemporary
developments in societies through the world. The books in this series
will cover the development and role of this sector in a broad cross-
section of nations, and also provide comparative, cross-
country analyses.

Johns Hopkins Nonprofit Sector Series 4

DEFINING THE NONPROFIT SECTOR

A cross-national analysis

Lester M. Salamon
and
Helmut K. Anheier

Manchester University Press

Manchester and New York

distributed exclusively in the USA by St. Martin's Press

hed by Manchester University Press
d Road, Manchester M13 9NR, UK
oom 400, 175 Fifth Avenue, New York, NY 10010, USA

uted exclusively in the USA
Martin's Press, Inc., 175 Fifth Avenue, New York
010, USA

Library Cataloguing-in-Publication Data
logue record for this book is available from the British Library

of Congress Cataloging-in-Publication Data
on. Lester M. Defining the nonprofit sector: a cross-national analysis /
Lester M. Salamon and Helmut K. Anheier.
    p. cm. — (Johns Hopkins nonprofit sector series: 4)
  ISBN 0–7190–4901–6. — ISBN 0–7190–4902–4 (alk. paper)
    1. Nonprofit organization—Cross-cultural studies.   I. Anheier
Helmut K., 1954–   II. Title.   III. Series..
  HD2769.15.S26   1997   95–39213
                                                                    CIP

ISBN 0 7190 4901 6 *hardback*
     0 7190 4902 4 *paperback*

First published 1997

01 00 99 98 97   10 9 8 7 6 5 4 3 2 1

Typeset in Great Britain
by Northern Phototypesetting Co Ltd, Bolton
Printed in Great Britain
by Bell & Bain Ltd, Glasgow

CONTENTS

v

Contents

FIGURES

TABLES

CONTRIBUTORS

Takayoshi Amenomori, Director of the Toyonaka Association for Intercultural Activities and Communication; he previously held the position of Senior Program Officer at the Japan Center for International Exchange in Tokyo, Japan.

Helmut K. Anheier, Associate Director of the Johns Hopkins Comparative Nonprofit Sector Project, and Associate Professor of Sociology, Rutgers University, New Jersey, USA.

Edith Archambault, Professor of Economics, University of Paris I – Sorbonne, and Director of the Laboratoire d'économie sociale, CRNS, France.

Lawrence Atingdui, (deceased), Economist and senior researcher at the Institute of Statistical, Social and Economic Research at the University of Ghana, Legon, Ghana.

Gian Paolo Barbetta, Lecturer in Economics at the Università Cattolica del Sacro Cuore, Milan, and a senior researcher at the Istituto per la Ricerca Sociale in Milan, Italy.

Amani Kandil, Sociologist at the University of Cairo and senior researcher with the Follow-up Committee for Arab NGOs Conference, Cairo, Egypt.

Jeremy Kendall, Economist and Research Officer at the Personal Social Services Research Unit (PSSRU), London School of Economics, England.

Martin Knapp, Professor of the Economics of Social Care and Deputy Director, PSSRU, London School of Economics, and Head of the Centre for the Economics of Mental Health, London Institute of Psychiatry, England.

Éva Kuti, Head of the Section on Voluntary Sector Statistics at the Central Statistical Office, Budapest, Hungary.

Leilah Landim, Research Coordinator at the Instituto de Estudos da Religiâo and Professor at the Federal University of Rio de Janeiro, Brazil.

Tommy Lundström, Historian and researcher at Sköndalsinstitutet in Stockholm, Sweden.

Amara Pongsapich, Professor of Sociology and Director of the Social Research Institute at Chulalongkorn University in Bangkok, Thailand.

Lester M. Salamon, Director of the Johns Hopkins University Institute for Policy Studies, and Director of the Johns Hopkins Comparative Nonprofit Sector Project, USA.

Wolfgang Seibel, Professor of Political Science and Public Administration at the University of Konstanz, Germany.

Siddhartha Sen, Assistant Professor in the Institute of Architecture and Planning, Graduate Program in City and Regional Planning, Morgan State University, Baltimore, USA.

Filip Wijkström, Research Associate and Ph.D. candidate in the Department for Management and Organization Theory at the Stockholm School of Economics, Sweden.

SERIES EDITORS' FOREWORD

This book is one in a series of monographs on the voluntary or nonprofit sector throughout the world that have resulted from the Johns Hopkins Comparative Nonprofit Sector Project, a major inquiry into the scope, structure, history, legal position, and role of the nonprofit sector in a broad cross-section of nations.

Launched in May 1990, this project has sought to close the glaring gaps in knowledge that have long existed about the thousands of schools, hospitals, clinics, community organizations, advocacy groups, day care centers, relief organizations, nursing homes, homeless shelters, family counselling agencies, environmental groups and others that make up this important sector. Though known by different names in different places, these organizations are present almost everywhere, albeit to widely differing extents. More than that, there is significant evidence that they are growing massively in both scope and scale as faith in the capability of government to cope on its own with the interrelated challenges of persistent poverty, environmental degradation, and social change has declined. Indeed, we seem to be in the midst of a global "associational revolution" that is opening new opportunities for organized private action and placing new demands and responsibilities on private not-for-profit groups. As a result, it has becoming increasingly important to understand what the scope and contours of this nonprofit sector really are, and what its potentials are for shouldering the new demands being placed upon it.

The Johns Hopkins Comparative Nonprofit Sector Project was conceived as a way to meet this need, to document the scope, structure, revenue base, and background of the nonprofit sector, and to do so in a way that not only yielded solid and objective information about individual countries, but made it possible to undertake cross-national comparisons in a systematic way. For this purpose, we identified thirteen countries representing different religious and historical traditions, different regions of the world, and different levels of economic development. Included were seven advanced industrial societies (the U.S., the U.K., France, Germany, Italy, Sweden, and Japan), five "developing" societies (Brazil, Ghana, Egypt, Thailand, and India), and one former Soviet bloc country (Hungary). In each of these countries we recruited a Local Associate and undertook a similar set of information-gathering activities guided by a common definition, a common classification scheme, and a common set of data-gathering forms and instructions. The result, we believe, is the first systematic attempt to put the nonprofit sector on the social and economic map of the world in a solid and empirical way.

The present volume offers the first comprehensive look at the nature of the nonprofit sector cross-nationally. In its opening chapters, the book provides the building-blocks for a common definition and a common classification of the nonprofit sector, both of them crucial prerequisites for systematic comparative work. The subsequent chapters then demonstrate how this core definition and classification relate to the concepts and realities of the nonprofit sector in our project countries. The result is a rich panorama of the varying conceptualizations and defining characteristics of the nonprofit sector in a broad cross-section of countries, including the U.S., the U.K., France, Germany, Hungary, Italy, Japan, Sweden, India, Thailand, Brazil, Egypt and Ghana. Most important, *Defining the nonprofit sector* demonstrates beyond doubt that the traditional division of societies into two sectors – the public and the private, or the market and the state – is much too simplistic. The various contributions to this volume show that a third, or nonprofit, sector, with its own characteristics and defining features, has emerged as a clearly discernible presence in virtually all societies.

From its outset, the Johns Hopkins Comparative Nonprofit Sector Project has been a collaborative effort among an extraordinary group of scholars with support from a wide array of funders and advisors. The team of Local Associates – Martin Knapp and Jeremy Kendall in the U.K., Edith Archambault in France, Paolo

Barbetta and Pippo Ranci in Italy, Helmut Anheier, Eckhard Priller and Wolfgang Seibel in Germany, Éva Kuti in Hungary, Tadashi Yamamoto and Takayoshi Amenomori in Japan, Leilah Landim in Brazil, Lawrence Atingdui and Emmanuel Laryea in Ghana, Amani Kandil in Egypt, Amara Pongsapich in Thailand, Sven-Erik Sjöstrand, Filip Wijkström, and Thomas Lundström in Sweden – have worked together at every stage to perfect the information-gathering forms, develop the basic definitions and the classification scheme, and interpret the results. To all of them, we owe a deep debt of gratitude.

Thanks are also due to the numerous individuals who served on the International Advisory Committee to this project, to the members of the national advisory committees we formed to oversee the work, to Richard Purslow of Manchester University Press for the crucial encouragement he has provided in bringing this work to publication, and to the foundations, corporations, and government agencies throughout the world that provided support to make this work possible.

It was more than 150 years ago that the Frenchman Alexis de Tocqueville identified the "art of associating together" as the mother of all science. Today we appear to be in the middle of an extraordinary explosion of associational activity as new forms of organized citizen action are taking shape and expanding their role in widely disparate parts of the world. Our hope is that the series of monographs of which this volume is an important part will help make this process of change more visible and more understandable and thereby contribute to its success. We are convinced that important values hinge critically on this result.

L.M.S.
H.K.A.
Baltimore, Maryland
January 1996

Chapter 1

INTRODUCTION: IN SEARCH OF THE NONPROFIT SECTOR

Lester M. Salamon and Helmut K. Anheier

> *A book is made up of signs that speak of other signs, which in their turn speak of things.*
>
> Umberto Eco, *The Name of the Rose*

A glance across the institutional landscape of the world reveals often striking differences in the way human beings organize themselves for social, economic, and political action. Parliamentary democracies, one-party states, monarchies, tribal governments, plantations, small mercantile houses, multinational corporations, small-scale craftsmen, labor unions and many more dot the institutional landscape of the modern world in often complex and confusing patterns.

Despite the diversity of the resulting institutional reality, however, we have come to accept the existence of two grand complexes of organizations – two broad sectors – into which it has become conventional to divide social life: the *market* and the *state*, or the *private* and the *public* sectors. Notwithstanding the tremendous variety of actual institutional entities to which the abstract concepts of the market and the state actually refer, these abstractions have come to command acceptance as meaningful, indeed necessary, analytical notions without which it is impossible to understand or describe modern life.

No such agreement prevails, however, about the existence, let alone the precise contours, of a third complex of institutions, a definable "third sector" occupying a distinctive social space outside of both the market and the state. Although the existence of such a "third sector" with its own characteristic features and dynamics is increasingly coming to be accepted among a growing band of international scholars, nonprofit leaders, and international agency officials,[1] its existence remains at best a debatable proposition to the general public and much of the rest of the academic community.

There are doubtless many reasons for this state of affairs. One of the most compelling is the great diversity of the entities that tend to get lumped together in this third sector – ranging from tiny soup kitchens to symphony orchestras, from garden clubs to environmental groups. How a set of organizations with this much diversity can be considered a "sector" with significant common features is difficult for many to comprehend.

A second explanation for the failure to develop a clear understanding of a third, or nonprofit, sector is the far greater power and influence that the two other sectors have come to wield in the modern world. The emergence of the large-scale profit-making firm and of public administration represented the major institutional innovations of the eighteenth and nineteenth centuries, and the results have been institutional complexes of enormous social and economic power. The great political thinkers of the eighteenth and nineteenth centuries consequently struggled with analytical concepts to come to terms with these great developments and formulated a language of discourse and a set of labels such as capitalism, Marxism, liberalism, socialism, and social democracy to depict the alternative patterns for organizing these two broad spheres of life. Next to these immense institutional complexes, the roles of other social institutions, such as those in the so-called third sector, have seemed to pale in comparison. Apparently lacking sufficient power or influence to attract serious attention, these institutions, and the sector of which they are a part, tended to be ignored in many countries.

In fact, however, neither of these arguments is very persuasive. So far as the diversity argument is concerned, a similar argument could be made about the other "sectors" we have come to accept as meaningful concepts. How much similarity is there, after all, between a roadside vendor and the International Business Machines Corporation, or between an insurance company and a winery?

Similarly, the argument that the nonprofit sector has not attracted attention because it is not very powerful also turns out to be spurious. For one thing, even in economic terms the nonprofit sector is a far more significant force than is commonly recognized. In the U.S., for example, this sector accounts for over half of the hospital beds, half of the colleges and universities, most of the social services, and almost all of the cultural activity (Salamon, 1992). Beyond this, the third sector has given rise to a variety of social and political movements (for example, the environmental movement, the civil rights movement, and many others) that have successfully challenged the seemingly irresistible power of the market and the state.

In short, neither of these arguments suffices to explain the curious lack of appreciation for a distinctive third sector of private, nonprofit organizations in either our public discourse or academic debate. How, then, are we to explain this significant omission?

While there are doubtless many possible answers to this question, it is the argument of this book that one of the most important has been the absence of a sufficiently clear and workable definition of what this sector really encompasses. In other words, we suggest that the lack of attention to the third sector is a function less of the weakness of the sector than of the weakness of the *concepts* that have so far been used to comprehend and define it.

Such concepts are absolutely critical in the development of any field of study or in comprehending any social reality. As Karl Deutsch (1963:12) wrote in *The Nerves of Government* three decades ago: "It seems clear that we all use models in our thinking all the time, even though we may not stop to notice it. When we say that we 'understand' a situation ... we say, in effect, that we have in our mind an abstract model, vague or specific, that permits us to parallel or predict such changes in that situation as are of interest to us." The existence of analytical concepts is thus not a matter of choice: it is the *sine qua non* of all understanding. It is for this reason that Deutsch can argue that "progress in the effectiveness of symbols and symbol systems is ... basic progress in the technology of thinking and in the development of human powers of insight and action" (Deutsch, 1963:10).

Anyone who has examined the recent literature on the nonprofit sector during the past decade must appreciate this need for "basic progress in the technology of thinking." A significant outpouring of scholarly attention has now been lavished on the nonprofit sector both in the United States and abroad, yet far too little

3

attention has been given to the basic question of how this sector is defined or what it really contains. As a consequence, improper comparisons are drawn between one country and another and grand theories are developed about realities that are improperly or imperfectly specified.

Purpose of this book

The purpose of this book is to remedy this situation, at least in part. The book presents the results of an effort by a group of scholars in thirteen countries throughout the world who were involved in the Johns Hopkins Comparative Nonprofit Sector Project to formulate a common language and concept of the "nonprofit sector" that could guide systematic data-gathering on this sector cross-nationally. Without such clarification and consensus on basic concepts, on what we were trying to measure, little effective progress could be made in developing empirical estimates of the scope and scale of this sector that would have any validity cross-nationally. Yet the range of different national usages was such that no single national pattern could accommodate all of the relevant reality. Thus, as detailed more fully below, the common law countries of the U.S. and the U.K. draw distinctions between public and private institutions that are far more difficult to sustain in the civil law countries of Europe, where private nonprofit organizations often have the status of *public* law corporations. Similarly, in the developing nations of Ghana, Egypt, and India, activists often restrict the domain of nonprofit activity to a particular class of organizations – NGOs, or nongovernmental organizations – that, while quite broad in function, nevertheless represent a small portion of what is customarily included within the nonprofit sector in the more developed world.

To cope with this challenge, we proceeded along three major courses. First, we invited the team of scholars we had assembled to assist us with this project in the various countries to identify the terminology and concepts most often used to portray the "third sector" in their respective countries. Second, we examined these national usages against each other and against existing literature and concepts to identify alternative bases for defining this set of institutions. We then evaluated these types of definitions against a basic set of criteria and, in consultation with our local associates, settled on a hypothesized definition of the nonprofit sector, the so-called "structural–operational definition," that we concluded would be most fruitful for comparative work. Finally, because effective cross-national analysis requires consensus not only on what is *common* to the organizations within this sector but also on what the major *differences* are among them, we used a similar process to formulate a common classification scheme for this sector. This involved identifying a number of possible alternative bases for classification, evaluating these in the light of several crucial criteria, and then refining the resulting system through cross-checks against the realities in our project countries.

Although the range of experiences against which we formulated the definition and classification system outlined here was far from universal, pains were taken to include countries that represented considerable variation in terms of a number of crucial dimensions, such as level of development, relative scale of government social welfare spending, region of the world, religious tradition, and overall size (see Table 1.1).[2] The result, we believe, should therefore be applicable to a far larger range of countries throughout the world.

Table 1.1

Johns Hopkins Comparative Nonprofit Sector Project: project sites

	Government social welfare spending type				
	Low		**Medium**	**High**	
Developed	Japan (12%) U.S.A. (13%)		U.K. (20%) Germany (23%) Italy (23%)	France (29%) Sweden (36%)	
Developing	**South America**	**Africa**	**Middle East**	**South Asia**	**S.E. Asia**
	Brazil	Ghana	Egypt	India	Thailand
Former Socialist bloc			Hungary		

Structure of the discussion

To examine these results, this book is divided into four parts. Part I presents the basic conceptual equipment we developed for structuring inquiry into the nonprofit sector at the international level. The first chapter in this section (Chapter 2) describes the challenge we confronted in formulating a common definition of the nonprofit sector for comparative work given the treatments of this set of organizations in the different countries. Chapter 3 then reviews the alternative bases for defining this sector and the rationale for our choice of the "structural–operational definition" as the core definition of the nonprofit sector for this project. Chapter 4 then reviews the alternative bases for classifying nonprofit organizations and explains the International Classification of Nonprofit Organizations (ICNPO) we developed and the rationale for it.

Against this conceptual backdrop, Part II then examines how our structural–operational definition works in the context of the seven developed countries we covered (the U.S., the U.K., France, Germany, Italy, Sweden, and Japan). Each of the seven chapters in this part introduces what the third sector looks like in the respective country and assesses how the different terms and concepts used to depict this sector relate to the structural–operational definition we have proposed. Although the fit is far from perfect, the overall conclusion is that this definition works surprisingly well.

Parts III and IV then present a similar analysis for five developing countries (Brazil, Ghana, Egypt, Thailand, and India), and for one former Communist bloc country (Hungary). Here, again, the basic core definition of the nonprofit sector developed for this project turns out to fit much of the relevant reality.

A final chapter then pulls this discussion together. Drawing on the preceding country chapters it identifies a set of factors that seem to explain some of the observed variation in the basic structure and salience of the nonprofit sector from place to place. These factors then become the basis of hypotheses to be treated in subsequent work.

Conclusion

Definitions and classifications are hardly the stuff of high drama. Yet they are crucial to clear thinking and careful analysis. Particularly in a field as embryonic and lacking in basic information and conceptual clarity as this one, such definitional development and improvement in the basic "technology of thinking" is an absolute prerequisite to even the most rudimentary understanding. While we have no illusions that the concepts and descriptive insights presented here will be the last word on these issues, we hope that they will at least constitute useful first steps along the road.

Notes

1 Evidence of the growing awareness of the existence of a distinguishable "third sector" in societies around the world can be found in a recent series of international research conferences beginning in Bad Honnef, Germany in 1987, continuing in Jerusalem in 1989, and then in Indianapolis in the U.S.A. in March 1992; in the recent creation of *Voluntas*, the international journal of research on not-for-profit organizations; and in a number of recent books and articles reporting on this field. The latter include: Anheier and Seibel, 1990; James, 1989; Gidron, Kramer and Salamon, 1992; McCarthy, Hodgkinson and Sumariwalla, 1992; Salamon, 1994; Salamon and Anheier, 1994.
2 For a fuller discussion of the country selection criteria, see Salamon and Anheier, 1992; and Salamon and Anheier, 1994.

References

Anheier, Helmut K. and Wolfgang Seibel (eds) (1990), *The Third Sector: Comparative Studies of Nonprofit Organizations*. Berlin/New York: DeGruyter.

Deutsch, Karl (1963), *The Nerves of Government*. New York: The Free Press.

Gidron, Benjamin, Ralph Kramer and Lester M. Salamon (eds) (1992), *Government and the Third Sector: Emerging Relationships in Welfare States*. San Francisco: Jossey–Bass.

James, Estelle (ed.) (1989), *The Nonprofit Sector in International Perspective: Studies in Comparative Culture and Policy*. Oxford: Oxford University Press.

McCarthy, Kathleen D., Virginia Hodgkinson and Russy Sumariwalla (1992), *The Nonprofit Sector in the Global Community*. San Francisco: Jossey-Bass.

Salamon, Lester M. (1992), *America's Nonprofit Sector: A Primer*. New York: The Foundation Center.

Salamon, Lester M. (1994), "The rise of the nonprofit sector." *Foreign Affairs*, 73(4):109–122.

Salamon, Lester M. and Helmut K. Anheier (1992), "Toward an understanding of the international nonprofit sector: The Johns Hopkins Comparative Nonprofit Sector Project." Nonprofit Management and Leadership, 2:311–324.

Salamon, Lester M. and Helmut K. Anheier (1994), *The Emerging Sector: An Overview*. Baltimore: The Johns Hopkins Institute for Policy Studies.

Part I

CONCEPTUAL EQUIPMENT

A central argument of this book is that the nonprofit sector is poorly understood not so much because the data on it are so limited as because the concepts used to depict its boundaries are so murky and imprecise. Before effective efforts can be made to measure the scale and contours of this sector, therefore, progress is needed on the basic analytical equipment needed to conceptualize it and demarcate its basic character.

The three chapters in this part report on the efforts to fashion such conceptual equipment in the context of the Johns Hopkins Comparative Nonprofit Sector Project. Thus Chapter 2, the first chapter in this part, outlines the challenge that confronts analysts of the nonprofit sector as a result of the terminological and conceptual confusion that exists in this field and the wide variety of legal and popular treatments of these organizations in different countries around the world. Against this backdrop, Chapter 3 then examines how we approached the first part of this challenge: the task of formulating a coherent, core definition of the nonprofit sector that can be used in cross-national analysis. After evaluating several types of such possible definitions, the chapter concludes that what we term the "structural–operational" definition offers the best combination of economy, rigor, and organizing power. To demonstrate this, the chapter shows how this definition works in the context of three different national experiences: those of the U.K., Germany, and Brazil.

Chapter 4 then applies a similar approach to the other key conceptual challenge in comparative work on the nonprofit sector: the development of a classification scheme to differentiate the various types of entities the sector contains. After examining several possible existing typologies, including the U.N.'s International Standard Industrial Classification (ISIC), and the U.S. Independent Sector's National Taxonomy of Exempt Entities (NTEE), the chapter concludes that none is really adequate for the task at hand. Accordingly, it advances an alternative classification system, which we term the International Classification of Nonprofit Organizations, or ICNPO. The great advantage of the ICNPO is its ability to draw conceptually significant distinctions among the many different types of nonprofit organizations while remaining basically consistent with the U.N. Standard Industrial Classification system, which is the framework used for the collection of basic economic statistics around the world – a great advantage for systematic cross-national empirical work.

While hardly the last word on these topics, the structural–operational definition of the nonprofit sector and the International Classification of Nonprofit Organizations represent important conceptual equipment for the conduct of systematic empirical work in this field.

Chapter 2

THE CHALLENGE OF DEFINITION: THIRTEEN REALITIES IN SEARCH OF A CONCEPT

Lester M. Salamon and Helmut K. Anheier

Definition lies at the heart of all social analysis. Without a set of concepts to give some order to reality, there is no way to group perceptions and begin making sense of them. This is particularly true, moreover, in cross-national settings, where common language and common cultural understandings are not even available to help structure perceptions. Without a clearly articulated and understood set of definitions, the probability is high that different observers will perceive the same reality in far different ways, including or excluding aspects that others may view in a wholly different light. There are those who argue, in fact, that large-scale cross-national quantitative comparisons face insurmountable obstacles as a consequence, that definitions applied across national traditions inevitably distort more than they reveal (Centeno, 1994:126).

While the work reported here began from a very different premise, it is important to acknowledge at the outset the merit of this line of argument and the challenge that the task of forging a workable cross-national definition of the nonprofit sector entails.

The purpose of this chapter is to examine this challenge. To do so, we look first at the terminological tangle that envelops this field and the conceptual murkiness that lies behind it. Against this backdrop, we examine the diverse profusion of treatments of the nonprofit sector evident in the thirteen countries covered by our project, drawing heavily on the country studies reported in Parts II, III, and IV of this book. Finally, we identify some conclusions that seem to flow from the patterns of usage that we find. This, then, provides the context for the effort to forge a common definition described in Chapter 3.

The conceptual challenge

The terminological tangle

The challenge involved in forging a common definition of the nonprofit sector cross-nationally is evident, in the first instance, in the great profusion of terms used to depict this range of institutions – "nonprofit sector," "charitable sector," "independent sector," "voluntary sector," "tax-exempt sector," "nongovernmental organizations (NGOs)," "associational sector," *économie sociale*, and many more. As Salamon (1992) points out, each of these terms emphasizes one aspect of the reality represented by these organizations at the expense of overlooking or downplaying other aspects. Each is therefore at least partly misleading. For example:

- *Charitable sector* emphasizes the support these organizations receive from private, charitable donations. But private charitable contributions do not constitute the only, or even the major, source of their revenue.
- *Independent sector* emphasizes the important role these organizations play as a "third force" outside of the realm of government and private business. But these organizations are far from independent. In financial terms they depend heavily on both government and private business.
- *Voluntary sector* emphasizes the significant input that volunteers make to the management and operation of this sector. But a good deal of the activity of the organizations in this sector in many countries is not carried out by volunteers at all, but by paid employees.
- *Tax-exempt sector* emphasizes the fact that under the tax laws of many countries the organizations in this sector are exempted from taxation. But this term begs the question of what characteristics qualify organizations for this treatment in the first place. In addition, it is not very helpful in comparing the experience of one country with that of another, since it is dependent on the particular tax systems of particular countries.
- *NGO (nongovernmental organization)* is the term used to depict these organizations in the developing world, but it tends to refer only to a portion of what elsewhere is considered to be part of this sector – namely, the organizations engaged in the

promotion of economic and social development, typically at the grass-roots level.

- *Économie sociale* is the term used to depict a broad range of non-governmental organizations in France and Belgium, and increasingly within the European Community institutions, but it embraces a wide variety of business-type organizations such as mutual insurance companies, savings banks, cooperatives, and agricultural marketing organizations that would be considered parts of the business sector in most parts of the world.

- Even *nonprofit sector*, the term we will generally use here, is not without its problems. This term emphasizes the fact that these organizations do not exist primarily to generate profits for their owners. But these organizations sometimes do earn profits, i.e., they generate more revenues than they spend in a given year.

The question of scope

Behind this profusion of terms lie a number of ambiguities about the exact scope and character of the entities properly included within this sector. Three such ambiguities deserve mention here.

A crucial distinction: philanthropy vs. *the nonprofit sector*. In the first place, a crucial distinction needs to be drawn between *philanthropy*, on the one hand, and *the private, nonprofit sector*, on the other. Too often, these two terms are treated interchangeably and the nonprofit sector is considered essentially equivalent to private charity. In fact, however, philanthropy is really just a part of the nonprofit sector. In particular:

- The *private nonprofit sector*, as the term will be used here, is a set of private organizations providing a wide variety of information, advocacy, and services.

- *Philanthropy*, by contrast, is the giving of gifts of time or other valuables (money, securities, property) for public purposes. Philanthropy, or charitable giving, is thus just one form of income of private nonprofit organizations. To be sure, some nonprofit organizations have the generation of charitable contributions as their principal objective. But these are not the only types of nonprofit organizations, and private charitable contributions are not the only source of nonprofit income.

Sector vs. *subsectors: the "unit of analysis" problem.* In the second place, there is considerable ambiguity about the appropriate unit of analysis to use in the definition of the nonprofit sector. The concept of a "nonprofit sector" suggests that there are sufficient commonalities among a significant number of different entities to warrant treating them as part of a single group or sector even though they may have numerous differences as well. However, as the discussion below will make clear, this is far easier in some countries than in others. In the United States, for example, the entities commonly considered part of this sector are conveniently covered in a reasonably coherent and integrated body of law (Section 501 of the tax code and its relevant subsectors). In Japan, by contrast, no such coherent body of law exists. Rather, there are a variety of different laws that define entities that might be considered to be parts of the nonprofit sector even though they have their own distinctive legal personalities. More generally, the considerable variations that exist in the size, purpose, fields of activity, structure, and orientation of nonprofit organizations raise serious questions about whether a true sector exists and cause some experts to restrict their attention to particular subgroups of organizations, such as "charities" in the U.K., or "NGOs" in the developing world.

Formal vs. *informal institutions.* A third ambiguity involved in defining the nonprofit sector relates to the degree of organizational formality required of the entities considered part of it. In the United States at the present time, nonprofit organizations are typically formally incorporated under state laws. However, this is a relatively recent practice. Prior to the 1950s it was common for organizations to adopt constitutions or charters but not to incorporate formally, and this is still a practice followed by many self-help groups. In countries where legal incorporation is not permitted (for example, the former Communist countries of Central and Eastern Europe), or where informal associations are the norm (for example, village associations in parts of the developing world and much of the nonprofit sector in Italy), restricting the concept of nonprofit organization to entities that are formally incorporated or legally registered could artificially limit the scope and scale of the sector.

Thirteen realities in search of a concept

These conceptual ambiguities and terminological disparities find all too ample reflection in the varying perceptions of the nonprofit or "third" sector evident in our target countries. To be sure, cross-national research has long recognized fundamental differences in the scope and structure of the nonprofit sector and in the way it is constituted and defined from place to place (James, 1989; Anheier and Seibel, 1990). But the true nature of the conceptual challenge facing students of this field has only recently become clear. In point of fact, few societies have anything approaching a coherent notion of a distinct private nonprofit sector, and those that do often include entities that would be unrecognizable to students from other parts of the world. To a significant extent, therefore, the search for a nonprofit sector is thus a voyage of discovery in conceptual as well as empirical terms.

United States

Of all the countries examined here, the United States is probably the one with the clearest concept of a distinguishable nonprofit sector. While far from simple or homogeneous, the nonprofit sector at least has a coherent place in American law and usage, giving rise in some quarters to the mistaken notion that the nonprofit sector is an American invention. U.S. law thus recognizes a distinct sphere of private organizations serving public purposes and not organized principally to earn a profit. Such organizations are permitted to incorporate under state laws and to secure exemption from federal income taxes and most state and local taxes. No fewer than 26 different subsections of the tax law are available under which such tax-exempt status can be secured. Broadly, however, they fall into two groups – one covering essentially member-serving organizations such as business associations, social clubs, and labor unions; and the other covering organizations that operate principally to serve the needs of the public more broadly. The latter group, defined by section 501(c)(3) of the national tax code, form the core of what is generally regarded as the charitable nonprofit sector, and it not only enjoys exemption from federal income taxes, but also the privilege of receiving charitable gifts on which donors can claim a deduction on their own income taxes. Included here are organizations serving "religious, charitable, scientific, literary, or educational purposes," each of these a term of art derived from the English common law over some three hundred years of development. The term "charitable" in particular is quite broad in its interpretation, embracing organizations that promote the general welfare in any of a variety of ways, from providing child day care to promoting health, from guaranteeing free expression to offering family counselling (Hopkins, 1987:55–71). While the legal treatment of different types of organizations is far from simple, the U.S. nonprofit sector is perhaps unique in the extent to which popular conceptions of the sector correspond with basic distinctions in the law.

United Kingdom

The U.K. shares with the United States a reasonably clear concept of a nonprofit sector ("voluntary sector" in U.K. usage), but the legal boundaries of this sector are nowhere near as neatly demarcated. No single body of tax or other law embraces this set of institutions. One reason for this is the fact that different legal systems exist in the U.K. – one covering England and Wales, another Scotland, and a third Northern Ireland. Beyond this, however, the "common law" tradition, which puts a premium on flexibility and evolution rather than precise delineation of organizational types, has had a stronger hold in the U.K. than in the U.S., preventing even the kind of codification that the tax laws have achieved in the U.S. The result is a reasonably prominent notion of an organizational space outside the state and the market, but a far more complicated one than in the American setting.

The center of gravity of the U.K. nonprofit sector is the so-called "charities." These are organizations formally registered as "charities" by the U.K. Charity Commission and thereby accorded the protection of the Crown, the Courts, and the Charity Commission for their activities, including protection from taxation. The requirements for such classification have never been clearly and definitively specified, however. The listing provided in the Preamble to the Statute of Charitable Uses of 1601 has been a start, but it has been successively revised. Perhaps the most definitive ruling has been that in Pemsel's case in 1891, which approved four different classes of charities: those for relief of poverty, those for the advancement of education, those for the advancement of religion, and those for other purposes "beneficial to the community."

While they share a common set of basic purposes, charities can take any of a number of legal forms – trusts, unincorporated associations, companies limited by guarantee. But other types of voluntary organizations not recognized as "charities" by the Charity Commission can also take the same legal forms. These include such entities as "friendly societies," "industrial and benevolent societies," building societies, universities, private schools, and cooperatives. It has been estimated that at least half of the U.K. voluntary sector falls into these categories.

Defined in legal terms, therefore, the U.K. nonprofit sector is a bewilderingly confused set of institutions with poorly defined boundaries. For the most part, social science research has tended to focus on the registered charities (Posnett, 1987), but this overlooks a significant range of organizations. While the concept of a voluntary sector seems easy to identify in British usage, therefore, it is not easy to specify with any real precision.

Germany

Despite their differences, both the U.S. and the U.K. share a basic notion of an organizational universe distinct from the State and the market. In the countries of continental Europe, by contrast, such a notion is far less developed. There the right to form private organizations is more tightly defined by law and the concept of a public-serving nonprofit sector is complicated by the notion that the state is considered the truest embodiment of the public good.

In Germany, for example, a rather rigid and well-defined system exists for defining the status and rights of organizations. However, this system is not particularly designed to clarify the existence of a set of organizations that fit common notions of a private, nonprofit sector. On the contrary, they actually blur such a classification.

At the heart of the German system are two quite distinct systems of law, one of which (the civil law) applies to private individuals and organizations, and the other of which (the public law) applies to public institutions. Organizations must find a legal home in either the civil law or the public law. The problem, however, is that nonprofit organizations are private organizations that often serve essentially public purposes. They are thus civil-law in form and public-law in function, posing a challenge to the neat symmetry of the German legal order.

To cope with this challenge, a variety of special provisions have been made. In the first place, the civil law acknowledges the existence of a variety of types of civil law organizations that serve essentially public purposes. This includes: (1) so-called "ideal associations," or *Vereine*, which are essentially membership organizations serving other than commercial purposes (for example, political and civic organizations, local voters' groups, sports clubs); (2) certain limited liability companies and other forms of corporations considered to have a public mission, such as hospitals; and (3) foundations. Under German tax law, these civil-law organizations are tax-exempt and eligible to receive tax-deductible gifts to the extent that they are *gemeinnützige*, or public-benefit, organizations serving certain specified public purposes (for example, public health, youth and youth welfare, life-saving, prisoners' welfare).

These features of German usage are not far from the patterns evident in the U.S. and the U.K. The problem, however, is that not all of what would normally be considered part of the nonprofit sector in the U.S. and the U.K. falls under the civil law in Germany. A significant portion also falls under public law. Although theoretically reserved for public agencies, the public law category has been broadened to include a wide variety of organizations that are public in purpose but essentially private in structure, such as public television stations, the Bavarian Red Cross, the Jewish Welfare Agency, most universities, and even the Roman Catholic and Protestant Churches. Germany has thus included within the domain of public-law corporations, which applies mainly to government agencies, many types of organizations that would be classified as private, nonprofit organizations in other societies. Yet not all public-law corporations fit this criterion.

In the German setting, therefore, no clear line can be drawn between public and private institutions in defining the nonprofit sector. By law, some are public and some private. What is more, particular types of organizations can end up on both sides of this amorphous line, depending on peculiar historical circumstances. Thus, some German charitable foundations are chartered under civil law and some under public law. Similarly, the Church, commonly regarded as preeminently a private institution, is covered by the public law in Germany. Nor does the tax structure clarify what the legal structure leaves confused. While German law permits tax exemptions for private donations to public-benefit organizations, this category includes government agencies, civil-law organizations, and functionally independent public-law organizations.

In short, although Germany contains a rather rigid and formal legal structure and quite a sizable and well-developed set of nonprofit organizations, including some of the largest private social-welfare organizations in the world – the so-called "free welfare associations" – no coherent concept of a nonprofit sector exists. Rather, this sector is thoroughly mixed up with both the governmental and the private, for-profit spheres. The search for a nonprofit sector in Germany thus requires exceptional diligence and patience as well as a high tolerance for legal intricacy.

France

In France, the nonprofit sphere is somewhat more clearly specified, but it embraces a far wider range of organizations. The central organizing concept in the French setting is the concept of "solidarity," the need to join together to pursue common objectives. Although historically the State has been viewed as the highest expression of solidarity, since 1901 the law has acknowledged the legitimacy of a variety of other institutions that encourage the same goal. These organizations are embraced within what is known as the *économie sociale,* or the social economy. Included here are three broad sets of organizations – cooperatives, mutuals, and associations – each with its own set of laws, its own structures, and its own pattern of development.

The cooperative sector includes member-oriented nonprofit organizations that are engaged in some form of commercial activity, such as agricultural and consumer cooperatives and cooperative banks. Mutual associations include insurance funds and related schemes to provide for family, health and other social emergencies and risks, usually as an additional coverage to the public social security system. In recent years, many mutuals have moved closer to the for-profit sector, particularly in the insurance brokerage area, and would probably not be regarded as nonprofit organizations under U.S. usage.

Finally, associations form the third part of the French social economy sector. Included here are some 600,000–700,000 declared associations regulated by the Law of 1901 as well as an unknown number of undeclared associations with no legal status. These associations perform a wide variety of social welfare and representational functions, particularly in the areas of sports, recreation, health, and welfare. Also included are some 2,000 public utility associations, which, unlike other associations, may own real estate and receive tax-deductible gifts. These and other privileges are granted by the *Conseil d'État*, the highest administrative office in the Republic.

Italy

Italy in a way stands between the rather free-wheeling and open world of nonprofit action in the U.S. and the U.K. and the more tightly regulated and structured situation of Germany and France. On paper, Italy shares much of the formal structure of the French and German systems, including the strong presence of cooperatives and mutuals and a somewhat rigid civil-law legal system. But a long tradition of informality and the special position of the Catholic Church introduce a much more amorphous pattern in fact. Three rather distinct spheres thus exist in Italy: a public sphere, a secular private world, and the semi-autonomous realm of the Catholic Church, with its own body of law. Nonprofit organizations operate in each of these spheres, albeit without a great deal of clarity. Thus, some organizations, such as *Opere Pie* or Catholic social welfare agencies, began as private institutions under the auspices of the Catholic Church, but separate and partially contradictory legislative enactments since then have "assigned" them to either the private, the public, or the ecclesiastical sector.

Formally, organizations functioning for other-than-business purposes are supposed to secure formal legal status as incorporated entities under public or civil law. Very few such organizations become officially incorporated, however. Incorporation is time-consuming and requires a Presidential Decree. Incorporation is thus considered a privilege to be granted by the State, not a right inherent in the organization. Although it carries certain privileges and increases the potential array of business activities an organization can engage in, the high transaction costs keep most associations from seeking incorporation.

Most associations consequently remain unincorporated, giving rise to *associazionismo*, a large world of informal associations through which citizens join together to pursue common interests in such fields as culture, sport, recreation, social welfare, and religion. The act of establishing an unincorporated association requires only the drafting of a charter to be lodged at a notary's office. The great majority of Italy's secular nonprofit sector consists of such unincorporated associations and foundations, while Catholic organizations enjoy a separate legal status under ecclesiastical law.

Recent policies in social services and banking intend to reduce the constraints many nonprofit organizations face as unincorporated associations. For example, in the field of social services, a 1991 law addressed the problems of the many unincorporated associations that operated as *voluntariato*, or voluntary philanthropic institutions, and made it easier for them to administer grants, own real estate and receive donations. While these provisions have begun to systematize the nonprofit sphere in Italy, for the most part this sphere continues to operate in a largely inadequate legal environment that forces founders of nonprofit organizations to remain personally liable or to adopt legal forms typical for the business world that may be ill-suited for the type of activities carried out by nonprofits.

Sweden

Sweden is an even more complex mixture of the neatly demarcated organizational structure of the Continent and the far more amorphous and open systems characteristic of the Anglo–Saxon world. Because of the highly developed system of state welfare provision in Sweden, it has been common to assume that little or no substantial nonprofit sector exists there. Both common usage and the prevailing legal structure encourage this misconception, moreover. No coherent concept of a nonprofit sector exists in Swedish usage. What is more, although Sweden is a civil law country, no overarching body of law exists for this set of organizations, and what legal provisions do exist cover only a small portion of what elsewhere would be treated as part of this sector.

In fact, however, a quite sizable and important nonprofit sector does exist in Sweden, and has for centuries. This sector is far less deeply involved in the provision of services, however, and far more in promoting social integration and political participation. The Continental concept of "solidarity" thus lies at the heart of this sector. Reflecting this, popular movement organizations (*Folkrörelserna*), cooperatives, trade unions, and recreational organizations are particularly prominent. The central function of many of these organizations is not to deliver services but to provide a mechanism for mutual support and a vehicle for expressing the opinions and interests of particular groupings of citizens to the government. They are thus crucial devices for maintaining contact between government and citizens and thus for preserving the "policy of compromise" that forms the foundation of the "Swedish model." Little of this is enshrined in formal law, however. Only "economic associations," i.e., associations seeking to promote the economic interests of their members, are specifically authorized in positive law. The more common *ideell* associations, or associations serving ideal purposes, are covered only by a variety of judicial precedents and decisions by the Supreme Administrative Court, a situation akin to that in the common law tradition. A considerable variety of organizations is included here, however, ranging from sports clubs through social movement organizations to labor unions and employer associations. Complicating matters further is the position of the Swedish Church, which is formally part of the State but in practice increasingly private and autonomous in its operations. Similarly, foundations are quite numerous in Sweden, though few would consider them a part of a nonprofit sector in the American or English versions of the concept. In short, contrary to widespread beliefs, the growth of the welfare state has hardly obliterated associational life in Sweden. On the contrary, the Swedish population is actively engaged in a bewildering variety of associations, and these associations form a crucial part of Swedish social and political life.

Japan

In Japan, the nonprofit sphere is, if anything, even more restricted than in the European setting. A rather fully developed "welfare state," Japan has no general law authorizing the formation of non-profit organizations or granting them tax or other concessions. Although the status of *kōeki hōjin*, or charitable organization, is established under the Uniform Civil Code of 1896, such organizations are entitled to tax benefits only if they are specifically authorized under other legal provisions (in health, welfare, scientific research, and the like), and even then only if the responsible Ministry judges that the organization serves a valid public purpose as defined by the Ministry. As a result, next to *kōeki hōjin*, eight other major types of nonprofit organizations exist under laws establishing "nonprofit" social welfare corporations, private school corporations, religious organizations, health-related organizations, and research organizations. What is more, the narrow interpretation of public benefit has increased the requirements for the establishment of nonprofit organizations. The status of *kōeki hōjin* is granted by the State, and significant assets are required for incorporation. The amount required may vary from case to case, and in the absence of general procedural rules, registration forms the *de facto* equivalent of a state licensing system for nonprofit organizations. The one major exception to this are the numerous *jichikai* and *chōnaikai*, informal and formal multi-purpose associations at the local level. But these organizations generally operate on a voluntary basis, with little legal structure or protection. For the most part, the nonprofit sector hardly functions as a distinguishable sector in Japan. Its borderlines are often unclear, with no strict distinction in place to set apart nonprofit organizations, on the one hand, and the public, for-profit and household sectors on the other. What exists, rather, is a variety of separate institutional types in particular policy spheres, each governed by the laws and practices of that sphere with little general policy or conceptualization.

India

This general lack of a distinguishable nonprofit sector is also characteristic of the developing countries. Although a rich array of institutions often exists in these countries outside the formal boundaries of the State, these institutions are rarely considered to be part of a single entity called the nonprofit sector. Rather they represent the institutional manifestations of a variety of often discontinuous social and political developments stretching over centuries of history. In popular parlance, the closest one comes to the concept of a nonprofit sector in these countries is the range of organizations commonly associated with the term "nongovernmental organizations," or NGOs. But the range of entities masquerading under this label has evolved over time and is now quite broad, including the membership organizations represented at the League of Nations and later the U.N., Northern-based voluntary relief and development agencies operating in the developing world, indigenous umbrella groups providing technical assistance to local grass-roots organizations, and the local grass-roots organizations themselves.

India, in many respects, comes closest to a nonprofit sector in the sense in which the term is used in the West. Equipped with a British-inspired legal system that has generally facilitated the formation of nonprofit institutions, a set of Hindu, Buddhist, and Islamic religious traditions generally supportive of charitable activity, and popular political leaders in the Gandhian tradition who valued grass-roots organizing and action, India has provided fertile soil for the growth of nonprofit–type institutions. Indeed, a rich organizational tapestry exists on which can be read much of the history of this subcontinent. Included are Christian missionary and charitable organizations that entered the country under colonial rule, formal caste associations that formed early in the twentieth century, Gandhian organizations that emerged during the independence period at the village level, professional associations of various sorts, international NGOs, development-oriented technical assistance organizations, empowerment groups formed largely in the 1980s, indigenous foundations and corporate philanthropy programs, and grass-roots development organizations. Although these various organizational survivals hardly constitute a self-conscious sector, they nevertheless represent a significant "third sector" that exists with some meaningful degree of independence from the state and the corporate sectors.

Egypt

In most other parts of the developing world, the opportunities for nonprofit development are considerably more constrained. In Egypt, for example, six types of nonprofit organizations are in existence: associations and foundations, professional groups, business associations, foreign foundations, advocacy organizations, and religious organizations like the Islamic Brotherhood, Islamic charitable trusts, *wakf*, and the Christian Coptic charities. However, each of these is governed by a specific body of law that defines its rights and responsibilities. The broadest of these, Law 32 of 1964, allows for the establishment of a broad array of associations and foundations for social, cultural, religious, and charitable purposes, yet it imposes significant restrictions on the organizations, including the right of government to investigate the internal affairs of the association, to appoint board members, and to suspend and dissolve the organization if deemed necessary.

Brazil

A similar situation exists in Brazil, where a subset of associations and foundations is permitted to form "public-utility organizations," but only "under the discretionary jurisdiction of the President of the Republic, and the proper presentation of requests does not give the right to their approval ..." (Federal Ministry of Justice, 1990:7). Faced with these restrictions, people wanting to form organizations often have had to do so on a purely informal basis, outside the prevailing laws. The result in Brazil is a profusion of informal or semi-formal organizations, an *associativismo* movement seeking to create a "civil society," often under the protective auspices of the Church. Even staid professional organizations have often found themselves functioning as hotbeds of civil-society protest as a consequence, politicizing what in other parts of the world are often dismissed as narrow, member-oriented institutions.

Thailand

Similarly, in Thailand a complex set of registration requirements has led groups with any political or advocacy objectives to remain unregistered and to function as "forums," "units," or "working groups." What show up on official records as formally constituted nonprofit organizations, therefore, tend to be "safe" commercial organizations such as chambers of commerce and import-export groups, cremation societies, and employers' organizations, thus obscuring the diverse institutional universe that exists in fact.

Only slowly is the autocratic stance of the Thai government toward the nonprofit sector giving way to a more cooperative relationship. Joint coordinating councils between government and the NGO community have now been formed, and the current development plan acknowledges the role of nonprofit organizations in rural development particularly.

Ghana

In Ghana, nonprofit organizations include local self-help groups, village associations, women's societies, agricultural development groups, hospitals, local community groups, missionary societies and traditional ethnic associations. As part of its colonial past, Ghana inherited the British legal system, and with it the laws on incorporation and charitable trusts. Because of restrictions on incorporating independently and separately in the colonies, the British system of charities and voluntary associations could not take hold in Ghana, although charitable organizations and missionary societies had been present in the country since the early nineteenth century. After independence, the government followed the common law tradition in introducing numerous acts and ordinances to regulate particular segments of the nonprofit sector. The successive legal development came to a halt in 1982, when the new military government required nonprofit organizations, in particular religious bodies, to re-apply for charitable status, which was now granted by the government. In recent years, the status of established nonprofit organizations has improved, as the country's economy and political system have consolidated, and as international and local NGOs became part of development programs financed from abroad.

Hungary

Finally, Hungary represents a country in the midst of a transition from a largely informal to a more formal nonprofit sector, but in a situation in which the borders between the state and the business sectors are also very much in flux and where the concept of a for-profit sector is also very much a novelty. That a clear concept of a nonprofit sector has yet to emerge in Hungary or elsewhere in the former Soviet bloc should therefore come as no surprise. Indeed, the very concept of a voluntary sector encounters suspicion in this part of the world because of the use that was made of such institutions as instruments of social control under the Communist regime. As pressures emerged to allow the flowering of a true "civil society" in Hungary during the 1980s, laws on the formation of foundations and associations were liberalized, leading to a rapid upsurge of such organizations. In many cases, however, these bear very little relationship to their Western counterparts. In some cases, ministry officials fearful of being thrown from power transferred significant resources to supposedly independent "foundations" and then moved over to operate these foundations. In other instances, entrepreneurs utilized the foundation form as a way to avoid taxation. Alongside these are the thousands of hobby and recreational associations permitted under the Communist regime as well as large numbers of newer organizations formed to protest against state action, promote popular involvement, or provide basic services the state promised but did not deliver. As a consequence, the nonprofit sector quickly acquired a hybrid status that continues to haunt its development as a truly distinctive sector of national life.

Conclusions

Several conclusions can be drawn from this brief overview of the world of nonprofit organizations in thirteen countries. In the first place, it should be clear that the term "nonprofit sector" (or any comparable term) disguises as much as it reveals when applied cross–nationally. In point of fact, few countries have a coherent notion of an identifiable nonprofit sector. What exists in fact is a wide assortment of institutional types that varies greatly in basic composition from place to place. Under these circumstances, efforts to make cross-national comparisons using local definitions of this sector are destined to be seriously misleading at best.

In the second place, however, while no single "nonprofit sector" exists throughout the world, there are still striking similarities in the types of institutions that do exist outside the confines of the State. An explorer from outer space charged with locating "third-sector"-type institutions in different societies throughout the world would thus have no trouble coming up with significant examples in virtually every country and region.

How are we to make sense of this mixture of diversity and commonality? More particularly, is it possible to identify a set of common features that define the core of what can reasonably be considered a common "nonprofit sector" throughout the world? It is to the search for an answer to this question that we turn in the next chapter.

References

Anheier, Helmut K. and Wolfgang Seibel (eds) (1990), *The Third Sector: Comparative Studies of Nonprofit Organizations*. Berlin/New York: DeGruyter.

Centeno, Miguel Angel (1994), "Between rocky democracies and hard markets: dilemmas of the double transitions." *Annual Review of Sociology*, 20:125–147.

Federal Ministry of Justice [Brazil] (1990), *Entidade de Utilidade Publica Federal: Manual para Requerimento*. [Federal Public Utility: A Requirements Manual].

Hopkins, Bruce R. (1987), *The Law of Tax-Exempt Organizations*, 5th edn. New York: Wiley.

James, Estelle (ed.) (1989), *The Nonprofit Sector in International Perspective: Studies in Comparative Culture and Policy*. Oxford: Oxford University Press.

Posnett, John (1987), "Trends in the income of registered charities." *Charity Trends*, 10:6–8.

Salamon, Lester M. (1992), *America's Nonprofit Sector: A Primer*. New York: The Foundation Center.

Chapter 3

TOWARD A COMMON DEFINITION

Lester M. Salamon and Helmut K. Anheier

As Chapter 2 made clear, tremendous variations exist in the kinds of institutions that exist outside the market and the State in different countries throughout the world. Tremendous variations exist as well in the extent of coherence in the concepts and terminology used to depict this social space in the different countries. These variations pose a fundamental challenge to effective cross-national understanding of this set of situations, and hence to effective appreciation of the relative roles that these institutions play from place to place. Indeed, in the absence of a reasonably clear definition that can identify the elements of commonality among the organizations that make up this sector cross-nationally, there has been a pronounced tendency to ignore the sector and devalue its contribution to social, economic, and political life. Without an agreed-upon definition, in fact, this sector can hardly be said to exist.

But is it possible to overcome this problem, to identify certain common features shared by the entities that lie outside the market and the State, which thus justify their designation as a distinctive economic "sector" that can be found, in more or less developed form, in numerous societies throughout the world?

In this chapter we explore the answer to this question. To do so, we first identify a number of possible *bases* or factors in terms of which the nonprofit sector could be defined. We then introduce a set of criteria to the various types of definitions we have identified to determine which one seems most promising both empirically and conceptually.

Alternative bases for defining the nonprofit sector

As a first step in developing a common definition of the nonprofit sector, it is useful to examine the various types of definitions that are available. Fortunately, a number of these have been developed, each of them utilizing a somewhat different basis for differentiating third-sector organizations from the others. In this section we briefly outline four major types of such definitions before taking up in a subsequent section how to choose among them.

The legal definition

Perhaps the most certain and straightforward system for defining the nonprofit sector is the one provided in a country's law. As noted in Chapter 2 above, most countries of the world have specific legal provisions for classifying organizations that fall into the nonprofit or third sector. In the United States, for example, nonprofit organizations are legally defined as incorporated entities that qualify for exemption from the federal income tax under any of twenty-six specific subsections of the Internal Revenue Code (Hopkins, 1987). Organizations as diverse as burial societies and business leagues, garden clubs and "charitable, educational, religious, or scientific" institutions can thus qualify as parts of the nonprofit sector under this definition. Scholars using this legal definition can consequently construct rather precise, if sometimes complicated, typologies of the organizations included in this sector (e.g. Simon, 1987). Under this type of definition, a nonprofit organization is what the law (including judge-made law) of a country says it is.

The economic/financial definition

A second type of definition of the nonprofit sector emphasizes not the legal form of the organization but the source of its income. This is the approach taken by the U.N. System of National Accounts (SNA), which is the set of conventions adopted by governments around the world for official reporting on national income. The U.N. System of National Accounts breaks all economic activity into five major sectors, of which the nonprofit sector is one, and non–financial corporations, financial corporations, government, and households are the others (United Nations, 1993).[1]

What differentiates these various sectors are the financial transactions that dominate their operations. Thus, *non-financial corporations* are establishments created for the purpose of producing goods and services for sale in the market at a price that is normally designed to cover the cost of production (United Nations, 1993:90, 96). *Governments* produce "non-market" goods and services that are subsidized by taxes on the citizenry (United Nations, 1993:101).

The key feature that sets the *nonprofit sector* apart from the others according to this definition is that the institutions that constitute it receive the bulk of their income not from the sale of goods and services in the market, but from the dues and contributions of their members and supporters. The System of National Accounts consequently designates these organizations formally as *nonprofit institutions serving households* to emphasize that these are organizations that receive most of their income from contributions made by private individuals and households. To the extent that an organization receives the bulk of its income from fees and charges, i.e., from the sale of products "at prices that are economically significant" (United Nations, 1993:95), it is considered by the SNA system to be part of the business sector, regardless of its legal form or status.[2] Similarly, to the extent that an organization is mainly financed by government, it is considered in the SNA system to be part of the government, regardless of its otherwise private character.[3] Only organizations that receive half or more of their income from households on a contributory basis are considered to be "nonprofit organizations serving households" in the U.N. system.

The functional definition

A third type of definition of the nonprofit sector emphasizes the functions or purposes that organizations in this sector carry out. Perhaps the most common type of function attributed to the nonprofit sector is the promotion of what is variously termed the "public interest," or "public purposes." Thus O'Neill (1989:2) defines nonprofit organizations as "private organizations serving a public purpose," i.e., some cause related to "the good of the society." Another recent account defines the global nonprofit sector as a set of organizations designed "to serve underserved or neglected populations, to expand the freedom of or to empower people, to engage in advocacy for social change, and to provide services" (McCarthy, Hodgkinson and Sumariwalla, 1992:3). Perhaps the most comprehensive statement of such a "public-purpose" definition can be found, however, in the Preamble to the Statute of Charitable Uses of 1601 in England. According to this definition, nonprofit organizations are those engaged in the following activities:

> relief of aged, impotent and poor people … maintenance of sick and maimed soldiers and mariners, schools of learning, free schools, and scholars in universities … repair of bridges, ports, havens, causeways, churches, seabanks, and highways, education and preferment of orphans … relief, stock, or maintenance for houses of correction … marriages of poor maids, … supportation, aid and help of young tradesmen, handicraftsmen and persons decayed … relief or redemption of prisoners or captives, … aid or ease of any poor inhabitant concerning payments of fifteens,[4] setting out of soldiers, and other taxes (cited in Hopkins, 1987:56; see Picarda, 1977).

A second type of functional definition focuses not on the broad "public purposes" such organizations are supposed to advance but on a more narrow set of group interests or concerns. Such definitions emphasize "mutuality" or "solidarity" as the central distinguishing features of these entities. Reflecting this, they tend to utilize the term "association," which connotes a coming together of people for a common purpose, to refer to such entities rather than the term "organization," which connotes a greater degree of hierarchy and structure.

While this variant of the functional approach is particularly prevalent in Europe, where the tradition of guilds and the French Revolution's concept of "fraternity" still hold sway, the concept has recently found expression as well in the American setting through Roger Lohmann's concept of "the commons" as the defining focus of what we are here terming the nonprofit sector (Lohmann, 1992). Nonprofit organizations in this formulation are groups of people who join together voluntarily for some common or shared purpose and interact in a spirit of mutuality.

The structural–operational definition

A final set of definitions emphasizes not the purposes of the organizations or their sources of income but their basic structure and operation. A wide variety of such structural features have been advanced as crucial to the concept of the nonprofit sector (see, for example, Hatch (1980:12), Brenton (1985:9), Hansmann (1987:28)). The actual features included in the structural–operational definition of the nonprofit sector may consequently vary. Based on the input of the team of international experts on the nonprofit sector who served as Local Associates on the Johns Hopkins Comparative Nonprofit Sector Project, however, five of these have been identified as most compelling. Using these key features, the nonprofit sector can be defined as a collection of entities that are:

- *Organized*, i.e., institutionalized to some extent. What is important is that the organization have some institutional reality to it. In some countries this is signified by a formal charter of incorporation. But institutional reality can also be demonstrated in other ways where legal incorporation is either not chosen or not readily available – by having regular meetings, officers, rules of procedure, or some degree of organizational permanence. Purely ad hoc, informal, and temporary gatherings of people are not considered part of the nonprofit sector under this definition, even though they may be quite important in people's lives. Otherwise the concept of the nonprofit sector becomes far too amorphous and ephemeral to grasp and examine.
- *Private*, i.e., institutionally separate from government. Nonprofit organizations are neither part of the governmental apparatus nor controlled by government, i.e., governed by boards dominated by government officials. This does not mean that they may not receive significant government support or that no government officials can sit on their boards. The key here is that nonprofit organizations must be fundamentally private institutions in basic structure.
- *Non-profit-distributing*, i.e., not returning any profits generated to their owners or directors. Nonprofit organizations may accumulate profits in a given year, but the profits must be plowed back into the basic mission of the agency, not distributed to the organizations' "owners" or governing board. In this sense, nonprofit organizations are private organizations that do not exist

primarily to generate profits. This differentiates nonprofit organizations from the other component of the private sector – private businesses.

- *Self-governing*, i.e., equipped to control their own activities.
  Nonprofit organizations have their own internal procedures for
  governance and are not controlled by outside entities.
- *Voluntary*, i.e., involving some meaningful degree of voluntary
  participation, either in the actual conduct of the agency's
  activities or in the management of its affairs. This does not
  mean that all or most of the income of an organization must
  come from voluntary contributions, or that most of its staff
  must be volunteers. The presence of some voluntary input,
  even if only a voluntary board of directors, suffices to qualify an
  organization as in some sense "voluntary."

Needless to say, the five conditions identified in this
structural–operational definition will vary in degrees, and some
organizations may qualify more easily on one criterion than
another. To be considered part of the nonprofit sector under this
definition, however, an organization must make a reasonable
showing on all five of these criteria.

Selecting the best definition

Each of these definitions has its merits and demerits. How, then,
are we to choose the best approach? What criteria can be
employed to distinguish the most productive of these definitions
from the less productive ones?

Evaluation criteria

One potentially fruitful answer to these questions can be found in
the work of Karl Deutsch cited earlier (Deutsch, 1963:16–18).
Deutsch identifies three basic criteria for choosing among models
in either the physical or social sciences, and his observations have
great value in sorting out the best type of definition to use to
depict the nonprofit sector. On the basis of these, we suggest that
the quality of a concept or a model depends on its *economy*, its
significance, and its *explanatory or predictive powers*.

Thus, in the first place, the better model is the one that is more *economical*, the one that identifies the truly critical aspects of a phenomenon or process and thereby produces a picture of reality that is simpler than reality itself. In the second place, the better model is the one that has more *significance*, the one that focuses attention on aspects or relationships that are not already obvious or that are not trivial. Finally, the better model is the one that has the greater *explanatory or predictive capacities*. This is the most complicated of the three criteria. To be predictive, a model must have *rigor*, *combinatorial richness*, and *organizing power*. *Rigor* is the capacity of a model to produce unique answers regardless of who uses it. *Combinatorial richness* refers to the range of hypotheses the model generates, the number of interesting features and relations it identifies. *Organizing power* consists of the ability of a model or concept to explain processes other than those it was originally designed to explain, its ability to account for new phenomena.

Applying the criteria

All four of the types of definition of the nonprofit sector identified above have advantages in terms of these three basic criteria. But the "structural–operational" definition seems to have the most advantages and the fewest disadvantages.

The legal definition. The legal definition probably has the most *rigor* of all. At least where laws on the nonprofit sector exist, the combination of statutory language and legal interpretation provides a definitive road map about which entities are part of the nonprofit sector and which are not. The problem, however, is that such definitions typically lack *economy* and *organizing power*. They lack *economy* because legal definitions are often convoluted and overlaid with case law, regulatory interpretations, and informal understandings. Ferreting out the meaning of seemingly straightforward legal language is therefore often a difficult task. Even more serious, however, is the lack of *organizing power* that characterizes such definitions. This is so because legal definitions are almost by definition particular to individual countries. To be sure, some legal concepts travel across national borders, such as the concept of "charitable" in English common law, which infuses much of American, Canadian, Irish, and Australian law as well. But the specific meanings attached to similar words can diverge widely over time. Thus, the responsibility for defining what is "charitable" in England is vested by the courts in the Charity Commission, and there the concept has been much more narrowly construed than in comparable rulings in the U.S. What is more, "charities" as defined by law are only one type of nonprofit organization in the U.K., and the legal status of the others is somewhat murky (see Chapter 10 below). Even more difficult is the use of this type of definition in countries such as Japan, where the legal treatment of nonprofit organizations is exceedingly narrow. Thus Japanese law makes provision for so-called *koeki hojin*, or public benefit organizations, but not all of these qualify for special tax treatment. Such treatment is often a function of other specialized laws in particular policy fields that identify targeted classes of organizations that government agencies decide are sufficiently supportive of public objectives to warrant special tax advantages. Under these circumstances, the legal definition becomes largely useless for comparative purposes.

The economic definition. The *economic* definition shares with the legal definition a considerable amount of *rigor* and enjoys in addition a high level of *economy* and *organizing power*. As used in the U.N. System of National Accounts, for example, this model is capable of yielding definitive answers about the size and scope of the nonprofit sector in virtually every country in the world, and of doing so with only a few critical criteria. The problem with this type of definition, however, is that it has serious shortcomings with regard to *significance* and *combinatorial richness*. So far as significance is concerned, the economic definition severely restricts the scope of the nonprofit sector by limiting it to a set of institutions that verges on the trivial. Under the U.N. definition, for example, most of the organizations commonly considered part of the nonprofit sector in the United States would disappear from it and be classified in other sectors because they receive more than half of their income from either government or fees and service charges. This is true of most universities, hospitals, arts institutions, and social service providers. So restricted, the nonprofit sector that remains is an almost trivial shadow of its real self, consisting only of wholly voluntary organizations or organizations half or more than half supported by private charitable gifts. In the terms introduced in Chapter 2 above, this approach essentially collapses the definition of the nonprofit sector into the definition of private philanthropy. In the process, it reduces the *combinatorial richness* of the concept, the range of interesting relationships it highlights and encompasses. Under this definition, many of the most important interconnections between the nonprofit sector and other sectors of social life are essentially defined away: nonprofits that are engaged in such interconnections to a significant extent are simply treated, by definition, as parts of these other sectors and not part of the nonprofit sector at all.

The functional definition. The *functional* definition has a very different set of advantages and disadvantages. In many respects, this type of definition resembles the legal approach except that it goes beyond particular statutes in particular countries to ferret out certain underlying principles about the kinds of objectives that various countries reward with nonprofit status. This approach thus has much greater *organizing power* than does the legal approach since it can travel more easily across national borders. The problem, however, is that it purchases this greater organizing power at the cost of *economy, rigor,* and *combinatorial richness.* The functional approach lacks *economy* because it requires extensive listings of types of purposes that qualify organizations for nonprofit status. The listing provided in the Statute of Charitable Uses cited earlier is one illustration of this. At the same time, this approach lacks a certain *rigor* because some of the key functional categories are often ambiguous and others are highly time-sensitive. Serving the "public good," for example, is a difficult concept to define with precision and may depend on the eye of the beholder. A lawyer's association may be a potent force for ensuring individual rights in Egypt and thus an instrument for promotion of the public good, but the same type of organization may be an instrument for the self-promotion and aggrandizement of legal professionals in the United States and thus an instrument of private good only. Including this type of organization in one setting and excluding it in another could cause great confusion, however. By the same token, definitions of the public good change over time. The Weeks organization may have been considered charitable in medieval England for its work in distributing "faggots" used in burning heretics, but only a few die-hards would consider this a valid charitable purpose today. Finally this approach lacks *combinatorial richness* because it frequently tends to downplay certain types of entities that are widely considered parts of the nonprofit sector in particular parts of the world but are not often included in listings of charitable or nonprofit functions. These include artistic and cultural activities, recreation, sports, and other activities not targeted particularly on the poor or disadvantaged, as well as the characteristic "NGOs," or nongovernmental organizations, common in the developing world, which may appear more involved in business activities than the entities typically identified by the functional definition.

The structural–operational definition. The *structural–operational* definition avoids many of these pitfalls. This approach is relatively *economical* and *significant*, and has considerable *combinatorial richness* and *organizing power*. As far as its *economy* is concerned, this approach identifies a broad range of organizations with just five basic characteristics. The entities identified as part of the nonprofit sector are far from trivial, moreover. In countries such as those in the developing world, where the nonprofit sector has effectively been defined as "NGOs," this definition may in fact usefully broaden the focus of attention by making it clear that there is a much wider array of organizations with which NGOs share many crucial common features. Because of this, the approach has great *combinatorial richness*, permitting the examination of a wide assortment of characteristics and features. Indeed, with a suitable classification scheme, this definition permits focused attention on particular subsets of the nonprofit sector that are of particular interest. For example, primarily "public-serving" organizations can be separated out from primarily "member-serving" ones (Salamon, 1992), or sacramental religious organizations from others. This approach also has considerable *organizing power*, since it is not restricted to particular countries or substantive settings but rather defines a set of organizations that share certain structural and operational characteristics whatever their geographic location or field of activity.

This is not to say that this approach is without its drawbacks, of course. Compared to the economic definition it lacks *rigor* since some of the structural–operational criteria are difficult to apply with precision. In Japan, for example, many organizations that would normally be treated as parts of the nonprofit sector have influential government officials on their boards who often dominate organization affairs even though they do not constitute a majority of the board members. Does this mean that they fail the "nongovernmental" test? To get a precise answer might require interviewing the board members of the organizations. Similarly, concerns have been raised about the degree of control that government funding of nonprofit organizations brings in its wake. An organization that is institutionally separate from government yet receives 80 percent or 90 percent of its funding from government may consequently fail the "nongovernmental" test in fact if not in theory, though the evidence on this point suggests that funding yields less actual control than is sometimes assumed.[5] In addition, while it is more *economical* than some definitions, the structural–operational approach is less economical than others, requiring five rather complicated criteria to depict the nonprofit sector. Finally, the structural–operational definition is not without its troubling "borderline" cases. One of the most serious of these is the class of community-based development organizations and cooperatives in developing countries and other low-income communities. To the extent that these organizations primarily seek to stimulate economic activity and distribute the resulting "profits" to the communities that control the organizations, they would fall foul of the structural–operational definition's exclusion of profit-distributing organizations. However, to the extent that the fundamental objective of these organizations is not profit *per se* but general community betterment, they would fit the definition's requirements.

Despite these difficulties, compared to the other options this one seems to offer the most advantages and the fewest disadvantages, particularly for cross-national work. It makes it possible to define the nonprofit sector empirically without separately investigating every organization. It embraces within the sector a broad array of relevant organizations without opening it to every type of organized or unorganized entity that exists. And it makes it possible to generate hypotheses about the relationships between this sector and the other components of social and economic life.

Applying the structural–operational definition

To illustrate the utility of the "structural–operational" definition, it is useful to spell out more concretely the range of organizations it embraces, and to show how it accommodates the reality of organizational life in three quite different settings: first, the common law country of the U.K.; second, the civil law country of Germany; and third, the developing country of Brazil.

Components of the nonprofit sector

As is reflected in Table 3.1, a wide range of entities fits comfortably within the nonprofit sector as defined using our preferred "structural–operational" definition. This includes organizations engaged in culture and recreation, education, research, health, social services, development, housing, advocacy, philanthropy, religion, and business representation.[6]

Table 3.1

Types of entities embraced within the nonprofit sector according to the structural–operational definition

- Culture and recreation
- Education and research
- Health
- Social services
- Environment
- Development and housing
- Law, advocacy, and politics
- Philanthropic intermediaries and voluntarism promotion
- International
- Religion
- Business, professional associations, unions

The U.K. case[7]

The utility of the structural–operational definition can be further demonstrated by showing how it copes with the challenge of defining the nonprofit sector in a number of distinct countries. The U.K. is a good starting-point for such a discussion because it has both one of the most highly developed nonprofit or "voluntary" sectors and one of the most complex.

One reason for the complexity is the fact that different legal systems exist in the U.K. – one covering England and Wales, another

Scotland, and a third Northern Ireland. Beyond this, the shape of the U.K. nonprofit sector has been importantly shaped by the English "common law" tradition, which puts a premium on flexibility and evolution rather than precise delineation of organizational types.[8]

As noted in Chapter 2 above, the center of gravity of the U.K. nonprofit sector ("voluntary sector" in U.K. usage) is so-called "charities." These are organizations formally registered as "charities" by the U.K. Charity Commission and thereby accorded the protection of the Crown, the Courts, and the Charity Commission for their activities, including protection from taxation. The requirements for such classification have never been clearly and definitively specified, however. The listing provided in the Preamble to the Statute of Charitable Uses has been a start, but it has been successively revised. Perhaps the most definitive ruling has been that in Pemsel's case in 1891, which approved four different classes of charities: those for relief of poverty, those for the advancement of education, those for the advancement of religion, and those for other purposes "beneficial to the community."

Aside from this ambiguity, however, charities make up only half of the organizations typically considered part of the voluntary sector in the U.K. What is more, even charities come in a variety of legal forms – trusts, unincorporated associations, and companies limited by guarantee. In addition to this, there are so-called "friendly societies" and "industrial and benevolent societies."

Defined in legal terms, therefore, the U.K. nonprofit sector is a bewilderingly confused set of institutions with poorly defined boundaries. Implicitly, social science research followed the functional definition, and concentrated on either registered charities (Posnett, 1987) or voluntary associations (Brenton, 1985). Consequently, there is no commonly accepted concept that captures the basic contours of the sector as a whole, and that spells out the defining components of the organizations which in the aggregate constitute the nonprofit sector.

To what extent does the "structural–operational" definition proposed here overcome this problem and succeed in giving some coherence to what the law leaves bewilderingly confused in the U.K. context? The answer, it appears, is fairly well.

In the first place, the criterion of "organized entity" in the structural–operational definition sets nonprofit organizations apart from voluntary activities and helping behavior within private households and local neighborhoods. While some unincorporated self-help groups might be overlooked as a result of this criterion, the definition is broad enough to encompass most of what would be considered "voluntary organizations" in the U.K.

The structural–operational definition also provides a convenient way to sort out a number of "borderline" situations that characterize the U.K. nonprofit sector, such as the quangos or quasi-nongovernmental organizations, the so-called "para-state apparatus" of private organizations outside the public sector (Wolch, 1990:4), the growing numbers of self-governing bodies within the public sector, and the wide variety of friendly societies, cooperatives, and mutual insurance companies. As for the quangos and "para-state" organizations, they would be treated as outside the nonprofit sector to the extent that they are created, controlled and fully financed by government, but included to the extent that they are truly self-governing bodies outside majority control by government. With regard to mutual benefit organizations, such as cooperatives, mutual insurance companies, and building societies, most have moved closer to for-profit firms and are now virtually indistinguishable from commercial organizations even though they are traditionally seen as part of the U.K. voluntary sector. Under the structural–operational definition they would be excluded from the nonprofit sector. So, too, would the "not-for-profit agencies" which have emerged in the field of social care; they have paid boards, and salaries are linked to organizational performance. According to the nonprofit criteria, they constitute borderline cases, and most would be excluded from the nonprofit sector.

In summary, applied to the U.K. circumstances, the structural–operational definition embraces almost all organizations commonly regarded as parts of the U.K. voluntary sector. Important borderline situations exist primarily in defining such features as "self-governing," "private," i.e., constitutionally separate from government, as well as "not profit-distributing." This last criterion excludes from the sector some cooperatives and community-based businesses that have historically been regarded as part of the sector (for example, building societies); but many of these have developed a commercial orientation that now makes them virtually indistinguishable from for-profit entities.

Germany[9]

As in other countries, the different legal and tax-based, economic, and functional as well as lay definitions of nonprofit organizations in Germany produce a complex and confusing terminology: unincorporated and incorporated associations, public benefit associations, public law associations, public and private law foundations, limited liability companies, cooperatives, communal economy corporations, and non-commercial organizations. Each term focuses on a particular subset of nonprofits, and significant overlaps among organizations exist.

In contrast to most of the United Kingdom, Germany is a civil law country in which two legal systems, public and private law, regulate the nonprofit sector. In addition, the German nonprofit sector is influenced by two overarching concepts: the principle of *subsidiarity*, which gives priority to private over public action in many areas of social and cultural policy, and the principle of *self-administration*, which affords considerable independence to many public law institutions. Both principles act as major organizing forces on the shape of the German nonprofit sector.

Several legal forms are consequently available for nonprofit organizations, usually based on the civil code for private law associations or special public and ecclesiastical charters and ordinances for public law associations:

- associations in the form of ideal, i.e., noncommercial, associations, which are nonprofit by definition;
- a smaller subset of recognized private public utility associations which enjoy additional tax privileges and can receive tax-deductible donations;
- private law foundations, non-membership-based trusts or endowments operating for the benefit of third parties, which include both grant-making and operating foundations;
- public law foundations and agencies that are created by governmental authorities but may enjoy far-reaching independence in terms of governance, administration and financing;
- the limited liability company regulated by the Commercial Code; and
- cooperative societies, as regulated by various special cooperative laws.

Taken together, however, the different legal forms do not add up to a distinct set of organizations: for example, registered associations may or may not be charitable; public law organizations vary from government agencies to largely independent institutions like public television stations, the Bavarian Red Cross Society, the Jewish Welfare Agency, and even the Roman Catholic and Protestant Churches; and public utility organizations include mutual benefit societies, and political parties, but exclude the Churches.

Thus legal definitions have limited utility in describing the non-profit sector in Germany. Moreover, the common understanding of the German nonprofit sector does not follow this legal structure. The parts of the nonprofit sector regulated by the principle of sub-sidiarity are usually referred to as "welfare associations" or "free carriers," a set of six relatively large conglomerates of nonprofit organizations delivering a wide range of health and social services. In fact, the "free carriers" are themselves made up of numerous establishments with different legal status. For example, the Protestant *Diakonie*, an umbrella for thousands of separate legal entities, consists of registered associations (43.2 percent), foundations (23.4 percent), public law foundations and corporations (29.4 percent), limited liability companies (5 percent), and other legal forms (Thermann, 1979). Members of the *Paritätischer Wohlfahrtsverband* include registered associations (88.6 percent) and limited liability companies (5.5 percent), with public law corporations and foundations making up the remaining 5.9 percent (Bockhacker, 1985).

The parts of the German nonprofit sector close to the principle of self-administration include public law corporations and foundations. Like quangos in the U.K., these "agencies of public law," as they are commonly understood and referred to, vary in the extent to which they are independent from government. Consequently, they include organizations that are operational arms of some federal or state ministry, as well as chambers of commerce and industry, radio and television stations, or institutions of higher education. Not all, however, qualify as nonprofit organizations under the structural–operational definition.

The great virtue of the structural–operational definition as applied to the German situation is that it pulls together the several overlapping subunits that national concepts treat separately. The structural–operational definition ties together the organizations regulated by these different bodies of law and commonly attributed to different sectors.

For example, the structural–operational definition makes it possible to get around one of the more serious complications in German treatment of the nonprofit sector: the differentiation between public and private law corporations. In practice, public law institutions are often virtually identical to their private law counterparts. Despite the clear distinction between public and private legal status suggested in the law, the choice of a public or private legal form seems often a matter of political and other circumstance rather than the strict application of civil law principles. For example, in matters involving both the federal and the state governments, the private nonprofit sector form is more practical, flexible and often less costly than the establishment of public law agencies. In such cases the virtue of the structural–operational definition is that it gets away from the narrow legal form and focuses on the operation of the organization.

Similarly, this definition makes it easy to encompass the political foundations which, aligned with major political parties, carry out a wide range of activities like political adult education, and management training and research. While they are relatively autonomous both legally and practically from individual party organizations, their objectives are nonetheless to support the party, however indirectly. In addition, many close personnel linkages exist.

Somewhat more complicated is the interpretation of the "voluntary" criterion in the German context. Church membership is quasi-automatic for children of Christian parents in Germany, and "opting out" rather than "opting in" is required to exercise the "voluntary" aspect of membership. A similar case can be made for the church tax, which is levied on the taxable income of every Church member to be collected by the public tax authorities. To treat the Church as part of the nonprofit sector in Germany, therefore, it is necessary to interpret voluntary as implying non-compulsory.

In short, the structural–operational definition usefully groups together what are otherwise considered separate types of organizations in Germany. It does so by de-emphasizing internal, often ill-defined, distinctions so as to allow us to focus in on aspects of the German nonprofit sector that are both important and difficult to conceptualize and measure, such as the distinction between the private and the public sector. The definition makes it possible to retain both private law and independent public law organizations in the nonprofit sector, yet to differentiate the nonprofit sector from a number of business-like institutions such as cooperatives, mutual insurance companies, housing associations, and marketing and promotional societies for businesses. It also differentiates the nonprofit sector from what in Germany are compulsory public law associations like the chamber of commerce, craft, and industry, and similar organizations for the medical and legal professions.

Brazil[10]

The utility of the structural–operational definition is perhaps best illustrated in the case of Brazil, a country in transition from underdeveloped to developed status.

As in many developing countries, the roles of both the State and the private sector are very much in flux in Brazil. In a context of extensive economic hardship and authoritarian politics, the nonprofit sector emerged as a focal point of political opposition closely allied, in many cases, with the Catholic Church. So politicized has the situation been, in fact, that even staid professional associations have often found themselves functioning as hotbeds of civil society protest. Beyond this are the countless unregistered community groups and grass-roots development associations that have provided a mechanism for mobilizing local communities for development activities.

In this turbulent climate, a narrow legal or functional definition of the nonprofit sector would miss much of the central reality of the sector as it operates in this context. For example, professional associations that would normally be excluded under most functional definitions need to be included in the highly charged political atmosphere of a developing society. Such organizations form part of an *associativismo* movement that includes labor unions, trade and professional associations, and membership organizations and that aims to build a "civil society."[11]

Community-based self-help and development organizations and cooperatives are a central part of the nonprofit sector in Third World countries like Brazil. As was pointed out above, this part also includes many "borderline" cases as seen from the standpoint of the structural–operational definition. If grass-roots efforts return profit generated by their activities primarily to owners, and to the community at large only secondarily, then such activities would be classified as businesses. If, however, profits are primarily distributed to the local communities that control the associations, we would treat them as part of the nonprofit sector. In actuality, the difference between real estate agency (business) and community development association (nonprofit) may be difficult to establish in the highly dynamic economy of the informal sector of Brazil and other developing countries. Nevertheless, we maintain that the structural–operational definition works better than some of the concepts employed locally. Perhaps the most common of these is the term "NGO." Though of relatively recent origin, this term has changed its meaning several times. While it was first used to refer to international, nongovernmental membership organizations represented at the League of Nations first and the United Nations later, its meaning changed to include development-oriented private organizations from the developed world, and then extended to cover indigenous self-help and advocacy groups, and educational, health and social service facilities. In other words, while the broadening of the term NGO reflects the social and economic situation in developing countries, it ranks low in terms of organizing power and rigor.

The structural–operational definition avoids the "catch-all" quality of the term NGO and the ambivalence of the term "association." As in the German case discussed above, this definition thus usefully de-emphasizes distinctions and similarities that reflect particular national, legal and political circumstances, while highlighting crucial common features.

Conclusion

The nonprofit sector has only recently emerged from obscurity as a distinguishable social sphere with its own characteristic features. At the same time, recognition of these features has been restricted to a relative handful of specialists, limiting popular understanding, systematic data assembly, and scholarly research. Crucial reasons for this have been the amorphousness of the definitions used to depict the sector and the absence of a workable concept with enough clarity and specificity to capture the central features of this field reliably and extensively. As we have argued, such concepts are the *sine qua non* of all understanding, and their absence has seriously impeded the development of this field.

The "structural–operational" definition of the nonprofit sector advanced here is doubtless not the last word on how to solve this problem. But we are convinced that it is a useful first step. As the chapters in Part II of this book will show, the components of this definition identified here have been tested against the realities of 13 countries spanning all the major continents, religious traditions, and social systems of the world, and have been found to work. Although more elegant, more rigorous, or more economical definitions may ultimately be found, we consider this one a useful foundation around which to organize serious thinking and research.

Notes

1 For a further discussion of the U.N. System of National Accounts and its treatment of the nonprofit sector, see Anheier, Rudney and Salamon, 1993.
2 In making these calculations, the SNA accountants are supposed to deduct any value of a product or service that is in excess of the fee received. In other words, if an organization is subsidizing a service and charging less than its true market value, the difference between the price charged and the value of the service is treated as a contribution by the organization.
3 In the case of government, an organization must not only be "mainly financed" but also "controlled" by government to be considered part of the government sector (United Nations, 1993:95). This added criterion picks up an element of the "structural–operational" definition described below.
4 *Fifteen*: "(=fifteenth), a tax formerly [and irregularly] imposed on personal property" (*Oxford English Dictionary*).
5 For a summary of this evidence, see Salamon, 1987, and Salamon, 1995.
6 For a discussion of the classification system reflected in this table, see Chapter 4 below.
7 This section draws heavily on Kendall and Knapp, Chapter 10 below.
8 The following discussion applies primarily to England and Wales, but not to Scotland, which is a civil law country.

9 This section draws heavily on Anheier and Seibel, 1993, and Chapter 6 below.
10 This section draws heavily on Landim, Chapter 12 below.
11 The term *associationalism* is also used to describe aspects of the non-profit sector in France and Italy. See Chapters 5 and 7 below.

References

Anheier, Helmut K. and Wolfgang Seibel (1993), "Defining the nonprofit sector: Germany." *Working Papers of the Johns Hopkins Comparative Nonprofit Sector Project*, no. 6. Baltimore: Johns Hopkins Institute for Policy Studies. (See also Chapter 6 in this volume.)

Anheier, Helmut K., Gabriel Rudney and Lester M. Salamon (1993), "The nonprofit sector in the United Nations System of National Accounts: definition, treatment, and practice." *Voluntas*, 4(4):486–501.

Bockhacker, Jürgen (1985), "Die Unternehmen in Deutschen Paritätischen Wohlfahrtsverhand." *Zeitschrift für öffentliche und gemeinwirtschaftliche Unternehmen*, 8:6–16.

Brenton, Maria (1985), *The Voluntary Sector in British Social Services*. London: Longman.

Deutsch, Karl (1963), *The Nerves of Government*. New York: The Free Press.

Hansmann, Henry (1987), "Economic theories of nonprofit organizations," in *The Nonprofit Sector: A Research Handbook*, ed. W. W. Powell. New Haven: Yale University Press.

Hatch, Stephen (1980), *Outside the State: Voluntary Organizations in Three Towns*. London: Croom Helm.

Hopkins, Bruce R. (1987), *The Law of Tax-Exempt Organizations*. 5th edn. New York: Wiley.

Lohmann, Roger (1992), *The Commons*. San Francisco: Jossey-Bass.

McCarthy, Kathleen D., Virginia Hodgkinson and Russy Sumariwalla (1992), *The Nonprofit Sector in the Global Community*. San Francisco: Jossey-Bass.

O'Neill, Michael (1989), *The Third America: The Emergence of the Nonprofit Sector in the United States*. San Francisco: Jossey-Bass Publishers.

Picarda, Hubert (1977), *Law and Practice Relating to Charities*. London: Butterworth.

Posnett, John (1987), "Trends in the income of registered charities." *Charity Trends* 10:6–8.

Salamon, Lester M. (1987), "Partners in public service: the scope and theory of government–nonprofit relations," in *The Nonprofit Sector: A Research Handbook*, ed. W. W. Powell. New Haven: Yale University Press.

Salamon, Lester M. (1992), *America's Nonprofit Sector: A Primer*. New York: The Foundation Center.

Salamon, Lester M. (1995), *Partners in Public Service*. Baltimore: Johns Hopkins University Press.

Simon, John (1987), "The tax treatment of nonprofit organizations: a review of federal and state policies," in *The Nonprofit Sector: A Research Handbook*, ed. W. W. Powell. New Haven: Yale University Press.

Thermann, Gottfried (1979), "Einrichtungen der Diakonie als gemein-wirtschaftliche Unternehmen." *Zeitschrift für öffentliche und gemein-sirtschaftliche Unternehmen*, 2:443–56.

United Nations (1993), *System of National Accounts, 1993* (E.94.XVII.4, ST/ESA/STAT/Ser.F/2/Rev. 4). New York: United Nations.

Wolch, Jennifer R. (1990), *The Shadow State: Government and Voluntary Sector in Transition*. New York: The Foundation Center.

Chapter 4

TOWARD A COMMON CLASSIFICATION

Lester M. Salamon and Helmut K. Anheier

If, as we have argued, the lack of attention that has historically been given to the nonprofit sector around the world has been due to factors that are as much conceptual as empirical, then the task of defining the nonprofit sector and identifying its common characteristics, which we addressed in the previous chapter, still represents only half of the conceptual challenge involved in coming to terms with this sector. At least as important is a second crucial task: the task of classification, of identifying the systematic *differences* among the organizations in the sector and an appropriate basis for grouping them.

Definition and classification are, in a sense, two parts of a related process. The first specifies what the entities in a group have in common; and the second spells out the ways in which they nevertheless differ.

Such differentiation is absolutely essential for serious analysis, and even casual description. As a recent United Nations report (1990:6) puts it: "… all economic processes that are to be described in the form of statistics require systematic classification. Classifications are, so to speak, the system of languages used in communication about … phenomena."

This general need for a classification system is particularly applicable to the nonprofit sector. Because of the diversity of this sector, comparisons at the level of the sector as a whole can be at best incomplete and at worst seriously misleading. Countries that have major differences in the overall scale and character of their nonprofit sectors can nevertheless have significant commonalities with respect to particular types of organizations. Without some systematic basis for grouping information in terms of the component parts of this sector, little progress can be made in describing the sector, let alone conducting serious cross-national research on it.

The challenges of classification

Two key issues

While classification is essential, however, it is also very difficult. No single classification system is perfect for all possible purposes. In a sense, the ultimate value of a classification system is dictated by the use to which it will be put. For some uses, it is sufficient to group all organizations that are part of a class simply by size. For others, more complex classifications are necessary.

Broadly speaking, two basic issues have to be settled in the design of any classification system. The first of these is the *unit of analysis* to be used; and the second is the *basis of the classification*, the central variable, or variables, in terms of which entities are to be differentiated from each other.

Unit of analysis. So far as the unit of analysis is concerned, the task is to find the unit that is both sufficiently homogeneous in terms of the classification factor of interest (so that entities can really be grouped in terms of this factor) and also sufficiently manageable in terms of being a unit about which relevant information is collected. A complex organization such as Caritas, the Catholic human service agency in Germany, for example, may operate several hospitals, a number of day care centers, and a variety of family service agencies. If the organization is the unit of analysis, therefore, Caritas would likely be classified as a health provider, since that is probably the activity that accounts for the largest share of its expenditures. In the process, however, the classification system would obscure the probably more numerous family service agencies that the Caritas organization also encompasses. While it may be more precise to focus on the individual establishments or service units, however, Caritas may not keep its data in this form.

Basis of classification. Even when the unit of analysis can be established, important questions remain about the basis to use for classification. The possibilities here are almost endless: size, legal form, clientele, type of activity, product. All of these are reasonable possibilities, but each yields a different result. Thus a non-profit organization that conducts research on health matters could logically be grouped together with other research organizations or with other health organizations depending on whether the activity (research) or the product (health services) is used as the basis of the classification. Unless these matters are clearly under-stood and systematized, serious problems can arise in trying to interpret the basic parameters of the sector, especially in cross–national settings.

Alternative bases for classifying nonprofit organizations

Fortunately, a wide variety of systems for classifying nonprofit organizations are in existence, and they offer some insights into how to settle these issues. While these systems differ in many respects, there is some consensus that the appropriate unit of anal-ysis is the *individual establishment* and that the appropriate basis for classification, at least for assessing the economic character of the sector, is the *economic activity* that the establishment carries out, i.e., the product or service it generates.[1] This is the basis for the national income data used to generate estimates of national eco-nomic activity around the world, and it is also the basis for many of the more numerous national systems within which nonprofit organizations are classified.

To say that there are some basic commonalties among a num-ber of classification systems now in use for the nonprofit sector is not yet to say that the existing systems are the same. Most of the existing systems are built around *national legal codes* and embody an essentially legal definition of the nonprofit sector. A system developed by the Internal Revenue Service in the United States some years ago to classify nonprofit organizations, for example, identifies over 400 types of organizations, most of them subsets of the 26 different provisions of the Internal Revenue Code under which organizations can claim tax-exempt status. The *Nomenclature des domaines d'action associations* used by the French Statistical Office (INSEE, 1990), by contrast, utilizes an entirely dif-ferent grouping consisting of 10 general domains of activity, which are subdivided into 64 subdomains. Many of these are peculiar to French national circumstances, however, such as the distinction between university-based sport activities and other sport clubs, or the inclusion of the domain of "Transport and Communication."

Fortunately, however, a number of more general classification schemes are also available for differentiating the types of organizations that make up the nonprofit sector. These include the U.N. International Standard Industrial Classification (ISIC) of all economic activities, the General Industrial Classification of Economic Activities (NACE) developed by the European Statistical Office, and the National Taxonomy of Exempt Entities (NTEE) developed by the National Center for Charitable Statistics in the United States.

In the balance of this chapter, we assess the relative utility of these different classification systems and then suggest a modified system that we argue is more suitable than the existing alternatives for comparative international work in this field. We call this the *International Classification of Nonprofit Organizations (ICNPO)*. In order to explain why this alternative system is superior, however, we must first explore what the criteria are for choosing among classification schemes in this field.

Evaluation criteria

Since the utility of a classification scheme is determined in important part by the use to which it will be put, great care must be taken in declaring one system superior to another. For the present purposes, however, the evaluation criteria formulated by Karl Deutsch to choose among analytical models in the social sciences, and used in Chapter 3 above to choose among alternative definitions of the nonprofit sector, also provide an objective basis for choosing one classification scheme over another. In these terms, the best classification system, like the best definition, is the one that achieves the optimum combination of economy, significance, rigor, combinatorial richness, and explanatory power. Let us examine each of these in turn.

Economy. The temptation with any classification system is to multiply the number of categories so that it comes close to the number of separate organizations. So elaborated, a classification system loses its value as a way to simplify reality. What is more, it can make the system unworkable by requiring information that is not easily available.

As with a definition, therefore, a classification system to be effective must have a reasonable degree of economy. That is, it must group the welter of organizations that constitute the sector into a reasonable number of groupings, and it must do so with reference to only a limited set of crucial factors.

Significance. Economy, however, is only one factor in judging a classification system. Equally important is the preservation of distinctions that highlight the truly significant differences in the phenomenon under study. A classification scheme that is simple and economical but that permits comparison only in terms of factors that are trivial or unimportant is not the one that should command support. The classification must focus attention on differences that are truly meaningful and significant.

Rigor. Classification systems must also be rigorous or reliable in terms of measurement. Criteria must be defined in such a way that organizations that end up in one category in one country would be likely to end up in the same category in another country. What is more, the classification should not depend on special information known to only a small number of people. The basis for the classification should be capable of being made sufficiently clear to ensure that different people would group the same agencies the same way most of the time.

Combinatorial richness. A fourth crucial criterion of an effective classification system is the "combinatorial richness" it achieves. Combinatorial richness is the measure of the productivity of the classification system, the extent to which it surfaces a wide range of interesting relationships, comparisons, and contrasts. Combinatorial richness and economy are therefore partly in opposition to each other, since greater combinatorial richness can often be achieved only at the expense of a loss of economy, and vice versa. But these two criteria are not simply opposite sides of the same coin. On the contrary, it is possible to have a classification system that lacks *both* economy and combinatorial richness because it uses complex criteria of differentiation that are nevertheless not very suggestive.

Organizing power. The final test of a classification system is its "organizing power," its ability to fit circumstances other than the one it was originally developed to fit. This is obviously especially important in international comparative work. A classification system with the greatest organizing power is the one that can most comfortably encompass the circumstances of the largest number of different countries or types of national situations.

Summary. Clearly, no classification system can score equally high on all of these criteria, if for no other reason than that national circumstances do differ considerably. A system that is precise enough to demarcate the organizations in a particular country with great rigor is therefore likely to lack the organizing power to apply to another country very easily. Complex tradeoffs therefore exist among the various criteria, and systems that may be ideal for particular national circumstances may consequently not work well for international, comparative work. Since our objective here is to find a classification system that will work best comparatively, we necessarily put slightly more emphasis on some criteria (such as "organizing power" and "economy") than others. The discussion of various classification systems below must consequently not be taken to suggest that the various systems may not have great value in particular national circumstances. Rather, our question is different: How well do these systems work for the task of classifying the nonprofit sector for comparative, international work? The answer, we suggest, is "not very well", leading us to develop an alternative system. Let us examine, then, what factors led us to this conclusion and what the components of our recommended system are.

Existing classification systems: an assessment

Broadly speaking, three fairly comprehensive classification systems are available for differentiating the nonprofit sector at the international level: first, the U.N.'s International Standard Industrial Classification (ISIC) (United Nations, 1990); the European Communities' General Industrial Classification of Economic Activities (NACE) (Eurostat, 1985); and the National Taxonomy of Exempt Entities (NTEE) developed by the National Council of Charitable Statistics in the United States. How well do these systems stack up in terms of the criteria identified above?

The U.N. International Standard Industrial Classification System (ISIC)

The U.N. ISIC system was formulated to provide a basis for developing consistent economic statistics among the countries of the world. Modelled on the standard industrial classification system developed in the United States, it was adopted at the international level in 1948 and provides the most comprehensive and widely used system for classifying economic activity in the world.

Now in its third revision, the ISIC system essentially differentiates the many types of "establishments" in any national economy in terms of the principal "economic activity" they are in. Altogether, the ISIC groups establishments into 17 broad "sections" (e.g., Agriculture, Hunting, and Forestry; Manufacturing), subdivides these into 60 "divisions" (e.g., manufacture of textiles, manufacture of tobacco products, manufacture of rubber and plastics products), and further subdivides these 60 into up to nine "groups" each (e.g., "spinning, weaving, and finishing of textiles," "manufacture of knitted and crocheted fabrics and articles," etc.).

Like its cousin, the "economic definition of the nonprofit sector" described in Chapter 3, the International Standard Industrial Classification system has a great deal of *economy*, *rigor*, and *organizing power*. The system has evolved over more than forty years through the active involvement of statisticians from countries around the world. Although certainly not without its complexities, it provides a relatively efficient way to sort an immense amount of economic data on virtually every country, and has acquired, through extensive communication among statistical officials, a high degree of precision cross-nationally. What is more, it is a system that is already in place in the economic data systems of a wide array of countries, making it a very practical system for gathering economic data on the nonprofit sector.

Despite its considerable strengths, however, the ISIC system also has significant drawbacks as a mechanism for classifying the nonprofit sector. In the first place, as we pointed out in Chapter 3 above and elsewhere (Salamon and Anheier, 1992a; Anheier, Rudney, and Salamon, 1993), the ISIC system utilizes a definition of the nonprofit sector that excludes a significant portion of what is widely considered part of the sector, i.e., organizations that receive half or more of their income from fees or government support. Perhaps because of this, the types of nonprofit organizations that are differentiated in the ISIC classification are rather limited. Almost all the organizations meeting our definition for inclusion in the nonprofit sector would fall into one of only three broad classes identified in the ISIC: Education (M), Health and Social Work (N), and Other Community, Social, and Personal Activities (O) (see Table 4.1). Although the education category is usefully split apart into meaningful categories, the others are not. This is particularly true of "Health and Social Work," which groups a broad range of social welfare activities from counselling to adoption assistance to rehabilitation assistance under the broad catch-all "social work activities." What is more, the "Other Community, Social, and Personal Activities" category also contains an immense range of different types, from trade unions to libraries, museums, and religious congregations. The result is such a broad set of catch-all categories that it is difficult to use the scheme to make meaningful comparisons among countries at the level of subsectors of the nonprofit sector. In the terms we introduced earlier, the classification system thus lacks *significance* and *combinatorial richness* so far as the nonprofit sector is concerned.

Not only does it lack combinatorial richness, however, but also the ISIC system as currently constituted lacks *organizing power*. This is so because the system fails to give sufficient prominence to a type of nonprofit organization that has become increasingly important in many developing nations: the so-called nongovernmental organization, or NGO. These are combinations of housing, community development, economic development, and community empowerment organizations. During the past twenty years they have grown increasingly important in the life of many developing societies; yet they do not find a convenient or prominent home in the ISIC system. Developed for a different purpose, the ISIC does not seem able to accommodate this significant new phenomenon.

Eurostat's general industrial classification of economic activities (NACE)

As originally formulated, the General Industrial Classification of Economic Activities (NACE) developed by the European Statistical Office provided some useful improvements on the basic ISIC system (Eurostat, 1979:25–6; 1985). As reflected in Table 4.1, the NACE system added two major categories to the ISIC system: (1) "Research and Development"; and (2) "Recreation and Culture" (included as part of "other community services" under

ISIC). This usefully tightened the "Other Community, Social, and Personal Services" category and highlights the role of nonprofit research bodies.

Table 4.1

Existing and proposed classification systems for nonprofit organizations

Existing			Proposed
International Standard Industrial Classification (ISIC)	General Industrial Classification of Economic Activities (NACE)	National Taxonomy of Exempt Entities (NTEE)	International Classification of Nonprofit Organizations (ICNPO)
EDUCATION	EDUCATION	EDUCATION	EDUCATION &
• Primary	• High–Higher	• Elementary, secondary	RESEARCH
• Secondary	• Primary and secondary	• Vocational	• Primary and secondary
• Higher	• Vocational	• Higher	• Higher
• Adult and other	• Nursery	• Professional schools	• Other
		• Continuing	• Research
HEALTH AND SOCIAL	RESEARCH AND	• Libraries	
WORK	DEVELOPMENT	• Student services/	HEALTH
• Human health services		organizations	• Hospitals and
• Veterinary activities	MEDICAL/HEALTH	• Other	rehabilitation
• Social work activities	• Hospitals, nursing		• Nursing homes
	homes, sanitaria	HEALTH	• Mental health and
OTHER COMMUNITY	• Other medical care	• Hospitals, nursing	crisis intervention
SOCIAL AND	• Dental care	homes, convalescent	• Other
PERSONAL SERVICE	• Veterinary	• Outpatient facilities	
ACTIVITIES		• Reproductive health	SOCIAL SERVICES
• Sanitation	OTHER SERVICES TO	• Rehabilitation services	• Social services
• Business and	THE PUBLIC	• Health support	• Emergency aid relief
professional	• Social work	• Public health	• Income support
• Trade unions	• Social homes	• Health care financing	
• Other membership	• Professional	• Other	ENVIRONMENT
organizations	associations		• Environment
(including	• Employers' federations	MENTAL HEALTH	• Animals
religious, political)	• Trade unions	• Substance abuse	
• Entertainment	• Religious organizations	• Multipurpose	CULTURE AND
• News	and learned societies	treatment	RECREATION
• Libraries, museums,	• Tourism	• Crisis intervention	• Culture
culture		• Addictive disorders	• Recreation
• Sport and recreation	RECREATION,	• Others	• Service clubs
	CULTURE		
	• Entertainment	DISEASES, DISORDERS	DEVELOPMENT AND
	• Libraries, archives,	• Birth defects	HOUSING
	museums, zoos	• Cancer	• Economic, social, and
	• Sports organizations	• Leukemia	community
		• Organ diseases	development
		• Nerve, muscle, bone	• Housing
		• Allergies	• Employment and
		• Digestive diseases	training
		• Named diseases	
		• Medical specialties	
		• Other	

Table 4.1

(Continued)

Existing			Proposed
International Standard Industrial Classification (ISIC)	**General Industrial Classification of Economic Activities (NACE)**	**National Taxonomy of Exempt Entities (NTEE)**	**International Classification of Nonprofit Organizations (ICNPO)**
		MEDICAL RESEARCH • Birth defects • Cancer • Specific organs • Nerve, muscle, bone • Allergies • Digestive diseases • Named diseases • Medical specialties • Other	LAW, ADVOCACY, AND POLITICS • Civic and advocacy • Law and legal services • Political parties
		CRIME, LEGAL • Prevention • Facilities • Rehabilitation • Administration of justice • Law enforcement • Abuse protection • Legal services	PHILANTHROPIC INTERMEDIARIES, VOLUNTARISM • Philanthropic intermediaries, voluntarism INTERNATIONAL RELIGION
		EMPLOYMENT • Employment procurement • Vocation rehabilitation • Unions	BUSINESS, PROFESSIONAL ASSOCIATIONS, UNIONS OTHER
		FOOD, NUTRITION • Agricultural programs • Food service, distribution • Nutrition • Home economics	
		HOUSING, SHELTER • Housing development, management • Housing search • Low-cost, temporary • Owners (renters' orgs.) • Support services	

Table 4.1

(Continued)

Existing			Proposed
International Standard Industrial Classification (ISIC)	**General Industrial Classification of Economic Activities (NACE)**	**National Taxonomy of Exempt Entities (NTEE)**	**International Classification of Nonprofit Organizations (ICNPO)**
		PUBLIC SAFETY, DISASTER PREPAREDNESS • Disaster preparedness • Safety education	
		RECREATION, SPORTS • Camps • Physical fitness • Sports training • Recreation clubs • Amateur sports • Professional athletics	
		YOUTH DEVELOPMENT • Youth centers • Adult, child programs • Scouting organizations • Youth development	
		HUMAN SERVICES • Multipurpose • Children and youth • Family • Personal social services • Emergency assistance • Residential, custodial • Promotion of independence	
		ARTS, CULTURE • Multipurpose • Communications • Visual arts • Museums • Performing arts • Humanities • Historical societies • Arts service	

Table 4.1

(Continued)

Existing			Proposed
International Standard Industrial Classification (ISIC)	**General Industrial Classification of Economic Activities (NACE)**	**National Taxonomy of Exempt Entities (NTEE)**	**International Classification of Nonprofit Organizations (ICNPO)**
		ENVIRONMENT • Pollution abatement • Resource protection • Botanical, horticulture • Beautification • Environmental education	
		ANIMAL-RELATED • Animal protection • Wildlife preservation • Zoos • Specialty animals	
		INTERNATIONAL • International understanding • Development, relief • Peace and security • Human rights	
		CIVIL RIGHTS AND ADVOCACY • Equal opportunity • Specific groups • Voter education • Race relations • Civil liberties	
		COMMUNITY IMPROVEMENT • Neighborhood development • Economic development • Business services • Federated giving • Community service clubs	

Table 4.1

(Continued)

Existing			Proposed
International Standard Industrial Classification (ISIC)	**General Industrial Classification of Economic Activities (NACE)**	**National Taxonomy of Exempt Entities (NTEE)**	**International Classification of Nonprofit Organizations (ICNPO)**
		PHILANTHROPY • Private foundations • Public foundations • Voluntarism promotion • Philanthropy promotion	
		SCIENCE RESEARCH	
		SOCIAL SCIENCE RESEARCH	
		OTHER SOCIETY BENEFIT	
		RELIGION-RELATED	
		MUTUAL BENEFIT • Insurance • Pension funds • Fraternal • Burial societies	

Despite these improvements, however, the 1970 NACE system still suffered from many of the same problems as the ISIC system on which it rests. Thus, for example, it still failed to differentiate the many types of "social work" and related social welfare activities, grouping these under two rather broad categories – "social work" and "social homes." Nor did the 1970 NACE system depart from the overall definitional limitation of the ISIC system, its focus only on "donative" nonprofits and its exclusion of organizations that receive significant income from government or fees. In fact, the NACE is even more restrictive than the basic ISIC scheme. This is so because it restricts nonprofit organizations by definition to certain categories of services that it *a priori* treats as "nonmarket." Included in such nonmarket services are administration of cemeteries, social work, religious activity, and tourist information. Other services can be considered nonprofit, but only if the producer receives most of its resources from nonmarket sources (for example, charitable contributions). As a consequence, this system leaves out many important types of nonprofit activity and organizations, robbing the classification system of a considerable portion of its significance.

Finally, the NACE system also fails to leave adequate room for NGOs in the developing world. Such organizations are buried in the "other community services" category rather than being highlighted as a distinctive type of organization. While it makes some improvement, therefore, the NACE system thus still has serious deficiencies in terms of *significance, combinatorial richness,* and *organizing power.*[2] Created to classify economic activity in the for-profit sector, the NACE system, like its first cousin, the ISIC, does a poor job of differentiating types of nonprofit activity.

The National Taxonomy of Exempt Entities (NTEE)

A far more complete classification system for the nonprofit sector is available in the National Taxonomy of Exempt Entities (NTEE) developed by the National Center for Charitable Statistics, a division of the Independent Sector in the United States. Originally conceived as a way to get beyond the cumbersome classification system then in use by the Internal Revenue Service to classify charitable, nonprofit organizations in the United States, the NTEE system has elements that recommend it for comparative, international use as well. Most significant is the system's comprehensiveness and considerable *combinatorial richness.*

Where the ISIC system allocates only three broad classes to the economic activities in which nonprofits are active, the NTEE system provides for 26 "major groups," which are combined into 10 broad "functional categories." Thus, for example, the functional category "Human Services" includes such major groups as "Crime, Legal-Related," "Employment, Job-Related," "Food, Agriculture, Nutrition" (see Table 4.1).

Each of the major groups is then further divided into 17 "common activities" and up to 80 additional activities specific to the groups. The common activities include such things as "management and technical assistance," "research," and "fundraising and/or fund distribution." The additional activities then spell out the particular functions in more specific terms. Thus the major group "education" is further divided to differentiate such activities as "adult basic education, compensatory learning" (B60) from "continuing education, lifelong learning" (B64).

The NTEE system is thus an immensely rich classification system. From the point of view of the nonprofit sector, it is in some sense at the opposite extreme from the ISIC system: where the ISIC was skimpy in the categories it set aside for the activities of nonprofit organizations, the NTEE system is lush with distinctions. In the terms we introduced earlier, it thus has great *combinatorial richness*.

Despite this, however, the NTEE system has some significant drawbacks from the point of view of comparative analysis of the nonprofit sector. In the first place, as is always the case, its combinatorial richness is purchased at a considerable price in terms of *economy*. The differentiation of organizational types is so fine that it becomes difficult to make the distinctions called for. In fact, the NTEE system actually reserves some codes for certain named organizations rather than for certain *types* of organizations. Thus, Boy Scouts of America is assigned class O41, Big Brothers, Big Sisters class O31, the Urban League class P22, and so on. Clearly, a classification scheme that gets down to the level of actual organizations can become exceedingly complex and of questionable value in comparative work. In fact, taken to extremes, this is the opposite of a classification system: it comes close to a listing of agencies.

In addition to this, many of the categories of the NTEE do not line up well with the economic data within the Standard Industrial Classification System. As a consequence, the practicality of the system is open to serious question, because in many countries the only realistic body of meaningful data on the establishments in this sector is that embodied in the national income data systems, and these are categorized in terms of the ISIC. This consequently limits the *organizing power* of the NTEE system, its ability to apply to circumstances other than the one for which it was originally intended.

A further complication with the NTEE system arises from the comprehensive list of "common activity codes" it includes. In a sense, organizations are categorized on two bases at once: first, in terms of their "economic activity" as defined in the ISIC system (i.e., the product or field in which the entity is engaged); and second, in terms of what they do in that field. While this can be useful, it can also create difficulties. For one thing, the information needed to specify the activity may not be available. Thus, it may not be possible to determine, for example, whether a particular health-oriented organization is engaged in providing health services, or raising funds for health services, or advocating for health services. Even where such information is readily at hand, however, other problems arise. For example, foundations and other fundraising organizations focusing primarily on the education field are classified as education organizations, whereas other foundations and fundraising organizations with more general purposes are classified in Major Group T ("Philanthropy, Voluntarism, and Grantmaking Foundations"). Summary statistics on the scope of grantmaking activities can thus inadvertently leave out significant fundraising entities that are grouped in other activity areas. Perhaps even more seriously, this arrangement creates great opportunities for double-counting, since the grants made by an education foundation to other education organizations can end up being counted twice – once as an expenditure of the foundation and once as the expenditure of the organization to which the foundation made a grant.

These difficulties limit the *organizing power* of the NTEE system, making it difficult to apply the system in other settings, where the requisite level of detail is not available. It also limits the *rigor* of the system, particularly in cross-national settings. For example, NTEE places federated fundraising organizations such as United Way into a category called "Community Improvement, Capacity Building" (Major Group S) rather than in Major Group T, which is for "Philanthropy, Voluntarism, and Grantmaking Foundations." Observers from other countries applying this scheme objectively would probably have a hard time understanding this peculiar usage, since the principal activity of United Way and other federated funding organizations is to raise funds for the organizations affiliated with them. Placing these organizations in the "Community Improvement, Capacity Building" category is thus likely to be misleading.

Finally, the NTEE system also encounters other *organizing power* problems with respect to certain key components of the nonprofit sector elsewhere. Like the ISIC and NACE systems, it does not give much prominence to the types of nonprofit organizations that are most prominent and important in developing countries – namely, the so-called "NGOs" and grass-roots development organizations involved in community mobilization, village renewal, and small-scale economic development. The NTEE scheme does have a special code for organizations engaged in "Development and Relief Services," but only under International Activities. In other words, it provides a definitive category only for the international development organizations but not for the indigenous development organizations active in many developing countries. While some of these could be classified in the major group "Community Improvement, Capacity Building," many others would fall into a great number of other possible categories in the NTEE system.

The International Classification of Nonprofit Organizations (ICNPO): an alternative approach

If the ISIC and NACE systems are too limited and lacking in combinatorial richness and significance, and the NTEE system too complex and lacking in economy and rigor, is it possible to fashion an alternative approach that combines some of the advantages of each without falling into their respective pitfalls? What is more, is it possible to do so in a way that corrects the shortcomings that both of these models have in terms of *organizing power* so far as the developing world is concerned, so that a truly international system can be devised?

We believe the answer to these questions is yes, and have developed an alternative classification system for nonprofit organizations at the international level that we call the International Classification of Nonprofit Organizations, or ICNPO. We emphasize that this system may not be ideal for particular national experiences, since it may not capture the full range of nonprofit activity in particular national settings as fully as a purely national classification would do. However, we believe it provides a useful compromise between the level of detail that might be ideal for national work and the level that is feasible for comparative work, and that it does so while achieving a significant degree of *organizing power*.

This classification scheme was developed through a collaborative process involving the team of scholars working on the Johns Hopkins Comparative Nonprofit Sector Project (see Salamon and Anheier, 1992b). The system took shape by beginning with the International Standard Industrial Classification (ISIC) system, and elaborating on it as needed to capture most succinctly the reality of the nonprofit sector in the 13 different countries originally involved in this project (the U.S., the U.K., France, Germany, Italy, Japan, Sweden, Hungary, Brazil, Ghana, Egypt, India, and Thailand). Throughout, an effort was made to remain as close as possible to the ISIC system so that the existing national income data systems could ultimately be used to develop the information to document the scope of the organizations portrayed in the classification.

Central features

Reflecting this, the ICNPO utilizes the same basic approach to solving the central design issues of economic classification as the Standard Industrial Classification system developed over the past 45 years by the United Nations. This is apparent in its choice of the basis of classification and unit of analysis.

Focus on economic activities. So far as the basis of classification is concerned, the ICNPO uses the "economic activity" of the unit as the key to sorting. Units are thus differentiated according to the types of services or goods they provide (e.g., health, education, environmental protection). Unlike the NTEE system, which cross-cuts this kind of activity grouping with a grouping keyed to the type of service each entity provides within its activity area (e.g., fundraising, advocacy, research), the ICNPO sticks much more strictly to the ISIC practice of assigning dominance to the activity area and sorting units according to their area of primary activity. A research organization that specializes in health research would consequently be treated in the ICNPO structure, as in the ISIC structure, as a research organization rather than a health organization, since research is its principal activity.

Unit of analysis. As with the Standard Industrial Classification system, the key to making such an "economic activity"-based system work is to choose a unit of analysis that has enough homogeneity to avoid distorting the data. For this reason, the standard economic statistics use the "establishment" rather than the "enterprise" as the unit of analysis, since enterprises are frequently made up of many establishments, each of which may be engaged in a slightly different type of economic activity.

We have followed this practice in our proposed ICNPO. In particular, we seek to make the "establishment" rather than the "organization" our principal unit of analysis. An establishment is essentially a place of operation of an organization. In other words, it is a smaller unit than an organization. An organization may consequently run a number of different establishments, each of which may have its own economic activity. In the case of the German Caritas organization cited earlier, for example, the separate hospitals, family counselling centers, and related agencies that constitute the Caritas organization would be treated as separate "establishments," each of which would be classified according to its principal activity. Fortunately, this is also the format used by the German "census of workplaces," which focuses on the establishment, or workplace, as the unit of analysis.

Basic structure of the ICNPO

As reflected in Table 4.1, and in more detail in Table 4.2 and Appendix A, the ICNPO system groups the nonprofit sector as defined in Chapter 3 above into 12 *major activity groups*, including a catch–all "Not Elsewhere Classified" group. These 12 major activity groups are in turn further subdivided into 24 *subgroups*. Each of the subgroups has in turn been broken into a number of *activities*, but the ICNPO system as currently developed does not attempt to achieve standardization at the level of the activities because of the great diversity of the nonprofit sector in the different locales. The activities are nevertheless listed (though not coded) in the full specification of the system provided in Table 4.2, and in the fuller description offered in Appendix A, in order to illustrate the kinds of organizations that fall into each subgroup. To facilitate comparisons, Appendix B provides examples for a cross-walk between ICNPO major groups and subgroups and those of the ISIC, NACE and NTEE systems, in addition to national classifications in place in France, Japan and the U.S. Finally, Appendix C offers translations of ICNPO groups and subgroups into several languages.

Table 4.2

The International Classification of Nonprofit Organizations (ICNPO)

GROUP 1: CULTURE AND RECREATION

1 100 Culture and Arts
- media & communications
- visual arts, architecture, ceramic arts
- performing arts
- historical, literary and humanistic societies
- museums
- zoos & aquariums
- multipurpose culture and arts organizations
- support and service organizations, auxiliaries, councils, standard setting and governance organizations
- culture and arts organizations not elsewhere classified

1 200 Recreation
- sports clubs
- recreation/pleasure or social clubs
- multipurpose recreational organizations
- support and service organizations, auxiliaries, councils, standard setting and governance organizations
- recreational organizations not elsewhere classified

1 300 Service Clubs
- service clubs
- multipurpose service clubs
- support and service organizations, auxiliaries, councils, standard setting and governance organizations
- service clubs not elsewhere classified

GROUP 2: EDUCATION AND RESEARCH

2 100 Primary and Secondary Education
- elementary, primary & secondary education

2 200 Higher Education
- higher education (university level)

2 300 Other Education
- vocational/technical schools
- adult/continuing education
- multipurpose educational organizations
- support and service organizations, auxiliaries, councils, standard setting and governance organizations
- education organizations not elsewhere classified

2 400 Research
- medical research
- science and technology
- social sciences, policy studies
- multipurpose research organizations
- support and service organizations, auxiliaries, councils, standard setting and governance organizations
- research organizations not elsewhere classified

GROUP 3: HEALTH

3 100 Hospitals and Rehabilitation
- hospitals
- rehabilitation hospitals

3 200 Nursing Homes
- nursing homes

3 300 Mental Health and Crisis Intervention
- psychiatric hospitals
- mental health treatment
- crisis intervention
- multipurpose mental health organizations
- support and service organizations, auxiliaries, councils, standard setting and governance organizations
- mental health organizations not elsewhere classified

3 400 Other Health Services
- public health & wellness education
- health treatment, primarily outpatient
- rehabilitative medical services
- emergency medical services
- multipurpose health service organizations
- support and service organizations, auxiliaries, councils, standard setting and governance organizations
- health service organizations not elsewhere classified

GROUP 4: SOCIAL SERVICES

4 100 Social Services
- child welfare, child services, day care

- youth services and youth welfare
- family services
- services for the handicapped
- services for the elderly
- self–help and other personal social services
- multipurpose social service organizations
- support and service organizations, auxiliaries, councils, standard setting and governance organizations
- social service organizations not elsewhere classified

4 200 Emergency and Relief
- disaster/emergency prevention, relief and control
- temporary shelters
- refugee assistance
- multipurpose emergency & refugee assistance organizations
- support and service organizations, auxiliaries, councils, standard setting and governance organizations
- emergency and refugee assistance organizations not elsewhere classified

4 300 Income Support and Maintenance
- income support and maintenance
- material assistance
- multipurpose income support & maintenance organizations
- support and service organizations, auxiliaries, councils, standard setting and governance organizations
- income support and

maintenance organizations not elsewhere classified

GROUP 5: ENVIRONMENT

5 100 Environment
- pollution abatement & control
- natural resources conservation & protection
- environmental beautification & open spaces
- multipurpose environmental organizations
- support and service organizations, auxiliaries, councils, standard setting and governance organizations
- environmental organizations not elsewhere classified

5 200 Animals
- animal protection & welfare
- wildlife preservation & protection
- veterinary services
- multipurpose animal services organizations
- support and service organizations, auxiliaries, councils, standard setting and governance organizations
- animal-related organizations not elsewhere classified

GROUP 6: DEVELOPMENT AND HOUSING

6 100 Economic, Social and Community Development
- community and neighborhood organizations
- economic development
- social development
- multipurpose economic, social and community development organizations
- support and service organizations, auxiliaries, councils, standard setting and governance organizations
- economic, social and community development organizations not elsewhere classified

6 200 Housing
- housing associations
- housing assistance
- multipurpose housing organizations
- support and service organizations, auxiliaries, councils, standard setting and governance organizations
- housing organizations not elsewhere classified

6 300 Employment and Training
- job training programs
- vocational counseling and guidance
- vocational rehabilitation and sheltered workshops
- multipurpose employment and training organizations
- support and service organizations, auxiliaries, councils, standard setting and governance organizations
- employment and training organizations not elsewhere classified

GROUP 7: LAW, ADVOCACY AND POLITICS

7 100 Civic and Advocacy Organizations

- civic associations
- advocacy organizations
- civil rights associations
- ethnic associations
- multipurpose civil and advocacy organizations
- support and service organizations, auxiliaries, councils, standard setting and governance organizations
- civic and advocacy organizations not elsewhere classified

7 200 Law and Legal Services
- legal services
- crime prevention and public safety
- rehabilitation of offenders
- victim support
- consumer protection associations
- multipurpose law and legal service organizations
- support and service organizations, auxiliaries, councils, standard setting and governance organizations
- law and legal organizations not elsewhere classified

7 300 Political Organizations
- political parties
- political action committees
- multipurpose political organizations
- support and service organizations, auxiliaries, councils, standard setting and governance organizations
- political organizations not elsewhere classified

GROUP 8: PHILANTHROPIC INTERMEDIARIES & VOLUNTARISM PROMOTION

8 100 Philanthropic Intermediaries
- grantmaking foundations
- voluntarism promotion and support
- fundraising intermediaries
- multipurpose philanthropic intermediaries and voluntarism organizations
- support and service organizations, auxiliaries, councils, standard setting and governance organizations
- philanthropic intermediary organizations not elsewhere classified

GROUP 9: INTERNATIONAL ACTIVITIES

9 100 International Activities
- exchange/friendship/cultural programs
- development assistance associations
- international disaster & relief organizations
- international human rights & peace organizations
- multipurpose international organizations
- support and service organizations, auxiliaries, councils, standard setting and governance organizations
- international organizations not elsewhere classified

GROUP 10: RELIGION

10 100 Religious Congregations and Associations

- Protestant churches
- Catholic churches
- Jewish synagogues
- Hindu temples
- Shinto shrines
- Muslim mosques
- multipurpose religious organizations
- associations of congregations
- support and service organizations, auxiliaries, councils, standard setting and governance organizations
- religious organizations not elsewhere classified

GROUP 11: BUSINESS AND PROFESSIONAL ASSOCIATIONS, UNIONS

11 100 Business and Professional Associations, Unions

- business associations
- professional associations
- labor unions
- multipurpose business, professional associations and unions
- support and service organizations, auxiliaries, councils, standard setting and governance organizations
- business, professional associations and unions organizations not elsewhere classified

GROUP 12: [NOT ELSEWHERE CLASSIFIED]

12 100 N.E.C.

Although it is based on the ISIC system, the basic Activity Group structure of the ICNPO differs from the ISIC in a number of significant ways. Most fundamentally, it elaborates on the basic ISIC structure to take better account of the components of the non-profit sector. Thus:

- The Health and Social Work "section" of the ISIC system is broken into two "major activity groups" in the ICNPO scheme: *Group 3, Health*, embracing "Hospitals and Rehabilitation" (3 100), "Nursing Homes" (3 200), "Mental Health and Crisis Intervention" (3 300), and "Other Health Services" (3 400); and *Group 4, Social Services*, embracing "Social Services" (4 100), "Emergency and Relief" (4 200), and "Income Support and Maintenance" (4 300).
- The catch-all "Other Community Social and Personal Service Activities" section in the ISIC system is broken into eight major

activity groups in the ICNPO system: "Culture and Recreation" (Group 1); "Environment," including animal-related activities that ISIC classified under "Health" (Group 5); "Law, Advocacy and Politics" (Group 7); "Philanthropic Intermediaries and Voluntarism Promotion" (Group 8); "International Activities" (Group 9); "Religion" (Group 10); "Business and Professional Associations and Unions" (Group 11); and "Other" (Group 12).

- A special *Development and Housing Group* (Group 6) is created for the NGOs that have taken such a distinctive place in the nonprofit sectors of the developing countries. Included in this group are three subgroups of organizations: those involved in "Economic, Social, and Community Development" (6 100); "Housing" (6 200), and "Employment and Training" (6 300).

While relying most heavily on the ISIC structure, however, the ICNPO system also borrows from the NTEE system discussed above. This is most clearly apparent in the inclusion of a special category of "Philanthropic Intermediaries and Voluntarism Promotion" organizations (Group 8). However, the ICNPO system would put all organizations engaged in this function in this category rather than grouping some of the foundations and other fund-distribution organizations with the service organizations with which they are most closely affiliated and others in an ambiguous "Community Improvement" classification.

Advantages and disadvantages

The proposed ICNPO is certainly not without its drawbacks. Certain of the distinctions proposed may be difficult to make in practice. Numerous environmental organizations are principally engaged in advocacy activities, for example. Should they be classified according to their area of activity or the nature of their activity? Similarly, German trade unions are often deeply involved in vocational training, adult education, and the provision of social services. Should they be treated as trade unions, educational facilities, or social service agencies?

Beyond this, the nature of a particular type of organization may vary depending on the stage of political and economic development in a country. For example, associations of doctors or lawyers that would be treated as member-serving trade or professional

associations in most developed countries often function as significant promoters of free speech and human rights in developing
societies. Unfortunately, the ICNPO system does not take this into
account. All professional associations are grouped together,
despite the differences that may exist among them. In the terms
introduced earlier, this inevitably makes the classification less
rigorous than might be desired. The one saving grace is that most
other classification systems suffer from a similar shortcoming.

Finally, though more *economical* than the NTEE system, the
ICNPO system is considerably *less* economical than the ISIC
approach, which contains far fewer categories in terms of which to
differentiate nonprofit organizations. This will naturally make the
ICNPO system harder to use than the far simpler ISIC one. What
is more, the ICNPO categories do not line up perfectly with the
often very different groupings spelled out in national legal systems.

Fortunately, however, these shortcomings are more than balanced by a number of advantages. In the first place, though it
triples the number of major groupings allocated to the nonprofit
sector in comparison with the basic ISIC system, the proposed
ICNPO system nevertheless retains considerable *economy*. The
entire nonprofit sector is embraced within 12 major activity
groups and 24 subgroups. What is more, it stays close enough to
the ISIC structure to give some reasonable hope that the basic
national income data systems can be used to generate the data
needed to analyze this sector in the terms the classification suggests.

In the second place, the additional complexity that the ICNPO
introduces is done in order to increase the *significance* and *combinatorial richness* of the resulting classification structure. The
ICNPO system makes it possible for the first time to differentiate
the many different types of nonprofit organizations that have
emerged in recent years – environmental organizations, civil
rights organizations, business associations, foundations, and
many more. Under the ISIC system, as we have seen, these were
all bundled together in a large, undifferentiated mass of "Other
Community, Social, and Personal Service Activities."

In the process, the ICNPO makes it possible to group and
regroup organizations in order to shed light on a number of significant dimensions of the nonprofit sector. One of the more interest-

ing distinctions found in the literature, for example, is that between primarily "public-serving" and primarily "member-serving" organizations (see, for example, Salamon and Abramson, 1982; Sumariwalla, 1983; Salamon, 1992). This distinction is crucial in American law, which permits tax-deductible gifts only to the former category of organizations. Under the ICNPO system, the member-serving organizations can be separated out by focusing on Group 11, "Business and Professional Associations and Unions," plus the "Social, Recreational, and Sports Clubs" classified in Subgroup 1 200 under Arts and Culture.[3]

The ICNPO system also easily accommodates two other crucial distinctions frequently drawn among nonprofit organizations: the first between essentially partisan political organizations and those that are nonpartisan; and the second between churches, synagogues, mosques and other religious congregations and all other organizations. The former is handled by a separate category (7 300) set aside for political parties and other similar organizations whose principal purpose is to assist particular candidates to secure political office (as opposed to promoting a particular cause or policy position). The latter is handled in a major group (Group 10) set aside especially for religious congregations. This analytical flexibility is a crucial advantage of the ICNPO system. In the terms introduced earlier, it demonstrates the *combinatorial richness* of the scheme.

Cross-national application: a partial test

Ultimately, however, the real test of the ICNPO system is its *organizing power* and *rigor*, its ability to perform well in coming to terms with the realities of different national systems. Although the proof here will be some time in developing, the early indications are quite promising. A review of the fit between the ICNPO and the national circumstances of some of the countries included in the Johns Hopkins Comparative Nonprofit Sector Project should make this clear. (See also Appendix B.)

France. As noted in Chapter 5 below by Edith Archambault, the French notion of the nonprofit sector, *économie sociale*, is broader than the structural–operational definition that is the foundation for the ICNPO classification, since it includes cooperatives and mutuals in addition to associations. Within the world of "associations," however, the ICNPO provides a useful and workable system for differentiating organizational types in terms that permit cross-national comparisons. As such, it usefully bridges a number of peculiarities of French law and practice.

Under French law, for example, there are four major types of associations: "declared associations," i.e., organizations that are registered under the French Law of 1901 and active in a variety of social and economic fields; "undeclared associations," i.e., Churches, some political parties, and informal neighborhood groups; "public utility associations," which operate in the fields of health and welfare and enjoy certain fiscal advantages not available to other declared associations; and "foundations," which are typically operating agencies with the privilege of owning real estate and other assets.

This legal structure provides only the most limited basis for differentiating French nonprofit organizations in terms of what they do, however. The only system in use for doing this is the French version of the European NACE classification scheme, which is called *Nomenclature d'activités et produits*, or NAP. In French practice, every economic organization with wage-earners is listed on a formal file called the SIRENE file, which records, in addition to its name, address and certain economic data, the legal status of the organization and its NAP code. SIRENE is thus potentially an immensely valuable tool for gathering information about French nonprofits. Unfortunately, however, the NAP system suffers from the same limitations as its parent NACE so far as the nonprofit sector is concerned. Although education and health and social service activities are separately identified in the classification system, the rest of what we have defined as the nonprofit sector is lumped into a catch-all category called "Other collective nonmarket services."

The ICNPO system, by contrast, would divide these remaining types of nonprofits into a number of major groups, including "Environment," "Law, Advocacy and Politics," "Philanthropic Intermediaries and Voluntarism Promotion," "International Activities," and "Religion." It thus provides greater *combinatorial richness* than the existing French classification scheme. What is more, it does so while accommodating some of the peculiar French types of nonprofit organizations. For example, the so-called *comités d'enterprise*, or "worker councils," which operate in every enterprise with more than 50 employees and manage canteens, day care and holiday centers, cultural activities, and other personal or family social services, would fit into ICNPO Category 4 100, "Social Services." Similarly, the so-called *tourisme populaire*, or "social tourism" organizations, which provide tourism, sport, and cultural opportunities for working-class families on a sliding fee basis geared to family income, would fall into Group 1 200, "Recreation." In the terms introduced earlier, the ICNPO system thus offers both *combinatorial richness* and a considerable degree of *organizing power*, so far as the French system is concerned.

But is the system workable? Is it possible to gather information about French nonprofits at this more refined level of aggregation? The answer to date appears to be a qualified yes. At the very least, a beginning can be made thanks to the existence of a number of umbrella or "peak" associations that collect some information on key components of the nonprofit sector. Thus, for example, UNIOPSS (Union Nationale Interprofessionelle des Oeuvres Privées Sanitaires et Sociales), a coalition of some 7,000 nonprofit health and welfare associations, gathers important information on the employment and activities of its member organizations. Similarly, UNAT gathers comparable data on popular recreation and tourism associations, CNOSF (the Olympic Committee) on other sports federations, UNAF (the family associations' national union) on some 5,700 family service agencies, and FONJEP on youth and popular education associations. While far from adequate, these sources provide some basis for applying the ICNPO in practice, at least until national income classification schemes are modified sufficiently to incorporate the ICNPO more fully.

Japan. A similar situation exists in Japan, though here the legal structure provides a bit more detail on the character of the organizations embraced within the sector. This is so because Japanese law does not provide a blanket authority to form nonprofit organizations. Rather, such organizations are restricted to particular purposes, each of which is governed by a separate legal provision. Thus, for example, Japanese law separately permits the formation of *kōeki-hōjin* (public benefit corporations), *shakaifukushi-hōjin* (social welfare corporations), *iryō-hōjin* (medical corporations), *shūkyo-hōjin* (religious organizations), and private school corporations (Amenomori, 1993).

In the case of the nonprofit organizations established by special legislation (for example, the social welfare or medical corporations), the legal class can be translated into the ICNPO categories with only limited difficulty. The situation is a bit more complicated in the case of the *kōeki hōjin* category, because it embraces a wide assortment of organizations spanning virtually all of the ICNPO categories. However, Japanese tax law distinguishes 137 types of *kōeki hōjin*, providing some basis for sorting these organizations. More difficult still is the situation with "unincorporated associations," such as the *kudomokai* (children's associations), the *seinendan* (youth clubs), and the *jichikai* (community self-help bodies). Even here, however, the ICNPO has a place to classify these organizations and thus to pick up some of the special features of the Japanese nonprofit sector. For example, the so-called *jichikai* organizations, which are local community organizations that provide certain social services but also maintain a registry of citizens residing in a community, would seem to fall into ICNPO Major Group 7, "Law, Advocacy and Politics." In other words, the ICNPO seems to have considerable *organizing power* for coming to terms with the special characteristics of the Japanese nonprofit sector as well.

India. The ICNPO also seems capable of embracing the rich diversity of nonprofit organizations in a country like India, which contains a variety of traditional associations representing caste, ethnic, and religious communities; various missionary societies and associations related to the Gandhian movement; Western-style nonprofit organizations in such fields as social services, recreation, and health; and an important set of so-called "nongovernmental organizations" or NGOs. Under the ICNPO system, for example, caste and ethnic organizations would fall under Group 7 100, "Civic and Advocacy Organizations;" religious groups in 10 100, "Religion;" Gandhian or religiously based development organizations under Group 6, "Development and Housing."

The identification of a separate category – Major Group 6, "Development and Housing" – that can accommodate NGOs is a special advantage of the ICNPO system for countries like India. Such organizations have grown increasingly important in the developing world. They function as crucial transmission belts for development activities, embracing community organizing and local economic development. Despite their importance, they are not easily accommodated in the existing national income classification systems. By providing a definable category for them, the ICNPO system achieves greater *organizing power* and *combinatorial richness*.

Conclusion

Classification efforts of the sort discussed in this article often get short shrift in the development of new bodies of knowledge. It is, after all, somewhat dry work, lacking the drama of new empirical discoveries. Yet the importance of such work to our understanding cannot be overemphasized. Classification is the crucial prerequisite for scientific progress in any field of study. The development of clear definitions and classification systems is fundamental progress in the technology of thinking. Abstract words like the nonprofit or voluntary sector have no real meaning without it, and serious empirical work cannot proceed in its absence. Regrettably, the development of this kind of conceptual equipment has lagged badly in the newly emerging field of nonprofit sector studies. While the ICNPO system outlined here may not be the last word on this topic, it is our hope that it will at least get the topic on the agenda, and perhaps provide a foundation on which to build.

APPENDIX A

THE INTERNATIONAL CLASSIFICATION OF NONPROFIT ORGANIZATIONS: EXPLANATORY NOTES

GROUP 1: CULTURE AND RECREATION

Organizations and activities in general and specialized fields of culture and recreation.

1 100 Culture and Arts

- *media and communications:* production and dissemination of information and communication; includes radio and TV stations, publishing of books, journals, newspapers and newsletters, film production, libraries.

- *visual arts, architecture, ceramic art:* production, dissemination and display of visual arts and architecture; includes sculpture, photographic societies, painting, drawing, design centers and architectural associations.
- *performing arts:* performing arts centers, companies, and associations; includes theaters, dance, ballet, opera, orchestras, chorals and music ensembles.
- *historical, literary and humanistic societies:* promotion and appreciation of the humanities, preservation of historical and cultural artifacts, commemoration of historical events; includes historical societies, poetry and literary societies, language associations, reading promotion, war memorials, commemorative funds and associations.
- *museums:* general and specialized museums covering art, history, sciences, technology, culture.
- *zoos and aquariums.*

1 200 Recreation
- *sports clubs:* provision of amateur sports, training, physical fitness, and sport competition services and events.
- *recreation and social clubs:* provision of recreational facilities and services to individuals and communities; includes playground associations, country clubs, men's and women's clubs, fitness centers.

1 300 Service Clubs
- membership organizations providing services to members and local communities, for example Kiwanis, Lions or Zonta International.

GROUP 2: EDUCATION AND RESEARCH

Organizations and activities administering, providing, promoting, conducting, supporting and servicing education and research.

2 100 Primary and Secondary Education
- *elementary, primary and secondary education:* education at elementary, primary and secondary levels; includes pre-school organizations other than day care.

2 200 Higher Education

- *higher education (university level):* higher learning, providing academic degrees; includes universities, business management schools; law schools; medical schools.

2 300 Other Education

- *vocational/technical schools:* technical and vocational training specifically geared towards gaining employment; includes trade schools; paralegal training, secretarial schools.
- *adult/continuing education:* institutions engaged in providing education and training in addition to the formal educational system; includes schools of continuing studies, correspondence schools, night schools, sponsored literacy and reading programs.

2 400 Research

- *medical research:* research in the medical field, includes research on specific diseases, disorders, or medical disciplines.
- *science and technology:* research in the physical and life sciences, engineering and technology.
- *social sciences, policy studies:* research and analysis in the social sciences and policy area.

GROUP 3: HEALTH

Organizations that engage in health-related activities, providing health care, both general and specialized services, administration of health care services, and health support services.

3 100 Hospitals and Rehabilitation

- *hospitals:* primarily inpatient medical care and treatment.
- *rehabilitation:* inpatient health care and rehabilitative therapy to individuals suffering from physical impairments due to injury, genetic defect or disease and requiring extensive physiotherapy or similar forms of care.

3 200 Nursing Homes

- *nursing homes:* inpatient convalescent care, residential care as well as primary health care services; includes homes for the frail elderly, nursing homes for the severely handicapped.

3 300 Mental Health and Crisis Intervention

- *psychiatric hospitals:* inpatient care and treatment for the mentally ill.
- *mental health treatment:* outpatient treatment for mentally ill patients; includes community mental health centers, and halfway homes.
- *crisis intervention:* outpatient services and counsel in acute mental health situations; includes suicide prevention and support to victims of assault and abuse.

3 400 Other Health Services

- *public health and wellness education:* public health promoting and health education; includes sanitation screening for potential health hazards, first aid training and services and family planning services.
- *health treatment, primarily outpatient:* organizations that provide primarily outpatient health services – e.g., health clinics, vaccination centers.
- *rehabilitative medical services:* outpatient therapeutic care; includes nature cure centers, yoga clinics, physical therapy centers.
- *emergency medical services:* services to persons in need of immediate care; includes ambulatory services and paramedical emergency care, shock/trauma programs and lifeline programs; ambulance services.

GROUP 4: SOCIAL SERVICES

Organizations and institutions providing human and social services to a community or target population.

4 100 Social Services

- *child welfare, child services, day care:* services to children, adoption services, child development centers, foster care, includes infant care centers and nurseries.
- *youth services and youth welfare:* services to youth; includes delinquency prevention services, teen pregnancy prevention, dropout prevention, youth centers and clubs, job programs for youth; includes YMCA, YWCA, Boy Scouts, Girl Scouts, Big Brothers/Big Sisters.

- *family services:* services to families; includes family life/parent education, single parent agencies and services, family violence shelters and services.
- *services for the handicapped:* services for the handicapped; includes homes, other than nursing homes; transport facilities, recreation and other specialized services.
- *services for the elderly:* organizations providing geriatric care; includes in-home services, homemaker services, transport facilities, recreation, meal programs and other services geared towards senior citizens. (Does not include residential nursing homes.)
- *self-help and other personal social services:* programs and services for self-help and development; includes support groups, personal counseling, credit counseling/money management services.

4 200 Emergency and Relief

- *disaster/emergency prevention and control:* organizations that work to prevent, predict, control, and alleviate the effects of disasters, to educate or otherwise prepare individuals to cope with the effects of disasters, or provide relief to disaster victims; includes volunteer fire departments, life boat services, etc.
- *temporary shelters:* organizations providing temporary shelters to the homeless; includes travellers' aid, and temporary housing.
- *refugee assistance:* organizations providing food, clothing, shelter and services to refugees and immigrants.

4 300 Income Support and Maintenance

- *income support and maintenance:* organizations providing cash assistance and other forms of direct services to persons unable to maintain a livelihood.
- *material assistance:* organizations providing food, clothing, transport and other forms of assistance; includes food banks and clothing distribution centers.

GROUP 5: ENVIRONMENT

Organizations promoting and providing services in environmental conservation, pollution control and prevention, environmental education and health, and animal protection.

5 100 Environment
- *pollution abatement and control:* organizations that promote clean air, clean water, reducing and preventing noise pollution, radiation control, hazardous wastes and toxic substances, solid waste management, recycling programs, and global warming.
- *natural resources conservation and protection:* conservation and preservation of natural resources, including land, water, energy and plant resources for the general use and enjoyment of the public.
- *environmental beautification and open spaces:* botanical gardens, arboreta, horticultural programs and landscape services; includes organizations promoting anti-litter campaigns, programs to preserve the parks, green spaces and open spaces in urban or rural areas, and city and highway beautification programs.

5 200 Animals
- *animal protection and welfare:* animal protection and welfare services; includes animal shelters and humane societies.
- *wildlife preservation and protection:* wildlife preservation and protection; includes sanctuaries and refuges.
- *veterinary services:* animal hospitals and services providing care to farm and household animals and pets.

GROUP 6: DEVELOPMENT AND HOUSING

Organizations promoting programs and providing services to help improve communities and the economic and social well-being of society.

6 100 Economic, Social and Community Development
- *community and neighborhood organizations:* organizations working towards improving the quality of life within communities or neighborhoods – e.g., squatters' associations, local development organizations, poor people's cooperatives.
- *economic development:* programs and services to improve the economic infrastructure and capacity; includes building of infrastructure like roads, and entrepreneurial programs, and technical or management consulting assistance, rural development organizations.
- *social development:* organizations working towards improving

the institutional infrastructure and capacity to alleviate social problems and to improve general public well-being.

6 200 Housing

- *housing associations:* development, construction, management, leasing, financing and rehabilitation of housing.
- *housing assistance:* organizations providing housing search, legal services and related assistance.

6 300 Employment and Training

- *job training programs:* organizations providing and supporting apprenticeship programs, internships, on-the-job training, and other training programs.
- *vocational counseling and guidance:* vocational training and guidance, career counseling, testing, and related services.
- *vocational rehabilitation and sheltered workshops:* organizations that promote self-sufficiency and income generation through job training and employment.

GROUP 7: LAW, ADVOCACY, AND POLITICS

Organizations and groups that work to protect and promote civil and other rights, or advocate the social and political interests of general or special constituencies, offer legal services and promote public safety.

7 100 Civic and Advocacy Organizations

- *advocacy organizations:* organizations that protect the rights and promote the interests of specific groups of people – e.g., the physically handicapped, the elderly, children, and women.
- *civil rights associations:* organizations that work to protect or preserve individual civil liberties and human rights.
- *ethnic associations:* organizations that promote the interests of, or provide services to, members belonging to a specific ethnic heritage.
- *civic associations:* programs and services to encourage and spread civic-mindedness.

7 200 Law and Legal Services

- *legal services:* legal services, advice and assistance in dispute resolution and court-related matters.

- *crime prevention and public safety:* crime prevention to promote safety and precautionary measures among citizens.
- *rehabilitation of offenders:* programs and services to reintegrate offenders; includes halfway houses, probation and parole programs, prison alternatives.
- *victim support:* services, counsel and advice to victims of crime.
- *consumer protection associations:* protection of consumer rights, and the improvement of product control and quality.

7 300 Political Organizations

- *political parties and organizations:* activities and services to support the placing of particular candidates into political office; includes dissemination of information, public relations and political fundraising.

GROUP 8: PHILANTHROPIC INTERMEDIARIES AND VOLUNTARISM PROMOTION

Philanthropic organizations and organizations promoting charity and charitable activities.

8 100 Philanthropic Intermediaries and Voluntarism Promotion

- *grantmaking foundations:* private foundations; including corporate foundations, community foundations and independent public law foundations.
- *voluntarism promotion and support:* organizations that recruit, train, and place volunteers, and promote volunteering.
- *fundraising organizations:* federated, collective fundraising organizations; includes lotteries.

GROUP 9: INTERNATIONAL ACTIVITIES

Organizations promoting greater intercultural understanding between peoples of different countries and historical backgrounds and also those providing relief during emergencies and promoting development and welfare abroad.

9 100 International Activities

- *exchange/friendship/cultural programs:* programs and services designed to encourage mutual respect and friendship internationally.

- *development assistance associations:* programs and projects that promote social and economic development abroad.
- *international disaster and relief organizations:* organizations that collect, channel and provide aid to other countries during times of disaster or emergency.
- *international human rights and peace organizations:* organizations which promote and monitor human rights and peace internationally.

GROUP 10: RELIGION

Organizations promoting religious beliefs and administering religious services and rituals; includes churches, mosques, synagogues, temples, shrines, seminaries, monasteries, and similar religious institutions, in addition to related associations and auxiliaries of such organizations.

10 100 Religious Congregations and Associations

- *congregations:* churches, synagogues, temples, mosques, shrines, monasteries, seminaries and similar organizations promoting religious beliefs and administering religious services and rituals.
- *associations of congregations:* associations and auxiliaries of religious congregations and organizations supporting and promoting religious beliefs, services and rituals.

GROUP 11: BUSINESS AND PROFESSIONAL ASSOCIATIONS, UNIONS

Organizations promoting, regulating and safeguarding business, professional and labor interests.

11 100 Business and Professional Associations, Unions

- *business associations:* organizations that work to promote, regulate and safeguard the interests of special branches of business – e.g., manufacturers' associations, farmers' associations, bankers' associations.
- *professional associations:* organizations promoting, regulating,

and protecting professional interests – e.g., bar associations, medical associations.

- *labor unions:* organizations that promote, protect and regulate the rights and interests of employees.

GROUP 12: [NOT ELSEWHERE CLASSIFIED]

12 100 N.E.C.

APPENDIX B

CROSS-WALK BETWEEN ICNPO AND ISIC, NACE, NTEE, AND SELECTED NATIONAL CLASSIFICATION SYSTEMS

ICNPO	ISIC	NACE[a)]	US[b)]	FRANCE	JAPAN	NTEE	INDIA
GROUP 1: CULTURE AND RECREATION							
1 100 Culture and Arts	923*	971–7 966*	792 84	8601–08 9611–22	943 918 782	A B70	950 952 956
1 200 Recreation	924 9199*	978–9*	799* 703*	67 9617–18 9624–25 9712	785*	N	959
1 300 Service Clubs	9199	97	8641*	96	949	S80	95
GROUP 2: EDUCATION AND RESEARCH							
2 100 Primary and Secondary Education	801 8021	932	8211	8201 9211–14	911,916 912,913	B21–28	920*
2 200 Higher Education	803	931	8221	8203	914,949*	B41–43	921*
2 300 Other Education	809 8022*	933 934*	8222 823,824 829	8202 9216–18 9221	915 917 918	B50 B60 B80 B90	920*
2 400 Research	73 75 8532*	94 952* 911*	8922 8733 9321	77 9311	93	H* U* V*	922*
GROUP 3: HEALTH							
3 100 Hospitals and Rehabilitation	8511 667.4	951 8069	8062	8402–06	871–73 E22 E24 E26	E50	930*
3 200 Nursing Homes	8519	951 805	8051–2	8502–04	876	E25	930.9*
3 300 Mental Health and Crisis Intervention	8511–9	951	8063 8051*	8402–06	871–73	F	930.9*
3 400 Other Health Services	8519	*952*	809	8407–13	875	G, H	930

ICNPO	ISIC	NACE a)	US b)	FRANCE	JAPAN	NTEE	INDIA
		954 955	808	9411 9421	879 949*	E60–80 E30–40	
GROUP 4: SOCIAL SERVICES							
4 100 Social Services	8531 8532	934* 961 962	83	9511–13 9522–23	92	B21 P, O K40–50	941* 969*
4 200 Emergency and Relief	8531 8532	961 962	83	9511–13 9522–23	92	M	941* 949*
4 300 Income Support and Maintenance	8531 8532	961 962	83	9524	92	P K30*	94*
GROUP 5: ENVIRONMENT							
5 100 Environment	900 37 9233	0 96	8641* 8699*	9723	949	C K20	910 956.3
5 200 Animal Protection	8520 0140	956 0*	8641* 8699* 075*	9723	949	D	931
GROUP 6: DEVELOPMENT AND HOUSING							
6 100 Economic, Social and Community Development	919	963 968	8399	0–66, 77	949	S*, W* Q30–31	94*
6 200 Housing	7010 452C	50* 834*	6513* 704*	55* 79* 81*	949	K, L	50* 82*
6 300 Employment and Training	8022* 8090* 919*	96* 933*	8331*	9218	919*	J20–30	942
GROUP 7: LAW, ADVOCACY AND POLITICS							
7 100 Civic and Advocacy Organizations	919	966 968	8641 8651 8699*	9723	949	R Q70 P80*	942 949
7 200 Law and Legal Services	7411* 919*	835 963*	8111	7708	949	I	830
7 300 Political Organizations	9192	968	8651	9723	949	W*	949
GROUP 8: PHILANTHROPIC INTERMEDIARIES AND VOLUNTARISM PROMOTION	919	96	6732 8699* 8399*	9723	949	T S70	949
GROUP 9: INTERNATIONAL	919	96	6732* 8699* 8641*	9723	949	Q*	94 980
GROUP 10: RELIGION	9191*	966·	8661	9723	949	X	940
GROUP 11: BUSINESS AND PROFESSIONAL ASSOCIATIONS, UNIONS	9111 9112 9120	963 964 965	8611 8621 8631	7715 9711	941 949*	S41 Y J40	942*
GROUP 12: [NOT ELSEWHERE CLASSIFIED]	9199 9249 9309	968 979 984	8699 8999	87 9723	949	Z	99

* indicates a significant mismatch between ICNPO and other classification; however, some equivalence exists

▒ indicates that ICNPO activity is not captured by other classification, or that such activities are grouped into a catch-all or residual category.

a) 1970 NACE

b) 1987 SIC

APPENDIX C

ADAPTATION OF ICNPO GROUPS AND SUBGROUPS IN VARIOUS COUNTRIES

ICNPO	Brazil	Egypt	France	Germany
GROUP 1: CULTURE AND RECREATION	Cultura e Recreação	الثقافة والاستجمام	Culture et loisirs	Kultur und Erholung
1 100 Culture and Arts	Cultura e Artes	الثقافة والفنون	Culture et beaux-arts	Kunst und Kultur
1 200 Recreation	Recreação	الترويج والاستجمام	Sports et loisirs	Sport, Freizeit, Erholung
1 300 Service Clubs	Clubes* (De Serviços)	نوادي الخدمات العامة	Tourisme social**	Sonstige Klubs
GROUP 2: EDUCATION AND RESEARCH	Educação e Pesquisa	التعليم والبحث	Éducation et recherche	Bildungs- und Forschungswesen
2 100 Primary and Secondary Education	Educação de Primeiro e Segundo Graus	التعليم الابتدائي والثانوي	Enseignement préélementaire, primaire et secondaire	Schulen, Primar- und Sekundarstufe
2 200 Higher Education	Educação Superior	التعليم العالي	Enseignement supérieur	Universitäten und Hochschulen
2 300 Other Education	Educação Alternativa e de Adultos	أنواع أخرى من التعليم	Autres enseignements et formation continue	Sonstige Organisationen des Bildungswesens
2 400 Research	Pesquisa	البحث	Recherche	Forschungswesen
GROUP 3: HEALTH	Saúde	الصحة	Santé	Gesundheitswesen
3 100 Hospitals and Rehabilitation	Hospitais e Reabilitação	المستشفيات ومراكز التأهيل	Hospitaux et établissements de rééducation	Krankenhäuser
3 200 Nursing Homes	Sanatórios	دور النقاهة والمسنين	Maisons de convalescence et ～	Pflegeheime

ICNPO	Brazil	Egypt	France	Germany
3 300 Mental Health and Crisis Intervention	Saúde Mental e Pronto-socorro Psiquiátrico	الصحة النفسية ومعالجة الأزمات	Santé mentale	Psychiatrische Krankenhäuser
3 400 Other Health Services	Outros Serviços de Saúde	خدمات صحية أخرى	Autres services de santé	Sonstige Organisationen des Gesundheitswesen
GROUP 4: SOCIAL SERVICES	Assistência Social	خدمات اجتماعية	Services sociaux	Soziale Dienste und Hilfen
4 100 Social Services	Assistência Social	خدمات اجتماعية	Services sociaux	Soziale Dienste
4 200 Emergency and Relief	Emergências	الطوارئ والإغاثة	Secours et aide d'urgence	Katastrophenschutz und -hilfe
4 300 Income Support and Maintenance	Geração e Manutenção de Renda	دعم الدخل والإعالة	Associations caritatives	Finanzielle Unterstützung und Beihilfen
GROUP 5: ENVIRONMENT	Ambientalismo	البيئة	Protection de l'environnement	Umwelt- und Naturschutz
5 100 Environment	Ambientalismo	البيئة	Protection de l'environnement	Umwelt- und Naturschutz
5 200 Animal Protection	Proteção de Animais	الحيوانات	Protection des animaux	Tierschutz und Tierheime
GROUP 6: DEVELOPMENT AND HOUSING	Desenvolvimento e Habitação	التنمية والإسكان	Développement local et logement	Entwicklung, Wohnungswesen, Beschäftigungsinitiativen
6 100 Economic, Social and Community Development	Desenvolvimento Econômico, Social e Comunitário	التنمية الاقتصادية والاجتماعية والمحلية	Développement local	Entwicklung, Gemeinwesenarbeit
6 200 Housing	Habitação	الإسكان	Logement	Wohnungswesen
6 300 Employment and Training	Emprego e Capacitação	التوظيف والتدريب	Aide l'emploi et formation professionelle	Beschäftigung und berufliche Fortbildung

ICNPO	Brazil	Egypt	France	Germany
GROUP 7: LAW, ADVOCACY AND POLITICS	Defesa de Direitos e Atuação Política	القانون والحقوق والسياسة	Services juridique, défense des droits, organisations politiques	Rechtswesen, Bürger- und Verbraucherinteressen, Politik
7 100 Civic and Advocacy Organizations	Entidades de Defesa de Direitos Civis	جمعيات الدفاع عن الحقوق	Associations civiques et de défense des droits	Staatsbürgerliche Vereinigungen, Bürgerinitiativen, Verbraucherorganisationen
7 200 Law and Legal Services	Serviços Jurídicos e de Proteção Legal	الخدمات القانونية	Services juridiques	Rechtswesen und Rechtsberatung
7 300 Political Organizations	Entidades de Atuação Política	المنظمات السياسية	Organisations politiques	Politische Organisationen
GROUP 8: PHILANTHROPIC INTERMEDIARIES AND VOLUNTARISM PROMOTION	Intermediários Filantrópicos e Promoção de Voluntariado*	الجمعيات الخيرية وتشجيع التطوع	Intermédiaires philanthropiques et promotion du bénévolat	Stiftungswesen, Spendenwesen, allgemeine ehrenamtliche Arbeit
GROUP 9: INTERNATIONAL	Atividades Internacionais	الأنشطة الدولية	Activités internationales	Internationale Aktivitäten
GROUP 10: RELIGION	Religião	الدين	Religion	Religion
GROUP 11: BUSINESS AND PROFESSIONAL ASSOCIATIONS, UNIONS	Sindicatos e Associações Profissionais de Empregadores, de Empregados e de Autônomos	الجمعيات المهنية ونقابات العمال وأصحاب الأعمال	Associations professionnelles et syndicats	Wirtschaftsverbände, Berufsverbände, Gewerkschaften
GROUP 12: [NOT ELSEWHERE CLASSIFIED]	Outros	أخرى	Non dénommé ailleurs	Sonstiges

* Literal Translation. These are not currently used expressions.

** No exact equivalent.

IONPO	Hungary	India	Italy	Japan	Thailand
GROUP 1: CULTURE AND RECREATION	Kultúra és pihenés	Samskruti avam Manoranjan	Attività Culturali e Ricreative	文化とリクリエーション	ศิลปวัฒนธรรมและสันทนาการ
1 100 Culture and Arts	Kultúra és müvészetek	Samskruti avam Kala	Attività Culturali ed Artistiche	文化と芸術	วัฒนธรรมและศิลป์
1 200 Recreation	Pihenés	Manoranjan	Attività Ricreative	リクリエーション	สันทนาการ
1 300 Service Clubs	Pihegklubok	Seva Sanghattan	Club	サービスクラブ	สโมสร/สมาคม
GROUP 2: EDUCATION AND RESEARCH	Oktatás és kutatás	Shiksha avam Shoda	Istruzione e Ricerca	教育と研究	การศึกษาและวิจัย
2 100 Primary and Secondary Education	Alapfokú és középfokú oktatás	Prathamikaa avam Madhyamika Shiksha	Istruzione Primaria e Secondaria	初等・中等教育	การศึกษาระดับประถมและมัธยม
2 200 Higher Education	Felsőoktatás	Utham Shiksha	Istruzione Universitaria	高等教育	การศึกษาระดับสูง/ อุดมศึกษา
2 300 Other Education	Egyéb oktatás	Anya Shiksha	Istruzione Professionale ed Istruzione degli Adulti	その他の教育	การศึกษาอื่นๆ
2 400 Research	Kutatás	Shoda	Ricerca	研究	วิจัย
GROUP 3: HEALTH	Egészségügy	Swasthya	Sanità	ヘルス	สุขภาพ อนามัย
3 100 Hospitals and Rehabilitation	Kórházak és egészségügyi rehabilitáció	Aspathal avam Rogi Samarthikaran	Servizi ospedalieri Generali e Riabilitativi	病院とリハビリテーション	โรงพยาบาลและสถานพักฟื้น
3 200 Nursing Homes	Szanatóriumok, és egészséggíároultak szociális otthonai	Arogyalaya	Case di Cura	療養所	บ้านพักคนชรา

ICNPO	Hungary	India	Italy	Japan	Thailand
3 300 Mental Health and Crisis Intervention	Mentális betegségek kezelése, krízisintervenció	Manasika Arogya Avam Sankhat Nirvarthna	Servizi Psichiatrici Ospedalieri e non Ospedalieri	精神衛生と危機回避	ความบริการบำบัดทางจิตและบริการในภาวะวิกฤต
3 400 Other Health Services	Egyéb egészségügyi szolgáltatások	Anya Arogya Seva Kendra	Altri Servizi Sanitari	その他のヘルスサービス	การบริการสุขภาพด้านอื่นๆ
GROUP 4: SOCIAL SERVICES	Szociális szolgáltatások	Samajika Seva	Assistenza Sociale	社会福祉	บริการสังคม
4 100 Social Services	Szociális szolgáltatások	Samajika Seva	Servizi Sociali	社会福祉	บริการสังคม
4 200 Emergency and Relief	Katasztrófaelhárítás menekültügy	Apathkaline Sahayatha	Servizi di Assistenza in caso di Calamità Naturale, di Protezione Civile e di Assistenza a Profughi e Rifugiati	緊急救援	เหตุการฉุกเฉิน และการบรรเทาทุกข์
4 300 Income Support and Maintenance	Jövedelemkiegészítő pénzbeni támogatások	Utpan Adhar avam Nibha	Servizi di Sostegno ai Redditi ed Alle Condizioni di Vita Individuale e Servizi di Beneficenza	所得保障・・・	สนับสนุนรายได้ และการยังชีพ
GROUP 5: ENVIRONMENT	Környezetvédelem	Paryavaran	Attività Ambientalista	環境	สิ่งแวดล้อม
5 100 Environment	Környezetvédelem	Paryavaran	Attività a favore dell'ambiente	環境	สิ่งแวดล้อม
5 200 Animal Protection	Állatvédelem	Pashu Rakshan	Attività a favore degli Animali	動物	สัตว์

ICNPO	Hungary	India	Italy	Japan	Thailand
GROUP 6: DEVELOPMENT AND HOUSING	Település-, gazdaság- és közösségfejlesztés, lakásügy	Vikas avam Avas	Promozione dello Sviluppo Economico e Sociale della Comunità Locale; Tutela degli Inquilini E Sviluppo del Patrimonio Abitativo	開発と住宅	การพัฒนา และที่อยู่อาศัย
6 100 Economic, Social and Community Development	Település- és közösségfejlesztés	Arthik, samajik avam Nagarik vikas	Promozione Dello Sviluppo Economico e Sociale Della Comunità Locale	経済・社会・コミュニティ開発	การพัฒนาชุมชน ด้าน และเศรษฐกิจ
6 200 Housing	Lakásügy	Avas	Tutela degli Inquilini e Sviluppo del Patrimonio Abitativo	住宅	การเคหะ
6 300 Employment and Training	A munkanélküliség kezelése képzés	Udyog avam Parishikshan	Addestramento ed Avviamento Professionale	雇用と訓練	การจ้างงานและ ฝึกอบรม
GROUP 7: LAW, ADVOCACY AND POLITICS	Jog, érdekvédelem, politika	Kanoon, Vakalath avam Rajneethi	Diritti Civici, Tutela Legale e Politica	法律・代言活動（アドボカシー）・政治	กฎหมาย การปกครอง และการเมือง
7 100 Civic and Advocacy Organizations	Polgárjogi és érdekvédelmi szervezetek	Jan Chetna Sanstha avam Jan Adhikaar Samrakshan	Organizzazioni Civiche e di Tutela dei Diritti	市民と社会運動団体	องค์การประชาชนและการพิทักษ์ สิทธิ
7 200 Law and Legal Services	Jogi szolgáltatások	Kanoon avam Kannoni Jankaari Kendra	Servizi di Tutela Legale	法的サービス	กฎหมายและการบริการ ด้านกฎหมาย
7 300 Political Organizations	Politikai szervezetek	Rajneethik Samstha	Organizzazioni Politiche	政治団体	การจัดตั้งทางการเมือง

ICNPO	Hungary	India	Italy	Japan	Thailand
GROUP 8: PHILANTHROPIC INTERMEDIARIES AND VOLUNTARISM PROMOTION	Jótékonyság, az öntevékenység támogatása	Paropkari Madhyam Sanstha avam Swayam Seva Bhav Prothsahin	Intermediari Filantropici e Promozione del Volontariato	フィランソロピー的仲介組織と ボランティア	องค์กรการกุศลและ ส่งเสริมงานอาสาสมัคร
GROUP 9: INTERNATIONAL	Nemzetközi kapcsolatok	Antharashtriya Karyakaram	Attività Internazionali	助成団体	กิจกรรมระหว่างประเทศ
GROUP 10: RELIGION			Organizzazioni Religiose	国際的活動	ศาสนา
GROUP 11: BUSINESS AND PROFESSIONAL ASSOCIATIONS, UNIONS	Üzleti és szakmai szövetségek, testületek	Vyaparik avam Vyavasayak Sanghattan, Mazdoor dal	Organizzazioni Economiche, di Titolari di Impresa, Professionali e Sindacali	業界団体と専門的団体 組合	สมาคมธุรกิจและ วิชาชีพ สหภาพ สมาคม
GROUP 12: [NOT ELSEWHERE CLASSIFIED]	Egyéb	Anya	Altri	その他 分類されないもの	อื่นๆ

Source: *Voluntas*, 3(3):301–307

Notes

1 An "economic activity" in national income statistics is defined as "the combination of actions that result in a certain set of products" (United Nations, 1990:9).

2 A 1992 revision of the NACE system makes the classification nearly identical to the ISIC, although some more detail is provided at the sub-group level, allowing for a more refined treatment in some industries (Eurostat, 1992).

3 Some analysts would include Service Clubs (Subgroup 1 300) as member–serving organizations also.

References

Amenomori, Takayoshi (1993), 'Defining the nonprofit sector: Japan', *Working Papers of the Johns Hopkins Comparative Nonprofit Sector Project*, no. 15, ed. L. M. Salamon and H. K. Anheier. Baltimore: The Johns Hopkins Institute for Policy Studies.

Anheier, Helmut K., Gabriel Rudney and Lester M. Salamon (1993), 'The nonprofit sector and the United Nations System of Accounts: country applications of SNA Guidelines', *Voluntas*, 4(4) (1993): 486–501.

Eurostat (1979), *European System of Integrated Accounts (ESA)*, 2nd edn. Luxembourg: Office for Official Publications of the European Community.

Eurostat (1989), *NACE. General Industrial Classification of Economic Activities within the European Communities*. Luxembourg: Office for Official Publications of the European Community.

INSEE (Institut National de la Statistique et des Etudes Economiques) (1990), *Enquête sur les Associations*. Paris: INSEE.

Salamon, Lester M. (1992), *America's Nonprofit Sector: A Primer*. New York: The Foundation Center.

Salamon, Lester M. and Alan J. Abramson (1982), *The Federal Budget and the Nonprofit Sector*. Washington, DC: The Urban Institute Press.

Salamon, Lester M. and Helmut K. Anheier (1992a), "In search of the non-profit sector I: the question of definitions". *Voluntas*, 3(3):125–151.

Salamon, Lester M. and Helmut K. Anheier (1992b), "In search of the non-profit sector II: the problem of classification." *Voluntas*, 3(3):267–309.

Sumariwalla, Russy (1983), "Preliminary observation on scope, size, and classification of the sector" in *Working Papers for the Spring Research Forum: Since the Filer Commission*. Washington, DC: Independent Sector.

United Nations (1990), *International Standard Industrial Classification of All Economic Activities*, 3rd rev. edn, Statistical Papers Series M, no. 4, rev. 3. New York: United Nations.

Part II

DEFINING THE NONPROFIT SECTOR IN DEVELOPED SOCIETIES

Ever since Alexis de Tocqueville in the mid-1830s proclaimed the penchant of Americans to form associations as one of the distinctive features of U.S. society, it has been customary to treat the nonprofit sector as a preeminently, and almost distinctively, American phenomenon.

In fact, however, the existence of a wide range of organizations outside the market and the State is hardly uniquely American. Third-sector organizations have long played major roles in virtually every developed society in the world, and in many developing ones as well. Indeed, this role often exceeds that played by these organizations in the U.S. itself.

In this part we examine the position of private, nonprofit, or voluntary organizations in the seven developed countries covered in the Johns Hopkins Comparative Nonprofit Sector Project – the U.S., the U.K., France, Germany, Italy, Sweden, and Japan. The chapters in this section represent the responses of the team of Local Associates who collaborated in this project to a field guide seeking information on the basic terminology used to depict third-sector organizations in their respective countries, on the concepts and organizational realities that lie behind this terminology, and on the viability of our proposed "structural–operational" definition to depict the resulting organizational universe.

Though the countries covered in this section share a similar level of social and economic development, they differ markedly along a number of other dimensions thought to influence the development of a nonprofit sector. Included are thus countries representing both common law (U.S. and U.K.) and civil law

(Germany, France, Italy, Japan, and Sweden) legal traditions; countries with high levels of government social welfare spending, such as Sweden and France, as well as countries with much lower levels, such as the United States and Japan; countries with long traditions of decentralization, such as the United States and Germany, as well as countries with long traditions of centralized government, such as France and Japan.

By examining the patterns of third-sector structure in these countries, it should therefore be possible to gain useful insights not only into the diverse character of this sector, but also into the viability of some of the theories advanced to explain its presence and into the suitability of the conceptual equipment developed here for coming to terms with its basic contours.

Chapter 5

FRANCE

Edith Archambault[1]

Introduction

The difficulty of defining and measuring France's nonprofit sector derives largely from its relative official invisibility in the country's institutional landscape. As in most other countries, statistics on the sector as a whole are simply not kept. And while such terms as *économie sociale, tiers secteur, and secteur sans but lucratif* may be cited occasionally by specialists or employees of nonprofit organizations, they are not used in general discourse. Indeed, until recently, most nonprofits were sometimes even viewed as components of an informal economy, which also included household activities and illegal trade (Archambault and Greffe, 1984). Finally, understanding of the sector has been impeded by the sector's internal balkanization into distinct sub-components – a consequence of both the different legal treatments afforded to nonprofit organizations, and the distinct political and religious orientations of major subsectors.

During the 1980s, however, the Socialist government supported the emergence of the sector as an important tool for social policy. Since 1982, nonprofit organizations have been employed by successive Socialist governments as mechanisms through which to implement decentralization – a hallmark of political change in France during the last decade.

To grasp the dimensions of the sector, therefore, it is useful to begin with a historical overview of the relationship between the French State and religious and other nongovernmental associations. The following pages provide this review; specify the sector's four components or subsectors; describe the organizational types, and some of the laws to which they are subject, within each subsector; and elaborate on the rapidly changing relationship between the State, the nonprofit sector, and French society in general. The resulting definition of the sector, most commonly referred to as *économie sociale*, is then compared to the "structural–operational definition" which has been developed to facilitate international comparisons.

Historical note

The relative underdevelopment of France's nonprofit sector has its roots in the 1789 French Revolution. In 1791, the *Le Chapelier Act* suppressed guilds and all other associations which had existed under the previous *ancien régime*. Its rationale was a Rousseauian concept of the state as the achievement of the collective interest of the French people: "No one is allowed to incite citizens to have an intermediary interest [between their own and the State's], to separate them from the Nation by a spirit of cooperation."

Despite this restriction, voluntary associations and mutual benefit societies appeared again at the start of the nineteenth century, largely in response to the onset of the industrial revolution and its by-product of working-class poverty. Social clubs, Catholic health and youth charities, and worker-support groups flourished in urban areas (Gueslin, 1987; Fenet, 1989).

Successive centralized Jacobin governments, whether Republican or Bonapartist, were suspicious of both religious organizations and labor movements. Anticlerical governments viewed Catholic charities and mutualist societies as a revival of *ancien régime* religious and corporatist tendencies. Public authorities saw in the labor movement in general, and in workers' self-help organizations in particular, the specter of anarchism and working-class dominance – a movement which reached its apex with the Paris Commune of 1871, when the frightened authorities battled the illegal coalitions of the workers' groups.[2]

It was not until the latter part of the nineteenth century that the nonprofit sector began to shed its illegality. The crime of coalition itself was abolished in 1864; of labor unions two decades later; and of mutual benefit societies in 1898. Voluntary associations were made legal by 1901. But these legal changes did not eliminate the long-term, deep-seated animosity between an omnipotent, centralized government and the Catholic Church and its subsidiaries, especially schools and charities. In fact, the 1901 Law was enacted during an intensely anticlerical political era. While it legalized voluntary associations, it imposed considerable restrictions on religious congregations.

In 1905, the Disestablishment of the Church Act fully severed the Roman Catholic Church from the State, and secular–religious conflicts began to subside. During the same period, as the industrial era evolved, mutual societies and cooperatives diverged from the workers' movement. The former became middle-class-oriented; the latter more radical and Marxist (Hatzfeld, 1971).

By the twentieth century, the evolving relationship between public authorities and what came to be known as the "social economy" had become more peaceful and, indeed, complementary. The expansion of government social welfare programs between the two World Wars not only accompanied a growing number of mutual benefit societies, but affected the very direction of those organizations by motivating them to reorient their aims and operations.

In 1945, France incrementally established a comprehensive social security system, protecting virtually the entire French population against four "social risks": illness, old age, unemployment, and family expansion. Programs to meet these risks included reimbursement of medical expenditures and free hospitalization; retirement pensions and other old age benefits; unemployment compensation; and family allowances for all but the first child. As a consequence, mutual benefit societies found it necessary to develop innovative measures to complete the protection – to fill the gaps left by the public social security system (Caire, 1984).

Since 1965, the "associative" component of the nonprofit sector (see the following section) grew rapidly, almost as if in compensation for its historical lag. During the 1970s and 1980s, characterized in part by a deepening fiscal crisis of the welfare state, the complementary relationship between the government and nonprofit services was reinforced.

With the slowing of economic growth and the rise of unemployment, many public health and welfare agencies found their income imperiled, since they were linked to the social security system which, in turn, depended on employment-related contributions. As a result, public agencies sought the cooperation of organizations in what was increasingly referred to as the *économie sociale*, or social economy. These organizations included groups offering home services to reduce increasing admission rates to hospitals and nursing homes, self-help day care centers, continuing education for unskilled youth or unemployed people, job training, income maintenance, and temporary shelters for the "new poor."

By 1982, the Socialist government, which had come to power the year before, had instituted a decentralization policy, which was further developed and implemented by successive Socialist administrations. The policy strongly encouraged the incorporation and development of the social economy as a tool of decentralization. It also had the effect of promoting public awareness of the social economy as an entity in its own right, notwithstanding the diverse legal standings of its components such as cooperatives, mutual benefit and insurance societies, foundations, works councils, and other organizations.

Components of the social economy

Legal status is the main criterion for membership in the social economy. Differences in legal treatment of social economy organizations are, however, considerable, which helps explain why these organizations do not share a common awareness of belonging to the same sector. But a sense of commonality is growing in spite of these differences. It is aided by the proliferation of coalitions, sometimes referred to as umbrella or "peak" organizations, conferences on social economy, and the creation of the *Délégation à l'Economie Sociale*, a high-level policy-making body attached to the central government.

The social economy includes four distinct components:

- the cooperative sector;
- the banking sector;
- the mutualist sector; and
- the associative sector.

To facilitate the following discussion, Figure 5.1 offers a schematic representation of the various components, and Table 5.1 provides some indication of the size of the social economy by showing the number of organizations operating in each sector and subsector.

The cooperative sector

Cooperatives are member-oriented organizations, engaged in some form of commercial activity. They are governed by the 1947 General Status of Cooperation Act (revised in 1983 and 1985), and may adopt any legal "enterprise status." The Act defines cooperatives as enterprises with two aims: "to reduce, by common effort and to the benefit of members, the price of goods and services produced and directly marketed, and to better the quality of products supplied to members or sold to consumers." Financially, the capital in a cooperative belongs to each of the organization's members, that is, it is not shared. The organizations are exempt from corporate taxes, but if they develop operating surpluses they must establish reserve funds, and/or distribute the surplus to members in the form of reduced fees or prices.

Cooperatives in France take three forms: workers' cooperatives, consumers' cooperatives, and enterprise cooperatives (producer cooperatives). *Workers' cooperatives*, or *sociétés co-opératives ouvrières de production* (SCOP), are essentially producers of industrial goods, although a quarter of them deliver services. Relatively few in number (around 1,500), they experienced an expansion during the recent manufacturing crisis as workers created cooperatives to avoid the consequences of bankruptcies afflicting regular business enterprises. Members are salaried, and contribute some capital. Traditional banks tend to view workers' cooperatives with suspicion, and are loath to grant them loans. Lack of capital keeps the size and number of workers' cooperatives fairly small.

Consumers' cooperatives' members are either suppliers of goods or customers. Supplier groups, in particular those marketing agricultural products, are expanding; but customer groups – which took the form of the "chain retail stores" widely popular during the nineteenth century – are rapidly declining and being driven out by for-profit firms. Housing cooperatives, another form of consumers' cooperatives, are also declining. Widespread after the Second World War, many today are short-lived, dissolving once housing is built. Some housing cooperatives offer rental facilities for low-income populations.

Figure 5.1

Scope of the social economy

Cooperatives	producer cooperatives	worker cooperatives (SCOP) enterprise cooperatives cooperatives of agricultural sector
	consumer cooperatives	distribution cooperatives housing cooperatives
Cooperative Banks	*Crédit Agricole, Crédit Mutuel, Banque Centrale des Coopératives et Mutuelles, Crédit Coopératif, Banques Populaires*	
Mutuals	mutual benefit societies (*Code de la Mutualité*)	*Fédération Nationale de la Mutualité Française Fédération des Mutuelles de France*
	Mutualité Sociale Agricole	
	mutual insurance companies	
Associations	undeclared associations	
	declared associations	ordinary declared associations public utility associations
	foundations	
Borderline organizations	works councils business and trade associations labor unions property-owners and condominium associations	

Enterprise (producer) cooperatives are numerous in agriculture and fishing, offering members the opportunity to share farm equipment, boats, trucks, and the like. Beyond economizing or "rationalizing" purchasing, production and transformation or processing of goods, the cooperatives seek to protect independent small-scale producers against the power of market concentration. Cooperatives are very prominent in agriculture, entailing the participation of four out of five French farmers. Roughly 25,000 agricultural cooperatives are currently in operation, employing some 200,000 people, and reporting annual revenues of 500 billion FF (around $90 billion) (Padieu, 1990). In the French national accounts, cooperatives are treated as businesses and part of the corporate sector.

Table 5.1

Number of organizations recorded in the *Système Informatique pour le Répertoire sur les Entreprises et les Etablissements* (SIRENE) file[a]
(Padieu, 1990)

Cooperatives	25,920	worker cooperatives	1,540
		cooperatives in the agricultural sector	21,350
		other enterprise (producer) cooperatives	3,030
Banks	4,516[b]		
Mutuals	2,870	mutual benefit societies	2,020
		agricultural mutual benefit societies	100
		insurance mutuals and other	750
Associations[c]	160,705		
Foundations[d]	357		
Borderline organizations	9,718	works councils	2,699
		property-owners/condominium associations	4,594
		labor unions, business and trade associations	2,425

a   The SIRENE file records all enterprises irrespective of legal status if they hire wage earners and pay taxes. Some of the additional data figures quoted in the text are provided by the umbrella organizations and similar groups.

b   Number of establishments.

c   The SIRENE file includes only associations which hire one or more wage-earners and/or those which paid Value-Added Tax (VAT) over the five previous years.

d   Largely operating foundations.

The banking sector

Cooperatives of a substantially different nature from those described above are credit establishments created initially to bypass ordinary banks, and to serve the credit needs of low-income farmers and workers. Founded initially on the principle of collective self-help, in which the surpluses of some members finance the deficits of others, the network's participants today operate increasingly like regular banks. The *Crédit Coopératif* and the *Banque Centrale des Coopératives et Mutuelles* also serve the financial needs of nonprofit organizations. Their members are organizations rather than individuals.

Crédit Agricole remains the most important French bank; 20 years ago, before the rise of the Japanese banks, it ranked among the largest in the world. Its role in financing the modernization of French agriculture was decisive, and was integral to the activity of agricultural cooperatives. Like *Crédit Mutuel* and *Banques Populaires*, *Crédit Agricole* is sustained by small-scale deposits and savings accounts, owing to its widespread branches, especially in rural areas.

Assets of the cooperative banking network in 1989 amounted to 1,800 billion FF (around $330 billion at the rate of exchange that year). They employed 130,000 workers, or 29 percent of total employment in the banking industry. This compares to 33 percent employed by for-profit banks, and 38 percent in state-owned, public banks. *Crédit Agricole* represents about two-thirds of the total assets in the nonprofit banking sector, and more than half the employment in cooperative banking (Padieu, 1990). In the national accounts, banks in the social economy are treated as *Institutions de Crédit*, that is, as belonging to the financial sector, along with private for-profit and nationalized banks.

The mutualist sector

Mutuals are heirs to the oldest part of the French nonprofit sector. Some provide direct services to members; others are insurance companies operated on a nonprofit basis.

Mutual societies, the major component of this subsector, are basically nonprofit organizations, descended from the friendly societies of the nineteenth and early twentieth centuries. Subject to the 1955 Mutual Societies Code, they are defined as "organizations that promote with their members' subscriptions an activity of providence, solidarity and philanthropy to the benefit of families. This activity aims to prevent social risks, to encourage motherhood, to protect childhood and the family, and to promote the moral development of their members."

Since the establishment of the public social security system in 1945, the role of these organizations has changed from one of meeting the basic needs of members, to one of supplementing the social security allowances (Caire, 1984). Although 99 percent of the French population is covered by compulsory social security, half the population chooses mutual supplementary insurance. Why? Because compulsory health insurance requires a 20 percent patient contribution, which the mutual societies cover.

Mutual societies also expanded guarantees of income in the events of illness, accident, or death, which brought them into direct competition with insurance companies. However, the societies differ from insurance firms in two important respects, aside from the fact that they are nonprofit. First, they charge according to income, rather than age, risk, or other actuarial factors. Thus, wealthier participants subsidize the less wealthy, in accordance with the principle of solidarity. Second, mutual societies are administered by volunteer boards, while insurance company trustees receive directors' fees. Some 100,000 volunteers reportedly operate local mutual societies.

Beyond insurance, mutual societies provide health and welfare services, including medical clinics, day care hospitals, pharmacies, nursing homes or centers, optical and dental clinics, social service centers for the elderly and handicapped, and "holiday centers" for children with disabilities. Around 1,070 such facilities or services were in operation in 1988, reporting revenues of 6.4 billion FF (around $1.1 billion).

Finally, in addition to providing insurance and offering direct services, mutual societies manage some programs that are part of the national social security system. In this respect they serve as *de facto* government agencies, providing compulsory social security for civil servants, the self-employed, students, teachers, professors, and farmers. Because this activity is not independent of the government, it must be excluded from the social economy in the strict sense.

Mutual societies are organized into federations. The *Fédération Nationale de la Mutualité Française* (FNMF) employs 50,000 people, delivers services to 25 million beneficiaries, and is financed by fees amounting to 35 billion FF ($6.4 billion). FNMF is the most important Federation and encompasses 90 percent of the groups. The remaining 10 percent belong to the *Fédération des Mutuelles de France* (FMF), which employs 5,500 people, delivers services to seven million beneficiaries, and is financed by fees amounting to 6.5 billion FF or $1.2 billion (Padieu, 1990). FMF is close to the Communist Party.

Mutual insurance companies are best viewed as a borderline component of the social economy. Often subsidiaries of mutual societies, mutual insurance companies guarantee primarily against property damage, as opposed to personal risk. They hold about 35 percent of automobile policies, and 25 percent of other property policies. Premiums are paid on the basis of actuarial risk, as is the custom with for-profit insurance firms, rather than according to member income, as is the case with mutual societies.

For these reasons, and because they are subject to the Insurance Code rather than the 1955 Mutuality Code, it is debatable whether one should include them as a subset of the social economy. The French system of national accounts, for example, treats them as regular insurance firms. Still, they provide no capital remuneration (the equivalent of profits) to members, and some of them perform no brokerage services. Eventual "profits" or surpluses are distributed only in the form of reduced premiums the following year. Finally, all trustees are volunteers. Thus, we may consider mutual insurance companies part of the social economy if they do not provide brokerage services. This is the case for the *Groupement des Sociétés d'Assurance à Caractère Mutuel*. Otherwise, they are part of the for-profit economy. Together, in the late 1980s, the mutual insurance industry received 42 billion FF or $7.7 billion in premiums annually, and employed 28,000 people (Padieu, 1990).

The associative sector

The associative sector is the most diverse and least understood component of the social economy. Legally, the sector comprises three types of associations:

- undeclared associations, i.e., those with no legal status;
- declared associations, which are subject to the 1901 Act; and
- public utility associations, which is a status granted by the State to a select group of declared associations.

Undeclared associations constitute a diverse set of organizations; they include religious organizations at the parish level, such as *associations cultuelles*, relating to religious activities, sacraments, and rituals, or *associations diocésaines*, serving as financial distribution channels for Catholic churches; neighborhood groups; or political groups advocating a specific cause. In some instances, newly founded nonprofit organizations select the "undeclared status" in an initial "try-out" phase before becoming a declared association after some consolidation period.

Declared associations are by far the most numerous in the associative sector. The reason is entirely juridical: an association usually opts for "declared" status offered by the 1901 Act, which remains the most liberal and flexible under French law.

This Act defines an association as "a convention according to which two or more individuals permanently pool their knowledge or activity with an aim other than the sharing of profit." Since the creation of an association must be declared at the *préfecture*, a local authority, reliable data are available on the founding of these groups, which are booming; for example, 17,500 formed in 1965, and more than 60,000 in 1990, according to the official government register. Unfortunately, the associations do not have to declare their dissolution, so the actual number of declared groups currently active is unknown. A reasonable "guesstimate" is between 600,000 and 700,000 (see Padieu, 1990).

Declared associations are limited in their capacity to engage in certain types of financial transactions. For example, they may not own real estate or receive legacies. This restriction, which severely reduces the financial options available to associations, dates back to the early part of the twentieth century, and to the conflict between the State and religious congregations. Nevertheless, they are exempt from income and profit taxes, and partially from value-added taxes. Further, gifts to declared associations are deductible up to 3 percent of taxable income, and up to 1/1000 of enterprise revenue.

Public utility associations, technically a form of declared associations, operate as charities, primarily in the fields of health and welfare. Status as a public utility association is granted by the *Conseil d'Etat*, following a two-year application procedure. Unlike other declared associations, these groups may own real estate and other financial assets, and receive legacies. Gifts to them are deductible up to 5 percent of taxable income; legacies are encouraged by exemption from inheritance taxes (Alix and Castro, 1986). Their number is few – 1,948 in 1990 – but they tend to be large in size.

Foundations enjoy the same fiscal privileges as public utility associations, in terms of owning real estate and other financial assets. Of the nation's 428 foundations in 1990, almost all are operating foundations such as the *Institut Pasteur or Fondation Cousteau.* Only 13, or 3 percent, are grantmaking institutions, the most important of which is the *Fondation de France.*[3]

Another classification distinguishes between operating, advocacy and sociability associations.

Operating associations are nonprofits that receive most of their public financing either through the central or local governments, or through social security. They provide both market and non-market services, and are staffed by both wage earners and volunteers (Archambault, 1986). Most operating associations are active in health, welfare, research, education, professional training, recreation, and "social tourism."

Advocacy or sociability associations, as the term implies, are either pressure groups or social clubs. Advocacy associations today promote feminism, minority rights, environmental protection, family values, consumer rights, and so forth. Examples of sociability associations include recreation or sports clubs, veterans and senior citizens groups, etc.

Reliable statistical data on the social economy's associative sector as a whole do not exist. We know neither the number of active associations, nor the number of volunteers, nor the hours spent in volunteer work. Data that are available reveal the following:

- The sector employs some 800,000 people, and wage work increased rapidly during 1980–1985, largely in establishments serving the needs of the elderly and handicapped (see Padieu, 1990).
- Half the adult French population belongs to one or more associations (Hauesler, 1990).

Additional information on small segments of the sector is available from umbrella or "peak" associations, but the data may be overstated. Key umbrella groups include:

- *Ligue de l'Enseignement,* or Education League, created in 1866, governs lay school social institutions, or nonprofits linked to public schools: 33,000 associations, 930,000 members.
- Union Nationale Interfédérale des Oeuvres Privées Sanitaires et Sociales (UNIOPSS), created in 1947, represents 7,000 non-profit health or welfare operating associations. The members employ 300,000 people, and provide services to 450,000 users. Nonprofits within UNIOPSS account for about 15 percent of the

services provided in the health field, and 51 percent in social welfare.

- *Union Nationale des Associations de Tourisme* (UNAT), established in 1920, works in the field of popular recreation and tourism; it has a million members and employs 57,000 people.
- *Comité National Olympique du Sport Français* (CNOSF), created in 1908, represents 73 sports federations. Total membership is about 11 million, and includes more than a million active volunteers.
- *Union Nationale des Associations Familiales* (UNAF), created in 1945, represents 5,700 associations and 650,000 families.
- *Fonds de Coopération de la Jeunesse et de l'Education Populaire* (FONJEP), created in 1964, is a federation of youth and popular education associations. A significant amount of data pertaining to the members is available as a result of a survey by Fouquet, Tabard and Villac (1990).

The national accounts

How is the social economy treated in the national accounts? Figure 5.2 presents a summary picture and shows that most components of the social economy are allocated to other sectors. In accordance with the European System of Accounts, French national accounts single out as *administrations privées* some private nonprofit and nongovernmental organizations, such as churches, labor unions, political parties, consumer groups, youth and cultural associations, and charities. However, the structure and development of the national accounts are widely criticized (Anheier, Rudney and Salamon, 1993). For example, operating associations are treated as *outside* the *administrations privées* if their sales are more than 50 percent of total resources. Such groups are instead recorded in the business sector, which includes social tourism, recreation, and professional training associations.

Further, the most important health and welfare associations and private religious schools are recorded in the government sector, because public financing accounts for more than 50 percent of their resources. Smaller associations, hiring fewer than two wage-earners, are included in the household sector (Archambault, 1988). Finally, national accounts depictions of the insurance sector (*entreprises d'assurance*) treat mutual societies as separate from for-

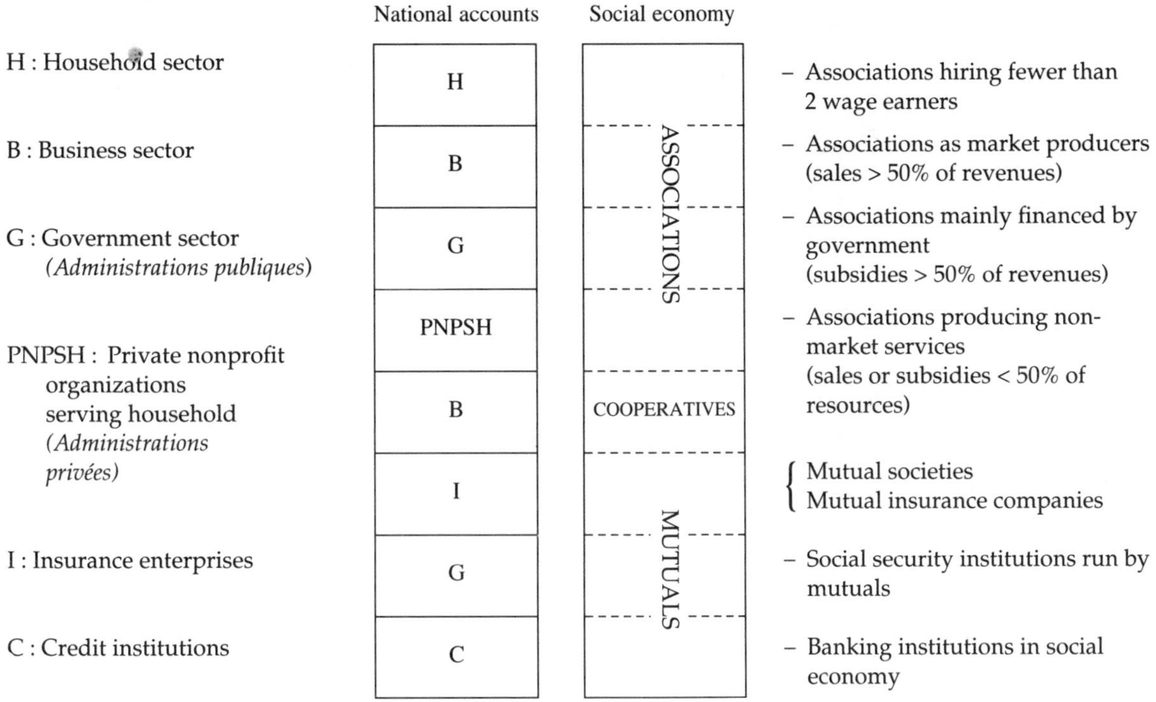

National accounts	Social economy	
H		– Associations hiring fewer than 2 wage earners
B	ASSOCIATIONS	– Associations as market producers (sales > 50% of revenues)
G		– Associations mainly financed by government (subsidies > 50% of revenues)
PNPSH		– Associations producing non-market services (sales or subsidies < 50% of resources)
B	COOPERATIVES	
I	MUTUALS	{ Mutual societies Mutual insurance companies
G		– Social security institutions run by mutuals
C		– Banking institutions in social economy

H : Household sector

B : Business sector

G : Government sector (*Administrations publiques*)

PNPSH : Private nonprofit organizations serving household (*Administrations privées*)

I : Insurance enterprises

C : Credit institutions

Figure 5.2 National accounts and social economy

116

profit insurance companies, and the national accounts record defines cooperatives in the business sector (*Sociétés et quasi-sociétés*) as ordinary for-profit companies.

The State, French society, and the nonprofit sector

The relationships between the nonprofit sector, French society, and the State today have been shaped by two factors: the different legal treatment afforded the social economy's member institutions, and fierce social and political conflicts, some of which can be traced to medieval times. The previous section examined some of the legal issues; this section provides an overview of the historically-rooted cross-currents in present-day French society that are the product of longstanding conflicts. In brief, these cross–currents include: centralization versus regionalism, Catholicism versus socialism, non-Marxist versus Marxist socialism, left versus right Catholicism, large-scale charities versus small grass-roots organizations, welfare state versus self-help ideologies, and, lately, the issue of immigration. Obviously, these conflicts are hardly separate and distinct. They overlap and intertwine, rendering the relationships between the sector, the State, and society in general highly complex.

Centralization and homogeneity

While France today is increasingly multicultural, traditionally it has had a less diversified society than other European nations, a consequence of both monarchical and Jacobin governmental policies. As de Tocqueville pointed out, between the twelfth century and the 1789 revolution, the monarchy moved successfully to centralize government authority and reduce regionalism.

After the revolution, successive Jacobin governments, either Bonapartist or Republican, went beyond political centralization and sought to promote social homogeneity through such institutions as compulsory public schooling. At the end of the nineteenth century, public schools served as a powerful "melting pot," both diffusing republican ideology and all but destroying minority regional languages such as Breton, Basque, Provençal, and Alsatian. Until the beginning of the twentieth century, however, the Church resisted the standardization of French society, opposing social change, and allying itself with the monarchy.

Successive waves of immigration have made French society far more diversified today than in previous eras, and this too affects the social economy. After the Second World War and up to 1973, domestic manpower shortages were filled initially by Spanish and Portuguese immigrants, and later by Algerians, Moroccans, Tunisians, and Africans from former French colonies. So long as the economy was reasonably vibrant, the immigrants were welcomed. But as unemployment increased during the 1980s, it was accompanied by a rising aversion towards immigrants among the French population. Perhaps the most visible manifestation of this is the growing extreme right vote for Jean Marie Le Pen. A counter-movement has also grown, consisting of organizations like SOS-Racism, and ethnic and Muslim groups. Both the central and local governments have sought to work with these associations to deal with unemployment and other social problems faced by first- and second-generation immigrants. Today, as a result, the nonprofit sector plays an important role as the State's partner in employment policies, particularly for youth.

Catholicism *vs*. Republican egalitarianism

The historical relationship between these two ideologies contributed to perhaps the most prominent cross-current in French society: opposition between Catholicism and Republicanism. Revolutionary tradition notwithstanding, the Church had remained a considerable power; as late as the turn of the twentieth century, it was able to rally a majority of the population. Integral to its history and, of course, to its ideology was the practice of charity. Ultimately, this ideology came into conflict with the Republican movement, which, rooted in an industrializing and urbanizing economy, emphasized the public provision of social services.

French philanthropists such as Le Play (1806–1825), Ozanam (1813–1853), and De Mun (1841-1914) represented Catholic charity in its modern form. Saint-Simon (1760–1825), Fourier (1772–1837), and Proudhon (1809–1865) were the theoreticians of French utopian socialism. With the rapid advancement of French urbanization, however, the influence of the Church has waned. At present, church attendance is lower in France (11 percent of the population) than in any other European country. France also has the highest percentage of people defining themselves as atheists (Djider and Marpsat, 1990).

Nevertheless, conflicts between Catholic charity and socialism continue to affect some parts of the nonprofit sector. In 1984, for example, the streets of Paris were filled with two million teachers, members of parent–teacher associations and alumni demonstrating against a Socialist policy to combine public and Catholic schools. Even though Catholic schools are financed with public grants, and teachers paid by the central government, opponents saw the move as undermining their pedagogic and ideological independence. Faced with such vehement opposition, the government withdrew the policy.

The Catholic–socialist schism does not coincide neatly with a right–left demarcation. For example, while Catholic schools tend to be largely maintained by conservative support, nonprofit health and welfare associations in UNIOPSS – the most important of the umbrella organizations – veer to the left or center. UNIOPSS, in fact, represents Catholic social thought in the tradition of the *Rerum novarum* encyclical of 1891.

French socialism, likewise, has its own internal divisions, primarily between Marxists and non-Marxists. This division, too, influences the character of the social economy. Within the nonprofit sector, in fact, French socialism is almost entirely non-Marxist, since Marxists, as a matter of principle, seek a state monopoly on education, health, welfare, and cultural services.

Perhaps the most important of the non-Marxist socialist umbrella organizations is the *Ligue de l'enseignement*, encompassing nonprofits linked to public education. The *Ligue* also operates cultural, sports, leisure, and social service programs.

Finally, freemasonry is yet another, though more covert, current affecting the social economy, especially the *Ligue de l'enseignement* and the *Federation nationale de la mutualité française* (FNMF). Today, freemasons tend to be close to the socialist government, and have maintained strong anticlerical attitudes.

Conflicts between large and small institutions

Another cross-current within French society affecting the nonprofit sector is the conflict between large, national organizations and small, local groups. Large organizations, heavily dependent on public funding, are opposed to smaller or "lighter-weight" voluntary organizations, which they argue have access to more diversified resources. To an extent, this opposition overlaps the conflict between operating associations and advocacy groups; it also mirrors the ideological strains between welfare state advocates and proponents of private initiative and self-help, and between centralization and regionalism.

The Decentralization Act of 1982 was an effort to respond to critics of centralized authority, and to facilitate entry into a European market whose other members were increasingly adopting decentralization policies. But because decentralization confers upon local communities both prerogatives and resources, it places nonprofit organizations in a dilemma: on the one hand, the groups are better able to participate in local development and policy formation; on the other hand, their consequent political and financial dependence on local government imperils them when these governments change or cut back funding.

French social economy and the nonprofit sector

Widely divergent historical, religious, and cultural traditions among nations make it difficult to compare nonprofit sectors across national boundaries. To facilitate such comparisons, the common structural–operational definition specifies five key characteristics of nonprofit organizations: formal, private, self-governing, nonprofit-distributing, and voluntary (Salamon and Anheier, 1992). How does this definition relate to the French notion of social economy?

The French "Charter of Social Economy"

In 1980, the *Charter of Social Economy*[4] formally acknowledged the existence of a nonprofit sector, notwithstanding the legal diversity of its components. The charter also specified the basic principles underlying the sector's member organizations. These include:

- *Personal and voluntary participation.* Free entrance and free exit of individual members, in contrast to compulsory adhesion and contributions to social security.
- *Solidarity among members.* The concept of solidarity is very

important to the French nonprofit sector. It implies interdependence, a sense of belonging, joint responsibility, and income redistribution. In many French social economy organizations, members either pay the same flat fee for different types of services, or they pay according to income.

- *Democratic management.* General meetings of nonprofit organizations are conducted in accordance with "one person, one vote." By contrast, meetings of joint-stock companies operate under the principle of "one share, one vote."
- *Independence from government.* The organizations must not be part of the government. This is important, because quasi-governmental agencies with the legal status of associations are often created to circumvent administrative regulations and public accountability. Many such entities had been created during the preceding decade. Trustees are often civil servants or municipal representatives. As such, these groups are not self-governing, and hence not part of *l'économie sociale.*
- *Volunteer board of directors.* Directors may receive no compensation, other than cost reimbursement.
- *Profit is not the aim of the organization,* and remuneration of capital, as in the form of dividends, is not present. Income in excess of expenses is reinvested in the organization. This applies strictly to organizations in the associative sector, but less tightly to mutuals or cooperatives. The latter may either reinvest profits, or distribute them to members and clients in the form of reduced fees and prices.
- *Capital cannot be shared.* In the event of a nonprofit's dissolution, its capital assets must be given to another nonprofit organization.

Comparing the charter and the structural–operational definition

As can be seen, some of the Charter's principles coincide with those of the structural/operational definition, while others do not. The first three principles of the Charter reflect basic themes in French history. Personal and voluntary participation contrasts with compulsory membership in *ancien régime* guilds. Solidarity derives from the workers' movement, and contrasts with the ideology of a free or atomized market, in which individuals compete against each other. Democratic management contrasts with the basic law of capitalist governance, under which decisions are made in accordance with wealth (one share, one vote).

The Charter's fourth principle of independence from government is, in its intent, similar but not identical to the structural–operational definition's "self-governing" criterion. Some associations are in fact quasi-governmental agencies. Examples include the *Association pour la Formation Professionnelle des Adultes*, which works in continuing education, and the *Institut National de la Consommation*, the main umbrella group for consumer protection. According to the structural–operational definition, both these groups would have to be excluded from the nonprofit sector, because they are not in fact self-governing.

Where the Charter specifies a volunteer board of directors, the structural–operational definition stipulates voluntarism. The concept of "non-profit-distributing" in the structural–operational definition matches the Charter's specifications that profit is not the aim of the organization, and that capital is not shared or remunerated. However, the nonbusiness criterion included in the characteristic "non-profit-distributing" has no equivalent in the Charter. Where the Charter would include most cooperatives, the structural–operational definition would exclude them as businesses (except, perhaps, for housing cooperatives). Likewise the entire banking sector and mutual insurance societies would *not* meet the structural–operational definition's criteria, but do qualify under the Charter.

Figure 5.3 offers a comparison of the nonprofit sector and the social economy. While we have already discussed most commonalities and differences, it is useful to examine several types of organizations in more detail, and to see how, within the French context, they might fit the nonprofit and social economy concept.

Public foundations. While France has few private foundations, it has no governmental or public foundations. Despite the absence of public foundations, the State, public agencies, and towns often create associations, governed by the 1901 Act, to manage social services, especially since the Decentralization Act of 1982. The aims of creating these associations include easing the welfare state's financial burdens, circumventing regulations, avoiding public accountability, escaping civil service requirements, and obtaining more flexible management. Associations so created are dependent on public subsidies, and are often not self-governing. Therefore they are not part of the social economy.

Figure 5.3

Terminology and type of organization

TYPE OF ORGANIZATION		Economie sociale	Nonprofit Sector
Adult education agencies	formation professionnelle des adultes		
Advocacy organizations	associations de défense		
Business associations	syndicats patronaux	borderline	borderline
Clinics	cliniques		
Cooperatives	coopératives		x
Cultural organizations	associations culturelles		
Elementary and secondary schools	écoles primaires et secondaires		
Hospitals	hôpitaux		
Labor unions	syndicats de travailleurs	borderline	borderline
Mutuals	mutuelles		x
Neighborhood / ethnic organizations	associations de voisinage / d'étrangers	x	
Nursing homes	maisons de retraite		
Political parties	partis politiques	borderline	
Popular tourism organizations	tourisme social		
Private foundations	fondations privées		
Public housing	logement social	borderline	borderline
Public foundations		x	x
Religious congregations, Churches	congrégations religieuses, églises	x	
Self–help groups	entraide	x	borderline
Service clubs	amicales		
Sheltered workshops	ateliers protégés		
Social service agencies	services sociaux		
Sports clubs and associations	clubs sportifs		
Trade associations	associations professionnelles	borderline	borderline
Universities, research organizations	universités, instituts de recherche		
Works Councils	comités d'enterprises	borderline	
Young workers or students residence	foyers de jeunes travailleurs, cités univ.		
	entreprises intermédiaires		

x = not included

Universities. Most French universities are public. Only five are private and Catholic, with 1 percent of the student body. However, higher education in France is also delivered by *grandes écoles.* Engineering schools and institutes of technology are public, but most business schools are private and managed by the

Chamber of Commerce or by trade associations. Theoretically, therefore, they are included in the social economy.

Schools. Most elementary and nursery schools are public. Some specialized kindergartens are operated as either nonprofits or for-profits. Likewise, most secondary schools are public, but France has some 11,000 private schools, which enroll 2.3 million pupils. Most of these schools are Catholic and subsidized by government and local authorities. Teacher salaries are paid by the government.

Housing associations. Large-scale housing initiatives were a characteristic of the welfare state in France and other European countries. After the Second World War, the government established both public and private agencies to construct housing at below-market rents for low-income families. As the housing shortage ended, the market assumed a growing role in the housing sector, but some nonprofit housing associations are still in existence. Public housing agencies (*habitations à loyers modérés*) are excluded from the social economy; some housing cooperatives, however, are borderline.

Entreprises intermédiaires. These are organizations with associative or cooperative legal status. They provide temporary jobs to unskilled young people who have failed schooling, potential or former delinquents, and drug addicts. They seek to produce marketable goods or services in sectors overlooked by ordinary businesses. *Entreprises intermédiaires* are usually operated by former social workers; they are government-subsidized, and fit somewhere between ordinary businesses and adult education agencies. Sheltered workshops perform the same function for handicapped people.

Works councils (Comités d'entreprises). Works councils, specific to France, are borderline social economy organizations, operating in every enterprise with more than 50 employees. Administered by salaried employees elected from union lists, they manage canteens, day care and holiday centers, cultural activities, and other personal or family social services. They are funded by 1 percent of the total wage bill.

Social tourism. Like the works councils, social tourism is specific to France, though versions of it can be found in other European countries with strong socialist traditions. The establishment of social tourism dates back to 1936, when the first "vacation with pay" was created by a Socialist government. Leo Lagrange, a minister, instigated a network of holiday villages or camps for working class families. He also established youth hostels, holiday centers for children, and similar facilities. This nonprofit network developed more fully after the Second World War. Its aims included encouraging tourism among low-income people, promoting cultural and sports activities, and intermingling the working and middle classes. Payment is in proportion to income.[5]

In sum, the concept of the French social economy is broader than the set of organizations described by the structural–operational definition of the nonprofit sector. But the two are basically compatible. Perhaps it would be best to say that most organizations within the social economy other than associations are "borderline cases," neither completely within nor completely outside either typology.

Conclusion

The growing importance of the French nonprofit sector, in particular the associative sector, is due largely to the decentralization policy initiated by the Socialist Government in the 1980s. Basic to this policy, which runs counter to a long tradition of centralization, is the use of independent nonprofit or "social economy" organizations as vehicles through which the government administers welfare and employment programs. In the context of the budgetary constraints facing the public sector, many local governments began to include nonprofit organizations in the provision of social services. A striking example of the emergent partnership between the State and the nonprofit sector is the introduction in 1989 of a minimum income for the poor, coupled with an "insertion contract" between the State and the beneficiary that aims at integrating clients into the labor force ("insertion"). While the central state provides the funds, nonprofit organizations and local government agencies implement the insertion contract.

Even before decentralization, however, French society had been "catching up" with other European countries and the United States in the development of the nonprofit sector, at least since the mid-1960s. Today, the most important challenge the sector faces is the creation of a unified European Community in political, economic, and social spheres. If French social economy organizations can bridge their own conflicts and divisions, deriving from legal differences and divergent historical traditions, they will contribute immensely to the European Community as a cultural and social entity, and not merely as a huge market for social services and sports and cultural activities.

Notes

1 The French portion of the Johns Hopkins Comparative Nonprofit Sector Project is funded by the *Fondation de France*, the *Délégation à l'é-conomie sociale*, the *Ministère des Affaires Sociales*, and the *Credit Coopératif*. The author expresses her gratitude to those funders and to all who provided her with valuable information. She also thanks Helmut Anheier, Christine Bon, and Nathan Weber for editing the manuscript, and the Project Directors for their comments on earlier drafts of this chapter. Responsibility for the contents of this chapter is entirely her own.

2 The *Commune*, lasting only three months, was a popular insurrection attempting to establish a democratic political system. Its ideology was utopian socialism, based on worker education and welfare.

3 By comparison, the United States has approximately 32,000 foundations, of which almost 96 percent are grantmaking. Great Britain, Germany, Italy, and other European countries of comparable size have more foundations than France.

4 The Charter (*Charte de l'économie sociale*) is a formal declaration signed by representatives of major nonprofit organizations and umbrella groups. Based on a 1976 *protocole d'accord* among the signatories, the Charter is an expression of an emerging awareness of French social economy organizations as a distinct *sector*. The following principles are either stated in the Charter itself, or otherwise commonly agreed upon.

5 *Club Mediterranée* applied the basic concept to a for-profit business, catering to middle- and higher-income clients.

References

Alix, N. and S. Castro (1986), *Associations et activités économiques, approche juridique*. Paris: UNIOPSS.

Anheier, Helmut K., Gabriel Rudney and Lester M. Salamon (1993), "The nonprofit sector and the United Nations System of Accounts: country applications of SNA Guidelines." *Voluntas*, 4(4):486–501.

Archambault, Edith (1986), "L'économie sociale est-elle associée aux grands fonctions economiques des pouvoirs publiques", *Revue des études coopératives, mutualistes et associatives,* 18:3–35.

Archambault, Edith (1988), *Comptabilité nationale,* 4th edn. Paris: Economica.

Archambault, Edith and X. Greffe (1984), *Les économies non-officielles.* Paris: La Découverte.

Caire, Guy (1984), "Syndicalisme, sécurité sociale et mutualité," *Revue de L'Économie sociale,* 1(2): 56–67.

Djider, Z. and M. Marpsat (1990), "La vie religieuse: chiffres et enquêtes," in I.N.S.E.E., *Données sociales,* pp. 376–385. Paris: I.N.S.E.E.

Fenet, F. (1989), *L'aide sociale à l'enfance: stratégies de redéploiement.* Paris: Centre Technique National d'Etudes et de Recherches sur les Handicaps et les Inadaptations – Presses Universitaires de France.

Fouquet, A., N. Tabard and M. Villac (1990), *La vie associative et son financement.* Paris: La Documentation Française.

Gueslin, A. (1987), *L'invention de l'économie sociale: le XIXe siècle français.* Paris: Economica.

Hatzfeld, H. (1971), *Du pauperisme à la sécurité sociale.* Paris: A. Colin.

Hauesler, L. (1990), "Le monde associatif de 1978 à 1986," in I.N.S.E.E., *Données Sociales.* Paris: I.N.S.E.E.

Padieu, Claudine (1990), *Statistiques de l'économie sociale.* Rapport présenté à M. Dreyfus, Secrétaire d'Etat à l'Economie Sociale, mimeographed, February 1990.

Salamon, Lester M. and Helmut K. Anheier (1992), "In search of the non-profit sector I: the question of definitions." *Voluntas,* 3(2):125–151.

Chapter 6

GERMANY

Helmut K. Anheier and Wolfgang Seibel

Introduction

This chapter offers a conceptual analysis of the nonprofit sector in Germany in the context of major characteristics of German society.[1] Definitions and concepts about the institutions located in the area between the state agency and the market firm reflect distinct national histories, styles of organizing, and institutional cultures. Such conceptualizations are closely tied to the methods societies develop to define and provide public goods and social services, to resolve political conflicts, and to coordinate opposing interests. In the following we intend to examine these factors in the way they relate to the nonprofit sector in Germany.

In Germany, the area between market and State is not commonly understood as a single institutional sector. Likewise, the nonprofit sector is not seen as one entity, neither in everyday language, nor in legal, economic, or political discourse. Several general terms are used to refer to organizations located between state agency and market firm: *Vereine* and *Verbände* (associations), *gemeinnützige Organisationen* (public benefit organizations), with the important subset of the "free welfare associations," *gemeinwirtschaftliche Unternehmen* (communal economic corporations) and *Organisationen ohne Erwerbszweck* (organizations with no commercial character). The adjectives (*freiwillig, gemeinnützig, gemeinwirtschaftlich*) or modifiers (*ohne Erwerbszweck*) can then be used to describe the sectors or systems (*Wesen*): *Vereins- und Verbandswesen* (associational system), *Gemeinnützigkeitswesen* (public benefit system), *Gemeinwirtschaftswesen* (communal economy), and *Nicht-Erwerbssektor* (non-commercial sector).[2]

As in other countries, the different legal, tax, national accounting, social science and "street" usages produce a complex terminology. Each term focuses on a particular subset of nonprofits, and significant overlaps exist among the organizations included and excluded. But there are also important differences which reflect specific historical developments and how they, in turn, shaped the nonprofit sector. We will sketch these historical developments and describe how they influence both the nonprofit sector itself and the ways the sector is conceptualized and defined. These factors are closely related to different principles which emerged in the complex course of the last two centuries of German history:

- the principle of *self-administration* or self-governance, originating from the nineteenth-century conflict between State and citizens, allowed parts of the nonprofit sector to emerge and develop in an autocratic society, where the freedom of association had only partially been granted;
- the principle of *subsidiarity*, originally related to secular–religious frictions, and fully developed after the Second World War, assigns priority to nonprofit over the public provision of social services; this created a set of six nonprofit conglomerates ranking among the largest nonprofit organizations worldwide; and finally:
- the principle of *Gemeinwirtschaft* (communal economics), based on the search for an alternative to both capitalism and socialism, led to the cooperative movement and the establishment of mutual associations in the banking and housing industries.

To varying degrees the three principles shaped the various parts of the nonprofit sector, each institutionally linked and oriented to a specific sector of society.

Why de Tocqueville's problem did not apply to Germany

The evolution and political economy of Germany's nonprofit sector may best be understood by way of comparison with two classic examples of the political role of intermediary institutions, the French and the American, as they appear in Alexis de Tocqueville's influential analysis *Democracy in America* (1835–40). His analysis of American associations was meant as a critique of France's post-revolutionary political order and society. Long before the revolution of 1789 took place, France had been a centralized nation-state, and it was the very centralization of the State which had facilitated the revolution's effectiveness. The *ancien régime* was replaced by a new ruling class that used the existing centralized state structure as a tool for rebuilding the country's political system and societal order. In accordance with the strict individualistic, anti-corporatist ideology of the Revolution, the *Loi le Chapelier* (1791) stipulated that no "intermediary associations" were allowed to exist between the individual as citizen and the State.

Individualism provided the basis of America's "Voluntary Spirit," too (O'Connell, 1983; see also Herbert Hoover's *American Individualism*, 1922). But in contrast to the French case, American society was quasi-stateless and pragmatically oriented towards the maintenance of individual mobility and free choice, with a general mistrust of central state power. Accordingly, voluntarism and associational life evolved as an appropriate compromise of individualism and political collectivity. Whereas the French State had been conquered by a revolutionary regime which saw associations as premodern elements of the feudal and clerical order, the State in the United States emerged only gradually, while local community and associational life remained the focus of a democratic identity.

In both countries, *either* state *or* associational structures formed the basis of political progress and initial democratic identity. In this respect, the German case is fundamentally different. Politically, Germany's history of the eighteenth and nineteenth centuries is one of compromises between a "self-modernizing" feudal order on the one hand and the emergent bourgeoisie on the other. Germany did not witness a successful anti-feudal revolution, nor the building of the nation-state. Its 300 kingdoms, dukedoms and baronies remained religiously and politically divided, with the Protestant Kingdom of Prussia and the Catholic Empire of Austria as two dominant and autocratic powers.

When elements of a bourgeois culture in the sense of civil society first evolved in the eighteenth century in the field of literature, newspaper publishing, music societies, and educational associations (Habermas, 1962; Nipperdey, 1976), government and state administration, however, continued to remain under the exclusive control of the aristocracy. The new middle class, or *Bürgertum*, did not share political responsibilities. However, there was a tradition of bourgeois associations in the form of *corporations* that dated back to medieval times. These corporations, usually with compulsory membership and fairly comprehensive coverage of virtually all trades, crafts and professions, formed the backbone of German society well into the eighteenth century. The beginning of political modernization in the eighteenth and nineteenth centuries implied a "de-corporatization" by transforming the mandatory system of corporations into a field of *voluntary* associations. As a result, the emergence of the modern third sector in Germany reflects a dual pattern whereby the elements of a structural legacy from the medieval, pre-modern society were transformed into the building blocks of genuine modernization (see Dann, 1993; Scheuch, 1993).

In contrast to what happened in other European countries, the latent tension between the aristocratic and autocratic state on the one hand, and the emergent middle class, with its political aspirations and associations, on the other, never led to ultimate rupture, despite serious conflicts during the nineteenth century. Though the early associational initiatives in the eighteenth century were anti-status quo – since their explicit purpose was to assemble people regardless of rank within the feudal order – early forms of cooperation between the State and associations soon developed. This was particularly the case when the interest of the feudal State and *Bürgertum* coincided, for example, in the areas of education, free trade, and economic development (Nipperdey, 1976). Especially in Prussia, where the State acted as the main driving force of modernization, an increasingly stable and more widely applied pattern of cooperation provided the seed for what was to become a major aspect of the nonprofit sector in Germany. To a large extent, the German nonprofit sector did not develop in antithesis to the State, but in interaction with it. This pattern led to the development of characteristic types of organizations that are located and understood in German society in ways different from what is implied in de Tocqueville's dichotomy of state-centered versus association-centered society – a dichotomy that does not apply to the German situation.

The emergence of the principle of self-governance

With respect to the modernization of State and economy, Prussia's defeat by France in 1806 brought a wave of unprecedented reforms to government, State administration, and the State–society relationship.[3] Prussia's civil code, only ten years old, was stripped of almost all corporatist elements to allow for free trade, free choice of profession, and personal mobility (Koselleck, 1967). Trade and business associations were officially recognized as representative institutions and the State's official interlocutors (Hendler, 1984). In 1809, the cities were exempted from the feudal system and obtained the status of self-governing authorities with a limited form of citizen participation.

The political effect of granting limited civil rights was to mitigate the underlying conflict between the aristocratic State and the bourgeoisie (*Bürgertum*). The economic effect was the liberalization of trade and commerce, which provided the basis for much improvement in subsequent economic development. The institutional effect, however, was the construction of "state-free" organizations for both economic purposes and political integration, such as the chambers of trade and commerce as well as "free" professional associations.

The principle of *self-government* that was enacted in the chambers of commerce and professional associations and the new municipal constitutions, created a far-reaching pattern of institutional memory and experience. Licensing by the State and the transfer of considerable autonomy to some associations occurred while full freedom of association continued to be banned. Therefore, the historical experience was that the State would grant limited freedom to citizens while maintaining control over its institutional and political dynamics.

A new period of State–society relations began with the Congress of Vienna in 1815 and the upcoming era of the "restoration." What was to be restored was the Old Regime in the once French-occupied Europe. Napoleonic occupation, though the result of national imperialism, had disseminated some crucial elements of an anti-feudal social and political order, such as the *code civil* which treated everyone as an equal citizen. It had also substantially shattered the political role of the Catholic Church and reduced the role of the Church as an important landowner. Moreover, the war of 1813 had mobilized the common man and, accordingly, had strengthened the people's political self-confidence.

The Congress of Vienna, however, and the Karlsbad Decisions of 1819 in particular, brought a conservative backlash against any kind of political liberalism. The effect was a newly emerging conflict between the State and the politicized citizenry and their associations. The Prussian General Order of 1816 declared *Vereine* (associations) "useless" and banned them as a potential source of political unrest and upheavals. As a consequence, existing associations were forced to change into clandestine organizations, or *Geheimbünde* (Dann, 1993:133–135). From 1815 to 1848, the right of association was a central claim of political liberalism in Germany, and became even a synonym for democratic constitutionalism (Müller, 1965; Dann, 1976; 1993; Scheuch, 1993:154–158; Hueber, 1984). This idealization of political associations was even intensified after the failed bourgeois revolution of 1848 – with characteristic consequences for the political embeddedness of Germany's future intermediary (nonprofit) sector.

In Germany as well as in all the other European countries, the revolution of 1848 ultimately failed, though it led to the first national parliament. What followed, however, was another conservative political backlash and, again, associations were subject to authoritarian persecution. The repeated failure to seize state power led to a new idealization of associational life as the "true" locus of politics. In the face of political suppression, associations became a surrogate for democracy, which had not been achieved within the political realm of the state-order itself. With political suppression being slowly relaxed, the association became a broadly accepted institutional type of local everyday life in sports, culture, folklore, and, last but not least, quasi-politics (Wurzbacher, 1971).

The revival of associational life after 1848 showed important structural similarities in the political culture of the bourgeois middle class and the emerging workers' movement. The latter grew from associational initiatives of journeymen and young workers aiming for risk protection in industry and improvement of education. In everyday life, associations for sports and singing formed a common cultural experience for workers and the middle class. Thus, even without the full right of association granted to the citizens, associations as an institutional form had been fully developed and culturally acknowledged *within* an autocratic political system when Germany became a nation-state in 1871.

Alongside the latent political conflict between the autocratic State and the middle class, a new conflict developed, this time between the State (and the still ruling aristocracy) and the workers' movement. From 1878 to 1890 the Social-Democratic Party and its related associations were banned from political life. Yet once more, this conflict, too, was mitigated through modernization of governmental policy and political integration: beginning in 1883 and throughout the rest of the century, state legislation on health insurance, accidents and invalidity and pension funds was passed. The deliberate purpose of the policy was to integrate the workers into the new nation-state, and thereby weaken the social-democratic movement, which was considered to be the most important challenge to political order and stability. While Germany's civic associational culture remained underdeveloped in political terms, its social security legislation itself was among the most advanced in the world.

Still more important, however, was the institutional form under which the legislation was administered, which until today has remained the model of collective risk protection in Germany. Again, self-government became the institutional mechanism to achieve two objectives at the same time: to maintain political control through a system of quasi-public service administration, and to integrate parts of the population that might otherwise pose a threat to political legitimacy and stability. Social insurance corporations were independent bodies with boards of directors composed of representatives of the employers and the employees. Nonetheless, their self-administration was and still is subject to close state supervision and control. It is a repeated pattern of *loose coupling* between the State and quasi-independent agencies, a kind of state-controlled autonomy within a triangular setting: two sides with more or less antagonistic interests, plus the State as the neutral intermediary (Lehmbruch, 1982). This was to become the classic model of *neocorporatism* as a pattern of German politics in general and of the government–nonprofit relationship in particular (Seibel, 1990).

The emergence of the principle of subsidiarity

After 1871 a significant conflict developed, primarily between the (Protestant) Prussian government of the Reich under Chancellor

Bismarck on the one hand and the Catholic Church on the other. The conflict was not as threatening to the political order as the one between the conservative élite and the social-democratic workers' movement, since it mostly affected the Catholic parts of the country. Nevertheless, the tension between State and Church, and the ultimate compromise, laid the ground for the gradual development of the principle of subsidiarity, which after the Second World War became an important aspect of much of the government–nonprofit relationship in Germany (Anheier, 1992).

One reason for mistrust of the Prussian State and the Reich government was the intensified political Catholicism, and the founding of the Catholic political party, *Zentrum* (Center) in 1871. This meant a challenge for (Protestant) Prussia which had only recently gained political dominance in Germany by defeating (Catholic) Austria in the war of 1866. As the Social-Democrats would later, the Catholic Church and related groups became subject to restrictive or even suppressive measures. All Catholic schools came under state control in Prussia in 1872, in addition to the general administration of the Church (1873), and all state subsidies to the Catholic Church were suspended in 1875.

Though the open conflict with the autocratic State was settled during the 1880s, it remained a traumatic experience for the Catholic Church as well as for the Catholic élite in Germany. An appropriate ideological response came late; but when it came, it was especially influential. The Pope's encyclical *Qudragesimo anno* (1931) insisted on the priority of individual compassion and solidarity instead of state-organized assistance and public welfare programs. The State's role in this matter ought to be only a "subsidiary" one (Nell-Breuning, 1976). The principle of subsidiarity of public welfare became the most influential ideological counterweight to state-centered ideas of welfare provision.

A Catholic principle by origin, subsidiarity became a synonym for any sort of institutional alternative to the State as provider of social welfare. In the German context, subsidiarity also implied an alternative to a *public* welfare state, which continued to be propagated by the Social-Democratic Party. In (West) Germany, the complicated conflicts between State and Church, and between Catholicism and Social Democracy in the field of social welfare, were legally settled only in 1961 by the German Supreme Court (see below). This settlement endorsed the constitutionality of the

Bundessozialhilfegesetz (Federal Social Assistance Act) and related legislation which stipulated the general subsidiarity of public action, giving preference rather to the free welfare associations (see below) in the provision of social services (Rinken, 1971).[4]

The ideological success of the principle of "subsidiarity" also led to another compromise in terms of institutional effects. Ultimately, the German welfare state is not a state affair at all. Not only are the huge administrative bodies of social insurance (health, pension funds, accidents) subject to self-government – which makes them largely independent from direct governmental control and influence – but so are most of the social services provided through the free welfare associations. The latter, however, though independent in terms of governance, are dependent on public subsidies to considerable degrees (Seibel, 1990; Anheier, 1992).

The emergence of the principle of the *Gemeinwirtschaft*

The principle of self-government and the idealization of associational life, combined with the vision of a socialist organization of the economy, gave birth to a set of institutions that influenced the notion of the German nonprofit sector for several decades until the mid-1980s: the principle of the *Gemeinwirtschaft*, or communal economy. The principle implies nonmarket, non-competitive production of commodities and delivery of services (cf. Thiemeyer, 1970). The principle rested on a vision of a non-capitalist order of economic production which was less radical than Karl Marx's, since it required neither revolution nor working-class domination. The principle of *Gemeinwirtschaft* became important in the cooperative and workers' movement, and favored an economic system in which actors attempt to maximize common as well as private returns. This communal, socialist tradition is most clearly expressed by the term *Gemeinwirtschaft* itself, which bears some affinity with Toennies' (1935) notion of *Gemeinschaft* (community), and can be understood as a form of communal, though not necessarily local, economy, and as a third way between "free market capitalism" and "bureaucratic socialism." Moreover, it revitalized rural traditions of self-help among independent producers, e.g. the *Raiffeisen Cooperatives* for small-scale farmers, or cooperative banks for small-scale businesses in urban areas.

In practice, however, *Gemeinwirtschaft* was the ideological justification for the growing property of the unions and the Social-Democratic Party and a symbol for the vision of a non-capitalist future. The term gained much currency after the Second World War, particularly in public housing, where excess demand existed until the mid-1970s. The decline of the communal economy set in at about that time, and by the mid-1980s, many organizations had closed (following several scandals of corruption and mismanagement) or changed to commercial firms, like banks and insurance companies.

The principles in action

Before the three principles came to exert their full influence on what had begun to emerge as the German nonprofit sector, the Nazi period (1933–1945) resulted in significant discontinuities in the country's institutional setup and political economy. The Nazi policy of *Gleichschaltung,* the organizational levelling, streamlining, and incorporation of all major aspects into the political party machine, brought much of the nonprofit sector under party control. Other parts were brutally suppressed. For example, independent, private welfare associations were first regrouped under a single (Nazi-controlled) umbrella organization, and soon, with the exception of the Red Cross, reorganized as the National-Socialist People's Welfare (NSV) (Bauer, 1990; Sachße and Tennstedt, 1992:110–150).

The era after the Second World War saw a Germany pacified in domestic terms, too. Many previous conflicts, while never resolved or settled, no longer mattered: regional and religious differences, as well as separatist tendencies, became much less manifest, and no regional party has been represented in the Federal Parliament since 1957. The weakened and displaced agrarian groups were incorporated into the Christian parties, which in turn made attempts to avoid religious politics. It was only in postwar Germany that the three principles which emerged between 1870 and 1929 came to full fruition:

- The principle of subsidiarity became the cornerstone of German social policy and the general principle to govern public–private relationships in a great variety of areas, most prominently in the case of the free welfare associations.

- The principle of self-administration became an important ingredient of labor and industrial policy through the establishment of business and professional associations, the formation of many public law institutions in the cultural, educational, health, and social services fields, and the institutionalization of the social market economy, wherein unions and employers' associations enjoy quasi-statutory power in a system of "tariff autonomy" in setting and enforcing wage policies and disputes.
- The principle of communal economy was influential in the period of reconstruction in the 1950s and 1960s, and declined gradually as a consequence of privatization efforts under the Kohl government, and a series of corruption scandals that shattered the nonprofit housing industry in the 1980s.

The associational system maintained its largely apolitical character until the mid-1970s, and the nonprofit sector became a cornerstone of political stability. The aristocratic agrarian élite in the East had disappeared; the new party system managed to incorporate virtually all social groups and strata within a democratic system. More importantly, however, the party system acted as a mediator between the State and the organized interests of society. By contrast with what occurred under the Weimar Republic, all significant interest groups were able to find political representation in the democratic party system.

The loose alliances that emerged among the interest groups under the new system were a precondition for the establishment of paragovernmental coordination to influence public policy, for instance in industrial relations and social security. This neo-corporatist style of policy-making, which seeks to establish consensus prior to parliamentary decisions, bypasses the constitutional order and weakens the power of parliament. However, it relieves government of the "costs" of coordination as well as from the need to establish legitimacy for particular policies. Since the mid-1970s, neo-corporatism has provided the political "elasticity" needed to support welfare measures during economic crisis.

This pattern is even true for the so-called New Social Movements which emerged in the context of the economic crisis of the 1970s (Windhoff-Héritier, 1982). These movements – formed by environmentalists, feminists, grass-roots activists – were ideologically ambivalent at first because they did not fit into the left–right scheme of traditional politics. On a different level, however, they corresponded to a general trend toward relieving government from increased demands, which in turn made the new social movements legitimate partners in both economic and ideological terms within the grass-root philosophy of neo-liberalism. This trend meant a certain containment of the expanding West German welfare state.

Moreover, the new social movements are influenced by the very same institutional and ideological tradition of the German nonprofit sector in general: on the one hand, the political myth of a state-free associationalism as the locus of "true" democracy – or *Basisdemokratie* (basic democracy) – was revitalized. On the other hand, through a new political party, the *Grüne* (Greens), parts of the movement became integrated into the "regular" political system. Other self-help groups that emerged as part of the new social movements became associated with one of the several large welfare associations (see below).

According to Vilmar and Runge (1986), the estimated 35,000 self-help groups in the mid-1980s fall into six main fields of activity: unemployment, training, and employee-managed enterprises (40 percent); handicapped and health problem (28.7 percent); homeless, homosexuals, ethnic minorities, delinquency (15.4 percent); the economically disadvantaged (11.9 percent); leisure, education, and culture (2.9 percent); and neighborhood initiatives (1.3 percent). Thus, self-help groups contributed primarily to easing employment and health-related problems.

Major types of organizations in the nonprofit sector

Figure 6.1 offers a schematic representation of the principal types of organizations in the nonprofit sector. These types are the building-blocks for the major systems that may form either conceptual equivalents or components of what we will define below as the German nonprofit sector: associations, public benefit organizations, the communal economy, and organizations with no commercial character.

As we can see in Figure 6.1, the German legal system distinguishes between member-based and nonmember-based institutions. Among member-based forms, we can separate private law associations (like a sports club) and public law cooperatives (local savings and loan associations) from commercial law bodies, businesses and corporations (partnerships, limited liability companies, stock corporations), and public law corporations, like some professional and business associations (chambers of notaries, chambers of commerce), and some religious organizations. On the other side, among the nonmember-based forms, we can separate foundations and trusts as endowed institutions from public law corporations as operating agencies, such as universities, schools, public insurance funds, the Federal Post or most radio and television stations. It is important to keep in mind that the notion of a nonprofit organization cuts across all the different types of legal institutions that German associational and corporate law treats as separate. Thus, the nonprofit sector includes organizations that vary greatly in terms of legal personality (public versus private), taxation (commercial versus noncommercial), or financial structure (stock corporations versus tax-financed institutions versus endowments).

Associations and the associational system (*Vereins- und Verbandswesen*)

The associational system includes a great variety of organizational forms, ranging from village improvement associations, singing clubs, amateur theaters, and sports clubs, to professional and business associations and foundations. In general, the term excludes organized religion, cooperatives, and political parties. However, it generally includes political and civic organizations and local voters' groups, as well as compulsory economic associations like chambers of commerce and craft unions.

"*Verein*" (association) has several meanings in the German context.[5] First it implies sociability, and refers generally to any social group outside family, business, and public administration. "*Verband*" is similar to "*Verein*," but tends to be used more in reference to formal, means-oriented associations that combine common or mutual interests, like a business association. Other terms used are *Vereinigung*, which is similar to *Verband* and refers primarily to mutual interest associations among businesses in the same branch of the economy; and *Gesellschaft*, which is often used to refer to scholarly associations and learned societies. Finally,

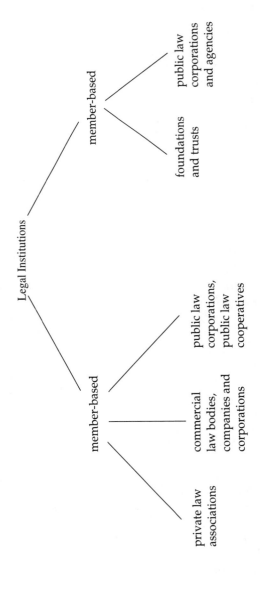

Figure 6.1 Major types of legal institutions

association in the terms *Innung* or *Kammer* (chamber) tends to refer to modernized versions of medieval corporations, such as guilds among local businesses and organizations of the members of a profession, often with compulsory membership.

Participation in society via associational membership and volunteering has long been identified as a major aspect of social integration. The number of registered voluntary associations is estimated to range between 180,000 and 250,000 for 1990 (Agricola and Wehr, 1993:11–12), which, relative to population size, is considerably less than in other countries of comparable economic development, such as the United States (1.4 million) or France (500,000–700,000). A poll (Commission of the European Communities, 1987) shows that somewhat less than half (45 percent) of the German adult population are members of associations, compared to 43.9 percent in France. Combined with the number of associations, this suggests that German associations tend to be, on average, larger than their French counterparts. Membership in a political association or party is at 4.6 percent for the German adult population, which is slightly higher than the percentage for France (3.1 percent), but lower than in Great Britain (6.4 percent). German membership rates in human rights organizations are the lowest in Northern Europe, and are, at 3.1 percent, below the European average of 6.3 percent for environmental organizations. Certainly, such survey data may be affected by problems of cross-national validity; however, the data seem to give some support to the thesis of the continuing relatively underdeveloped state of political civil society in Germany when measured in individual membership of typical civic associations.

Second, "association" is a legal term, based on the right of association granted in Article 9 of the Basic Law (Constitution), "All Germans have the right to found associations and societies," and the law of associations, grounded in the German Civil Code of 1900 (*Bürgerliches Gesetzbuch* [BGB], §§21–79). An association is based on a contract among natural personalities. The contract may stipulate any objective (§145 BGB), provided it does not violate existing legal (§134 BGB) or moral and ethical provisions (§138 BGB). Associations may be registered (*eingetragener Verein*) or not (*nicht eingetragener Verein*). The registered association becomes a legal personality endowed with its own legal rights. To achieve legal personality, an association must be registered in the

Association Registry (*Vereinsregister*) maintained locally at the approximately 800 local county courts (*Amtsgerichte*). To register, an association must pursue a noncommercial (*ideal*) objective, have at least seven members, a charter, and a Board (*Vorstand*). A registered association can be recognized by the acronym "e.V." which many associations attach to their name, for example the German Alp Association, e.V. A nonregistered association possesses no legal personality; it is legally represented by the Board, and members are personally liable.

At this point, it is important to recall the distinction between two principal types of nonprofit organizations: *Vereine* (private law associations) and *Körperschaften* (public law corporations). As a civil law country, Germany is based on the fundamental distinction between private law, regulating the rights and responsibilities among individuals and private legal personalities, and public law (for instance administrative, fiscal, and ecclesiastical law), dealing with the relations between individuals and the State, public agencies, and public law corporations. The central point is that the State is regarded as a legal actor *sui generis*, relatively independent of the political party in power, and in possession of its own legal subjectivity that requires laws and regulations qualitatively different from those addressing private individuals. Moreover, the distinction between public and private law equates the State with the public good, and puts the burden of proof of public utility on private law associations only.

By definition, public law corporations are set up for public benefit, and their charter may include an explicit reference to serving a public good or a common goal. For example, many muncipalities established savings and loan associations (*Sparkassen*) in the form of public law corporations charged to provide financial services to local populations not covered by the commercial banks. In order to make sure that the local savings and loans associations should not diverge from their objective of serving low-income groups, a "common good clause" (*Gemeinwohlklausel*) was explicitly written into their charter.

The actual legal status of nonprofit organizations varies. The BGB differentiates between ideal associations (those with no primary business interest) and commercial associations. The law classifies associations according to their underlying *raison d'être*, and not according to their profit motive. The basic point is that bodies with primarily commercial objectives are usually prohibited from assuming associational status, and must either use a noncorporate form (e.g., private partnerships) or choose a corporate status envisioned in the Commercial Code, such as limited liability companies or stock corporations. Thus we have a situation whereby nonprofit organizations may be associations or corporations in legal terms, whereas commercial for-profits may not.

Other legal forms

While associations are the most important organizational type in the German nonprofit sector, other legal forms are the *Gesellschaft mit beschränkter Haftung* (limited liability company), *Stiftung* (foundation) and *Genossenschaft* (cooperative).

Limited liability companies are common in the nonprofit hospital industry. They are also used for some quasi-commercial nonprofits (Hansmann, 1980), such as workshops employing handicapped people. Overall, the limited liability company is the form of choice for the great majority of for-profit corporations in Germany. Relatively easy to found, with minimal capital requirements and limited public oversight, they also provide useful legal form for nonprofit organizations that need relatively large capital investments.

Foundations are treated separately in the Civil Code (§§80–88), and are defined not as associations but in terms of their endowment. Actual foundation law is a matter of *Länder* legislation (see Neuhoff, 1978). Because of secularization and the development of a state-centered welfare system, church-related foundations had already lost their crucial function for charity in the nineteenth century. In addition, two periods of hyperinflation (1923 and the late 1940s) wiped out the liquid assets of many foundations. The majority of foundations existing today were created after the Second World War. One German peculiarity is the "Political Foundations" which form the legal umbrella for the educational and international activities of political parties. With the exception of the Social Democratic Friedrich Ebert Foundation (created in 1925) they are a product of the postwar period, and largely financed by public funds.

Cooperatives play an important role in some segments of the (West) German economy – mainly farming, housing, banking, and insurance – but have lost their not-for-profit stance to a large extent. Initially considered as an alternative to the capitalist economy (Oppenheimer, 1896), cooperatives as nonprofit organizations persisted only in public housing. Cooperatives in the farming and banking industry, however, have largely changed into businesses.

The public benefit status

Whereas the legal status of associations was at center stage in the emergence of civil society within the context of an autocratic political system, the issue of public benefit is closely linked to the social question of the nineteenth and early twentieth centuries. The definition of what constitutes public benefit is essentially defined by provisions in various tax laws.

Gemeinnützigkeit, or "public benefit status," is today first and foremost a fiscal term. Its definition and application serves to differentiate the tax-exempt from those liable to various forms of taxation. Tax-exemption on the basis of *Gemeinnützigkeit*, i.e., whether or not an association meets the criteria of public benefit, is generally regulated in §§51–68 of the German Fiscal Code (*Abgabenordnung* or AO).[6]

The promotion of the following objectives is covered by the definition of *Gemeinnützigkeit*:

- public well-being in the material, spiritual, and moral spheres;
- charitable and benevolent activities to support persons in need and unable to care for themselves; and
- church-related activities, including the construction, maintenance, and administration of churches and church property, religious instruction, religious services, and training of the clergy.

The following types of activities are mentioned as exemplars of *Gemeinnützigkeit* in Article 52 (2) of the AO:

- support of science and research, education and instruction, art and culture, religion, international understanding and exchange, development aid, environmental protection, historical preservation, and local customs;
- support of youth welfare, the elderly, public health, welfare, and sport;
- the general support of a democratic State and community; and

- the support of animal husbandry, plant cultivation and gardening (all noncommercial), traditional customs, veterans' affairs, amateur radios, model airplane clubs, and dog shows.

This list is meant to be non-exclusive and, its exemplary character notwithstanding, reveals a great deal of arbitrariness, particularly in the last point. According to the AO (§§55 to 68) (see Bundesministerium der Finanzen, 1988), public service activities designated as *gemeinnützig* must be:

- *selfless*, in the sense of altruistic, whereby members of the organization are allowed to receive neither profits nor any other profit-like recompense. This strict nondistribution constraint excludes many mutual membership associations, as well as business and professional associations. It also implies that the cost behavior of nonprofits must be "reasonable" in terms of salaries and fringe benefits.
- *exclusive*, in the sense that the organization pursues only purposes defined as *gemeinnützig* in the AO. If an organization carries out other activities, it may lose the nonprofit tax status altogether. In practice, the organization may declare some of its activities as *gemeinnützig* and others as "commercial." This has the effect that those activities which are classified as *gemeinnützig* receive preferential tax treatment, whereas commercial activities may be subject to taxation.
- *direct*, in the sense that the charitable purpose has to be served by the organization itself rather than through third parties. This provision contains many exceptions which basically relate to inter-organizational structures (peak associations), financing (transfers to developing countries), and special institutions (foundations), whereby a third party may provide services on behalf of a tax-exempt organization.

The tax regulations on donations and deductions follow essentially the same logic. According to §10(b) of the income tax law, only donations to legal personalities under public law (for example, municipal administration, churches) and organizations with *Gemeinnützigkeit* status can be deducted from taxable income.

To achieve the status of *Gemeinnützigkeit*, an organization must have a formal status, and be, for example, a registered or an unregistered association, a foundation, a limited liability company, a cooperative, or even a stock corporation. The application is submitted to the local tax authority, which also decides on the matter. To qualify for tax exemption, the activities of the organization must meet the requirements stipulated in relevant tax provisions. Special regulations apply to housing associations. The nonprofit status is examined by the local tax authorities every three years. This usually light public oversight involves a routine inspection, and rarely a full audit. Nonprofits found in violation of the tax-exempt provision of the relevant tax laws may lose their nonprofit status.

Gemeinwirtschaft (the communal economy)

As was mentioned earlier, the term has become less important in recent years, and many organizations in the communal economy have changed to commercial enterprises. The communal economy refers to that part of the economy which is guided by the principle of maximizing the public good rather than private returns only (Himmelmann, 1985; Eichhorn and Münch, 1983). Often, *Gemeinwirtschaft* is contrasted to *Erwerbswirtschaft*, the commercial (but not necessarily for-profit) sector. The term "communal economy" does not imply that organizations disown the profit motive; the profit objective is subordinated to other goals such as public and social welfare or economic equity considerations. The principle of *Gemeinwirtschaft* states that the chief objective of business is to improve social and economic conditions and not to maximize profits.

Several types of organization are regarded as typical for the communal economy: public enterprises and utilities, self-help groups, cooperatives, union-related corporations and banks, housing societies, foundations, and charities. The term excludes political parties and organizations, business and professional associations, and organized religion. Note that an employers' association would not fall under the definition of *Gemeinwirtschaft*, whereas workers' unions may be included.

A statistical term: organization without commercial motive

This term comes in some ways close to "nonprofit organization," but shows several substantial differences. In addition to organizations serving charitable purposes and membership associations, this terms includes Churches, political parties, unions, some types of foundations, and employers' and business associations as well as public law economic and professional associations, such as chambers of commerce, or groupings of physicians, pharmacists, or notaries. It excludes commercial-law cooperatives, nonprofit housing associations, public utilities and related public corporations, and mutual organizations.

The term is widely used in official statistical accounts. Unlike most other systems of national accounts, the German System of Economic Activity, the national equivalent of the Standard Classification of Industries, identified (until 1992) nonprofit organizations as a separate sector in economic and labor-related statistics (see Statistisches Bundesamt, 1987).

The German system of national accounts defines nonprofit organizations as "associations and institutions which either provide public goods and serve the common weal, or meet the specified interests of their members or other groups. These organizations are not primarily active for economic gains; they meet their expenses largely through membership contributions, public subsidies and, in the case of the Churches, through taxes, and only to a lesser extent through production income, usually in the formed sales and services" (Statistisches Bundesamt, 1979).

The State and the nonprofit sector

Historically, the institutional features of the nonprofit sector resulted from conflicts between the State and its political challengers, such as the workers' movement or the Churches. What persisted is, accordingly, a peculiar organizational pattern of political compromise, with state-licensed and state-controlled independence as its major characteristics. In this section, we will focus on how the State and the nonprofit sector relate to each other in two areas that are most indicative of this relationship: the principle of subsidiarity and the free welfare associations, and the principle of self-governance and the role of public law corporations in particular.

Subsidiarity

The Church-State relationship in Germany is highly complex in historical and political terms. Although the Basic Law does not recognize a State Church, ecclesiastical law is constitutionally equivalent to public administrative law. Thus, Churches are established not under civil but under public law, and form corporations of public law. This legal privilege applies only to the member Churches of the Council of Protestant Churches in Germany (41.5 percent of the West German population) and the Roman Catholic Church (43.3 percent of the population) and the Jewish congregations. Other religious communities, in particular the numerous "free religious associations" and the close to two million Moslems, would form civil law organizations, if they decided to incorporate.

Because of its public law status, church property is not taxed. Since public benefit status is a private law category, the classification of Churches as public law entities means that the Protestant and Catholic Churches as such are tax-exempt by definition, yet they become *gemeinnützig* only through the appplication of §§52–68 AO. In other words, while public law status implies tax exemption, it does not necessarily equate with *Gemeinnützigkeit*, which enables organizations to receive tax-deductible donations. As legal personalities under public law, the Churches can set up civil law associations and foundations, which can then apply for preferential tax treatment provided their activities meet the criteria of §52(1), which states that only organizations pursuing charitable, religious, or public good-related objectives can be *gemeinnützig*.

The Churches maintain their own tax administration, and are in a constitutional position to collect "church tax," which is levied by the State through employee payroll deductions and transferred to the Churches. The church tax provides Churches with a stable, inflation-proof income. The church tax is only voluntary in the sense that taxpayers can "opt out" by denouncing their church membership. Leaving the Protestant or Catholic Church is more than the cancellation of membership in a voluntary association: it is an official legal act like a change in marital status, to be recorded in both civil and church registries.

The implications of the church tax system and the special status of the Churches become clear if considered in the context of the principle of subsidiarity. While the Basic Law does not explicitly mention the principle of subsidiarity, legislation and judiciary derive it from several Basic Law articles, in particular Article 20 ("The Federal Republic is a democratic and social federal state"), and passages granting religious freedom and administrative autonomy to the Churches (Article 140 of the Basic Law).

Between 1950 and 1975 the principle of subsidiarity was introduced in three significant bodies of legislation which pertain to the role of private nonprofit providers in the field of social services and welfare. This applies primarily to the Social Code, which includes the Federal Social Assistance Act, and the Children and Youth Welfare Act. Legislation establishes the "overall responsibility" of the public sector for the provision of social services and assistance, and successively implements the principle of subsidiarity as a form of protected, state-supported system of private service and assistance delivery (see Anheier, 1992).

In §2, the *Bundessozialhilfegesetz* (Federal Social Assistance Act) introduces the primacy of individual help and care over any form of private or public social assistance and service provision. In §10(3)(1) the Federal Social Assistance Act mandates public–private cooperation in providing assistance and services:

> In cooperating with nonprofit-making, voluntary establishments and organizations, the [public] social assistance institutions seek to ensure that their activities and those of the [nonprofit and voluntary] establishments and organizations effectively complement one another for the benefit for those receiving assistance.[7]

The general concept of cooperation is further specified in §10(2) of the Federal Social Assistance Act:

> 2. In the implementation of this Act, the [public] bodies responsible for social assistance shall collaborate with the public law churches and religious communities and with the free welfare associations, acknowledging in so doing their independence in the targeting and execution of their functions ...

Within the context of cooperation and independence, §10(3)(2) of the Federal Social Assistance Act requires the public sector to provide financial and other support to the free welfare associations:

> 3. ... The (public] social assistance bodies shall support the Free Welfare Associations appropriately in their activities in the field of social assistance.

The principle by which cases of individual assistance are allocated between public assistance organizations and the free welfare associations is established in §10(4) of the Act:

4. If assistance in individual cases is ensured by Free Welfare Associations, the [public] social assistance bodies shall refrain from implementing their own measures; this does not apply to the provision of cash benefits.

While this section establishes the primacy of private delivery of social assistance over public assistance, irrespective of the mandate for public support, §93 of the Federal Social Assistance Act provides additional protection for the free welfare associations by virtually limiting and restricting the number and type of service providers at local levels (similarly, §5 of the Children and Youth Welfare Act):

1. The [public] social assistance bodies shall seek to ensure that establishments appropriate to the provision of social assistance are sufficiently available. They may not create their own new establishments if suitable establishments of the free welfare associations ... are available, or can be extended or provided.

The principle of subsidiarity is more than a formula for public subvention; it is primarily an organizational principle for the division of labor between the public and the private sector (Anheier, 1992). As mentioned earlier, it has been politically controversial. In the 1960s, the Social Democratic government of the state of Hessen challenged the constitutionality of the Youth Welfare Act.

The legal case against the principle rested on four charges: first, the law establishes privileges for the free welfare associations that amount to an embargo of public organizations in the field of social service delivery and assistance at the local level; second, the law introduces a hierarchy among assistance and service providers whereby public organizations are devalued and put into a position of "second choice;" third, the principle of subsidiarity, based on Catholic moral philosophy and theology, stems from the idea of natural law and of a pre-state social order which cannot serve as a guiding principle for legislation affecting all citizens; and fourth, the privileges accorded to the free welfare associations, in particular their quasi-monopoly once established in a local area, lead to a restriction in the number of choices available to individuals seeking help.

In a controversial 1967 ruling, the Federal Supreme Court (Bundesverfassungsgericht, 1968) rejected the charges and argued that, primarily, the translation of subsidiarity into a ranked system

of providers does not imply a depreciation of public organizations. The Supreme Court emphasized the role of the public sector
in the "overall responsibility" for provision of services at the local
level. Secondly, the language in which subsidiarity is described in
the law does not imply any theological or natural law principle; it
is primarily a principle dealing with the division of labor between
the public sector and the free welfare associations. Thirdly, neither
the public nor the private nonprofit sector would be able to provide social services and assistance to all citizens, neither financially nor organizationally. This necessitates the cooperation and joint
efforts that had characterized the relationship between sectors
since the creation of the Federal Republic. The intent of the Youth
Welfare Act (later: Children and Youth Welfare Act) and similar
legislation was to formalize and enhance such cooperation. Lastly,
the right of choice of a suitable and personal form of assistance (§3
of the Federal Social Assistance Act) co-exists with the right to
assist and the freedom of association for the free welfare associations in accordance with their own beliefs and convictions.

We can take it that the free welfare associations occupy an
important position in social welfare and services in Germany
(Goll, 1991). They run 68,466 institutions in the area of health care,
youth, and family services, as well as services for the handicapped, the elderly, and the poor (Bundesarbeitsgemeinschaft,
1990). They provide 70 percent of all family services, 60 percent of
all services for the elderly, 40 percent of all hospital beds, and 90
percent of all employment for the handicapped. The free welfare
associations employ 548,420 full-time and 202,706 part-time staff.
The number of volunteers is estimated at 1.5 million, with a self-
reported average number of 15.8 volunteer hours per month
(Spiegelhalter, 1990). To put the combined size and economic
weight of the free welfare associations into perspective, it is useful
to consider that CARITAS alone employs more people than the
industrial conglomerate Siemens, one of the largest employers in
the Federal Republic. Together, the free welfare associations
employ three times as many people as the Federal Post Office.

The free welfare associations present a special and perhaps
unique case both in the field of social service delivery and in the
area of interest mediation. Most welfare associations are closely
linked to a religious or political belief. As interest associations they
aggregate the interests of the social group they represent *vis-à-vis*

the State; as instruments of government policy they participate in the formulation, financing, and implementation of public programs and activities. Thus, their role is inherently ambiguous (see Bauer and Dießenbacher, 1984).

Legal stipulations based on the principle of subsidiarity tend to protect the nonprofit organizations from both for-profit and public sector competition. In this case, the principle of subsidiarity led to quasi-monopolistic supply structures. In terms of *law* and *taxation*, the public law status of the Catholic and the Protestant Churches and the church tax system provide those parts of the nonprofit sector linked to the Churches with a stable source of income, making church-related nonprofit organizations less dependent on the State in general, and on competitive grants, consumer fees, and charges in particular. Because the principle of subsidiarity is deeply imprinted in Germany's constitution and laws, it allows organizations access to sources of funds largely independent of the current political situation.

Self-governance

As we have seen above, the principle of self-administration or self-governance originated from the nineteenth-century conflict between State and citizens. It allowed parts of the nonprofit sector to emerge and develop in an autocratic society, where the freedom of association had only partially been granted. In the course of the last century, and particularly since 1949, the principle has become incorporated in numerous aspects of economic and social life, and is a dominant force in the field of research, higher education, and the arts.

Many of these aspects relate to labor and industrial policy within the general framework of the social market economy. First, unions and employers' associations enjoy far-reaching autonomy in the area of collective bargaining over wages as well as working and social conditions. These negotiations are legally protected from any government interference, and the results are binding for all employers and employees in a particular branch, independent of actual union membership and representation in firms. Nonmembers, however, are not bound to adhere to the agreements reached at collective bargaining.

The *de facto* system of unitary labor unions (only one union per industry) under the umbrella of the Federation of the German Trade Unions, finds its counterpart in the employers' associations. Therefore, each employers' association tends to deal with only one union, which reduces industrial conflicts and contributes to stable labor–management relations. In addition, the system of co-determination requires labor representation as well as participation in the management of all larger enterprises.

Whereas the employers' associations deal with collective bargaining and social policy, the several thousand business associations organized under the Federation of German Industries deal with economic policy, and are active lobbyists in matters relating to trade, industrial, and business affairs. Both the employers' associations and the business associations are registered associations under private law. The chambers of commerce and industry, however, are public law corporations with comprehensive and compulsory membership, and are responsible for the interests of the local and regional business community in general, and carry out some regulatory and governance functions. The organization of economic interests is a special feature of the German system. The business community, represented in a triple system of interest associations, and the unions, organizationally in a relatively strong and somewhat protected position, are responsible for a wide array of social and economic policies independent of the State.

Other areas show different manifestations of the principle of self-government. Broadcasting is one area that for long seemed indicative both of the continued mistrust felt by the German State *vis-à-vis* uncoordinated and unregulated political and market forces and of the protective or care-taker role the State tends to assume in relation to the public at large. The example of broadcasting is also useful to highlight some of the reasons that lead to the creation of public law corporations. Until recently, when private for-profit broadcasting corporations entered the television and radio market, the right to broadcast rested exclusively with nine regional corporations and one national. As nonprofit, public law corporations they were created by treaty among the various *Länder* (states), and by choosing public law status they ensured that the corporation could remain relatively independent from disproportionate influence from any particular *Land*, as well as from any special private and political interests.

By law, the broadcasting corporations are required to remain politically neutral. Consequently, the composition of the governing bodies of these corporations has assumed high levels of complexity, because of the meticulous attempt to arrive at a balanced representation for major interest groups. For example, the Television Board of the Second German Television channel (ZDF), a nonprofit organization under public law, includes 66 members: one representative from each of the *Länder* party to the Treaty, to be delegated by the state government; three delegates from the federal government; 12 representatives from political parties in proportion to their number of seats in parliament; two representatives each from the Catholic and the Protestant Churches; one from the Central Council of Jews; three from the trade unions; two from the Federation of Employers' Associations; one from the Central Committee of German Agriculture; one from the Central Association of Crafts and Trades; two from the Federation of Newspaper Publishers; two from the Journalists' Association; one each from the four largest free welfare associations; one each from the Conference of Cities, the Conference of Counties, and the Conference of Communities; one from the German Sports' Federation; one from the Federation of Expellees; ten from the fields of education, science and the arts; one representative of the free professions, and one each from fields of family services, youth services and women's issues.

The composition of the Television Board highlights a style of organization and a mode of interest regulation typical of many aspects of Germany's institutional landscape: conflict management of potential sources of contention by the accommodation of special interests. In many ways the systems lead to an over-representation of political parties, since many delegates tend to be party members at the same time.

Defining the nonprofit sector

In this section we provide an evaluation of how well the structural–operational definition fits the German situation. According to this definition, the nonprofit sector is a collection of organizations that are formal, private, not-profit-distributing, self-governing, and voluntary. As in other countries, the different legal and tax-based, economic, and functional as well as the street definitions of nonprofit organizations produce a complex and confusing terminology: unincorporated and incorporated associations, public benefit associations, public law corporations, public and private law foundations, limited liability companies, cooperatives, communal economy corporations, and non-commercial organizations. Each term focuses on a particular subset of nonprofits, and significant overlaps exist among the organizations included or excluded.

As we have seen, the different legal forms available to nonprofit organizations do not add up to a distinct sector: for example, registered associations may or may not be nonprofit, or charitable; public law organizations vary from government agencies to largely independent institutions like public television stations, the Bavarian Red Cross Society, the Jewish Welfare Agency, and even the Roman Catholic and Protestant Churches; and public utility organizations include mutual benefit societies, and even political parties, and exclude the Churches.

Thus legal definitions have limited utility in describing the full scope of the German nonprofit sector. Moreover, the common understanding of the German nonprofit sector does not follow this legal structure. The parts of the nonprofit sector regulated by the principle of subsidiarity are usually referred to as "welfare associations." In fact, the "free welfare associations" are themselves made up of numerous establishments with different legal status: for example, the Protestant *Diakonie*, an umbrella for thousands of separate legal entities, consists of registered associations (43.2 percent), foundations (23.4 percent), public law foundations and corporations (29.4 percent), limited liability companies (5 percent), and other legal forms (Thermann, 1979). Members of the *Paritätischer Wohlfahrtsverband* are 88.6 percent registered associations, to 5.5 percent limited liability companies, with public law corporations and foundations making up the remaining 5.9 percent (Bockhacker, 1985).

The parts of the German nonprofit sector close to the principle of self-administration include civil law associations, public law corporations, and foundations. These vary in the extent to which they are independent from government. Consequently, they include organizations that are an operational arm of some federal or state ministry, as well as chambers of commerce and industry, radio and television stations, and institutions of higher education.

Not all, however, qualify as nonprofit organizations under the structural–operational definition. These include the public radio and television corporations or the German Association for Technical Corporation.

As we will see below, the great virtue of the structural–operational definition as applied to the German situation is that it pulls together the several overlapping subunits that national concepts treat separately. The structural–operational definition ties together the organizations regulated by these different bodies of law and commonly attributed to different sets of institutions.

Formal. The criterion "formal" applies to Germany: the definition includes nonregistered associations and informal groups, which are not fully captured by legal definitions. One example is the citizen initiatives. Most such groups were ad hoc, informal associations of individuals who shared common concerns that they did not find appropriately addressed by local authorities or political parties. The issues were varied, and ranged from waste disposal to traffic regulation and child day care. The initiatives were basically local and small, with only 4 percent having more than 1,000 members (Kodolitsch, 1975). They added a local element to the centralized associational landscape of Germany's civil society. Beginning in the mid-1970s, they tended to form extended regional and national networks, which later benefited the creation of the Green Party (the first environmentalist party worldwide) as well as the peace movement of the 1980s.

Private. The distinction between public and private law has become blurred ever since forms of public–private partnerships and cooperative arrangements emerged in the field of social security and services. The principle of subsidiarity has contributed to the increasing complexity of the public–private borderline, as have the numerous private and public law institutions created by public agencies to take on auxiliary administrative and service tasks. As some authors have remarked, the choice of public or private organizational form seems often a matter of political and other circumstances rather than a strict application of legal principles (Schuppert, 1981). For example, in matters involving both federal and state governments, the private nonprofit form is a more practical, and therefore less costly, solution than establishing joint public law corporations, which, according to legal form, would be the logical choice.

Thus, it may seem inappropriate to employ a strict distinction between public and private law categories in defining the non-profit sector in Germany. It may be useful to extend the notion of "private" to include also "self-governing public law organiza-tion." This, however, would appear to open a Pandora's box: uni-versities, public broadcasting stations, and many other public law organizations would qualify as nonprofit. Are we willing to grant nonprofit status to the University of Eichstätt, which is an inde-pendent Catholic university and legally a Church foundation, but not to the (secular) University of Cologne, which sees itself as an independent learned corporation? Both are established as public law bodies, one by the Catholic Church, the other by a regional government. Should the public TV stations be regarded as private nonprofit organizations, despite the fact that they collect revenue from a "captive" audience through a "fee collection agency" endowed with quasi-regulatory power to enforce compliance?

As we have seen, "public" does not necessarily mean "state" in Germany, and "private" may neither imply "non-state" nor "non-public." It is one of the consequences of the distinction between civil law and public law that the private versus public distinction ends up being not very useful for our purposes. The governance of an organization (primarily private and relatively independent versus state-appointed and governmental) may be better in con-structing the dividing line needed to separate public from private nonprofits than the legal status of both the organization itself (public law, private law) and its founder (individual or parlia-ment, by decree or other legal instrument). In this case the virtue of the structural–operational definition is that the combination of two criteria, i.e. private and self-governing (see below), will allow for a refined treatment of borderline cases. Other such cases, how-ever, will have to examined on their own merit.

Self-governing. Much of the history of association in the nine-teenth century is a history of the allocation of social, political, and economic spheres into either private or public realms, and there-fore, private and public law status. Well into the first part of the century, the law says little about *Gemeinnützigkeit* (public useful-ness), but much about public oversight and political restrictions to associational freedom. The nineteenth century set a pattern whereby the legislature has tended to opt for public law status, whenever the State saw a special need to protect its own rights and sovereignty *vis-à-vis* private interests (as in the case of the Churches), or felt the necessity to balance public and private needs (as in the creation of public law broadcasting corporations or the public railroad network), or when the general public-good character of institutions could be separated from individual motivations (as in universities). However, contrary to the abstract legal principles that underlie the public–private law distinction, legal reality had always been mediated by political opportunism and practicality, and the dividing lines have become more fluid in the course of recent decades.

The for-profit versus nonprofit status of associations was much less a contested issue, when compared to the degree of public control. The issue of self-governance poses problems whenever the private or public character of a nonprofit organization is unclear. In addition to the typical cases mentioned in the discussion of private–public distinctions above, the issue of self-governance becomes less focused in the relationship between political parties and the nonprofit organizations located in their ideological vicinity.

Non-profit-distributing. In the German case, the monetary equivalent of economic activities directly linked to the charitable purpose of the organization is exempt from certain forms of taxation but not necessarily from all. Nor are all of the organization's activities exempt: beyond a certain threshold any "commercial activity" not directly related to a charitable purpose is subject to taxation. The tax law divides nonprofits into the charitable segment inclusive of related business income, the commercial segment, and the financial segment of endowments, assets, and liabilities. It then applies different tax-liability and tax-exemption regimes to each. Thus, in some ways, nonprofit versus for-profit status is less of a dichotomy than it would appear. Like the various forms of the 501(c) exempt categories in the US, the nonprofit/for-profit difference is closer to an ordinal ranking than a strict dichotomy. In addition, for small associations below a certain threshold of annual turnover (DM60,000), the nonprofit constraint does not apply; they are not required to file tax reports and tax authorities do not examine their balance sheets. They are nonprofits by default. *In toto*, however, it should be possible to draw a relatively clean boundary for nonprofit organizations.

It is, however, the combination of the public–private, self-governance and nonprofit issues which contributes to the complexity of defining the German nonprofit sector. We should recall the distinction between tax exemption and *Gemeinnützigkeit*. Keeping this in mind, it becomes apparent why a regional water works association and a cultural foundation are, as public law bodies, both tax-exempt, but only the latter can achieve the status of *Gemeinnützigkeit*, i.e. receiving tax-deductible donations and exemption from many forms of taxation: while the AO foresees a category for the support of culture, no such stipulations are made for water treatment. Similarly, the Churches are tax-exempt, privately-governed public law corporations which are *gemeinnützig* because religious objectives are classified as such in the AO. By implication, the public benefit status of the Churches, as granted in the AO, refers only to religious activities, and does not necessarily extend to non-religious objectives, like science or education, even though the latter are classified as *gemeinnützig*. In such cases, religious organizations must set up legally separate branches or institutions. Finally, the tax law recognizes a number of special cases that regulate the *Gemeinnützigkeit* status of municipalities, universities, or chambers of commerce in the support of certain activities.

Voluntary. It is at the intersection of participation and volunteering that we find additional differences between Germany and other countries: historically, the notion of volunteering carries a different connotation. The equivalent German terms *Ehrenamt* (honorary office) and *ehrenamtliche Tätigkeit* (honorary office activity) emphasize the honorary component, officialdom and public legitimation rather than voluntarism as such (see Müller and Rauschenbach, 1988). The notion of honorary office was popularized in the nineteenth century in an attempt to reconcile the need for citizen participation and voluntary labor input with the political control felt necessary by the autocratic State. During the Third Reich, honorary office was widely propagated and employed as a means of both political control and infiltration of the Nazi Party into ever more aspects of society. Today, however, the notion of honorary office has been freed of much of its origins, and has moved closer to the concept of voluntarism. Information on volunteering is incomplete; available data suggest a lower rate of volunteering than in other countries, with about 6 percent of the population volunteering at least once a week, and 42 percent reported to have volunteered at least once within the last two years (Braun and Röhrig, 1986; Institut für Demoskopie, 1979).

Somewhat different is the notion of voluntarism in the case of membership in the Protestant and Catholic Churches. Church membership is quasi-automatic for children of Christian parents, and "opting out" rather than "opting in" is required to exercise the "voluntary" aspect of membership in this regard. A similar case can be made for the church tax, which is levied on the taxable income of every Church member and which is collected by the public tax authorities. Thus, in some cases "voluntary" would primarily imply non-compulsory.

In summary, the structural–operational definition groups together otherwise separate types of organizations. It does so by de-emphasizing internal, often ill-defined, distinctions, so as to allow us to focus in on aspects of the German nonprofit sector that are both important and difficult to conceptualize and measure, for example the distinction between the private and the public sector. In summary, with some simplification: "formal" brings into focus the entire range of formal organizations located between the state agency and the market firm; "private" and "self-governing" retain private law and independent public law organizations; "non-profit-distributing" excludes cooperatives, mutual insurance companies, and most housing associations, as well as marketing and promotional societies for businesses; and the criterion "voluntary" excludes compulsory public law associations like the chambers of commerce, craft, and industry, and similar organizations for the medical and legal professions.

Conclusion

Historically, the world of associations emerged in a complex process marked by several extreme positions: the anti-associational, individualistic tradition of the French Revolution; the corporatist influences of a late medieval society that were soon used and modified by self-modernizing economic and political élites; the anti-liberal policies and administrative reforms of the autocratic State; the failure of the new middle class to achieve political power; and the increased cultural differentiation of society. These conflicting, and sometimes overlapping, currents shaped a nonprofit sector that is both the terrain and the result of the conflict between organized religion, political opposition, and the State over the division of labor and spheres of influence. We argued that de Tocqueville's problem, formulated as a dichotomy of either a state-centered or an association-centered society, does not apply to the German situation. The early development of the modern German nonprofit sector happened in antithesis to an autocratic State. During much of the nineteenth century, Catholic and Protestant associations were often seen as a challenge to the autocratic State, and found little public support, even though the situation varied significantly across different parts of the country. Similarly, the conflict between the new middle class and the established political order found its expression in demands for a greater freedom of association, and the workers' movement began to create its own associational system, often against the fierce opposition of employers and public authorities alike. However, unlike what occurred in other countries, these conflicts did not lead to ruptures and severe discontinuities; rather, within the complicated course of German history, and beginning with Bismarck's social insurance policies, they were channeled into a mode of interaction between the nonprofit sector and the State. This mode emerged as the dominant pattern, ranging historically from more or less subtle forms of coercion, cooptation, and corporatist arrangements, to voluntary cooperation and far-reaching coordination.

We conclude by pointing to some of the implications for the German nonprofit sector today. First, within the legal and programmatic context of subsidiarity, the free welfare organizations are in a complex relationship with the State that goes well beyond monetary transfers (see Goll, 1991, for a recent analysis). There are several points of view regarding free welfare organizations. According to Heinze and Olk (1981), they are a corporatist arrangement whereby the State extends into the area of social services and welfare. Thränhardt (1983) sees free welfare organizations as tools of the Churches and other "conservative" political forces to control a vital area of social welfare by creating quasi-monopolies, whereas Spiegelhalter (1990) views them as part of an efficient, responsive, and decentralized system in which the advantages of private and public involvement in the field of social services are realized to everybody's benefit.

In terms of policy, as a result of both the principle of subsidiarity and the principle of self-governance, nonprofit organizations tend to be relatively well integrated into the policy-making function of government. In many areas of legislation, public authorities are required to consult nonprofit organizations in matters of economic, social, and cultural policy. Moreover, as we have seen above, the State needs the endorsement of the free welfare associations for the establishment of public sector organizations in the field of social welfare and assistance. In this case, the principle of subsidiarity resulted in what others called the neocorporatist system (Heinze and Olk, 1981).

Second, larger interest associations, particularly business associations, are part of a system of "nonplanning" – a system whereby policy initiatives are "tested" or "rehearsed," often informally, with an emphasis on cooperation and conflict-avoidance. Relatively independently of political ideology, all governments since 1949 have operated with a minimum of direct state planning. The unspoken maxim of nonplanning, which leaves many policy initiatives and their implementation to nongovernmental agencies and local governments, involves the participation of the numerous mandatory and voluntary associations. In this way, they become incorporated in a political system that demands and encourages cooperation by "controlled delegation" of tasks – a learned institutional behavior first introduced in the nineteenth century.

Third, the largely apolitical associational system has shown signs of change, as participation in nontraditional social movements has increased since the 1970s in the form of citizen initiatives. However, true to the organizational environment in which they operate, citizen initiatives began to form peak associations. The most visible of the new peak associations grew from 15 member organizations in 1972 to about 1,000 by the mid-1980s, representing between 300,000 and 500,000 individual members. Thus, while the citizen initiatives introduced new elements into civil society, they nonetheless replicate some of the characteristics of Germany's society and nonprofit sector alike (Katzenstein, 1987): the centralization of decentralized organizations and constituencies through nonprofit institutions.

Politically, the integration of citizen initiatives and self-help groups was provided by a political party which also originated in the late 1970s in the context of the emerging New Social Movements: the "Greens" count the self-help movement as their clientele. Moreover, as a political party they serve as intermediary between government and this part of the nonprofit sector (cf. Seibel, 1990). In local politics, the "Greens" act as the protectors of grass-roots and self-help initiatives. This tripartite relationship between new social movements, political parties, and government is a "softer" version of the pattern which generally prevails in the German nonprofit sector. Thus, this arrangement indicates the stability of a deeply rooted institutional pattern of political integration.

In general terms, the nonprofit sector in Germany, how it developed and how it is conceptualized, is a history of why "State" and "society," "public" and "private" are no zero sum. It shows that the dichotomy "association-centered" versus "state-centered" societies can be quite misleading. In Germany, the public and the private nonprofit sectors developed sometimes in open conflict with each other, but often in a mutually reinforcing manner. In this sense, the structural–operational definition allows for a refined conceptual treatment of the interaction between government, public sector and nonprofit sector.

Notes

1 Although the legal, economic, and political system of the Federal Republic of Germany now includes the former German Democratic Republic, we will focus on West Germany in this chapter. This is, at least partly, justified by the fact that the West German institutional setting had been formally transferred to East Germany by 3 October 1990, although significant differences continue to exist in legal and administrative aspects.

2 In addition, three terms are used in the social science literature which have usages that are similar to those in other countries: *intermediäre Organisationen* or intermediary organizations (see Bauer, 1990), *Dritter Sektor* or third sector (Anheier and Seibel, 1990), and finally, *Nicht-Regierungsorganisationen* or nongovernmental organizations.

3 For reasons of shortness and clarity, we use the Prussian example as the paradigmatic case. While other parts of Germany show significant deviations from the course of Prussian history in the nineteenth century, Prussia became the dominant political actor in the formation of the German nation-state.

4 Significantly enough, it was the Social-Democratic government of the state of Hesse which filed suit with the Constitutional Court against

the Federal Social Assistance Act and its stipulation of "subsidiarity" (see below).

5   In its contemporary meaning, the term is a creation of the nineteenth century (Hardtwig, 1990). Several major bodies of law, from the Prussian Land Law of the late eighteenth century to the Civil Code of 1900, and the various laws on commercial associations like the stock corporation or the limited liability company, established uniform definitions for associations, corporations, societies, or cooperatives, terms previously often used interchangeably. The imprecision and overlap in definition is an indication of the early (and – in comparison with common law countries – late) development of various forms of private associations.

6   Similar provisions for tax privileges in the case of *Gemeinnützigkeit* are found in special tax laws. They all relate to the AO as the basic legal reference for the definition of tax-exempt status. Examples are §5(1) No. 9 corporate income tax law, §3(6) trade tax law, §3(1) No. 12 property tax law, §3(1) No. 2b real estate tax law, §13(1) No. 16b inheritance tax law, §7(1) No. 1 capital transfer tax law, and the provisions of §4 of the turnover tax law.

7   The translation of §2 and the following legal passages in this section are, in part, adopted from Deutscher Verein, 1986.

References

Agricola, Sigurd and Peter Wehr (1993), *Vereinswesen in Deutschland: Eine Expertise*. Vorgelegt im Auftrag des Bundesministeriums für Familie und Senioren durch die Deutsche Gesellschaft für Freizeit. Stuttgart: Kohlhammer.

Anheier, Helmut K. (1992), "An elaborate network: Profiling the third sector in Germany," in *Government and the Third Sector: Emerging Relationships in Welfare States*, ed. Benjamin Gidron *et al.* San Francisco: Jossey-Bass.

Anheier, Helmut K. and Wolfgang Seibel (eds) (1990), *The Third Sector: Comparative Studies of Nonprofit Organizations*. Berlin/New York: DeGruyter.

Bauer, Rudolph (1990), "Voluntary welfare associations in Germany and the United States." *Voluntas*, 1(1): 97–111.

Bauer, Rudolph and Hartmut Dießenbacher (eds) (1984), *Organisierte Nächstenliebe: Wohlfahrtsverbände und Selbsthilfe in der Krise des Sozialstaats*. Opladen: Westdeutscher Verlag.

Bockhacker, Jürgen (1985), "Die Unternehmen im Deutschen Paritätischen Wohlfahrtsverband." *Zeitschrift für öffentliche und gemeinwirtschaftliche Unternehmen*, 8:6–16.

Braun, Joachim and Peter Röhrig (1986), "Umfang und Unterstützung ehrenamtlicher Mitarbeit und Selbsthilfe im kommunalen Sozial- und Gesundheitsbereich," in *Freiwilliges soziales Engagement und Weiterbildung*, ed. Bundesminister für Bildung und Wissenschaft. Bonn: The Bundesministerium.

Bundesarbeitsgemeinschaft der Freien Wohlfahrtspflege (1990), *Gesamtstatistik 1990*. Bonn: Bundesarbeitsgemeinschaft der Freien Wohlfahrtspflege.

Bundesministerium der Finanzen (1988), *Gutachten der unabhängigen Sachverständigenkommission zur Prüfung des Gemeinnützigkeits- und Spendenrechtes*. Schriftenreihe Heft 40. Bonn: The Bundesministerium.

Bundesverfassungsgericht (1988), "Urteil Nr. 19 vom 18. Juli 1967." *BVerfGE*, 22:180–220.

Commission of the European Communities (1987), *Eurobarometer 2*. Brussels: Commission of the European Communities.

Dann, Otto (1976), "Die Anfänge politischer Vereinsbildung in Deutschland," in *Soziale Bewegung und politische Verfassung*, ed. Ulrich Engelhardt, Volker Sellin, and Horst Stuke, pp. 197–232. Stuttgart: Klett.

Dann, Otto (1993), "Vereinsbildung in Deutschland in historischer Perspektive," in *Vereine in Deutschland: Vom Geheimbund zur freien gesellschaftlichen Organisation*, ed. Heinrich Best, pp. 119–142. Bonn: Informationszentrum Sozialwissenschaften.

Deutscher Verein für öffentliche und private Fürsorge (1986), *Voluntary Welfare Services*. Frankfurt: Deutscher Verein (in-house publication).

Eichhorn, Peter and Paul Münch (eds) (1983), *Aufgaben öffentlicher und gemeinwirtschaftlicher Unternehmen im Wandel*. Baden-Baden: Nomos.

Goll, Eberhard (1991), *Die freie Wohlfahrtspflege als eigener Wirtschaftssektor*. Baden-Baden: Nomos.

Habermas, Jürgen (1962), *Stukturwandel der Öffentlichkeit*. Frankfurt: Suhrkamp. (Further edn. 1990.)

Hansmann, Henry (1980), "The role of nonprofit enterprise," *Yale Law Journal*, April, 835–898.

Hardtwig, Wolfgang (1990), "Verein," in *Geschichtliche Grundbegriffe*, vol. 6, ed. Otto Brunner, Werner Conze, and Reinhart Koselleck. Stuttgart: Klett.

Heinze, Rolf G. and Thomas Olk (1981), "Die Wohlfahrtsverbände im System sozialer Dienstleistungspoduktion: zur Entstehung und Struktur der bundesrepublikanischen Verbändewohlfahrt." *Kölner Zeitschrift für Soziologie und Sozialpsychologie*, 1:94–114.

Hendler, Reinhart (1984), *Selbstverwaltung als Ordnungsprinzip. Zur politischen Willensbildung und Entscheidung im demokratischen Verfassungsstaat der Industriegesellschaft*. Cologne/Berlin/Bonn/ Munich: C. Heyman.

Himmelmann, Gerhard (1985), "Public enterprises in the Federal Republic of Germany." *Annalen der Gemeinwirtschaft*, 3:365–391.

Hoover, Herbert (1922), *American Individualism*. New York: Doubleday.

Hueber, Alfons (1984), "Das Vereinsrecht im Deutschland des 18. Jahrhunderts," in *Vereinswesen und bürgerliche Gesellschaft in Deutschland*, ed. Otto Dann, pp. 115–132, Munich: R. Oldenbourg.

Institut für Demoskopie (1979), *Die Stellung der freien Wohlfahrtsverbände*. Allensbach: The Institute.

Katzenstein, Peter J. (1987), *Policy and Politics in West Germany: The Growth of a Semisovereign State*. Philadelphia: Temple University Press.

Kodolitsch, Peter (1975), "Gemeindeverwaltungen und Bürgerinitiativen: Ergebnisse einer Umfrage." *Archiv für Kommunalwissenschaften*, 3:318–332.

Koselleck, Reinhart (1967), *Preußen zwischen Reform und Revolution: Allgemeines Landrecht Verwaltung und soziale Bewegungen von 1791 bis 1848*. Stuttgart: Klett.

Lehmbruch, Gerhard (1982), "Neo-Corporatism in comparative perspective," in *Patterns of Corporatist Policy-Making*. Beverly Hills and London: Sage.

Müller, Friedrich (1965), *Korporation und Assoziation. Eine Problemgeschichte Vereinigungsfreiheit im deutschen Vormärz*. Berlin: Duncker & Humblot.

Müller, S. and T. Rauschenbach (eds) (1988), *Das soziale Ehrenamt*. Weinheim/Basel: Beltz.

Nell-Breuning, Oswald von (1976), "Das Subsidiaritätsprinzip." *Theorie und Praxis der sozialen Arbeit*, 27:6–17.

Neuhoff, Klaus (1978), "Stiftungen §§80–88 BGB." *Materialien aus dem Stiftungszentrum*, 10. Essen: Stiftungszentrum im Stifterverband für die deutsche Wissenschaft.

Nipperdey, Thomas (1976), "Verein als soziale Struktur in Deutschland im späten 18. und frühen 19. Jahrhundert," in *Gesellschaft, Kultur, Theorie*, ed. T. Nipperdey, pp. 1–44. Göttingen: Vandenhoeck & Rupprecht.

O'Connell, B. (1983), *America's Voluntary Spirit: A Book of Readings*. New York: The Foundation Center.

Oppenheimer, Franz (1896), *Die Siedlungsgenossenschaft*. Jena: Gustaf Fischer.

Rinken, Alfred (1971), *Das Öffentliche als verfassungstheoretisches Problem dargestellt am Rechtsstatus der Wohlfahrtsverbände*. Berlin: Duncker & Humblot.

Sachße, Christoph and Florian Tennstedt (1992), *Der Wohlfahrtsstaat im Nationalsozialismus: Geschichte der Armenfürsorge in Deutschland*, vol. 3. Stuttgart/Berlin/Cologne: Kohlhammer.

Scheuch, Erwin K. (1993), "Verein als Teil der Privatgesellschaft," in

Vereine in Deutschland: Vom Geheimbund zur freien gesellschaftlichen Organisation, ed Heinrich Best, pp. 143–201. Bonn: Information-szentrum Sozialwissenschaften.

Schuppert, Gunnar F. (1981), *Die Erfüllung öffentlicher Aufgaben durch verselbständigte Verwaltungseinheiten.* Göttingen: Schwartz.

Seibel, Wolfgang (1990), "Government/third-sector relationship in a comparative perspective: the cases of France and West Germany." *Voluntas*, 1(1):42–60.

Spiegelhalter, Franz (1990), *Der Dritte Sozialpartner.* Bonn: Lambertus.

Statistisches Bundesamt (1979), *Systematik der Wirtschaftszweige.* Mainz: Kohlhammer.

Statistisches Bundesamt (1987), Unternehmen und Arbeitsstätten: Arbeitsstättenzählung vom 25. Mai 1987, vol. 1, 2, 4, 5, 11. Stuttgart: Metzel-Poeschel.

Thermann, Gottfried (1979), "Einrichtungen der Diakonie als gemein-wirtschaftliche Unternehmen." *Zeitschrift für öffentliche und gemein-wirtschaftliche Unternehmen*, 2:443–456.

Thiemeyer, Theo (1970), *Gemeinwirtschaftlichkeit als Ordnungsprinzip. Grundlegung als Theorie gemeinnütziger* Unternehmen. Berlin: Duncker & Humblot.

Thränhardt, Dietrich (1983), "Ausländer im Dickicht der Verbände: ein Beispiel verbandsgerechter Klientelselektion und korporatistischer Politikformulierung," in *Sozialarbeit und Ausländerpolitik*, ed. F. Hamburger et al. Neuwied/Darmstadt: Luchterhand.

Toennies, Ferdinant (1935), *Gemeinschaft und Gesellschaft: Grundbegriffe der reinen Soziologie*, 2nd edn. Leipzig: Buske.

Vilmar, Fritz and Brigitte Runge (1986), *Auf dem Weg zur Selbsthilfegesellschaft?* Essen: Lambertus.

Windhoff-Héritier, Adrienne (1982), "Selbsthilfeorganisationen: eine Lösung für die Sozialpolitik der mageren Jahre?" *Soziale Welt*, 33:49–65.

Wurzbacher, Gerhard (1971), "Die öffentliche freie Vereinigung als Faktor Sozio-kulturellen, inbesondere emanzipatorischen Wandels im 19. Jahrhundert," in *Zur historischen Herausbildung des Dritten Sektors als intermediäter Zone zwischen Bürger und Staat und somit als institutioneller Ersatz für die Ständeordnung des Ancien Regime*, ed. Walter Ruegg and Otto Neulch, pp. 103–122. Göttingen: Vanderhoeck & Ruprecht.

Chapter 7

ITALY

Gian Paolo Barbetta[1]

Introduction

The Italian nonprofit sector is a vast and vague universe that falls in the blurred or shaded area created by the overlapping of the *nominally* separate realms of private and public institutions. This gray area is the legal result of two parallel conflicts that took place in the second half of the nineteenth century, when the process of unification of the country came to an end. On one hand, the new Italian political élite tried to limit the power and the influence of the Catholic Church, while on the other, it struggled to integrate the growing socialist movement into the political structure of a capitalist economy.

As a result of the first struggle, many Church-affiliated organizations that historically met the bulk of the nation's collective needs in health, education, and social welfare became part of the public welfare system and enjoyed a peculiar legal position. Today, their status can best be described as private/public, or as secular/religious. Examples include *Istituzioni pubbliche di assistenza e beneficenza* (IPAB or public charity and assistance institutions) and hospitals managed by the *enti ecclesiastici civilmente riconosciuti* (ecclesiastic bodies recognized by civil law). Under the 1968 hospital reform law, some religious hospitals were required to serve the entire public without discrimination based on religious belief, and at fees regulated by the government. In fact, they became part of what later emerged as the National Health System. As members of a public administration, they receive funds from the central and/or local governments, and are perceived by the general population as public service providers. However, as private, religiously affiliated organizations, they continue to appoint their own administrators.

As a result of the second conflict, the Italian State took responsibility for attending to the "collective needs" of the people, advancing their well-being or general welfare. Today, public responsibility does not necessarily imply public administration. Often, private organizations that first addressed some collective needs are granted partial *de jure* public status. Such groups range from the Red Cross to the Touring Club of Italy, organizations which the United States or Great Britain might typically classify as nonprofit. While legally viewed as private, they exert governmental authority in specific fields. Their boards are sometimes appointed by the government, and they often retain fiscal and labor-related privileges not allowed other organizations.

Historical note

Crucial events in the evolution of the Italian nonprofit sector took place in the second half of the nineteenth century with the establishment of Italy as a nation-state (the *Risorgimento*), the onset of the industrial revolution, and the struggle for power among the new State, the old Church, and a growing socialist movement. As the century drew to a close, social, welfare, and health services were provided largely by religious institutions founded during the medieval era. At the same time, a rising socialist workers' movement began to establish its own mutual care organizations.

Catholic welfare was mainly administered by the *Opere Pie*, consisting of some 18,000 institutions endowed with donations and bequests, which met most of the social and health needs of the very poor. Almost all *Opere Pie* were under the direct control of religious congregations. Their services far surpassed those provided by public institutions: according to one study, the government spent only 60 percent of the money spent by the Opere Pie on similar services (Ranci, 1990).

In terms of the workers' movement, the "development of *Società operaie di mutuo soccorso* (Workers Mutual Aid Societies) from the remaining traces of *corporazioni di mestiere* (professional guilds) was also extremely promising" (Paci, 1989).

Legal attacks against the Catholic organizations were initiated by the State in its quest for authority, which began in 1866 (described further below). Efforts to incorporate the autonomous workers' mutual benefit societies under the State were enacted towards the end of the nineteenth century and into the twentieth. Indeed, it can be said that the Italian welfare system derived from an attempt by the State to drive private nonprofit initiatives, of both Catholic and socialist origin, into public channels, with the consequent increase in state political control.

Reducing Catholic influence

In 1860, numerous regions of what is now central and southern Italy, formerly belonging to the Papal State and to the Kingdom of the Two Sicilies, were militarily annexed to form a new Italian state. Ten years later, the new Kingdom of Italy conquered the remaining Papal areas, including Rome, which was established as its capital. The cessation of war did not end the hostility between the new State and the Catholic hierarchy; instead the battle moved to the political and legislative arenas.

The establishment of the State generated a new political élite, which saw as its first major challenge the need to reduce the strength and influence of the Catholic Church and its institutions. Between 1866 and 1890, the State enacted laws confiscating the assets of various Catholic orders and congregations, forcing organizations like the *Opere Pie* to adhere to state jurisdiction.

In 1866, as a first attempt to diminish the influence of the Pope, the State passed a law suppressing some 1,800 religious orders and congregations, and confiscating their belongings. Expropriated buildings were given to local government authorities to house schools, hospitals, and social institutions. Books and works of art were assigned to public libraries and museums.

At the time, religious ministers were mostly supported by the income given by their *benefici* (endowments in land and buildings erected in the legal form of a foundation); different ministers had different standards of living according to the income given by the endowments to which they were entitled. Presumably in an effort to ease the harshness of the expropriation of these endowments, the law passed in 1866 created the *fondo per il culto* (worship fund), the goal of which was to provide support to the members of the suppressed orders whose assets had been confiscated. Subsidies from the fund, called *supplemento di congrua*, were made possible through a government endowment consisting of 5 percent in treasury bonds as well as a portion of the previously confiscated land and buildings.

An additional 25,000 religiously-affiliated institutions had their assets confiscated and auctioned off under a second law passed in 1867. These were not parishes and local churches, which the law left untouched, but were organizations that offered no direct sacramental service ("cure of souls"), i.e., largely charitable institutions.

To compensate the members of these groups, the government endowed in perpetuity the *fondo per il culto*. The law also mandated a minimum level of income for the priests. Therefore priests whose *benefici* (assets) had not been confiscated, but whose income was below the mandatory minimum level, were entitled to get public subsidies from the *fondo per il culto*. However, the government then established an *una tantum* tax on ecclesiastic wealth, effectively reducing the amount of irredeemable bonds given to the fund by 30 percent.

A third and final law was passed in 1890 aimed at decreasing Catholic influence on Italian society and at creating a state-controlled social services system. It was known as the *legge Crispi*, after the ruling Prime Minister. Under the law, *Opere Pie* offering health, education, and job training were defined as *Istituzioni Pubbliche di Assistenza e Beneficenza* (public charity and assistance institutions) and became part of the public sector.

Under the Crispi law, additional organizations offering social services which were willing to be incorporated (to receive *personalità giuridica*, or juridical standing) were required to obtain a public IPAB charter, which placed them within the public sector. Ultimately, the law required any institution offering public assistance and having some "economic relevance" to submit to public control.

This effort at secularizing Italian society, however, was far from total. Over the decades, social service organizations and the religious élite managing them retained considerable autonomy. This autonomy increased during the fascist era (1922–1943), when the hostile relationship between the State and the Church ceased with the signing of the *Concordato* (general agreement) in 1929. The Concordato not only granted a great deal of freedom of action to the Church, it declared Catholicism the official state religion, com-

pletely disavowing the liberal principle of Church–State separation. As a result of this complex historical evolution, it could be
said that the Catholic Church has been considered as part of the
State, and Catholic institutions as public ones.

Integrating the working class

The political integration of the working class was viewed as the
second challenge of the new state-based political élite. The aim
was to reduce the level of social discontent, paving the way for
widespread industrialization (Ascoli, 1984). Toward this end, the
State passed sweeping social legislation as the old century gave
way to the new. Under the Giolitti administration, the legislature
established a system, organized and regulated by the State, of
voluntary, worker-contributed insurance through mutual funds.
Providing illness and retirement insurance, the mutual funds,

> behind the pro forma appearance of autonomous control, allowed for
> substantial control on the part of the central authorities. State control
> resided not in the administration of the funds, but in the political
> appointments of the directors – in effect, the state's "clients." The *Cassa
> Nazionale di Previdenza* for aged and disabled workers, approved in
> 1898, was characterized by its status as a state institution of popular
> insurance and by a formally autonomous board whose members, how-
> ever, were (as it was then said) morally dependent upon the state gov-
> ernment. (Paci, 1989)

This approach was preferred to compulsory insurance programs
adopted increasingly by other European countries. The Italian
state did, however, enact in 1898 compulsory insurance for industrial accidents. Compulsory insurance for retirement (pensions)
and unemployment was instituted in 1919 and during the ensuing
Fascist era (1922–1943). In this last period, the State suppressed
workers' mutual societies (along with all political parties and
freedoms), substituting mandatory public health and pension
insurance, and government-administered services.

The postwar era to the present

The 1948 Constitution left the Crispi law unchanged, notwithstanding a provision – Article 38 – which allowed for private social
assistance. Some scholars such as Cavalari (1988) have argued that

the discrepancy was tolerated because the 1890 law generated many advantages to newly created IPABs. These included public funding for capital items such as buildings renovation and medical instruments; and the availability of contracts from the National Health System. Further, the public status of the IPABs did not prevent them from being administered in accordance with the will of their founders, especially the Catholic Church.

In 1977, as part of an attempt by the government to decentralize health and social services, the State enacted a law to subject IPABs to local authorities. This greatly constrained the organizations' freedom of action, and led to a legal challenge to the constitutionality of the Crispi law. By 1988, the Constitutional Court declared unconstitutional the *legge Crispi's* Article 1, which prohibited the existence of IPABs as private entities. Consequently, new organizations can now be incorporated under a different law, and existing IPABs may apply for a private charter. The situation today remains in flux, however, because few IPABs have applied for privatization (50 out of 800 in Lombardy, for example).

An agreement signed by the Holy See and the State in 1984–1985 allows entities of the Catholic Church having religious purposes to apply for a "legal personality," thereby becoming *enti ecclesiastici civilmente riconosciuti* (ecclesiastic bodies recognized by civil law). While these organizations must pursue religious aims, nothing in the law prevents them from undertaking other activities, including health services, education, arts and culture, or even commerce. Thus, in addition to the types of organizations described in the next section, some of the *enti ecclesiastici civilmente riconosciuti* may operate within the nonprofit sector.

The Italian welfare system came to develop the following characteristics:

- a high degree of state intervention, and a limited role for private organizations, except those religiously affiliated; and
- a "corporative-guarantistic" and "clientelistic-assistential" nature. "The former expressed itself in the primacy of professional solidarities based on private insurance, which, once inserted into the public code … assumed guarantistical institutional characteristics. The latter manifested itself primarily in assistential programs left to the political and administrative discretion of the public authorities, thus leading to the clientelistic dependence of the beneficiaries" (Paci, 1989).

The Italian welfare system expanded greatly after the Second World War. The role of nonprofit organizations decreased, while that of the State increased, largely through public provision of health and education services. As it expanded, the system developed a kind of service separation. Social security, health, and education tended to be provided largely by the government, a consequence of state incorporation of the socialist mutual benefit societies and related worker self-help groups. This remains the case today. By contrast, most other social services, although funded by public authorities, are administered primarily by Catholic organizations (albeit under government charter), which historically have devoted their efforts to relieving the conditions of the poor, regardless of working status.

In addition, the welfare system's expansion proceeded incrementally, meeting the needs of specific groups of people, rather than through any overall effort to create a general welfare system available to all citizens. This piecemeal approach lasted until 1978, when a general health reform act guaranteed equality to all citizens in terms of access to health care. But even this reform reinforced the trend towards a limited role for nonprofits, and the inclusion of private institutions in the public National Health System.

Recent years have seen a reversal of this trend. The fiscal crisis of the welfare system has motivated the State to contract services to private nonprofit organizations, primarily in the field of social welfare, but also, to a limited extent, in health. Many of these contractors derive from a Catholic tradition. Others, however, are of recent vintage and reflect a new secular social awareness of altruism, the importance of caring for other people.

Major types of organizations

An accepted definition of nonprofit organizations does not exist as such in the Italian legal system. Little by way of explanation can be found in general legislation (the codes), which means that any usable definition must be inferred from the abundant special legislation, such as the national law establishing incentives for private organizations operating in the Third World, or various regional laws governing health and welfare.

The most common popular terms used to refer to components or subsectors of the nonprofit sector include:

- *terzo settore*: third sector, or *terzo sistema*: third system;
- *associazionismo:* the world of private associations, including foundations; and
- *volontariato*: the world of voluntarism.

The American term "nonprofit" is also gaining wider acceptance.

Terzo settore

The term that most closely resembles the American idiom is *terzo settore* (third sector) or *terzo sistema* (third system). However, while this generic expression serves to distinguish Italian nonprofit organizations from those in the market and government sectors, it often includes organizations omitted from the nonprofit sectors of other countries, such as trade unions and cooperatives. It is the term used by the *Istituto per la Ricerca Sociale* (Ranci and Bassanini, 1990).

Associazionismo

Associazionismo refers to the widespread world of associations regulated by the Civil Code. Associations are in the areas of sports, culture, religion, social care, and virtually every other field. The term applies to any group of people who organize to engage in any activity other than business. Therefore it does *not* necessarily suggest "social concern," a concept applicable to the *volontariato* (see below). Associations, in fact, can simply pursue the well-being or aims of their own members, as in leisure and sports associations.

Civil Code Regulation. The Italian Civil Code regulates the basic legal aspects of both business corporations and associations. The Code's fifth book applies to business corporations, or *società*, which undertake economic activities and distribute profits to the owners. The Code's first book applies to associations, foundations, and committees.

As happens in most civil law countries, the distinction between the two types of organizations is *not* based on whether profits or assets are distributed, a constraint never actually imposed by law in Italy. Rather, the difference pertains either to the objectives or *to the nature of activities* performed by the organization. Thus, a self-interested or business aim is typical of a corporation; an altruistic aim would suggest associations and foundations.

Legal scholars have explored the distinction at length, but wide areas of disagreement remain (Ponzanelli, 1985). Some scholars focus on organizational objectives. They argue that the aim of a business corporation is economic, while that of an association is "idealistic," pertaining to the sphere of ideals. Yet this distinction is only partially satisfactory, in so far as economic activity may be needed to obtain "ideal" goals. Other scholars define the distinction between corporations and other organizations in terms of their respective activities. Business corporations, they argue, produce goods and services, while other organizations satisfy needs, such as the need to gather and discuss political issues, or listen to music, or help neighbors.

Forming an association. While foundations must be incorporated to acquire legal or juridical standing *(personalità giuridica)*, associations can apply for a decree of incorporation and become *associazione legalmente riconosciute* (incorporated associations), or they may simply remain as *associazione non riconosciute* (unincorporated associations).

The formation of an unincorporated association is a simple matter. It is a "private act" which requires writing a charter and registering with a notary. The entity receives no public recognition, and is exempt from registering with a public agency. Because of this easy and inexpensive procedure, associations have mushroomed in the last forty years.

By contrast, a complex and time-consuming procedure is entailed in an association's incorporation. Its charter must be legally recognized with a public deed, inquiries must be made to ensure that the association's wealth is appropriate to the achievement of its goals, and juridical standing must be conferred by Presidential decree – a concession of the State, not a right of the organization. The incorporation process takes several years, and any modification of the association's charter must be approved by governmental authority.

Why, then, would an association go through the process of acquiring the status of *associazione legalmente riconosciuta?* An association would want to become incorporated primarily to guard its members against liability for losses or damages. An association with this status is solely liable; its members' wealth cannot be touched. Secondarily, an association would seek incorporation because unincorporated associations cannot own real estate, nor receive donations or bequests. Buying and selling real estate or accepting donations and bequests, however, is not much easier for incorporated associations. Those actions, in fact, require specific governmental authorizations.

Fiscal and tax regulations. Fiscal regulations provided by the *Testo Unico sulle Imposte Dirette* introduce a taxonomy different from the Civil Code. The regulations treat *enti commerciali* (commercial bodies or entities) separately from *enti non commerciali* (non-commercial entities). The former include societies specified in the Italian Code's fifth book, such as joint stock companies, cooperatives, other private organizations whose main aim is a commercial activity, and associations operating some type of commercial enterprise. Non-commercial entities include both public organizations and private non-business societies whose main aim is other than commercial.

Commercial bodies pay income taxes according to their total annual income, currently at a 46 percent rate. Non-commercial bodies enjoy income tax exemption for all activities, regardless of whether they are intended to generate profits, with the exception of those specified under Article 2195 of the Civil Code. The Code lists the following non-exempt activities:

- industrial operations involved in the production of goods and services;
- commercial operations involved in distribution;
- transportation of goods and people;
- banking and insurance; and
- activities that supplement the above.

Any income derived from these specified activities is subject to taxation.

Any other activity, including one which generates a profit, is exempt from taxes so long as it meets two criteria: it must be strictly connected to the main goal of the organization; and it must provide services "at cost" and without "specific organization." Non-commercial entities are also exempt from value added tax for selected operations. It bears repeating that tax exemption does not apply to the absence of a profit aim; it applies only to income generated by activities that are legally defined as "non-commercial."

Tax deductibility of donations. Tax deductibility is allowed mainly for donations made to associations and foundations. By Presidential Decree (917/1986, Articles 10 and 65), individual and business donations may be deducted from income tax:

- Without limit for gifts to incorporated foundations and associations dealing with the study, exhibition, preservation, maintenance, and restoration of prominent art works (Law 512/1982). Research and exhibitions, however, must be approved by the Ministry of Cultural Heritage.
- Up to 2 percent of total income for gifts to qualified organizations operating relief and development projects in developing countries (Law 49/1987).
- Up to 2 percent of total income for gifts to incorporated foundations and associations active in performing arts (Law 163/1985).
- Up to 2 million lire (about $1700 at the 1990 rate of exchange) for donations to *organizzazioni di volontariato* (voluntary organizations) regulated by Law 266 of 1991 (see below).

Businesses, in addition, may deduct up to 2 percent of income for gifts to incorporated organizations (not limited to foundations or associations) active in scientific research, education, instruction, recreation, and social and health insurance (Law 512/1982), and for donations to universities. Moreover, they can deduct 50 percent of their donations, or up to 100 million lire (about $83,000), to *organizzazioni di volontariato* regulated by Law 266 of 1991 (see below).

Increasing donor choice. Italian donors may choose not only where to donate their own money, but also where certain government funds may be allocated. This tendency toward donor choice was begun by a 1985 agreement between the State and the Holy See (Law 222). According to the law, the government dispenses 0.8 percent of its annual tax revenues (roughly 800 billion lire in 1989, or almost $583 million at that year's exchange rate) to public organizations with social or humanitarian goals, and to private "religious, educational, or charitable programs under direct control of the Catholic Church or of any other Church that has signed an agreement with the State." When filing annual tax returns, each individual may recommend how these revenues shall be allocated. The amounts eventually distributed to various recipients reflect the proportion of taxpayer choices (not the share of taxes paid by each individual).

It has been estimated that about three-quarters of the 0.8 percent of government revenues for charitable purposes goes to the Catholic Church – an amount equal to more than 600 billion lire (almost $501 million). Part of it supports charitable purposes both in Italy and abroad. The remainder, perhaps 350 billion lire in 1990 ($292 million), is allocated to support clergy and other church personnel. Moreover, 10 billion lire ($8.3 million) in clergy support is generated through individual donations. The agreement, in fact, allows individuals to make tax-deductible donations to the clergy. As previously noted, the government had provided a *congrua* (subsidy) to some 29,000 Catholic priests to supplement the income they received from ill-paying *benefici* (endowments), and to compensate the Church for properties confiscated during the second half of the nineteenth century.

Under the law, this public support system changed effectively in 1990, when the Church established local, legally recognized *istituti per il sostentamento del clero* (institutes for support of the clergy), as well as a central institute. Individuals may deduct up to two million lire (around $1,700) each for donations to the central institute.

Volontariato

The term *organizzazioni di volontariato* (voluntary organizations), or simply *volontariato*, refers to a vast array of private organizations addressing problems primarily in health and social services (Ascoli, 1985; Prina, 1983). The term applies both to philanthropic organizations which assist the general public, and to mutual or self-help groups tending to the problems of their own members. The groups may choose which legal status to secure, or they may remain without legal recognition.

Workers may be either voluntary or salaried. While the roles of each are the subject of much debate, the recent trend is toward a significant percentage of paid staff members.

New legal trends

Since 1990, important legislation dealing with voluntary and non-profit organizations has been passed by the Italian Parliament. The new laws regulating voluntary organizations and *cooperative sociali* (social cooperatives) represent a major change to the piecemeal approach that characterized Italian legislation in this area in the past.

Regulating *Volontariato*

Law 266, enacted in 1991, defines *organizzazioni di volontariato* (voluntary organizations) as those that pursue participation and "solidarity" purposes – what in other countries might be called charitable aims. Although the law doesn't mandate any legal form to these voluntary organizations, it aims primarily at regulating the vast array of unincorporated associations acting in the health and social fields that rely heavily on volunteers. The law notes that such groups should not seek profits, and that volunteers should play a "prominent and conclusive" role in management and service provision.

Sources of income may include government grants and contributions and bequests from both members and nonmembers, while revenues from commercial and productive (industrial) activities must play a minor role. Unlike regular unincorporated associations, unincorporated *organizzazioni di volontariato* may purchase real estate and accept donations and bequests. Donations made to *organizzazioni di volontariato* are also tax-deductible.

Organizzazioni di volontariato, when not established as *società* (business corporations) regulated by the fifth book of the Civil Code, or as *cooperative* (cooperatives), are exempt from value added taxes on their "solidarity" services, and from income taxes on their marginal commercial activities.

Cooperative Sociali

The law regulating voluntary organizations deals mainly with bodies that generally do not run large operations. This differs from the law regulating *cooperative sociali* (social cooperatives) (Law 381/1991), a relatively new type of nonprofit organization previously known as *cooperative di solidarietà sociale* (social solidarity cooperatives). Essentially social cooperatives are:

- organizations providing social services to people in need; and
- organizations in which social workers and their clients work jointly to produce goods and services.

Typical activities of social solidarity cooperatives include job training for specific clientele such as the physically or emotionally disabled, drug addicts, former prisoners, etc., in community and personal social services, education, and so forth. Some of these activities are conducted through artisan workshops, agricultural enterprises or commercial businesses. Often, solidarity cooperatives sell their products and services on the open market; however, they tend to operate at a deficit, most likely because of the difficult nature of their labor force.

Prior to recent legislation (Law 381/1991), these organizations had the legal status of cooperatives, but by charter they were not allowed to distribute income earned in excess of expenses (that is, they were subject to a "non-distributive constraint"). The new law no longer requires the "non-distributive constraint" in the cooperative's charter, but relies on the classical definition of "mutual societies" instead:

- members may not obtain dividends higher than the legal interest (10 percent at present) on the amount of money given to the cooperative;
- financial reserves cannot be distributed to members; and
- in the event of dissolution, remaining assets or wealth must be disbursed for a public purpose.

Social cooperatives enjoy some fiscal advantages:

- donations and bequests are tax-exempt;
- registration fees are greatly reduced;
- sales of services in the social, educational and health fields are subject to reduced VAT rates; and
- disadvantaged people employed by the cooperatives are exempt from social security payments – roughly 65 percent of gross income for average workers (International Labor Office, 1991).

Usually, owing to their profit-making activities, cooperatives as a rule are not considered part of the nonprofit sector. Social cooperatives, however, are part of the Italian nonprofit sector. First, their business activities are in pursuit of a social goal, and not primarily for profit. Second, it is inappropriate for the cooperatives to accept the legal status either of "unrecognized association" – which means they have no legal standing – or of "recognized association," given the difficulty of obtaining that status. Other aspects of the law enforce nonprofit status on social cooperatives, too. For example, organizations must include volunteers as well as paid staff, and disadvantaged people must constitute at least 30 percent of the total labor force of programs aimed at job training.

Transformation of public banks

Until a few years ago, most public banks in Italy (about 100 savings banks and other large banks representing about 40 percent of total bank deposits) were established under the legal status of incorporated foundations or associations. Most charters stressed the "social concern" and the philanthropic attitude of the banks and their boards. This philanthropic attitude induced most public banks to donate quite a large share of their profits to nonprofit organizations (generally stated by the charters themselves), especially those acting in the areas where the banks run their business. Therefore, public banks were a hybrid of for-profit and nonprofit activities.

Law 280, passed in 1990, allowed the banks to change their legal status. Foundations (and associations) were allowed to create joint stock companies for the actual bank operations, whereas the foundations kept control of the majority of the new bank shares. Dividends paid by the bank therefore represent the income of the philanthropic foundation. The foundations may be active in scientific research, education, preservation of cultural heritage, or health. As a direct result of this law, the foundation subsector of Italy's nonprofit sector has greatly increased (Barbetta, 1992; Ranci and Barbetta, 1996).

Defining the Italian nonprofit sector

The structural–operational definition (Salamon and Anheier, 1992) gives the best available description of the Italian nonprofit sector. Nevertheless, the application of the core definition, which stipulates that nonprofit organizations be formal, private, non-profit-distributing, voluntary and self-governing, creates a few problems in the Italian context.

Formal. An organization must be formally constituted, as evidenced by either a legal charter or other form of institutional reality. Italian nonprofits meet this criteria, through both their own charters and the legal recognition granted them.

Private. An organization cannot be institutionally affiliated with the government. As previously stated, it is often difficult, if not impossible, to ascertain the public or private nature of many organizations in Italy. Legal criteria are of little utility here, in so far as the law confers some public authority on otherwise private organizations. One example is IPABs (public charities): the word "public" can be misleading, as some IPABs are legally defined as private institutions with private charters. Moreover, while IPABs are legally viewed as public entities, they are privately governed in so far as their administrators are appointed by the Church or some other nongovernmental body.

Furthermore, organizations such as the *Club Alpino Italiano* (Italian Alpine Club), the Automobile Club of Italy, the Italian Touring Club, and the *Aeroclub d'Italia* are privately constituted and governed, yet exert public powers such as issuing licenses, acting as legal monopolists in some fields, and enjoying various fiscal privileges.

At best, private incorporation will have to suffice as a measure of being privately owned in some cases. In other cases, the measure will pertain to the makeup of the governing board; and others yet must be analyzed on their own merits.

Self-governing. Internal decision-making should be uncontrolled by government or business. This criterion is problematic for two types of Italian nonprofits: Catholic hospitals, and foundations that have been generated from the transformation of certain public banks.

Hospitals owned by ecclesiastic entities recognized under civil law are legally public health organizations, subject to various controls by the Health Ministry (fees, facilities expansion or construction, new services, etc.). Nevertheless, these hospitals should be considered part of the nonprofit sector.

It may be too early to say whether the banking foundations should or should not be considered part of the nonprofit sector. At present both the banks and their newly created foundations are administered by officials appointed by the Minister of the Treasury and local authorities. Eventual inclusion of foundations will depend on what modifications, if any, are implemented to procedures used to appoint the governing board.

Non-profit-distributing. An organization should not distribute income in excess of expenses to its owners or members, but must instead use excess revenues for organizational purposes. With one curious exception, Italian law does not impose this constraint. Therefore, Italian nonprofits (such as incorporated or unincorporated associations, social cooperatives and, to a certain extent, *organizzazioni di volontariato* – those engaged in activities addressing social "ideals" rather than profit for its own sake) may, from a legal point of view, distribute profits.

According to some scholars (Preite, 1990), these nonprofits, and especially associations, may:

- engage in entrepreneurial activities, not only to pursue their main goals, but to provide services to their members. Business, in fact, can become an association's major activity (with the exception of *organizzazioni di volontariato*).
- engage in non-equal treatment of members and outsiders. For example, *de facto* profits (earnings above expenses) may be distributed to members alone.
- distribute assets to members in the event of dissolution (with the exception of social cooperatives and *organizzazioni di volontariato*).

The only Italian organizations required to abstain from profit distribution are those in the soccer business. Ironically, these groups are actually incorporated as joint stock companies (Law 91/1981), and they generally belong to large corporations or wealthy individuals. All profits must be allocated to the broad aims of the organizations – usually soccer practice – as decreed by their charters. Notwithstanding this constraint (probably enacted in response to bankruptcies in the 1970s), soccer companies should not be part of the nonprofit sector. They changed to *entrepreneurial* organization, primarily organized to promote the interests of their owners.

Conclusion

In spite of a legal system that has tended to blur the distinction between the public and private sectors in Italy, both the legislature and the general population appear to be increasingly aware of a nonprofit sector. New laws, for example, provide opportunities and fiscal advantages to voluntary organizations and social cooperatives, thereby acknowledging their social value and the role they play in the Italian welfare system. Hopefully, these and similar laws will reduce the present confusion between the public and private sectors, as they demonstrate that the satisfaction of collective needs can be accomplished by private or nonprofit organizations as well as by the State.

Notes

1   The author would like to express his thanks to Pippo Ranci for his direction, assistance, and general help in assembling and writing this chapter; and to Helmut Anheier for his useful comments on earlier versions of this chapter.

References

Ascoli, U. (ed.) (1984), *Welfare State all'Italiana*. Bari: Laterza.

Ascoli, U. (1985), "Volontariato organizzato e sistema pubblico di welfare: potenzialità e limiti di una cooperazione." *Democrazia e Diritto*, 5:75–90.

Barbetta, G. P. (1992), "La Legge Amato e le Fondazioni Bancarie: Nuovi Soggetti nel Mondo Delle Imprese Senza Fine di Lucro." *Economia e Credito*, 3(4):247–269.

Bassanini, M. C. and P. Ranci, (eds) (1990) *Non per Profitto*, Rome: Fondazione A. Olivetti.

Cavalari, P. (1988), "La legge Crispi sulle opere pie: una parabola lunga un secolo." *Prospettive Sociali e Sanitarie*, 22:6–8.

International Labour Office (1991), *Yearbook of Labour Statistics*. Geneva: International Labour Office.

Paci, M. (1989), "Public and private in the Italian welfare system," in *State, Market, and Social Regulation. New Perspectives on Italy*, ed. P. Lange and M. Regini. Cambridge: Cambridge University Press.

Ponzanelli, G. (1985), *Le nonprofit organizations*. Milan: Giuffrè.

Preite, D. (1990), "Aspetti istituzionali e normativi del terzo settore in Italia," in *Non per Profitto*, ed. M. C. Bassanini and P. Ranci. Rome: Fondazione A. Olivetti.

Prina, F. (1983), "Attualità del dibattito sul volontariato," in *Lo Stato Assistenziale tra Crisi e Trasformazione*, ed. G. Busso and C. Guala. Milan: F. Angeli.

Ranci, Ortigosa E. (1990), "La politica assistenziale," in *Le Politiche Pubbliche in Italia*, ed. B. Dente. Bologna: Il Mulino.

Ranci, P. and G. P. Barbetta (eds) (1996), *Le Fondazioni Barcarie Italiane verso l'Attività Grant-Making*. Torino: Fondazione G. Agnelli.

Salamon, Lester M. and Helmut K. Anheier (1992), "In search of the non-profit sector I: the question of definitions." *Voluntas*, 3(2):125–151. (See also Chapter 3 in this volume.)

Chapter 8

JAPAN

Takayoshi Amenomori[1]

Introduction

Recent years have seen significant changes in the Japanese non-profit sector. Within a relatively short period of time, a number of important initiatives were launched: the "1% Club" was created by the Federation of Economic Organizations, *Keidanren*, one of the major interest groups for business in Japan. Member companies of the Club pledge to donate at least one percent of their pre-tax profit for charitable purposes. As of February 1991, 203 companies have joined this club. The concept of *mecenat*, or corporate sponsorship of arts, which had previously been introduced in Japan, resulted in the establishment of the Association for Corporate Support for Arts in early 1991. At around the same time, a large public foundation for the support of art was created, and in Osaka, the Chamber of Commerce announced the start of the first community foundation in Japan. Moreover, the Council for Better Corporate Citizenship, an organization recently set up by *Keidanren*, represents a mechanism through which corporations can make tax-deductible donations to overseas recipients. Finally, in April 1991, another large public fund, the Fund for Global Partnership, was established "to help achieve closer relations between Japan and the United States, and to contribute to a better world through the cooperative efforts of both countries."[2]

To a certain degree, these initiatives, which typically involve the joint creation of a council or committee to coordinate activities as well as to allocate and to distribute funds, are in response to criticism from abroad. It was argued that while continuously expanding business overseas, Japan had not taken on broader responsibilities and was now urged to make a greater contribution to the international community. Moreover, the significant wealth accumulated in Japan since the 1960s and especially in the latter half of the 1980s may also have been a factor contributing to the expansion of nonprofit activities and philanthropy.

However, there may be other underlying reasons as well. For one, a new concern about quality of life emerged at the grass-roots level and people began to re-examine the fruits of economic success, achieved with considerable sacrifices such as long working and commuting hours, and often less enviable living conditions. Apart from that, Japanese society is now facing new kinds of social problems ranging from environmental issues and the weak integration of the foreign labor force to school violence and the situation of the elderly. These problems may require new institutional responses, and have, thereby, shifted more attention to the nonprofit sector.

It is therefore quite important and timely to seek a better understanding of the nonprofit world in Japan. That surprisingly little is known about it is, in part, a reflection of the way in which the sector is located in the institutional setup of Japanese society. Even though private nonprofit organizations have existed for centuries, they do not, in common understanding, form a sector distinct from both the public and the private business sectors. In fact, the nonprofit sector is so much influenced by the dominant other two sectors that the term *dai san sekutā* (third sector) refers to a hybrid sector of quasi-public, quasi-business organizations, but does not depict a distinct institutional sphere.

Certainly, the Japanese nonprofit sector is difficult to define and measure: many organizations are not registered, let alone incorporated. Although quite a lot of statistical material is routinely collected from nonprofit organizations, it is often impossible to separate out the nonprofit sector. Many nonprofit organizations are virtually treated as part of government. There are also many mass organizations and community-based groups which, deeply rooted in Japanese society and cultures, are difficult to describe in terms used to depict organizations in Western societies. The nonprofit sector in Japan is a mirror image of Japanese society, and a product of its complex history. Therefore, in order to understand the way the nonprofit sector is defined and located in contemporary society, it is useful to examine its history.

Historical note

Japan has a long tradition of philanthropy, though it usually represented a weak rather than strong historical current in the development of Japan. As a consequence, historical accounts and analyses too easily pass over the role and scope of traditional philanthropy in Japan, and little is known about the motives of founders as well as the activities and development of past institutions. The earliest records date back to the seventh and eighth centuries and suggest that hospitals and charities (for example, for feeding the hungry) were established within the precinct of large Buddhist temples like the *Tādaiji* and the *Shitennōji*. Such early examples of charity usually were initiated by benevolent nobles and high-ranking monks. It must be emphasized, however, that the Buddhist temples were by no means independent institutions; rather they were established in the interest of either the State or powerful clans.

Buddhist temples used to organize fundraising campaigns called *Kanjin*, in order to raise funds from the public for activities like casting Buddha images or running orphanages and homes for the aged, or for some other public purpose. *Kanjin* is considered to be one of the major indigenous forms of Japanese fundraising efforts. Buddhism in Japan was from the beginning utilized for political purposes, but became especially so after the seventeenth century, when every Buddhist temple was brought under the control of the central power, consequently losing its independence. Every household was required to register at some temple, so that the temples became part of the feudal administrative system.

However, the decline of Buddhism did not necessarily lead to an equal decline of charity itself. Charitable activities inspired by other beliefs and thoughts started to emerge, especially during the civil wars of the fifteenth and sixteenth centuries, and in the Edo period (1603–1868). For instance, wealthy merchants in Osaka, the center of commerce in the earlier Edo period, made generous contributions to private tutorial schools called *Shijuku*, where classical literature as well as modern and Western learning was taught.

These schools were organized as *Kō*, or private associations, which find their origin in the mutual-help groups gathered around temples. Private schools, however, were not confined to large cities like Edo or Osaka, and they also flourished in rural areas. In the first half of the nineteenth century, literacy was already a necessity for merchants and the better-off farmers. Thousands of village institutions known as *Terakoya* (temple schools) were in existence, and they paved the way for the modern educational system, established under the Meiji regime in the late nineteenth century.

The *Kan-on-kō* may be regarded as one of the first examples of large-scale organized philanthropy in the field of social welfare and relief. It was established in 1829, when Nawa Saburoemon Sukenari, purveyor to Lord Yoshiatsu Satake, offered to make a large donation to alleviate poverty in Akita Domain. Nawa proposed to purchase land for agricultural production, and to use the proceeds to assist local peasants and orphans. Eventually, 191 others contributed funds to this relief project. Historical documents praise *Kan-on-kō* as a financial asset that, belonging neither to the authorities nor to the people, has a special character. The *Kan-on-kō* established by Nawa still exists today as a social welfare organization (see below).

While Buddhism, and later Confucianism and Shintoism, played an important role in the development of philanthropy in Japan, there was also a short period of Christian influence. In the sixteenth century, the Jesuit missionaries established nursing homes and leprosy hospitals in different cities. Social service groups called *Misericordia* collected donations on a regular basis. Some of them survived well beyond 1638, the year Christianity was banned. It was only in the late nineteenth century that Catholic and Protestant missionaries were once again allowed to propagate Christianity. They began to establish missionary schools nationwide, especially at the secondary level.

With the exception of some prominent examples of private nonprofit initiatives, the shogunate and the provincial landlords were the main providers of public goods in general, and social services in particular. Together with a highly centralized system of governance, the dominance of the shogunate in delivering public goods left only a peripheral part to the nonprofit sector. It remained so throughout the Meiji period and much of the twentieth century until very recently.[3]

One of the first examples of organized private philanthropy in post-isolationist Japan is the *Onshi-Zaidan Saiseikai* (imperial relief association). Established in 1911, its purpose was to provide medical relief to the poor. The Emperor himself took the lead in its establishment by donating priming funds, expecting prefectural governors and leading industrialists to follow. A number of similar foundations were created in the years to follow, with or without the patronage of the imperial family. They became an important source of support for private social service institutions which had begun to emerge at around the same time after the Civil Code of 1896 provided the legal basis for incorporation in the form of a *kōeki hōjin*, or charitable association. It is important to note that the *kōeki hōjin* as regulated in Article 34 of the 1896 Civil Code were defined much more widely than is the case under current law (see below). For this reason, some nonprofit organizations which today would be established as medical corporations, religious corporations, or social welfare organizations were set up as *kōeki hōjin*, as either incorporated foundations or associations.

As Japan's economy expanded, wealthy families, especially those who owned large conglomerates called *Zaibatsu*, began to establish grantmaking foundations. Some foundations like the *Mitsui Ho-on Kai*[4] were very large indeed, even by today's standard: its annual grants to social service institutions exceeded the total amount of governmental subsidy to the same field. The creation of such large foundations, however, was not without political implications; at least in part, it was a response to criticism from ultra-nationalists, who accused the *Zaibatsu* of being corrupt, selfish, and primarily concerned with their own welfare at the expense of Japan's strategic interests.

In the 1930s and 1940s, under military dictatorship, all nonprofit organizations were subordinated to the State. Traditional youth groups which have their roots in the communities were merged into one single national organization; each industrial sector had to form a central coordinating body in Tokyo, and religious organizations were consolidated under government pressure or otherwise put themselves under common umbrella organizations. Moreover, the *Chōnaikai*, or community organizations for mutual help, were changed into instruments of government control. Sometimes called the *Showa 16 System*,[5] the totalitarian system had a lasting impact on Japanese society, including the nonprofit community, long after the war.

The war ended in Japan's total defeat. Under American occupation, Japan adopted a new constitution, and new laws facilitated the emergence of new and different types of nonprofit organizations. In the postwar period, labor unions and women's organizations began to flourish. Especially, the trade union movement, which was suppressed before and during the war, was encouraged by the occupying forces, and grew rapidly. Within a few years, labor unions were able to organize some 11 million workers. However, as the Cold War intensified, governmental control of the labor movement increased. In 1950, soon after the Korean War broke out, thousands of trade union leaders, especially members of the Communist party, lost their jobs and positions.

New social movements like the peace movement, the antinuclear movement, and the human rights movements in the 1950s and 1960s were strongly influenced by Western political currents, notably by socialist and communist ideologies. Large segments of the new social movements had a decidedly "anti-establishment" and anti-American character, often combined with pro-Soviet political attitudes. Their idealistic but confrontational style was one of the causes of factious tendencies, which led to a deep-seated distrust of movement-based nonprofit organizations on the part of the business community. By contrast, newly emerging foundations, most of which were sponsored by large corporations, were more conservative and restricted themselves primarily to grantmaking in the fields of science and technology. In the eyes of the government, they represented a useful vehicle for stimulating the modernization process of Japan, and donations to such foundations were encouraged by special tax treatment. The split between a politicized segment of associations and social movements on one hand, and the corporate world of grantmaking foundations on the other, impeded the common development of the nonprofit sector in Japan.

By the late 1960s, Japan had become one of the leading economic powers in the world, but the rapid growth also caused serious social problems such as industrial pollution and neglect of social infrastructure. Opposition movements against pollution led by local residents were generally apolitical, though confrontational. Residents exposed to extreme air and water pollution increasingly mobilized against the large corporations and the government. With the help of voluntary associations that formed around the issue, residents won all of the four major class action suits that were filed against corporations and government.

Civic movements began to mature gradually in the 1970s against the background of general affluence, increased leisure time, and a more diverse value system. Civic associations became less confrontational and more open. Concepts like "alternatives" and "networking" became popular in the 1980s. The increasing awareness of the limits to growth, triggered first by "oil shock," and later by global environmental problems, accompanied the "appeasement" of the previously confrontational process. External events influenced the shift in Japan's nonprofit sector, too. Especially after the late 1970s, when the refugees from South-East Asia (the "boat people") reached the coast of Japan, private relief agencies and non-governmental organizations (NGOs) began to proliferate. Parallel to this, many of the foundations established in the 1970s and 1980s created international programs. Today, more than half of the grantmaking foundations maintain international programs, although typically in the area of student exchange.

To summarize, several factors have contributed to the development of the nonprofit sector in Japan:

- Early on, Buddhism played an important role in the creation of indigenous philanthropic activities, although it later became less significant. Following the Buddhist influence, other religions and systems of thought, such as Confucianism and Christianity, influenced the development of the nonprofit sector in Japan.
- The acceleration of Japan's modernization in the first half of this century coincided with both an increased centralization of society and an expanded control of nonprofit activities by the State. The social and political space left for nonprofit organizations was significantly reduced. The dominance of the State culminated during the Second World War, when virtually every nonprofit organization had to put itself under an umbrella organization to serve the ends of Japan's military ambitions.
- Since the 1970s, when Japan's process of "catching up with the West" was virtually completed, social needs and values became more diverse. Owing to an increasing "internationalization" of Japan's economy, and the globalization of many social and

environmental issues, among others, the "space" for nonprofit organizations widened. It is increasingly felt that the public sector and the market alone cannot meet the needs of an increasingly diverse population. Thus, both public and private expectations of what nonprofit organizations can and should do in modern Japanese society have grown considerably. Parallel to increased expectations, the amounts of public and private support to nonprofit organizations have grown, particularly in recent years.

Major types of organizations

Before trying to define the nonprofit sector, it may be useful to know what types of private organizations exist in Japan. We will here use the legal form of establishment as a starting-point, since it is the usual way to do it in Japan, and because most official statistics use this classification for data compilation and reporting.

Below, we will examine the following types of organizations:

- *Kōeki hōjin* (charitable organizations, or public benefit organizations)
- *Shakaifukushi hōjin* (social welfare corporations)
- *Gakko hōjin* (private school corporations)
- *Shukyo hōjin* (religious corporations)
- *Iryo hōjin* (medical corporations)
- *Tokushu hōjin* (special public corporations)
- *Kōeki shintaku* (charitable trusts)
- *Kyōdō kumiai* (cooperatives)
- *Nin-i dantai* or *Jinkaku naki shadan* (unincorporated organizations)

Kōeki hōjin (charitable organizations)

Kōeki hōjin (charitable organizations) are defined in the Civil Code Article 34 as "associations or foundations relating to worship, religion, charity, science, art, or otherwise relating to public interest and not having for their object the acquisition of gain." Most private philanthropic organizations are established and incorporated under this provision. The total number of *kōeki hōjin* today is around 25,000.

The *kōeki hōjin*, sometimes also referred to as civil code corporations, may take two forms: the *zaidan hōjin* (incorporated foundation) and the *shadan hōjin* (incorporated association). In the case of incorporated foundations, the corporate status is given to assets dedicated in order to attain a given charitable objective, whereas in the case of incorporated associations, the same status is given to a group of associated persons whose aim is to attain a given charitable objective. In reality, however, the difference between the two may not be as clear as it appears in legal language.

The Civil Code of 1896, which was amended after the Second World War, defined *kōeki hōjin* much more widely, so that private schools, social welfare organizations, etc., were all included under this legal category. After that war, however, a number of separate laws were proclaimed for some of the more specialized nonprofit organizations. Even then, *kōeki hōjin* remained a diverse category. For one thing, organizations classified as *kōeki hōjin* cut across sectors and industries like social welfare, health, religion, and education, for which other forms of incorporation exist as well. Moreover, the legal interpretation of *kōeki hōjin* has changed over the years. For example, following a 1972 agreement between the relevant ministries and prefectural governments regarding the interpretation of "public benefit," only nonprofit organizations with clear, unambiguous, and direct "public benefits" are to be given the status of *kōeki hōjin*. Before the 1972 agreement, public benefit was usually interpreted in a much wider sense, but all *kōeki hōjin* approved before 1972 were allowed to retain their legal status, so that, at present, *kōeki hōjin* include the so-called *chūkan hōjin* or intermediate organizations, in addition to the purer public benefit organizations. The *chūkan hōjin* do not necessarily have the benefit of the public among their primary objectives as required by law. In most cases, they are membership associations like trade and business organizations, sports clubs, alumni associations, etc., established long ago, and would not qualify for incorporation as *kōeki hōjin* now, because they do not meet the public benefit criteria.

In addition, private nonprofit organizations co-exist with quasi-governmental entities. The latter group are established at the initiative or suggestion of governmental agencies, are usually heavily financed by governmental agencies, and are put under their tight control. Then there are the so-called *chūkan hōjin* or intermediate organizations, which do not necessarily have the benefit of the public among their primary objectives as required by the law.

In order to establish a *kōeki hōjin*, approval by the "competent governmental agency" is required. A local organization active within the borders of a prefecture may be approved by the governor, but if the organization will operate in more than one prefecture, the application for incorporation needs the approval of one of the agencies of the central government. In either case, it is a very difficult and time-consuming process, except when the government itself takes the lead in establishing a *kōeki hōjin*. Moreover, approval is also subject to the discretion of the officer in charge of the application case, and no clearly stated and standardized criteria for incorporation exist.

One of the major obstacles to creating a *kōeki hōjin* is the substantial amount of financial assets required by the public authorities prior to the actual establishment of the organization. The actual amount may vary from case to case, but it is very difficult for groups of citizens to accumulate assets of 300 million yen (US $2.3 million) or more, as required by the Ministry of Foreign Affairs. The public authorities set the actual amount of funds needed for the sustained operation of the organizations.

Once established, *kōeki hōjin* automatically enjoy several privileges, notably tax benefits. The most important ones are the exemption from corporate income tax as well as from taxation of interest income. Business activities of *kōeki hōjin* beyond a certain percentage are subject to taxation at a reduced rate.[6] Privileges as regards taxation of donors, i.e., the deductibility of donations, are also granted to corporate donors. Corporate donors may deduct donations to nonprofit organizations and political organizations up to a certain percentage of their income and capital,[7] regardless of whether the donee is incorporated or not. If a *kōeki hōjin* is given special public-interest-promoting corporate status, additional tax privileges are granted. However, individuals are usually not able to deduct donations, unless recipient *kōeki hōjin* are granted special status as *tokutei kōeki zōshin hōjin*, or "special public-interest-promoting organizations," the translation suggested by London (1991).

Shakaifukushi hōjin (social welfare corporations)

Shakaifukushi hōjin are defined and established under the Social

Welfare Services Law of 1951. Like the *kōeki hōjin*, they may be approved either by the prefectural governor or the central government, in this case by the Ministry of Health and Welfare. *Shakaifukushi hōjin* are active in such fields as services for the elderly, protection of women, maternal and child health services, and assistance to the handicapped. At present there are around 12,000 *shakaifukushi hōjin*, the single largest group being the day care centers for children under five.[8]

Article 25, clause 2 of the Constitution stipulates that the State should promote and develop social welfare. The article does not speak explicitly about the role of private institutions, and it is generally recognized that it is first and foremost the role of the State to provide social services. The role of private organizations is to supplement public services where the latter prove insufficient. This is in contrast to the situation in Germany, where the principle of subsidiarity establishes the primacy of the private nonprofit sector (Anheier and Seibel, 1993).

Most social welfare corporations are heavily dependent on public support, on average perhaps to 80–90 percent of total income. The rest is covered by fees, sales, and charges, as well as private donations largely originating from Community Chests. Very few funds are made available by private foundations. As a result, *shakaifukushi hōjin* are virtually quasi-public organizations to perform tasks entrusted to them by the central and local governments. Moreover, with the exception of a small minority, they hesitate to see themselves as private nonprofit organizations, although in legal form they are classified as private and nonprofit.

This is a peculiar situation if we consider the protection given to private nonprofit organizations by the Constitution of 1949, at a time when Japan was under occupation. According to Article 89 of the Constitution, public authorities are prohibited from providing public money to religious organizations and congregations as well as to private charitable, educational, and philanthropical activities. The original intent was to establish a clear legal and institutional separation between the public and the private sectors. This implies in essence that private organizations are ineligible to receive public sector funds, yet, at the same time, they are free from governmental control and interference. Over time, however, the interpretation of Article 89 changed significantly: now the government could support private organizations provided recipient nonprofits were under far-reaching governmental control. Thus social welfare corporations receiving public funds came under the strict supervision of the government. This, in turn, resulted in standardized social services, inertia, and loss of innovative capabilities on the part of the social welfare corporations.

The Social Welfare Services Law of 1951 provides the basis for the approval of establishment, change of statute, reporting, auditing, recommendation as to the dismissal of board members, etc. *Shakaifukushi hōjin* enjoy tax privileges similar to *kōeki hōjin*, but in order to encourage self-sufficiency, taxation on income from business activities is treated more favorably.

Gakkō hōjin (private school corporations)

Gakkō hōjin are established under the Private Schools Law of 1949. Together with other laws intended to promote and support private schools, the Law provides the legal framework for private schools. In general, the perceived role of private schools in the modernization process was similar to that of the social welfare corporations: to complement services provided by the public sector whenever these proved insufficient for financial or other reasons. Since education was seen by the authorities as one of the most important means of social control, the laws governing private schools were increasingly tightened in the course of Japan's modernization. For example, in the early Meiji period, private schools were just required to register with the Ministry of Education. After 1911, the Private Schools Order was amended and private schools were asked to seek the approval of the relevant government ministry in order to be allowed to operate. Private schools were also required to establish themselves as incorporated foundations, or *zaidan hōjin*, in order to strengthen their financial bases while at the same time moving them under closer public scrutiny. The extent of government control at that time becomes clear if we consider that the relevant public authorities had the power to dismiss teachers in private schools. Nevertheless, these schools still enjoyed a certain degree of independence, especially between 1913 and 1932 during the *Taisho* democracy. The growing militarization, however, ended this brief liberal interlude.

The postwar period saw drastic changes in public education. On the basis of the principles of the new Constitution and the Basic

Law on Education, private schools became more independent and achieved legal status equal to that of governmental schools. Private schools were established in response to increased demands for general and special education in the course of Japan's rapid economic development. To maintain financial stability and autonomy, private schools are required to establish themselves as *gakkō hōjin*, or private school corporations, based on the Private Schools Law. The Law provides for the possibility of financial support in the form of public subsidy, although this remains a controversial legal issue in view of Article 89 of the Constitution, which prohibits the authorities from extending financial support to independent organizations. Eventually, subsidies to *gakkō hōjin* became accepted on the ground that these schools had indeed a significant public character in the sense that they served the benefit of the public at large. This interpretation implied that public subsidies to private schools do not violate the intent of Article 89 of Japan's constitution. Today, about 15 percent of the revenue of private schools comes from public sources. Moreover, the portion of public subsidies has continually decreased since the 1980s, owing to the State's fiscal and budgetary difficulties.

Approval for the establishment of schools is in the hands of the Ministry of Education and Culture (for higher education) and the prefectural educational boards. Private schools can be classified into kindergartens, elementary schools, secondary schools (junior and senior high schools), institutions of higher education (colleges and universities, technical colleges), schools for the handicapped, and vocational schools. In addition to the *gakkō hōjin*, there are also a great number of schools run by individuals, especially kindergartens and vocational schools. Since no law regulates unincorporated schools, some of them may be business-oriented; but in most cases, they do not seek profits, and we treat them as part of the nonprofit sector.

As far as formal schooling is concerned, the educational services provided by the private schools are not substantially different from those supplied by the public sector: both types of schooling are under strict supervision of the Ministry of Education and Culture (or the local Board of Education), which gives detailed guidelines for curricula, facilities, teacher–student ratio, number of schooldays to be attended, and so on. The private schools have advantages over the public schools in that many of them provide education at primary, secondary, and tertiary levels successively, enabling the students to prepare themselves more thoroughly for the highly competitive entrance examinations for prestigious universities. Some private schools, notably those established by missionaries, tend to offer a more convenient learning environment. For these reasons, private schools have become an increasingly popular choice among parents and students against the background of a highly standardized public school system.

Shūkyō hōjin (religious corporations)

The basic law which governs religious organizations and congregations is the Religious Corporation Law of 1951. According to this law, religious corporations are organizations which have as their main purposes the dissemination of religious teachings and beliefs, the performance of ceremonies, sacraments and related functions, and the development of the believers or followers.

In the period before the Second World War, religion and State were not separated. What is more, a single religion, *Shintō*, was chosen to provide the emotional and ideological base for an increasingly totalitarian State. All *Shintō* shrines were put under the supervision of the Ministry of Home Affairs, unlike other religious sects and denominations, which were put under the control of the Ministry of Education. In fact, *Shintō* was for administrative reasons not considered a religion at all, and was administratively set apart and treated differently from other religious beliefs.

After the Second World War, governmental sponsorship, support, perpetuation, and control of *Shintō* was explicitly abolished, although *Shintō* was able to survive in denationalized form. Soon after the beginning of the Occupation, directives were issued by Allied Powers urging the removal of restrictions on political, civil and religious liberties, as well as the denationalization of *Shintō*. In 1951, when the occupation ended, a new law for the incorporation of religious organizations was put into effect. The basic principles underlying the Religious Corporation Law of 1951 are:

- eradication of militarism and ultra-nationalism;
- establishment of religious freedom, as stated in the Constitution; and
- separation of religion from the State.

To this end, *shūkyō hōjin* (religious corporations) provide the legal form of incorporation protected from external interference. It should be noted that it is not obligatory for religious groups to incorporate. Moreover, government officials are prohibited from requesting information about, or interfering in, religious teachings, rituals, or any other matters belonging to the religious domain. In order to strengthen their financial bases, religious corporations are assigned the legal capacity to possess, maintain, and dispose of worship facilities and other properties, and also to engage in business activities in support of their religious aims and purposes. Like *kōeki hōjin*, the *shūkyō hōjin* are exempt from corporate income tax, real estate tax, and registration tax. Although reliable data are lacking, there is evidence of significant misuse of these tax privileges by religious corporations.

As of 1989, some 184,000 religious corporations are registered with the Agency for Cultural Affairs under the Ministry of Education and Culture. Apart from these, there are a number of important liaison associations and coordinating councils at national, regional, and district levels. These organizations are established as *kōeki hōjin*, like the Association of Shinto Shrines, the Association of Shinto Sects, the All Japan Federation of Buddhist Sects, the Christian Liaison Committee of Japan, the Union of New Religious Organizations of Japan, and the National Christian Council.

Iryō hōjin (medical corporations)

Iryō hōjin are established under the Medical Service Law, proclaimed in 1948, and amended in 1950. Approval for the establishment of medical corporations is vested with prefectural governors or the Minister of Health and Welfare. Today, there are over 7,000 medical corporations. The Law of 1950 provides the basis for the supply of medical services, and enables the medical corporations to run hospitals, clinics, training institutes of personnel engaged in medical treatment, research institutes, etc. However, the law prohibits the establishment of hospitals and clinics for the purpose of making profits. Most medical corporations are actually able to sustain themselves from their own income in the form of fees and charges. For this reason the present Corporate Tax Law treats *iryō hōjin* in much the same way as business corporations. However, the Medical Service Law forbids the medical corporations to distribute profits, on the ground that their activities are closely related to the well-being of the public at large. Organizationally, medical corporations may take the form of a foundation or an association. As in the case of *kōeki hōjin*, medical foundations are defined by their endowment and financial assets, while medical associations are membership-based corporations. The capital of associations is usually owned by the members, each liable for his or her share. In order to improve the financial viability of marginal clinics, a legal amendment in law enables their incorporation on the condition that they employ at least one full-time physician or dentist.

Iryō hōjin that meet certain conditions[9] are given the status of *tokutei iryō hōjin* (special medical corporations), with tax privileges such as exemption from inheritance tax and a reduction in corporate income tax. However, their number is kept small. Finally, some long-established hospitals and clinics dating from before the Second World War are *kōeki hōjin*. They took this form because at that time, medical corporations did not exist, and they continue to enjoy tax privileges granted to *kōeki hōjin*.

Tokushu hōjin (special public corporations)

Tokushu hōjin (special public corporations) are quasi-governmental organizations created by specific legislation, either directly or through a deed of establishment by a government-appointed committee.[10] The reason why they are mentioned here is because many *kōeki hōjin* established under the civil code are quite similar to the *tokushu hōjin*; both are created and funded by the government. Moreover, some nonprofit organizations, while originally created as *kōeki hōjin*, changed into *tokushu hōjin* later. The Corporate Tax Law provides a list which names each *tokushu hōjin*, together with the specific laws that led to their creation. *Tokushu hōjin* can be classified into eight different categories, and include a diverse set of organizations: the privatized national railway companies, the Japan International Cooperation Agency (in charge of development assistance overseas), governmental banks like the Central Bank, the Japan Foundation, and many others. The Japanese Red Cross Society created in 1877 under the name of 'Philanthropic Society' may be an exception among the special public corporations, because it is a membership organization with thousands of volunteer groups. Although it does work in close coordination with the public sector, a senior official of the Red Cross Society has affirmed that it is an organization independent of government.

Kōeki shintaku (charitable trusts)

The *kōeki shintaku*, as defined in Article 66 of the Trust Act, do not possess legal personality. In their function they are quite similar to grantmaking foundations, though usually much smaller in size and with no full-time staff. Charitable trusts are simplified versions of grantmaking foundations. Except for a few cases, trusts and banking corporations assume the role of trustee. The day-to-day operations of *kōeki shintaku* are carried out by a trust officer, usually a clerk of a trust bank, unless a separate secretariat is formed by the Advisory Committee, a voluntary body which advises trustees on important matters pertaining to the *kōeki shintaku*, including the selection of grantees.

Kōeki shintaku are a relatively new phenomenon; the first was established only in 1977, when charges of unlawful management and an increasing number of defunct foundations became objects of public scrutiny. Unlike foundations, charitable trusts are usually created by individuals, and few by corporations and local governments. In the Japanese context, this form of grantmaking is perhaps best suited for well-defined programs like the provision of scholarships and the provision of financial support for the revitalization efforts of local communities.

Kōeki shintaku are exempt from income tax on financial revenues. Like *kōeki hōjin*, some *kōeki shintaku* may meet certain criteria set by the authorities to receive additional tax privileges, such as tax deductibility for individual and corporate donors. These are called *nintei tokutei kōeki shintaku*, or recognized special charitable trusts. As of March 1991, there were 344 charitable trusts, and their number has been increasing steadily in recent years.

Kyōdō kumiai (cooperatives)

Cooperatives are quite active in Japan. Farmers have their own agricultural cooperatives, and so do fishermen and foresters. They may be incorporated, and they enjoy some tax privileges. There are also quite a number of credit cooperatives. All of them are organized at the local, prefectural, and central level. At the central level, federations are mostly incorporated as *tokushu hōjin* (see above). However, here we would like to focus more on the consumer cooperatives. The larger consumer cooperatives appear very much like for-profit retailers, except for two aspects: first, they are membership-based organizations; and second, they are not profit-oriented. They do, however, distribute profits, although the amount distributed is rather nominal.

Many consumer cooperatives have a very high proportion of female members, moving such consumer cooperatives close to women's issues. Other cooperatives are actively involved in issues relating to food quality, organic farming, and the environment. Some cooperatives have even begun to participate in the electoral process and put up their own candidates in local elections.

Nin-i dantai or *jinkaku naki shadan* (unincorporated associations)

Unincorporated associations form the final component part of the nonprofit sector. In terms of number of organizations, it is the biggest part of the sector. The Economic Planning Agency refers to them as "groups for participating in social activities." Commonly called *shimin dantai* or civic groups, they are active in such fields as culture and sports, education and learning, health care, social services, improvement of the community, consumer movements, and international exchange and cooperation, among others. As the term used by the Economic Planning Agency suggests, they provide opportunities for actively participating in social life. *Shimin dantai* have proliferated in the recent decades: in 1983 the Economic Planning Agency estimated a figure of 556,000, not including community organizations and mass organizations.[11]

If one includes the community and mass organizations, the number would exceed one million. For example, the *Kodomokai* (children's associations), which have their roots in pre–modern *Kodomogumi*, are estimated to have around 150,000 groups. *Kodomokai* are formed in almost all primary school districts, and have umbrella organizations at the municipal, prefectural and national level. Among the most common activities are the organizing of traditional and modern festivals, outdoors activities, sports events, and fundraising through collection and sales of waste materials. Similarly, the *Rojin Clubs* for the elderly, which are also federated at three levels, claim to have 130,000 clubs throughout the country. Then there are the *Seinendan*, or youth clubs, which are still active in some rural areas, as well as grass-roots women's organizations.

Jichikai or *Chōnaikai*, depending on the locality, are community-based mutual help organizations. Their memberships are households, not individuals. The origin of the *Jichikai* is said to be the system of *Goningumi*, or "the group of five" in the Edo period. This system was introduced for mutual help and surveillance of the people. Approximately 90 percent of all households are members of a *Jichikai*, and their number is estimated to be around 275,000.

Jichikai have multiple functions: in most cases, they act as a communication channel between the residents and the local government. Circulation and distribution of information and official announcements, collaboration with the national census, or the distribution of insecticides are among the most common activities. The Community Chest, a mass fundraising campaign collecting more than 20 billion yen (approximately US $154 million) annually, relies heavily on the door-to-door collections of the *Jichikai* committee members, which are usually elected every year. The chairpersons of such community organizations are mostly informal leaders in that area, who often have some political influence, too. However, there are also cases where oppositional movements against the construction of highways, disposal sites, etc., are organized with the support of the *Jichikai*.

Although they are part of the "informal sector," recently the *Jichikai* were granted the possibility of incorporating with the Ministry of Home Affairs, with the purpose of giving clear ownership status to the facilities owned by the association.

In short, the *nin-i dantai* are a collection of different kinds of groups and organizations. Some of the most dynamic parts of the Japanese nonprofit sector are found here, in part because they are not subject to the complex requirements of incorporation. Moreover, lack of funds, smallness, and a loose organizational structure may contribute to the dynamism. Some organizations deliberately choose not to incorporate, and create separate bodies, often limited liability companies, to generate funds to support member activities and objectives.

The State, Japanese society, and the nonprofit sector

As already mentioned at the beginning of this chapter, it is difficult to judge whether Japanese nonprofit organizations form their own "sector" to constitute a relatively distinct institutional sphere. A large number of organizations are private, nonprofit in form, yet they may not qualify under the structural–operational definition (Salamon and Anheier, 1992), mainly because they neither are in a position to make decisions independently, nor include a sufficient element of voluntary participation. There is a fairly large gray area in the Japanese nonprofit community, and the dividing lines *vis-à-vis* both the corporate and the public sectors are blurred.

Central to our understanding of how the nonprofit sector is constituted and located in the context of Japanese society are the concepts of public and private in general, and how they relate to each other in particular. *Kan-min ittai* is a term referring to the interdependence, perhaps even a patron–client relationship, between the public and the business sectors in Japan. But to a certain extent, the term also applies to the relationship between the public and the nonprofit sector. In this section, we will try to describe this in some detail.

It is important to keep in mind the different notions of "public" and "private" in Japan when compared to Western concepts. Usually, the Japanese term for public is *kō*, while the term for private is *shi*. Hayashi and Yamaoka (1984) point out that, traditionally, *kō* refers to something which is done ostensibly or officially. It then represents the world of *tatemae*, which "refers to the standard, principle or rule to which one is bound at least outwardly" (Lebra, 1976). *Kō* as represented by the *okami* (the "above") is considered respectable and creditworthy, while *shi* as represented by *min* (the people) belongs to the sphere of one's natural, real, or inner wishes. It has the connotation of something secret, and therefore potentially dubious and suspect.

While the concepts of *kō* and *shi* are deeply rooted in Japanese culture and Confucianism, and while their connotations may have changed somewhat in recent decades, there remains nonetheless a strong tendency to regard *kō* as superior to *shi*. For example, public schools have been considered superior to private schools. An important consequence of the pattern is that private initiatives, whether for-profit or nonprofit, tend to seek the "official blessing" of the public sector. The most significant aspect of public approval is the status of legal personality granted by the government authorities to private organizations. Within the Japanese context, the complex and time-consuming registration process and over-sight procedures necessary do not carry negative connotations. Moreover, the close supervision of nonprofit corporations by pub-lic authorities implies considerable influence on the part of the government in nonprofit sector affairs. Depending on the actual public agency responsible for registering the different types of nonprofit organizations discussed above, applicants seeking incorporation are often advised to accept former bureaucrats as members of the board or as senior staff. In many cases, however, the situation is anticipated by applicants, and an offer is made to invite ex-government officials to the board of the new organiza-tions in the hope of achieving a positive impact on the public agen-cy in general, and those in charge of the registration procedure in particular.

Subsidies are also an important tool of public control. As dis-cussed above, Article 89 of the Japanese Constitution stipulates that private organizations not under public control may not receive public funds. This article was added to the draft constitu-tion in order to prevent private organizations from being mobi-lized for military purposes. As a consequence, social welfare organizations that had been supported by public funds since the pre-war period, faced serious budgetary problems. In response, Article 89 was interpreted by the Ministry of Health and Welfare in such a way that public support could be provided for private organizations under the condition that recipient organizations were put under public control. In this way, it was argued, social and welfare services that should have been provided by the pub-lic sector were supplied by private agencies, but at lower costs to the public sector.

Not only are nonprofit organizations and governmental agen-cies mutually dependent; quite a few nonprofit organizations are in fact established by the public sector itself. Local governments alone create around 100 *kōeki hōjin* yearly. There are several rea-sons for the proliferation of such organizations:

- Governmental agencies are often not able to increase the num-ber of staff, although needs may be pressing. In such cases, aux-iliary bodies are created, which take on routine activities like building management, maintenance of parks, and provision of various other services.

- Private organizations can be more cost-efficient, because they are able to generate their own income by running businesses, or through fundraising activities. They can collect fees, borrow money, and invite the participation of private investors more freely. Moreover, costs can be kept lower because of different salary scales, fewer fringe benefits, and smaller retirement payments and pensions.
- Some private organizations are created with the aim of implementing certain policies. For example, new organizations are established for starting international exchange programs or reforestation programs. Since the needs for public services are getting increasingly diversified, public service providers find it increasingly difficult to accommodate those needs. Separate organizations are also better suited as intermediaries between the government and the citizen and corporations.
- Nonprofit organizations provide acceptable positions for high-ranking government officials, who retired prior to normal retirement age, as part of personnel management schemes to promote younger staff members. Such a mechanism helps maintain the lifelong employment system of the public sector, where promotion remains based primarily on seniority.

The vertical interdependence between governmental agencies and nonprofit organizations can be observed in many fields, but it should be noted that the nonprofit organizations themselves are more often than not linked to each other in a vertical fashion that suggests government dominance. Let us examine this somewhat more closely, referring to the case of social welfare institutions.

The councils of social welfare, with their central office (National Council of Social Welfare) in Tokyo, maintain separate councils at prefectural levels as well. Both the National Council and the prefectural councils are social welfare corporations. The role of the 43 prefectural councils is to coordinate the activities of public and private agencies for social welfare in that prefecture. These agencies are categorized according to type of activities or clients, and form working groups consisting of organizations in the same field. Similarly, in every city and almost every town and village, there are councils of social welfare, which are coordinated by the council at the prefectural level. The task of the National Council then is to coordinate the work of all these councils, in close collaboration with the Ministry of Health and Welfare.

The Ministry has established centers for the promotion of volunteering at national, prefectural, and local levels. Their activities, like those of the councils, are highly standardized. Community volunteers called *minsei iin* and *jidō iin* assist the public institutions in performing their tasks. The standard number of such volunteers is now fixed at one for every 270 households in Tokyo and major cities, one for every 200 households in cities with a population of not less than a hundred thousand people, and so on. The volunteers usually serve for three years, and the standard number of them is set at 184,075 as of December 1989.

In order to supplement the income of social welfare institutions, community chest organizations are established "as an expression of mutual help among the people" (Japanese National Committee, 1990). Similarly to the councils and centers above, the Community Chest of Japan has branches at prefectural, municipal, and school district levels. Two million volunteers, consisting of students, women, *minsei iin* and others, help collect donations. Each year, more than 20 billion yen are raised and distributed. The whole fundraising campaign is coordinated by the Central Community Chest of Japan.

The above examples are characteristic for a significant part of the Japanese nonprofit sector. One could also refer to other examples, such as the youth organizations, which are similarly structured. At the grass-roots level, they are community-based, and thus the distinction between private and public becomes very blurred. And the more traditional and formal an organization, the less "voluntary" is the participation of volunteers. Many traditional volunteers may in fact respond to social pressure when deciding to volunteer.

Defining the nonprofit sector

We have described various types of what might be considered nonprofit organizations in Japan. Let us now examine whether they will indeed pass as nonprofit organizations, using the structural–operational definition as a frame of reference. The structural–operational definition specifies several criteria (Salamon and Anheier, 1992):

- formal
- private
- non-profit-distributing
- self-governing
- voluntary.

Let's turn to the criterion "formal" first. While it applies in general, there are nonetheless large numbers of groups and organizations that may not meet this criterion. These are groups at community levels, whose memberships are often limited to certain age groups, or by sex or locality. Some of them have their roots in traditional community organizations, and it may not be appropriate to label them "nonprofit organizations," a term heavily influenced by the Western world. Such organizations may be part of the "informal sector," and may not qualify as belonging to the nonprofit sector, because they are not formally organized as such. In most cases, however, they have a formal peak association at the prefectural and national level, and through such vertically structured networks assist local governments in implementing certain policies.

In general, it may be safe to say that the criterion "private" is not so much a problem in Japan, except in the case of special public corporations which have a hybrid public–private character. They should be considered as public institutions, and excluded from the nonprofit sector. Other organizations need to be examined on their own merit, such as the Red Cross Society and the Japan Foundation. Both, however, are treated as part of the nonprofit sector in Japan's National Accounts and in the annual survey of non-profit organizations conducted by the Economic Planning Agency.

The criterion "not-for-profit" is more difficult. For one thing, many "nonprofit" organizations, including private schools, charitable organizations, and religious corporations, are engaged in business activities. This is a problem in so far as *de facto* business enterprises may misuse the privilege of lower income tax rates and not reinvest profits for the benefit of the general public. There have been cases where nonprofit organizations were acquired for the sole purpose of being used as tax shelters. Finally, trade associations serve primarily their members' interests, and while they may neither generate nor distribute profits, they are at least indirectly related to for-profit activities.

The fourth criterion, "self-governing," causes problems too. The majority of *kōeki hōjin* (charitable organizations) and *shakaifukushi hōjin* (social welfare corporations), both important components of the nonprofit sector in Japan, are not able to make independent decisions. They are in reality part of the public sector, although legally they are in the private, nonprofit sector. It would be tempting to adopt two definitions: a wide definition, where all *kōeki hōjin, shakaifukushi hōjin* and the like are included in the nonprofit sector, and a narrower and more selective definition. However, the narrow definition would face practical difficulties, because no widely applicable set of criteria could be found to distinguish private from public and quasi-private from quasi-public nonprofit organizations. We therefore propose to adopt the wide definition and to add the necessary qualifications when necessary.

The community mutual-help organizations, vast in numbers but small in terms of economic size, present another set of problems. Are they not part of the government, considering their role as conduits for governmental agencies, especially in recent years? Are we talking about the same thing if we say in Western terms that they are run by "volunteers," whereas in fact not very many people would like to be one? In the Japanese context, there often is no clear dividing line between volunteering and mobilization through group pressure. Moreover, very few *kōeki hōjin* have volunteers as staff. Of course the board members usually work without compensation, and in that sense, they are volunteers. But then, we also have to keep it in mind that most board members tend to be passive and may take part in the decision-making process only nominally.

Conclusion

As we have seen, Japan does have a long history of philanthropic activities, and activities performed neither by the government nor by any commercial organization. Furthermore, there are a great number of groups and organizations which may at first sight be classified as part of the nonprofit sector. However, if we apply the structural–functional definition, parts of the Japanese nonprofit sector are moved to a borderline area. There may be several reasons for this. First, quite a number of the more established, incorporated organizations, while private in form, are in reality extended arms of governmental agencies. They were established at the initiative of the public sector to serve specific purposes, and remain under public sector control. Second, we saw that some groups and organizations at community levels, rooted in traditional Japanese culture, may be part of the informal sector.

While all this makes defining and measuring the nonprofit sector a difficult and complicated process, it is an important task if we want to find out how public and private domains relate to each other, and what the economic and social contribution of the nonprofit sector is in one of the world's most successful economies. It is often assumed that the nonprofit sector is insignificant in Japan. As we have discussed, the Japanese nonprofit sector is in fact not so small and insignificant if defined more broadly, and if we appreciate the complex relationship between the public and the private in this country.

Notes

1 The author and editors wish to thank Ms Mio Ohta and Helmut Anheier for their help in writing and editing this paper.

2 This quotation is taken from the "Program Guidelines of the Japan Foundation Center for Global Partnership."

3 The Meiji Restoration of 1868 opened the door to the Western world, ending the policy of national isolation that had lasted for more than two centuries. Beginning with the Meiji period, governments were determined to turn Japan into an affluent country with a strong military force.

4 *Ho-on* means repaying one's obligation, in particular the *on* to the State.

5 The 16th year of the *Showa* era corresponds to 1941, the year Japan started the war against the United States.

6 The reduced tax rate is 27 percent at present, against the normal corporate income tax rate of 37.5 percent.

7 The ceiling is derived from the following calculation: (0.5 (0.25 percent of net worth + 2.5 percent of taxable income)).

8 By contrast, kindergartens in Japan are educational facilities supervised by the Ministry of Education and Culture.

9   For example, the representation or family members on the governing
    board of the organizations may not exceed 40 percent; the organiza-
    tions must contribute to the "public benefit" by offering medical ser-
    vices in areas with acute shortages of clinics and hospitals, or at
    reduced rates to low-income people.
10 There are still other forms of public corporations. The National
    Institute for Research Advancement (NIRA) is neither a *tokushu hōjin*
    nor a *kōeki hōjin*, but a *ninka hōjin* or recognized corporation estab-
    lished under a separate law. It was created at the initiative of repre-
    sentatives of the central and local governments, business, labor
    unions, and others.
11 Community and mass organizations in Japan are based on the prin-
    ciple of opting-out rather than the principle of opting-in. In other
    words, inhabitants of local communities are members of community
    organizations by default. While still widely applying, the opt-out
    membership principle has been changing over the years.

References

Anheier, Helmut K., and Wolfgang Seibel (1993), "Defining the nonprof-
    it sector: Germany," *Working Papers of the Johns Hopkins Comparative
    Nonprofit Sector Project*, No. 6. Baltimore: The Johns Hopkins Institute
    for Policy Studies. (See also Chapter 6 in this volume.)
Hayashi, Yūjiro, and Yoshinori Yamaoka (1984), *Nihon no Zaidan*. Tokyo:
    Chuo-koronsha.
Japanese National Committee, ICSW (1990), *Social Welfare Services in
    Japan*, rev. edn. Tokyo: Japanese National Committee.
Lebra, Takie Sugiyama (1976), *Japanese Pattern of Behavior*. Honolulu: The
    University Press of Hawaii.
London, Nancy R. (1991), *Japanese Corporate Philanthropy*. New York and
    Oxford: Oxford University Press.
Salamon, Lester M., and Helmut K. Anheier (1992), "In search of the non-
    profit sector I: the question of definitions." *Voluntas*, 3(2):125–151. (See
    also Chapter 3 in this volume.)

Chapter 9

SWEDEN

Tommy Lundström and Filip Wijkström[1]

Introduction

Limited knowledge of the Swedish nonprofit sector has resulted in the lack of an adequate framework for discussing and debating the sector's nature and future. Existing terminology offers a complex mixture of sometimes overlapping, sometimes contradictory, terms and concepts. For these reasons, the idea of treating the diverse set of nonprofit or voluntary institutions as a more or less single entity, which this chapter attempts to accomplish, is relatively new in Swedish thinking. Some international researchers even question the existence of a nonprofit sector in Sweden (Boli, 1991).

Conceptual deficiencies notwithstanding, the Swedish nonprofit sector has received some attention from researchers interested in the comparative analysis of welfare service delivery systems. James (1989) argues that her findings of a small Swedish nonprofit sector result from the considerable homogeneity of Swedish society. In this undertaking, however, she seems to confuse the size of the service-delivery activities of the sector with its entire size. This is important, since the traditional welfare service production of the Swedish nonprofit sector is small in relation to its other activities, and especially when viewed from an international perspective. In context, by including a broader set of activities and types of organizations, such as the participation of voluntary movements and activities of church institutions, we obtain a quite different picture – one of a relatively large and significant nonprofit sector.

Likewise, focusing largely on service providers, Boli (1992) finds the Swedish nonprofit sector less independent of the State than is, for example, the case in the United States, and argues that the Swedish sector is too closely tied to the government. Because of such rather narrow conceptual frameworks, James and Boli underestimate the size and importance, as well as the independent role, of the Swedish nonprofit sector. There is substantial empirical evidence that the Scandinavian nonprofit sector has had a considerable impact on society during the twentieth century, and that it evolved consistently with the welfare state, rather than in opposition to or instead of it (Selle, 1993; Kuhnle and Selle, 1992a; 1992b; see also Salamon, 1987). In contrast to other countries, however, the Swedish nonprofit sector developed less in the fields of education, health and social services, and more in the areas of culture, leisure, and advocacy.

Some parts of the Swedish nonprofit sector have been studied by researchers specifically interested in political science and social movements. Social movements, or popular mass movements, play a major role in the Swedish nonprofit sector. Research has especially focused on the early movements: the labor movement, the cooperative movement, the temperance movement, the free church movement, and the sports movement (Engberg, 1986; Lundkvist, 1977; Olson, 1993; Pestoff, 1991). Other researchers proceed from a different perspective, from which they view nonprofit organizations as elements of a larger power structure in which the nonprofit organizations represent different interest groups, often in conflict with other interests or the State (Lewin, 1992; Micheletti, 1994; Pettersson *et al.*, 1989).

In our view, a comprehensive picture of the Swedish nonprofit sector that explores its historical roots, its political, economic, and legal environment, and its potential for adapting to changing demands, has not yet been developed. We intend to remedy this here with a conceptual framework that encompasses different parts of Swedish society not normally covered by a single concept. In so doing, we are aware that the types of organizations included do not constitute a homogeneous grouping, and that in all likelihood the various subgroups will differ in structure, will fulfill different functions, and will provide some services not normally seen in the nonprofit sectors of other countries. Nevertheless, we hope, by introducing this different framework, to stimulate a renewed interest in the Swedish sector and to encourage new angles for its analysis.

Historical notes

The history of the nonprofit sector in Sweden is largely one of its relation to the State. State–nonprofit relations are of vital importance, not only for the last 50 years, the era of the Swedish welfare state, but even as early as the sixteenth century. The key position of the popular mass movements, with their emphasis on membership, activism, and democratic decision-making, is another important element of the sector's history (Olson, 1993).

Before the Swedish Reformation began in the early sixteenth century, organized charity was a matter for the Church, as it was in the rest of the Catholic world at that time. The Reformation did not abolish Church responsibility for poor relief, and when King Gustav Vasa seized the property of the Church, he continued some of the existing arrangements for the poor and sick. According to the Lutheran faith, however, the peasants, the parish, and the State had different obligations to the poor. To differing degrees and at different times, conflicts concerning responsibility toward the poor came to characterize poor relief, and would influence poor-relief legislation for centuries to come. Because of these conflicts, but also in response to the persistent shortages in available resources for the poor, groups from the growing middle class, inspired by the example of medieval guilds, introduced social-insurance arrangements early in the eighteenth century, in an effort to provide support for widows and orphans. In addition, homes for the aged were started as an alternative to the poorhouses (Carlsson and Rosén, 1962; Qvarsell, 1993).

Although the overall power of the Church was diminished by the Reformation, representatives of the Church predominated in areas such as poor relief and education through the centuries. This was especially evident at local levels, where the clergy held important positions prescribed by law even into the twentieth century. A dominant Lutheran state Church with considerable influence in these areas could affect service production outside the state sector. For example, when a state compulsory public school system was introduced in 1842, there was no competition from strong religious movements. But the state Church acquired a powerful influence over local schools (Richardson, 1990; SOU, 1964).

Breakthrough for charity organizations

With the nineteenth century came a breakthrough for charitable activities, as new organizations emerged in response to social tensions and poverty. These associations drew no clear distinction between private charity and poor relief organized by municipalities. In fact, municipal poor relief was often financed by individual gifts and other charitable contributions (Qvarsell, 1993; Åberg, 1988).

At the beginning of the nineteenth century, charity organizations were dominated by middle-class men, but by the end of the century women had assumed a leading role in philanthropy both as to membership and the ideological commitment of the organizations. Consistent with this "feminization" was a transition from a patriarchal orientation to one of personal assistance that would supplement the recipient's own efforts. Institutions were set up for young people – orphanages and reformatories – providing for handicapped, deprived, and delinquent children. These initiatives came from individuals, associations, and foundations inspired by the increased and highly popular recognition of the need for child welfare at that time (Bramstång, 1964; Lundström, 1993; Qvarsell, 1993; Åberg, 1988).

In 1903 *Centralförbundet för socialt arbete* (The National Association for Social Work, CSA) was founded. This represented both a peak and a turning-point for organized charity. CSA was devoted to changing state policies on poor relief, child welfare, and other welfare policies. Because of CSA's work, leading members of nonprofit organizations came to occupy prominent positions in the social welfare State bureaucracy. This development is important in understanding the historically close links between the state and the nonprofit organizations that exist to this day.

During the twentieth century, many social welfare activities carried out by philanthropic organizations declined in importance with the growth of the welfare state. A number of activities were taken over by the State, often at the initiative of the organizations themselves. This process was mostly without conflict, but at times services run by nonprofit organizations were forced out of business by withdrawal of subsidies, or through legislation making it difficult to receive state support. Although the number of nonprofit service providers substantially declined, these organizations continued to serve as innovators in exploring alternative methods for meeting social needs (Boalt *et al.*, 1975; Höjer, 1952; Ström-Billing, 1991; Qvarsell, 1993).

Foundations

There are examples of foundations in areas such as poor relief and education, from before the beginning of the eighteenth century. By the end of the nineteenth century, foundations were commonly devoted to poor relief, immediately followed by child welfare and education. Economically, the foundations were strongest in education, where they often provided grants to students above the primary school level (Frii, 1985; 1989; Förslag till lagar om registrerade föreningar, 1903).

The internationally best-known Swedish foundation – the Nobel Foundation – was set up at the end of the nineteenth century, and its first prizes were awarded in 1901. In 1918, the Wallenberg family, one of the leading families in Swedish finance, established the most important of several foundations they created during the early part of the century. Its earliest charter stated that the foundation's purpose was to support religious, charitable, social, scientific, and cultural activities, but also to promote trade and industry (Hoppe *et al.*, 1992). Today, the largest Swedish foundations are major funders of research. And as the case of the Wallenberg foundations illustrates, some have been instrumental in controlling significant parts of Swedish industry (Holmström and Roos, 1985). As a consequence, concerns have been raised about the tax status of foundations, and some foundations are now subject to a certain degree of public control (Frii, 1985; 1989).

The development of the popular mass movements

The latter part of the nineteenth century saw the birth of the major popular mass movements, frequently inspired by similar movements in other countries. These movements created new forms of association that included the free churches, the modern temperance movement, the labor movement, consumer cooperatives, the sports movement, and the adult education institutes (Johansson, 1993; Lundkvist, 1977). The most important organizations among them were established during the last three decades of the nineteenth century: the initial growth of the sports movement took place during the 1870s and 1880s; the Social Democratic party was founded at the end of the 1880s; the Swedish Trade Union Confederation was founded about ten years later; and the labor movement and the consumer cooperatives were in their formative years just before 1900.

The period from the 1930s to the 1960s saw the labor movement at its peak in terms of both influence and membership. During this same period, however, the temperance movement and the free churches lost members and suffered a decline in influence (Johansson, 1980; 1993).

New social movements emerged after the Second World War. The growing number of immigrants after the war led to the founding of a number of immigrant organizations (H. Bäck, 1983). In the 1960s and 1970s, the movement of, and for, the handicapped gathered momentum (Holgersson, 1992). Similarly, the 1970s and 1980s were active years for the environmental and women's movements. The referendum on nuclear power in 1980 was an immense manifestation of the environmental movement's influence, and in 1988 a "green" party, *Miljöpartiet De Gröna*, was voted into parliament. The women's movement has not been marked by the establishment of a new distinct political party, but rather by the existence of loosely-linked networks within established political parties, within existing women's organizations and trade unions, and in the general public.

A Swedish nonprofit sector

The two main types of nonprofit organizations in Sweden are the nonprofit association (*ideell förening*) and the foundation (*stiftelse*). There is no specific legislation on these *ideell* associations, and the new legislation on foundations is very recent, but the distinction between association (*förening*) and foundation (*stiftelse*) is crucial. Other concepts that are important in defining the sector are the notion of membership, and the orientation toward the public good. An interesting and somewhat unique characteristic is the ambivalent stance of Swedish society towards the idea of charity. Finally, there are no direct counterparts in Swedish to the British and American concepts of a nonprofit sector.

The sector in Sweden is heterogeneous and difficult to fit under a single rubric. According to a recent survey, none of the major concepts used in Sweden covers more than 50 percent of the organizations in the sector,[2] and there have been no serious attempts to describe the whole of the sector with one single term or concept. The terms most frequently used at this time are: popular movement, interest organization, voluntary sector, and *ideell* sector. Other notions such as civil society, informal sector, social economy, informal network, or leisure sector are also used, though more infrequently. These different concepts often refer only to subgroups, and sometimes include organizations or activities not customarily included in the nonprofit sector, or those that serve primarily political purposes (see for example Blennberger, 1993; Burenstam Linder, 1983; Micheletti, 1994; Olson, 1990; 1993; Swedberg, 1993).

The association versus the foundation

An association is created in Sweden when a number of individuals (or legal entities) join to cooperate toward a common objective. The connotative emphasis of the Swedish term *förening* is more on the collectivity than on the individuals who join together to form it. This would distinguish it from the American usage of the term "association," which attributes more substance to the individuals, suggesting that they merely associate rather than unite (Boli, 1991).

The main characteristics of a foundation may be somewhat more troublesome to identify, since there is no specific legislation on the subject. However, a recent parliamentary resolution based on a government proposal (Proposition, 1993) has introduced completely new legislation governing foundations. Under these new laws, a foundation is created through the permanent designation of a certain property to be administered autonomously for a clearly specified purpose. Instead of resting on individuals as members, as is the core criterion for an association, the foundation is based solely on the autonomous property (or endowment) administered to ensure the accomplishment of its objectives (Norin and Wessman, 1993).

The idea of membership

A distinct and very important feature of the nonprofit sector in

Sweden is the high degree of association membership among the population, in both absolute and relative terms, as compared to other industrialized nations (Pestoff, 1977). Sweden is often described as a thoroughly organized nation. An official 1987 report identified 145,000 individual membership associations affiliated to regional or national organizations, and 50,000 local associations not connected to any umbrella organization. Most significant in terms of membership are cooperatives (mainly housing and consumer cooperatives), sports associations, and trade unions (SOU, 1987).

Membership is thus a central concept for understanding the specifics of the Swedish nonprofit sector. In fact, associations dedicated to the promotion of ideas and furthering the interests of their members as well as the public good are characteristic of the Swedish nonprofit sector. Further, nearly 50 percent of the Swedish people are active as volunteers in different associations. This figure contradicts the common belief that Swedes are passive where the nonprofit sector is concerned. Although comparisons must be made with great caution, it seems that Swedes are almost as active in the nonprofit sector as, for instance, the citizens of Great Britain (Jeppsson Grassman, 1993).

Association membership among the Swedish people has increased throughout the twentieth century. This is especially true for the labor unions and the sports movement, while the free churches and the temperance movement have suffered a substantial decrease in membership. Today, the total number of memberships amounts to approximately 30 million. However, membership numbers do not reveal the whole picture. The established popular mass movements and the political parties do, in fact, have problems with a low degree of member activity (Blomdahl, 1990).

Multiple umbrella organizations are another important aspect of the Swedish nonprofit sector. Especially in the labor market and in the older cooperative movement, joining forces into federations is very common. Since the nonprofit sector in Sweden is heavily organized and structured, such federations are often important actors on the national scene (Swartz, 1994). Some of these federations and umbrella organizations emerged when independent smaller groups joined forces, while others were established by larger parent organizations.

The public good

The concept of the "public good" is expressed by the terms *allmännyttig* and *ideell* both in everyday language and in the legal literature and legislation, but *ideell* has a broader meaning than *allmännyttig*. There is no good translation for the term *ideell*, which can refer to the input, such as unremunerated work (*ideellt arbete*), to the activity itself (*ideell verksamhet*) or to the aim of the activity (*ideellt syfte*). Although its connotations include concepts such as "altruistic," "nonprofit," "voluntary," or "public good," none of these English words alone captures the full meaning of *ideell* in Swedish.

Charity

The category "charitable organizations" is conspicuously absent from official Swedish social and economic statistics. From this it can be concluded that, since the State bears the responsibility for domestic social welfare, there may be less need for such organizations. While this conclusion is correct, we believe that the reasons are more complex and cannot be explained solely by reference to the welfare state. First, the Swedish notion of charity (*välgörenhet*) has a narrower meaning than its English counterpart, being reserved exclusively for activities in the field of social welfare. Further, the preliminary results of our survey (see Note 2) show that only 7 percent of responding organizations identify themselves as charities. If they do not identify themselves publicly as charitable organizations, it is because charity has a somewhat negative connotation in Sweden, stemming partly from the image of poor, helpless human beings heavily dependent on a wealthy, paternalistic, sometimes capricious upper class. As a result, not even internationally oriented charity organizations are labelled charities in Sweden. Most organizations prefer to be regarded as part of a popular mass movement or humanitarian activity (Blennberger, 1993; James, 1989; Kuhnle and Selle, 1992a; Qvarsell, 1993).

Folkrörelse (popular mass movement)

Folkrörelserna, the popular mass movements, are an interesting but not clearly defined type of organization found in Scandinavian countries. *Folkrörelse* indicates the existence of a strong bond and mutual trust between the movement and the general public. Many organizations seek to be publicly associated with the idea of "movement," even though they may not be a movement in the traditional sense of the word. In our survey, more than 40 percent of the respondents claimed to be popular mass movement organizations, but only 22 percent of the foundations so described themselves.

From an international perspective, the idea of a popular mass movement often carries a slightly revolutionary message. In the past, the Scandinavian, and Swedish, popular mass movements frequently were part of an anti-authoritarian – although comparatively peaceful – struggle against State and capitalist structures perceived as oppressive. During the Vietnam War era, demonstrations against the U.S. military presence in Indochina flared up, but these never consolidated into a strong student or civil-rights-type movement.

In a narrow sense, the popular movements in Sweden are divided into two groups. The older of these is generally associated with the powerful Swedish labor movement, but also includes the free churches and the temperance movement. The more recent grouping includes the women's movement and the environmental movement. While these younger movements still experience difficulties in establishing their own identities, the old movements of the working class continue to exercise a strong influence on political and social life (Eyerman and Jamison, 1991). In a broader sense, popular movements also include consumer cooperatives, the sports movement, and the adult education institutes (Elvander, 1972; Engberg, 1986; Johansson, 1980).

Some early attempts to define *folkrörelse* emerged from the works of Thörnberg (1943) and Heckscher (1951), who included in that concept both altruistic and interest-based organizations, provided that they are broadly-based and democratic. Broadness and democracy are also emphasized in later definitions, which also require that the organization carry an ideological message, be open to everyone, strive to create opinion, and be independent of government (Engberg, 1986; Jonsson, 1995; Svedberg, 1981). Engberg (1986) suggests that the notion of *folkrörelse* could be confined to only the large and successful organizations, and proposes a four-fold classification of such organizations: labor movements (*arbetets rörelse*), ideological movements (*idérörelse*), identity movements (*identitetsrörelse*), and movements of interaction (*interaktionsrörelse*). Other researchers stress the distinction between popular mass movements and popular mass movement *organizations*, most often taking the form of associations. The organization that emerges from the movement carries the same ideological message but has a more formalized and hierarchical structure. This transformation is explained by the efforts of a movement's activists to consolidate forces within the movement to maximize its public impact and political clout (Jonsson, 1995; Sjöstrand, 1985).

Interest organizations

Interest organizations play an important role in Sweden as well as in the rest of Scandinavia. This type of organization includes labor unions and farmer federations, both of which traditionally have had a significant impact on Swedish society. Interest organizations also include associations for the disabled and the temperance movement (Buksti, 1993; Elvander, 1972; Heckscher, 1951; Lewin, 1992; Rothstein, 1992). In our survey, 40 percent of the respondents described themselves as interest organizations. However, no more than 20 percent of the foundations claimed to be interest organizations. Since the Swedish nonprofit sector is primarily involved in advocacy and representation rather than service delivery, the interest element of the sector is of crucial importance. Interest organizations often exert considerable pressure on the government.

The voluntary sector

The term voluntary sector, *frivilligsektor*, generally refers to those segments of the nonprofit sector devoted to social service delivery (Kuhnle and Selle, 1992a; Micheletti, 1994). Further, the term focuses more on the activity than the purpose, emphasizing the voluntary aspect of participation. It implies the perspective of a donor rather than that of a receiver. It also sometimes encompasses voluntary work conducted under the auspices of local or central government (Blennberger, 1993). In our survey, fewer than 10 percent of the organizations identified themselves as part of the voluntary sector, and those that did were found mainly in the fields of health care and social service. Even in these fields, "voluntary" organizations represent only about one-eighth of the organizations.

The *ideell* sector

Another common label used in Sweden for the nonprofit sector is *ideell sektor*, perhaps the most politically-neutral term. In the legislation, *ideell* and *allmännyttig* (public good) are used interchangeably, even though *ideell* has a somewhat broader meaning. The concept of an *ideell* sector permits a clear and, we think, essential distinction to be made between the public-good efforts of the private realm and those provided, for example, by volunteers in different forms of public or semi-public organizations. In our study, 38 percent of the respondents declared themselves part of the *ideell* sector. The term has earlier been thought to apply principally to associations, excluding foundations. This is contradicted by our survey, in which more than one-third of the foundations claimed to be a part of the *ideell* sector.

Major types of organizations in the Swedish nonprofit sector

In Sweden, as in other modern industrialized states, the conflict between individual and collective rights and needs often resulted in the emergence of different forms of organizations, of which associations and foundations are the most common. Important also is the Church of Sweden, which, although formally a part of the State, lives a life of its own as a clearly separate and autonomous entity. We propose a typology of the nonprofit sector that includes the major categories of associations and foundations, and relevant parts of the Church of Sweden.

Associations

The largest and most important group in our typology comprises five different types of associations: recreational or service associations; associations with social or ideological objectives; economic or cooperative associations; business associations; and labor-market associations.

The most common organizations among recreational associations are sports-related. Others include people engaged in hobbies such as philately, model railways, or the preservation and management of rural or community centers. There are also societies devoted to the promotion of the arts or of science, or for outdoor activities, including scouting, boating, and tourism. The Swedish Touring Club (*Svenska Turistföreningen*) is one example.

Usually, the Swedish term *förening* indicates a group that is open and accessible to any interested individuals. By contrast, terms such as *klubb* (club), *sällskap* (society), *orden* (order), or *broderskap* (fraternity) often signal a more closed form of association. However, the names used by a particular organization depend, for the most part, on the period in which the association was created, the type of activity in which the association is engaged, or the international organization that served as the organizational model. Many international service organizations, such as the Rotary, Masonic Order, Odd Fellows, and Lions Clubs are found in Sweden. Social clubs, formed at schools or universities, or among groups of friends or employees, constitute another example of this type of association. Different minority organizations, among them associations for Finnish immigrants or the Sami people, are also included in this grouping.

Associations serving a social mission or presenting an ideological message include groups formed for the preservation and protection of the environment, such as the Society for Nature Preservation (*Naturskyddsföreningen*) and Greenpeace Sweden; ones organized to support the national defense, such as the Central Federation for Voluntary Military Training (*Centralförbundet för Frivillig Befälsutbildning*); and those representing the interests of the disabled and handicapped, such as the Association of the Visually Impaired (*Synskadades Riksförbund*) and Stockholm Independent Living – STIL. Others advocate a sober life; raise funds for research and education; provide relief and development assistance to the Third World; champion human rights; or work to further domestic welfare. Organizations such as the Swedish Red Cross, Save the Children, Amnesty International, the Salvation Army, and also political parties and religious congregations, fall into this grouping of associations.

A third type of association is devoted to various forms of economic cooperation, and includes different types of business associations. The older forms – common ownership and the village community – are often centered around some form of real property, such as a common ground or road. The traditional Swedish cooperative movement is dominated by large, well-established consumer and producer cooperatives and is highly visible at home, but also recognized abroad. Savings banks, cooperative banks, mortgage associations, and mutual insurance companies are distinguished from other financial service institutions both by their special legal status and by their cooperative form of organization. Some of them are major actors in the Swedish banking industry. The turnover of the six huge cooperative business groups together represents a substantial part of the Swedish gross national product.

A newly-emerging type of cooperative, labeled "*nykooperation*" (neo-cooperatives), consists of smaller organizations that usually operate on a local scale. Neo-cooperatives emerged in response to new market demands and declining confidence in the ability of the public sector to provide the bulk of social services. Well-known examples are the cooperative child care centers, established and run by parents. Others are cooperatives among disabled people, artists, and craftsmen.

Trade unions and employer associations are the two large groups of labor market associations. They both use the word *förening*, denoting organizations formed to defend their interests on the local or trade level. Labor unions are based on personal membership, although they also include federations of associations, such as national trade unions. By contrast, the members of employer associations at both trade and national level are companies. *Gille* or *skrå* (guild or craft) are ancient terms for associations of craftsmen of a particular profession or trade. By nature, these associations belong somewhere between the trade union and the trade association. They were dissolved in 1846 by anti-trust legislation, but some of their basic features are found today among professional organizations (Hemström, 1992; Nial, 1988).

The foundations

Foundations were earlier not required to register with the authorities and, as a consequence, precise data on their numbers and assets are generally not available. Estimates made in 1976 found that there were, at that time, approximately 50,000 foundations in Sweden, of which about 10,000 were governed by private independent boards. Their accumulated wealth was estimated at 50,000 billion Skr. Private "public good" foundations number 8,000. This type of foundation may be managed by an independent board of private citizens, or by another organization, such as the Swedish Red Cross or the Church of Sweden (Frii, 1989; Justitedepartmentet, 1987; Norin and Wessman, 1993; Proposition, 1993; SCB, 1979). Some foundations, apart from making grants, engage in different forms of business activity.

Frequently, foundations are connected to local or central governments and are established for the public benefit, as defined in the Swedish law. They may be private, but are supervised and administered by local governments, or created by central or municipal government to provide for a particular activity. A special type of foundation is created to raise funds from the public for a specific purpose, such as cancer research. Another type is the family foundation, established solely for the benefit of the members of one or a few families. Finally, there are retirement funds and personnel foundations which provide for the welfare of the employees of a particular company (Frii, 1989; Norin and Wessman, 1993; Proposition, 1993).

The Church of Sweden

The Church of Sweden (*Svenska kyrkan*) is a Lutheran Reformist church, incorporated by the State in the sixteenth century. Although its constitutional status has not changed, its organizational structure is now more or less independent from the rest of the State administration (Ekström, 1985). As in Germany (Anheier and Seibel, 1993), the Church is a public institution entitled to a church tax, amounting to about 1 percent of taxable income. This means that the Church has access to revenue elements not found elsewhere in the sector. Until recently, the Church of Sweden administered national population registration for the State, but this has changed as part of the ongoing process of separation between Church and State, and the national registration has been taken over by the local tax offices. Yet the Church still performs much of the social work carried on outside the local or regional government institutions.

The smallest organizational body in the Church of Sweden is the congregation; the next in size is a parish (*pastorat*). The largest unit of the Church of Sweden is the diocese or episcopate. In 1989 there were 2,563 congregations and 1,132 *pastorats* organized into 13 episcopates (Ekström, 1985). The Church has its own chain of command and a structure separate from the State. The highest decision-making body at the parish level is the select vestry, elected democratically every three years. At the national level, the synod is the highest decision-maker, and it elects the central board, which governs the Swedish Church.

The relationship between Church and State has been debated extensively, especially during the 1980s. Even though the Church already enjoys considerable autonomy within the State organization, this debate will probably result in an even greater separation. Therefore, though the Church is still legally and constitutionally part of the Swedish state, many Church activities are regarded as important elements of the Swedish nonprofit sector (Ekström, 1989; SOU, 1992a).

Concluding remarks on the typology of the Swedish sector

This section evaluates which of the nonprofit organizations in Sweden should be included in a definition of the sector, using the criteria set forth by the structural–operational definition of Salamon and Anheier (1992). These criteria are met by the associations in the recreational and social service fields. The status of a third group, economic or cooperative associations, is more complicated, since some of the organizations are, in fact, businesses with obvious elements of profit distribution. On the other hand, many of the activities in the "neo-cooperative" section are truly *ideell* or voluntary. We propose to include in the definition of a Swedish nonprofit sector these "neo-cooperatives" along with the different forms of business associations, but to exclude from it the traditional cooperative movement organizations.

The labor market associations are also difficult to classify, since they often work for the benefit of their members. However, it would be a mistake to exclude the important labor movement and related organizations, such as the educational associations, because they meet the conditions of the structural–operational definition. We also include those private foundations that provide some form of public service, but exclude those related to individual families or companies, or those that are created and entirely controlled by government entities, except those related to the Church of Sweden. The Church should be excluded, according to the structural–operational definition, because it is a state church. Referring to our previous discussion on the subject, however, we suggest including Church establishments that are clearly separated from the State.

Legal framework

The legal system in Sweden is based on civil law. However, since the principal legal forms of nonprofit organizations are not regulated by an overacting, explicit body of law, the legal status of these organizations has something of a common law character. It is largely based on scholarly doctrine and judicial precedent, and particularly on decisions of the Supreme Administrative Court. Since Swedish jurists are trained in the civil law system, the body of precedent is not as well developed as it might be in a country where the legal system rests on common law. The parts of the legal framework especially relevant to the nonprofit sector are the association law (*associationsrätten*) and various tax laws regarding associations and foundations, currently undergoing major revision.

Organizations in the Swedish nonprofit sector usually take one of two basic legal forms: either associations or foundations. There are, in turn, two principal types of associations: the *ideell* and the economic association. Although there is not yet any specific legislation governing the *ideell* associations and foundations have only recently been regulated, there is a substantial body of legislation regulating economic associations.

Economic associations

A common legal definition of an association is lacking from Swedish law (Mallmén, 1989). According to Hemström (1992), an association is created when a number of individuals (or legal entities) join to cooperate for a common purpose under organized forms and for a certain period of time. The law that pertains to economic associations (SFS 1987:667) roughly defines an economic association as one with the goal of promoting the economic interests of its members through economic activity in which the members participate, whether as consumers, suppliers, providers of their own labor, service recipients, or in any other similar way. The economic association is closely related to the legal institutions of joint ownership and common land, which are treated as economic associations in all relevant aspects. There are also some variants of the economic association active in the financial sector and governed by special legislation, but these will not be treated in this text, as they are not relevant to the concept of the nonprofit sector (Hemström, 1992; Mallmén, 1989; Rodhe, 1988).

Most cooperatives take the legal form of economic association and are the only form of association recognized by FL. The FL cooperative declaration refers to the following cooperative principles: the membership of the association should be open to anyone; the decision forms should be democratic (i.e., one member equals one vote); the return on invested capital should be limited; and the distribution of surplus should be based on the members' purchases from, or deliveries to, the cooperative (Rodhe, 1988).

Ideell associations

The *ideell förening, ideell* or private non-profit association (Hemström, 1972:252), is not defined in existing law. The *ideell* association is viewed as a more or less residual category consisting of all associations other than economic associations. Any association that fails to meet the criterion of conducting a business activity for the economic benefit of its members is automatically defined as an *ideell* association. In actual legal practice, however, an *ideell* association is treated either by legal analogy to the legislation on economic associations or by reference to general legal principles.

Two substantial obstacles in drafting legislation on *ideell* associations are that the existing associations vary considerably in character, and that the labor market associations oppose limits on their freedom of action (Rodhe, 1988). The legal distinction between *ideell* association and economic association is not identical to the one between protective and promotional organizations, since the Swedish system treats both trade unions and employer associations as *ideell* associations (M. Bäck, 1980).

Foundations

The legal status of foundations has not been very different from that of the *ideell* association, as a specific body of legislation on foundations has only recently been introduced. An important distinction between foundations and associations is that the foundation is not regulated by the association law. Whereas one of the basic elements of an association is its members, the foundation rests solely on property kept to further a certain purpose.

The legal situation of the foundation has changed very recently. For the first time ever, the legal situation of foundations in Sweden was regulated in January, 1996. However, the new Law on Foundations is very much a codification of existing case law and legal doctrine. According to the new law, a foundation is created when it is given a name, and when certain property has been definitely and irrevocably assigned to a person who has promised to administer the assets as an autonomous property in accordance with the instructions in the foundation's constitution, which must be in written form (SFS 1994:1220).

Two terms sometimes used for subsections of the group of foundations are the establishment or institution (*inrättning*), which refers to a foundation with assets in the form of a building or the like; and the fund (*fond*), a foundation with assets placed in securities or bank accounts. Foundations may own real estate and, under special conditions, also engage in business activities (Frii, 1989; Hessler, 1952; Norin and Wessman, 1993; Proposition, 1993).

The Church of Sweden in the law

Two principal bodies of legislation govern the Church of Sweden. The first is the Church Law (SFS 1992:300), a subdivision of public law, which is a single statute incorporating a previous system of piecemeal legislation dating back to the seventeenth century. The provision declaring the Church to be a democratic and nationwide institution is still contained in a separate statute, however, as a major constitutional modification would be required to change it. Under the new Church Law, the Church lost its previous legislative power, but the same law also gave the Church exclusive control over purely religious matters, a power it had formerly shared with the Swedish parliament. The second body of legislation is found in the tax laws, which contain specific provisions regarding the Church.

Nonprofit status

For an organization to receive and benefit from official nonprofit status in Sweden, it must qualify as an institution serving the public good. According to the Law on National Income Tax (SIL),[3] this status is based primarily on the purpose and legal form of the organization, but certain other limitations also apply. In determining the public good status of an organization's purpose, an important legal distinction is made between a "qualified" public good purpose and a general one.

The qualified public good purposes are defined in SIL (7 § 6 mom) as charitable institutions (*barmhärtighetsinrättningar*) and foundations which are primarily dedicated to strengthening the defense of the nation or furthering the care and upbringing of children and the support of education. Other qualified public good purposes include relief work among the needy, promotion of scientific research, and furthering cooperation among the Nordic countries.

The second group of public good purposes is much broader. It specifically relates to associations (SIL 7 § 5 mom), and includes religious, charitable, social, political, artistic, athletic, and other similar cultural purposes that are considered to be of public benefit. The purposes regarded as qualified in reference to a foundation are included as a subset of this larger category.

Benefits of nonprofit status include the right for certain organizations to organize lotteries and gambling, eligibility for subsidies from different levels of government, and the right to and the exemption from VAT (Value Added Tax) for activities traditionally used by nonprofit organizations to raise funds. Another example of the preferential treatment of associations under Swedish law is that only membership organizations are eligible for public subsidies.

There are also semi-official forms of nonprofit status that bring benefits to a number of organizations, achieved by being declared an *ideell* organization by the national telephone company, the postal service, or by the Foundation for Control of Fundraising (SFI).[4] The SFI's main role is to ascertain that funds raised by an organization are actually spent for the public good purpose for which they were collected. Along with the right to use the SFI insignia, qualifying organizations are also entitled to use special account numbers in an easily recognizable series reserved for nonprofit fundraising.

Tax exemption for foundations

Swedish society prefers the collective and democratic forms of organization of the associations to the more individualistic foundations. Foundations seeking tax exemption are held to much stricter legal standards than are associations, and associations are granted tax relief for a wider span of activities than foundations.

In principle, foundations are liable to taxation on all their income, but those foundations considered to be for the public good are exempt from tax under SIL. The most important tax relief, and also the most important form of nonprofit status, available to foundations in Sweden is the partial tax exemption on income. The foundations of interest may be divided into two subgroups: a small, exclusive group listed in a special "catalogue" (SIL 7 § 4 mom), and a larger group consisting of foundations designated as of "qualified public good purpose."

The "catalogue" lists more than 30 foundations (such as the Nobel Foundation) and other organizations, such as privately-run educational establishments and compulsory student unions, that are liable only to tax on income from property and are thus tax-exempt to a greater extent than those included in the larger group.

The majority of foundations granted tax-exempt status in Sweden are of the type referred to in SIL 7 § 6 mom ("qualified public good purpose"). These are exempt from tax on all income except income from property and business. Furthermore, they are only liable for the tax on capital to the extent of their investment in businesses engaged in the administration of capital or property. To qualify, a foundation must not only have a qualified public good purpose, but must also comply with two other conditions: the completion prerequisite, which stipulates that the major part of the yield must be used for the purpose claimed, and the recipient prerequisite, which states that the activities of the foundations may not be limited to a certain family or group of persons.

Tax exemption for associations

Associations eligible for tax exemption are generally *ideell* in legal form, but economic associations are not excluded. Roughly, the *ideell* associations may be divided into two groups: those serving a public good purpose and thus eligible for tax exemption, and those that do not serve any recognized public good and which are, therefore, subject to taxation.

As in the case of foundations, tax-exempt associations must also fulfill certain prerequisites. Four such prerequisites are mentioned in SIL (7 § 5 mom). The first requires that the organization's purpose serve the public good rather than families, or groups of private persons, and the second condition requires that the activities be exclusively for this purpose. The third prerequisite is that membership in the organization must be reasonably open to all who want to join. Finally, the fourth condition stipulates that the preponderant portion of the organization's income be used for the stated public good purpose. These conditions are critical in the determination of the association's tax-exempt status. For example, in June 1993, the county administrative court of Gothenburg partially denied Greenpeace Sweden its previous tax-exempt status for the years 1988 to 1991 on the grounds that the association did not fulfill the requirement of reasonable openness.

If these four conditions are met, the association's income is exempt from taxation, except for the portion that comes from property or business activity. Even business or property income can be exempt, if the property or business is naturally connected with the public good purpose of the association. Further, *ideell* associations are largely exempt from the Value Added Tax (VAT) since they are not generally considered businesses. If an association is declared to be for the public good, it will also be exempt from tax on the gifts it receives. This exemption applies as well to subsidies from governmental agencies. On the other hand, donors do not receive any favorable tax treatment. Changes in this matter have been proposed repeatedly over the years, most recently in an official government report (SOU, 1993a).

Finally, the eligibility of an *ideell* association to receive financial support from the government is also subject to certain conditions: the association must have an "ideological function," and must foster the formation of public opinion by promoting democratic values and social cohesion (SOU, 1988). The amount of government subsidies to different associations in the nonprofit sector is substantial and includes both direct financial contributions and indirect or in-kind support (Statskontoret, 1991).

Lotteries and concerts

Many Swedish nonprofit organizations derive a part of their income from various lotteries or forms of gambling. The popular mass movements, particularly the organizations in the sports and temperance movements, have traditionally organized large lotteries as a complement to other sources of income (Schwalbe, 1985). The total net income from different forms of lotteries and gambling is estimated close to one billion Skr. each year (SOU, 1992b). To receive a permit to conduct lotteries, the organizer, usually an *ideell* association, must fulfill requirements very similar to the four conditions imposed on *ideell* associations seeking tax exemption. One additional criterion found in the Law on Lotteries (*Lotterilagen*) is that the activities of the applicant should be of long duration. Other fundraising activities traditionally used by nonprofit organizations, such as concerts, are also excluded from VAT, provided the proceeds serve a nonprofit purpose.

The Swedish State and the nonprofit sector

Sweden, like other Scandinavian countries, has a reputation for being a leading welfare state with a stable labor market and a high degree of social protection. Although Sweden has a comparatively low degree of service production located in its nonprofit sector, relations between the State and nonprofit organizations are characterized by cooperation and close ties rather than by competition or conflict (Selle, 1993).

Social policy discourse and welfare reforms were first brought to Sweden by the struggle for universal and equal suffrage and rapid industrialization that caused the expansion of the working class. Social policy initiatives between the mid-1880s and the 1920s developed in an environment of growing popular mass movements, the emerging social sciences, and a new urban upper class inspired by German *Kathedersozialismus*, French revolutionary radicalism, and English liberalism (Olsson, 1990).

The reformists were successful in introducing gradual changes in the social welfare area throughout the second decade of this century. The organizations that took part in this movement, such as *Centralförbundet för socialt arbete* (CSA), were connected by their mutual membership in leading philanthropic associations.

Organizations like CSA, with its orientation towards public authorities, became a bridge between philanthropy and the state (Boalt and Bergryd, 1974; Boalt *et al.*, 1975; Olsson, 1990).

Until the 1930s Sweden had a rather weak social insurance system. The historical turning-point came with the depression and the forming of a parliamentary alliance between the Social Democratic and the Agrarian parties, laying the foundation for an active and massive state intervention. The 1930s also mark a turning-point in the development of the Swedish labor market. Important agreements were reached between the labor unions and employers' associations. These agreements became the basis of the Swedish "policy of compromise" or "the Swedish model."

However, it was not until after the Second World War that the foundations of the current welfare state were laid. The wave of reforms began in the mid-1940s with a universal flat-rate pension. The 1959 ATP reform (a supplementary pension based on income from gainful employment) represents the beginning of an earnings-related system that came to replace the earlier flat-rate pensions. The ATP reform caused protracted political conflicts. The non-socialist parties supported the idea of supplementary earnings-related pensions, but opposed the Social Democrats' proposals that the pensions be public and state-controlled. Ultimately the Social Democrats won out. The ATP decision was a milestone in the development of Swedish social policy: the social insurance system and other support systems were made compulsory, and financed and organized within the state sector (Esping-Andersen and Korpi, 1987; Lundström, 1989; Olsson, 1990).

The structure of the welfare model did not change much during the 1970s and 1980s, although Sweden had non-socialist governments for six years between 1976 and 1982. Adverse economic developments and the loss of consensus on the principles of the welfare state put the structure under pressure, but it retained its previous character; some improvements were even introduced.

Researchers analyzing the Swedish or Scandinavian welfare model emphasize the relatively high benefit levels and social service standards, commitment to universalism and equality going farther than that in many other nations. According to Esping-Andersen and Korpi (1987), the welfare states of Scandinavia seem to have a stronger "decommodifying" effect of moving the satisfaction of human needs from the market to a collective sphere. The traditional boundaries of welfare state policies have thus been exceeded to an exceptional degree, and have minimized the need for private care. Although such accounts might underestimate the role of the private for-profit and nonprofit sectors, there is extensive state provision, finance, and control, not only in the social security system, but also in areas such as education and health. Primary schools, for example, have long been under government control and, from the end of the 1940s, the absolute majority of schools on the secondary level have also been included in the state sector. At the end of the 1970s, less than 1 percent of children of compulsory school age attended private schools (SOU, 1981).

Even in an area of such state interest as education, however, there has been a place for nonprofit organizations. To a large degree, adult education, organized in study circles or residential colleges, has been conducted under the auspices of nonprofit organizations. In the delivery of some social services, nonprofit organizations have also held a prominent position. Institutional care for alcoholics and drug addicts, for example, has traditionally been an area with a significant share of nonprofit organizations (Richardson, 1990; SOU, 1987, 1990).

In Swedish political discourse the popular mass movements and the nonprofit sector are viewed as important schools for democracy, instruments for promoting both mutual and individual interests, and an integral part of the democratic civil society. Since the 1940s, but especially after the 1960s, state support to organizations in the nonprofit sector has grown substantially. State policy in this respect, however, has varied in regard to different areas of the nonprofit sector (Davidsson, 1993; SAP, 1993; SOU, 1987).

In areas such as culture, adult education, and sports, the State consistently supports nonprofit organizations through grants and in-kind assistance. However, in health services, social welfare, and education (except adult education), the State's policy has been directed toward equal rights reforms. Therefore, most of the important services in these areas have been produced within the public sector, while nonprofit organizations played a comparatively minor role.

At the local level, however, members and professionals from nonprofit organizations are making important contributions, often informally and through volunteer work, that supplement service production in the public sector. In social service and health these include activities that support the elderly, the homeless, persons with alcohol or drug-related problems, hospital patients, and persons under correctional care. Swedish municipalities have a high degree of autonomy and play a crucial part in areas such as education, social assistance, child care, care of the elderly, and leisure. In most of these areas nonprofit organizations cooperate with the municipalities and are highly dependent on them for support (SOU, 1993).

Conditions for the nonprofit sector today appear to be changing rapidly. Pressure on state budgets and changes in the ideological climate – including criticism of a growing, supposedly inefficient, welfare state bureaucracy – together with growing internationalization, call for a different social policy. They emphasize freedom and individual responsibility in the social welfare system and advocate a larger space for civil society. However, in spite of political controversy, there is a relatively strong consensus on the universal or institutional model. The proposed alternatives to the present system are rather vague ideas of a new welfare mix in which some form of civil society would have a more significant role (Olsson, 1993b).

Since the 1980s, with a shift in the dominant ideology towards more market-oriented concepts, criticism of bureaucracy, and a harsh economic climate, there has been a move in the direction of business-oriented management systems, deregulation, decentralization, service-orientation and privatization. These methods, intended to reduce public spending and increase productivity and efficiency in the public sector, have been introduced at both central and local levels. Accordingly, government policy will probably open up new space for nonprofit organizations providing services in such areas as social welfare, health, and education, especially on the local level (Regeringen, 1993; SOU, 1993b).

The Swedish welfare model is being challenged from outside and within, and is under pressure to move toward a "welfare mix" with more space for both business and the nonprofit sector and, one might add, with a risk of diminished social security for individuals. It is still too early to tell how nonprofit organizations will adapt to current and future changes. At present, there are several attempts from both local government and nonprofit organizations to initiate voluntary participation in areas traditionally run by government. However, considering Sweden's historical pattern of cooperation and mutual ties between organizations and government, and given the structure of its nonprofit sector today, one might reasonably predict that the future of the sector will not be a carbon copy of the structures in either continental Europe or the United States. The nonprofit sector in Sweden will more probably continue to develop along its present lines: with an emphasis on broad-based membership and participation; important roles allocated to popular mass movements, interest organizations, and organizations for mutual aid; and with close cooperation between the nonprofit sector and government.

Conclusion

This chapter has provided a conceptual framework for examining the nonprofit sector in Sweden that reaches beyond the traditional means and modes customarily employed for earlier comparable studies. It is true that the potential arenas for private nonprofit activity outside the State in Sweden have been limited as a consequence of the rise and expansion of the welfare state during the major part of the twentieth century. Nevertheless, it must be recognized that Swedish nonprofit organizations abound and are neither necessarily smaller nor less powerful than their counterparts in other countries. The Swedish nonprofit sector is uniquely characterized by the number and variety of its organizations and the effectiveness of its movements, and is not to be measured solely by the extent to which it is engaged in traditional welfare service delivery. When viewed in this way, the nonprofit sector is perceived as playing an undeniably significant role in Swedish society and history.

Although private nonprofit organizations have been encouraged to participate in the fields of culture, adult education, and sports and leisure, and also in politics and cooperative efforts, the core domains of the welfare state, such as compulsory education, health care, and social welfare have, by contrast, been characterized by large, State-provided, egalitarian reforms, which have left little room for organizations outside the state apparatus. The role of nonprofit organizations in these latter areas has been focused more on lobbying and acting as pressure groups to influence different levels of government to provide services than on actually providing these services themselves. This role of representation and advocacy has resulted in close ties between government and the nonprofit sector. At times it can be difficult to separate the span and activities of these entities from each other.

Historically, a main function of the strong, often government-supported, popular mass movements, beyond their primary purpose of representing the interests of their members, has been to organize and unite different groups of citizens, thereby fostering the democratic system. Foundations illustrate another aspect of the Swedish nonprofit sector where individuals or small groups may be able to influence the objectives and activities of the organization to a greater extent than is generally possible in a large popular movement. Nevertheless, foundations have often been neglected in the few existing attempts to describe the Swedish nonprofit sector.

The nonprofit sector in Sweden is facing a rapidly changing environment because of the reformulated role of the State. This includes questioning the degree of state involvement and the monopoly-like provision of services in such traditional welfare state sectors as social services and education. We see two reasons for this development. The first responds to liberal ideas of a smaller public sector. Some of the activities presently entrusted to this sector would be taken over by some form of civil society in the future. Another ideological explanation is to be found in the arguments of critics of the Scandinavian welfare state, who have sought to increase citizen participation and have demanded a decentralization of political decision-making.

Another significant factor contributing to the changing environment for nonprofit organizations is the economic recession of the early 1990s, which has diminished the capacity of government to finance and maintain all welfare institutions established during the second half of this century, as well as preventing it from expanding into new areas. One possible way out of this dilemma is to turn to for-profit businesses and the nonprofit sector to share some of the responsibility for service delivery. But another consequence of the recession is that general subsidies to the nonprofit sector are being questioned and cut back. As a result of these changes, the existing understanding between the Swedish State and the nonprofit sector is being renegotiated, and their respective roles are being reshaped and redefined.

We recognize that an attempt to develop a single, comprehensive concept that covers parts of society so disparate as the different organizations and components of the nonprofit sector, as we have presented it here, may well be open to questions. However, we hope that research and policy-making may ultimately benefit from this new perspective that views these different types of organizations as one sector.

Notes

1 The authors would like to express their thanks to Professor Erík Nerep and Jens Göthberg for research on the legal sections, and Helmut Anheier, Professor Sven-Erík Sjöstrand and Lars Svedberg for editorial comments and suggestions on earlier drafts. This chapter is part of a larger research project financed by grants from several institutions: The Swedish Council for Research in Humanities and Social Science; The Bank of Sweden Tercentenary Foundation; the Swedish Ministries of Public Administration and for Health and Social Affairs, respectively; and the Swedish Red Cross; which we would like to thank for their kind support.

2 In late 1993 and early 1994, a survey of over 2,500 nonprofit associations and foundations in Sweden was carried out as part of the Johns Hopkins Comparative Nonprofit Sector Project. The response rate for the total sample was 55 percent overall, and 75 percent for the 750 largest organizations in it. For the question referred to in the text, the organizations could choose more than one of seven alternative terms to describe a nonprofit organization.

3 *Lag om statlig inkomstskatt* (SIL). A recent Public State Report concerning the tax treatment of *ideell* associations and foundations has suggested changes. However, the changes suggested are rather minor and more or less in line with the previous legislation (SOU, 1995).

4 *Stiftelsen för Insamlingskontroll* (SFI) is an independent foundation established to monitor fundraising. The founders of SFI were the four most important associations in the labor market and the Association for Chartered Accountants, *Föreningen Auktoriserade Revisorer (FAR).*

References

Åberg, Ingrid (1988), "Revivalism, philanthrophy, and emancipation." *Scandinavian Journal of History*, 13: 399–420.

Anheier, Helmut K. and Wolfgang Seibel (1993), "Defining the Nonprofit Sector: Germany." *Working Papers of the Johns Hopkins Comparative Nonprofit Sector Project*, no. 6. Baltimore: The Johns Hopkins Institute for Policy Studies. (See also Chapter 6 in this volume.)

Bäck, Henry (1983), *Invandrarnas riksorganisationer*. Stockholm: Liber.

Bäck, Mats (1980), *Partier och organisationer i Sverige*. Stockholm: Liber Förlag.

Blennberger, Erik (1993), "Begrepp och modeller," in *Frivilligt socialt arbete*. SOU (Statens Offentliga Utredningar: Public State Reports) no. 1993:82. Stockholm: Allmänna Förlaget.

Blomdahl, Ulf (1990), *Folkrörelserna och folket, med utblick mot framtiden*. Stockholm: Carlssons.

Boalt, Gunnar and Ulla Bergryd (1974), *CSA – ett kapitel svensk socialhistoria*. Stockholm: Centralförbundet för Socialt Arbete.

Boalt, Gunnar, Ulla Bergryd, Arne Bjurman, Kaj Fischer and Eva Rappe (1975), *De socialpolitiska centralförbunden*. Stockholm: Centralförbundet för Socialt Arbete.

Boli, John (1991), 'Sweden: is there a viable third sector?" in *Between States and Markets – The Voluntary Sector in Comparative Perspective*, ed. Robert Wuthnow. Princeton: Princeton University Press.

Boli, John (1992), "The ties that bind: the nonprofit sector and the State in Sweden," in *The Nonprofit Sector in the Global Community*, ed. by Kathleen D. McCarthy *et al*. San Francisco: Jossey-Bass.

Bramstång, Gunnar (1964), *Förutsättningar för barnavårdsnämnds ingripande mot asocial ungdom*. Lund: Gleerup.

Buksti, Jacob A. (1993), "Interest groups in Denmark," in *Pressure Groups*, ed. by Jeremy J. Richardson. Oxford: Oxford University Press.

Burenstam Linder, Staffan (1983), *Den hjärtlösa välfärdsstaten*. Stockholm: Timbro.

Carlsson, Sten and Jerker Rosén (1962), *Svensk historia I. Tiden före 1718*. Stockholm: Svenska bokförlaget.

Davidsson, Inger (1993), "Individer, folkrörelser i folket," in *Folkrörelse och Föreningsguiden*. Stockholm: Civildepartementet and Fritzes.

Ekström, Sören (1985), *Svenska kyrkan – organisation och verksamhet*. 2nd rev. edn. Stockholm: Verbum Förlag.

Elvander, Nils (1972), *Intresseorganisationerna i dagens Sverige*. Lund: Gleerups.

Engberg, Jan (1986), *Folkrörelserna i välfärdssamhället*. Umeå: Statsvetenskapliga institutionen/Umeå universitet.

Esping-Andersen, Gösta and Walter Korpi (1987) "From poor relief to institutional welfare states: the development of Scandinavian social policy," in *The Scandinavian Model*, ed. Robert Erikson. New York: Armonk.

Eyerman, Ron, and Andrew Jamison (1991), *Social Movements*. Cambridge: Polity Press.

Sweden

Förslag till lagar om registrerade föreningar för annan än ekonomisk verksamhet (1903), Stockholm.

Frii, Lennart (1985), *Alla dessa fonder och stiftelser*, 2nd edn. Stockholm: Lehmann.

Frii, Lennart (1989), *Förvalta fonder och stiftelser*. Stockholm: Norstedts.

Heckscher, Gunnar (1951), *Staten och organisationerna*, 2nd rev. edn. Stockholm: Kooperativa Förbundets Bokförlag.

Hemström, Carl (1972), *Uteslutning ur Ideell förening*. Stockholm: PA Norstedt & Söners Förlag.

Hemström, Carl (1992), *Organisationernas rättsliga ställning – Om ekonomiska och ideella föreningar*, 4th rev. edn. Lund: Norstedts Juridik.

Hessler, Henrik (1952), *Om stiftelser*. Stockholm: Stockholms Högskola.

Holgersson, Leif (1992), *Socialtjänst – Lagtexter med kommentarer i historisk belysning*. Stockholm: Tiden.

Holmström, Leif and Carl Martin Roos (1985), *Stiftelser, en orientering*. Lund: Studentlitteratur.

Hoppe, Gunnar, Gert Nylander and Ulf Olsson (1992), *Till landets gagn, Knut och Alice Wallenbergs stiftelse 1917–1992*. Stockholm: KAW.

Höjer, Karl J. (1952), *Svensk socialpolitisk historia*. Stockholm: Norstedts.

James, Estelle (1989), "The private provision of public services: a comparison of Sweden and Holland," in *The Nonprofit Sector in International Perspective*, ed. by Estelle James. New York: Oxford University Press.

Jeppsson Grassman, Eva (1993), "Frivilliga insatser i Sverige – En befolkningsstudie," in *Frivilligt socialt arbete*. SOU (Statens Offentliga Utredningar: Public State Reports) no. 1993:82. Stockholm: Allmänna Förlaget.

Johansson, Hilding (1980), *Folkrörelserna i Sverige*. Stockholm: Sober.

Johansson, Hilding (1993), "Föreningsväsendet växer fram," in *Folkrörelse och föreningsguiden*, 2nd rev edn. Stockholm: Allmänna Förlaget.

Jonsson, Christer (1995), *Ledning: folkrörelseorganisationer – den interaktiva ledningslogiken*. Lund: Lund University Press.

Justitiedepartementet (1987), "Stiftelser – Förslag till lag om stiftelser," in *Ds Ju* (Government Office Report Series, Ministry of Justice) no. 1987:14. Stockholm: Allmänna Förlaget.

Kuhnle, Stein and Per Selle (1992a), *Government and Voluntary Organizations*. Aldershot: Avebury.

Kuhnle, Stein and Per Selle (1992b), "The historical precedent for government–nonprofit cooperation in Norway," in *Government and the Third Sector*, ed. Benjamin Gidron *et al*. San Francisco: Jossey-Bass.

Lewin, Leif (1992), *Samhället och de organiserade intressena*. Stockholm: Norstedts Juridik.

Lundkvist, Sven. (1977), *Folkrörelserna i det svenska samhället 1850–1920*. Stockholm: Sober.

Lundström, Tommy (1989), "On Swedish social policy." *International*

The nonprofit sector in developed societies

Social Work, 1 261–271.

Lundström, Tommy (1993), Tvångsomhändertagande av barn, en studie av lagarna, professionerna och praktiken under 1900-talet. Stockholm: Stockholms Universitet – Socialhögskolan.

Mallmén, Anders (1989), Lagen om ekonomiska föreningar. Stockholm: Norstedts Förlag.

Micheletti, Michele (1994), Det civila samhället och staten – Medborgarsammanslutningarnas roll i svensk politik. Stockholm: Publica.

Nial, Håkan (1988), Svensk associationsrätt, 4th edn. Lund: Norstedts.

Norin, Magnus and Lars Wessman (1993), Stiftelser – den nya lagstiftningen, redovisning, beskattning. Stockholm: Ernst & Young.

Olson, Hans-Erik (1990), Att forska om fritid! Plan för uppbyggandet av svensk fritidsvetenskap. Stockholm: Forum för fritidsforskning, Reprocentralen Stockholms Universitet.

Olson, Hans-Erik (1993), Föreningarna och den ideella sektorn. En forsknings- och kunskapsöversikt. Stockholm: Institutet för fritidsvetenskap.

Olsson, Sven E. (1990), Social Policy and Welfare State in Sweden. Lund: Arkiv.

Olsson, Sven E. (1993), "Models and Countries – the Swedish social policy model in perspective," in Social Security in Sweden and Other European Countries – Three Essays. In Ds (Government Office Report Series) no. 1993:51. Stockholm: Allmänna Förlaget.

Pestoff, Victor A. (1977), Voluntary Associations and Nordic Party Systems. Stockholm: Department of Political Science, University of Stockholm.

Pestoff, Victor A. (1991), Between Markets and Politics – Co–operatives in Sweden. Frankfurt: Campus Verlag.

Pettersson, Olof, Anders Westholm, and Göran Blomberg (1989), Medborgarnas makt. Stockholm: Carlssons.

Proposition (Regeringens proposition; Government bill) (1993), Stiftelser. no. 1993/94:9. Stockholm: Allmänna Förlaget.

Qvarsell, Roger (993), "Välgörenhet, filantropi och frivilligt socialt arbete – en historisk översikt," in Frivilligt socialt arbete. SOU (Statens Offentliga Utredningar: Public State Reports) no. 1993:82. Stockholm: Allmänna Förlaget.

Regeringen (Government) (1993), "Tillkallande av en beredning för främjandet av den ideella sektorns utveckling, PM, Bilaga till protokoll vid regeringssammanträde 1993–05–27." Stockholm: The Government of Sweden.

Richardson, Gunnar (1990), Svensk utbildningshistoria. Lund: Studentlitteratur.

Rodhe, Knut (1988), Föreningslagen – 1987 års lag om föreningar, 8th rev. edn. Stockholm: LTs Förlag.

Rothstein, Bo (1992), Den korporativa staten. Stockholm: Norstedts Juridik.

Salamon, Lester M. (1987), "Partners in public service: the scope and theory of government nonprofit relations," in *The Nonprofit Sector – A Research Handbook*, ed. Walter W. Powell. New Haven: Yale University Press.

Salamon, Lester M. and Helmut K. Anheier (1992), "In search of the non-profit sector I: the question of definitions," *Voluntas*, 3(2):125–151. (See also Chapter 3 in this volume.)

SAP (Socialdemokratiska Arbetarpartiet: The Swedish Social Democratic Party) (1993), *De nya uppdragen – för arbete, omtanke och framtidstro*. Stockholm: Socialdemokraterna.

SCB (Statistiska centralbyrån: Statistics Sweden) (1979), "Stiftelser – En statistisk undersökning utförd av statistiska centralbyrån på uppdrag av och i samverkan med stiftelseutredningen," in Ds Ju (Government Office Report Series, Ministry of Justice) No. 1979:4. Stockholm: Allmänna Förlaget.

Schwalbe, Rikard (1985), *Lotterilagen – Lotterinämnden samt lotterinämndens praxis*. Stockholm: PA Norstedts & Söners Förlag.

Selle, Per (1993), "Voluntary organisations and the welfare state: the case of Norway." *Voluntas*, 1:1–15.

Sjöstrand, Sven-Erik (1985), *Samhällsorganisation*. Lund: Doxa Ekonomi.

SOU (Statens Offentliga Utredningar: Public State Reports) (1964), *Kyrkastat IV. Historisk översikt. Kyrkobegreppet*. no. 1964:16. Stockholm: Almqvist & Wiksell.

SOU (Statens Offentliga Utredningar: Public State Reports) (1981), *Fristående skolor för skolpliktiga elever*. no. 1981:34. Stockholm: Allmänna Förlaget.

SOU (Statens Offentliga Utredningar: Public State Reports) (1987), *Ju mer vi är tillsammans* (del 1) no. 1987:33. Stockholm: Allmänna Förlaget.

SOU (Statens Offentliga Utredningar; Public State Reports) (1988), *Mål och resultat – nya principer för det statliga stödet till föreningslivet*. no. 1988:29. Stockholm: Allmänna Förlaget.

SOU (Statens Offentliga Utredningar: Public State Reports) (1990), *Folkhögskolan i framtidsperspektiv*. no. 1990:65. Stockholm: Allmänna Förlaget.

SOU (Statens Offentliga Utredningar: Public State Reports) (1992a), *Ekonomi och rätt i kyrkan*. no. 1992:9. Stockholm: Allmänna Förlaget.

SOU (Statens Offentliga Utredningar: Public State Reports) (1992b), *Vinna eller försvinna – folkrörelsernas lotterier och spel i framtiden*. no. 1992:30. Stockholm: Allmänna Förlaget.

SOU (Statens Offentliga Utredningar: Public State Reports) (1993a), *Organisationernas bidrag*. no. 1993:71. Stockholm: Allmänna Förlaget.

SOU (Statens Offentliga Utredningar: Public State Reports) (1993b), no. 1993:82. *Frivilligt socialt arbete: Kartläggning och Kunskapoversikt*. no. 1993:82. Stockholm: Allmänna Förlaget.

SOU (Statens Offentliga Utredningar: Public State Reports (1995), *Översyn*

The nonprofit sector in developed societies

av skattereglerna för stiftelser och ideella föreningar. no. 1995:63. Stockholm: Allmänna Förlaget.

Statskontoret (1991), Statligt föreningsstöd – en kartläggning. no. 1991:6. Stockholm: Statskontoret.

Ström-Billing, Inger (1991), Ungkarlshotell – Föreningen Söderhem, enskild filantropi och allmän socialvård 1900–1986. Stockholm: Stockholms stad and Seelig.

Svedberg, Lars (1981), Ej till salu. Stockholm: Statens ungdomsråd.

Svedberg, Lars. (1993), "Socialt inriktade frivilligorganisationer – grundläggande karakteristika", in Frivilligt socialt arbete. SOU (Statens Offentliga Utredningar: Public State Reports) no. 1993:82. Stockholm: Allmänna Förlaget.

Swartz, Erik (1994), Ledning och organisering av federationer. Stockholm: Nerenius & Santérus Förlag.

Swedberg, Bo (1993), "Den ideella sektorn," in Organisationernas bidrag. SOU (Statens Offentliga Utredningar: Public State Reports) no. 1993:71, Appendix 4. Stockholm: Allmänna Förlaget.

Thörnberg, E. H. (1943), Folkrörelser och samhällsliv i Sverige. Stockholm: Albert Bonniers Förlag.

Chapter 10

THE UNITED KINGDOM

Jeremy Kendall and Martin Knapp[1]

Introduction

There is little doubt that the voluntary sector – to use the most common term for the nonprofit sector in the United Kingdom – is important. What must be in considerable doubt, however, is quite *how* important, for the sector's boundaries are poorly defined, many of its activities go unremarked, and its full contributions to the UK economy and society are uncharted. This chapter examines the issues surrounding the treatment and definition of the voluntary sector in the UK. We first provide a short account of the sector's historical development, and then set out the major organizational types to be found in the UK voluntary sector. We then examine some issues of political economy, particularly the links between the State, society, and the voluntary sector. In the final substantive section we move to a definition, concentrating on the criteria to be met for an entity to be termed a "voluntary organization," and examine the boundaries around the sector and some of the issues which surround these.

Historical note

The history of the formal voluntary sector in the UK is one of gradual secularization and formalization of voluntary action, and of changing roles in relation to the State (see Owen, 1964, for the leading account of the sector's history in England up until 1960). It concerns equally important traditions of philanthropy and mutual aid – and collective action combining elements of both – and charts the development of charitable giving and its conduits. An important set of subthemes concern the changing balances in service provision between the four principal domestic economic sectors – the formal voluntary sector, government, households and informal community action, and private for-profit enterprises. In the UK as in most other countries, the voluntary sector's roles as substitute and complement have been determined by, and have themselves determined, the inter-sectoral balances of provision of key services. The history of the voluntary sector is also about both reactionary agencies, and a dynamic set of organizations which through their campaigning and innovations have performed a pivotal role as catalysts for change in the wider society. These developments have taken place against a backcloth of sometimes focused, but more often seemingly piecemeal and *ad hoc* policy reform.

The formalization of philanthropy began in earnest with the Elizabethan Statute of Charitable Uses in 1601. Passed in the wake of the religious upheaval of the Reformation, it marked the beginnings of the secularization of philanthropy (Ware, 1989), but, in common with the Poor Law passed in the same year, it was also a response to the economic and social upheaval of the period, including the emergence of a class of landless and indigent people. As the movement from the land accelerated with industrialization in the eighteenth and nineteenth centuries, the pressures of industrial development, rapid population growth, and blighted cities made increasing demands on both philanthropy and the State (Prochaska, 1988). The reluctance or inability of the State to intervene left the way open for the development of formal voluntary organizations at local and national level.

During the eighteenth and nineteenth centuries, philanthropic organizations were often formed by members of the middle class, sometimes combining exemplary and innovative service provision with a strong campaigning role, highlighting new needs and bringing old injustices to public attention. Many of these agencies evolved into what we refer to below as *professional non-profit organizations* and *voluntary service organizations*. These range from social welfare agencies like Barnardo's, which grew to develop national remits providing orphanages and services for children across the country (albeit unevenly), through Church-based local

activities with missions and visiting societies concerned to preserve family life in the face of severe poverty, particularly in towns
and cities, to federal bodies working through local branches. The
latter included women's organizations, which provided "a compelling, and relatively unrestricted, avenue for expression and status" (Prochaska, 1988:24–25). Many of the other prominent fields
of activity in which organizations emerged over this period
remain important today, including housing provision, schools
and adult education, culture and the arts, and the environment
(preserving common land and urban open spaces). These constitute just a few examples of the sector fulfilling its "historic role as
pioneer" (Nathan, 1952).

Mutual aid organizations were also established at this time by
working-class people, particularly in the latter part of the nineteenth century. Rose's Act of 1793 gave formal recognition to the
friendly societies, bodies of (typically) men who pooled their
resources to create a contingency fund for sickness, burial, and old
age, meeting in the local inn or chapel. *Trade unions, consumer cooperatives, building societies*, and *housing societies* were also part of
this trend, recognized by the Royal Commission of 1871–4 as
examples of "the working spirit of self-help ... by which that
portion of the population which is most within the risk of pauperism endeavours to escape from it" (Beveridge, 1948:85–86). The
benevolent societies performed a similar role for the indigent higher
classes.

The sector's profile was perhaps highest during the nineteenth
century as a bulwark against poverty in areas as yet deemed inappropriate for state support, combining the direct provision of
resources with its quintessential advocacy role. Re-emphasizing a
division of responsibility between State and voluntary sector
which can be traced back to fourteenth-century legislation
(Chesterman, 1979), the reform of the Poor Law in 1834 delineated
the State's control of the "undeserving poor" through the deter-
rent of the workhouse, while the voluntary sector's role was principally to provide for the "deserving poor." Over this period, the
Charity Organisation Society (COS) or, to give it its more descriptive full title, the *Society for Organising Charity and Repressing
Mendicity* (begging), attempted to act as umbrella and coordinator
for the philanthropic wing of the sector, though with mixed success. The nineteenth century also witnessed the social surveys of

major philanthropic reformers and the settlement movement mobilizing "citizens of public spirit to undertake civic tasks," who both lived and worked in the newly emerging ghettos of increasingly divided cities.

Moving into the twentieth century, many aspects of formal voluntary action were increasingly being coordinated by umbrella groups such as the local and national councils for voluntary service.[2] The need for effective coordination was made all the more crucial by the upheavals of the First World War and the subsequent economic depression. All the while, state action was growing, though slowly and unevenly. The Second World War saw a strong partnership of state and voluntary effort, as manifested in the contributions of women's groups, the Red Cross and Citizens' Advice Bureaux, for example. It was not until the foundations of the welfare state were laid through the social legislation of the 1940s that the public sector came to dominate the funding and provision of education, health, social welfare, and income maintenance services. This redefinition of the role of the State and its responsibilities naturally had implications for the voluntary sector. The pioneers of state socialism saw the voluntary sector moving away from, to use the terminology of the Webbs (Webb and Webb, 1912), the "parallel bars" role in social provision of the Poor Law and COS period, with more emphasis now to be placed on the "extension ladder" role, complementing and supplementing the new universalism. Although stability and acquiescence were common reactions among some of the health, social service, and education organizations which were not absorbed into the mainstream state system (Wolfenden, 1978:20), many parts of the sector were invigorated rather than marginalized by the reforms – for example, in the mental health field, MIND (the National Association for Mental Health) and the Mental Health Foundation were both established in the late 1940s. Into the 1950s and 1960s, the vibrancy of the sector was beyond doubt, as established organizations pioneered new technologies, particularly in health and social care, while many new organizations were formed, including innovative self-help groups, international aid and awareness agencies, and a myriad sporting and leisure bodies.

During the 1960s and 1970s, then, voluntary organizations continued to be at the forefront of social change. As the broadened boundaries of the State became more apparent, so too did its limitations. Realization of these limitations, combined with a desire to combat newly emerging problems, such as urban decay and racial tension, and enhanced expectations from the general public prompted public sector bodies, at national and local level, to fund community-based groups and consumer and service-user organizations to a much greater extent than before. Lobbying groups in the voluntary sector such as the Child Poverty Action Group and Shelter called for the extension of the rights and entitlements of those adjudged to be in need. Government agencies were also increasingly being characterized as inefficient and unresponsive in their provision of services. It was in this context that a new Conservative government came to power in 1979, under Margaret Thatcher's premiership, with a commitment to reduce or limit the role of the State in practically all fields of activity, and with an especial emphasis on rolling back the boundaries of state social provision.

Major types of organization

There is no single or simple route in the UK to the identification of "types" of voluntary or nonprofit organization; as with definitions, the most useful categorizations will depend on the reasons for using them (Johnson, 1981). In this section, however, we start by considering some categorizations which provide an overview of some important characteristics of the sector, and we then describe the legal and tax environments in which the sector operates.

Functions and types of voluntary organization

A useful descriptive prelude to the consideration of legal and tax structures and frameworks, and a way to highlight the niche occupied by these organizations in UK society, is to categorize them by primary *function*, even though most voluntary bodies would characterize themselves as *multi-functional*. Such typologies are neither substitutes for a definition of the sector, nor of a classification of the "industries" or fields of activity within it. Brenton (1985) suggests the following set of functions for voluntary sector social service organizations, but it could equally well be applied in other industries (Murray, 1969; Wolfenden, 1978; Johnson, 1981; Handy, 1988; Nathan, 1990).

1. The *service-providing function* "typifies those voluntary agencies which supply a direct service to people, in kind or in the form of information, advice and support" (Brenton, 1985:11). In the social services field, agencies such as Barnardo's, as providers of child care, have this as their primary function, as do voluntary hospitals and schools. Law centers and independent advice centers are legal service providers.

2. The *mutual aid function* is "about self-help and exchange around a common need or interest" (Brenton, 1985:12), and is the main feature of organizations like Cruse (for widows), Alcoholics Anonymous, and a whole range of local community-based organizations in education, health, and recreation.

3. A third function identified by Brenton is the *pressure-group function*, "the marshalling of information around some specific cause or group interest and the application of this to some public arena through direct action, campaigning, lobbying and advocacy to achieve a desired change" (Brenton, 1985:12). The Child Poverty Action group, Liberty, and Oxfam are three well-known campaigning or pressure groups. Organizations whose primary activities are mutual aid or lobbying are less obviously producing a tangible good or service than direct service providers, since social participation is a key dimension of the value added to society by their existence.

4. Finally, we have what Brenton terms the *resource* and *coordinating functions*, which typically involve blending service provision to other voluntary sector bodies, often in particular industries, acting as "a central catalyst or repository of expertise, information, research, etc., on a specialist subject," with "represent[ing] a membership of other voluntary bodies and seek[ing] to liaise between them and coordinat[ing] their activities, their public relations or their connections with government" (Brenton, 1985:12). Included here are sector-wide national and local intermediaries (Wolfenden, 1978) such as the National Council for Voluntary Organisations, the Charities Aid Foundation, the Volunteer Centre and Local Development Agencies, together with industry-specific bodies such as the National Youth Agency and the National Federation of Housing Associations.

Another way to categorize the voluntary sector is to identify different structural types, depending on the method of resourcing and the nature of the organization (Home Office, 1990:3; Chanan, 1991:14). One type would be the intermediary bodies referred to above. Following Chanan (1991) another three varieties can be distinguished. *Professional non-profit organizations* are providers of professional services – employing paid staff at national and local level – where the national organizations directly run the local offices and raise funds for local work. *Voluntary service organizations* have professionally-organized national headquarters but autonomous local groups which raise their own funds and use volunteers. *Independent local community groups*, finally, are "self-standing bodies with no head office to provide support" (Home Office, 1990:3); their overwhelmingly important resources are their volunteer members' unpaid labor. In common with the (local) mutual aid and pressure group functional varieties in Brenton's taxonomy, the essence of the "output" of many of the latter groups will not be some identifiable service. Such bodies are difficult to classify in terms of an "industry" or market, since conventional distinctions between demand and supply, user and volunteer, or process and output often conflict with their underlying ideologies and operating principles.

Legal framework and tax treatment

The legal situation in the UK is complicated by the existence of three different legal frameworks. England and Wales are covered by English law. It is based on *common law*, the ancient law of the land deduced from custom and interpreted by judges, which has been exported to the USA, Ireland, Canada, Australia, and some other countries. Scotland falls under the auspices of separately developed Scots law, which is based on *Roman law*, a close relative of civil law, in common with legal systems in mainland Europe. Northern Ireland is something of a "half-way house" between the two (Woodfield *et al.*, 1987). In all the constituent countries of the UK, government legislation and European Community law are the other main sources of law. The treatment of the voluntary sector in the English and Scottish systems has been closely scrutinized of late, culminating in fresh legislation (see below), although this has not altered the definitional approach adopted by the law.

In none of the constituent countries of the UK is there such a neat and tidy concept of "nonprofit status" as is apparently available to entities which are the nearest equivalent to voluntary organizations outside the UK. *Charitable status*, and the comprehensive and automatic constitutional and fiscal privileges granted to bodies which attain it, is available to independent organizations which have legally recognized public benefit objectives or "purposes" written into their constitutions, but probably less than a half of all UK voluntary sector organizations are thus recognized in law (Kendall and Knapp, 1996). Moreover, there is no particular legal structure or form uniquely associated with either charities or non-charity voluntary organizations, and the same types of legal form are often adopted by both varieties (see below).

In practice, in England and Wales it falls to the Charity Commission to decide whether or not an organization is charitable in law. The Commission must be satisfied that the purposes or objects are *exclusively* charitable. Once recognized as a registered charity – as were over 170,000 organizations at the end of 1990 – these bodies "at once have the protection of the Crown, the Courts and the Commission for their purpose" (Guthrie, 1991). The Commission has had a number of supervisory, administrative, and pro-judicial roles since its inception in its present form in 1853, although many of its powers were put in place or enhanced by the *Charities Act 1960*. Its duties now include the maintenance of a register, an administrative function performed on behalf of Parliament, and attempting to identify, control, and remedy abuse in individual charities, in which it acts on behalf of the courts (Charity Commission, 1991). The Charity Commissioners thus act in a dual role, on behalf of the High Court on legal matters, and on behalf of Parliament (as any other government department) on administrative matters, attempting to safeguard charitable assets and the confidence of the public in charities and their trustees. The *Charities Act 1992*, and the consolidating *Charities Act 1993*, strengthen the Commission's powers by enhancing its ability to obtain information about the management of individual charities, and give it greater powers to act quickly upon the detection of abuse. The new legislation also clarifies the responsibilities of trustees (the members of the unpaid governing boards of charities), introduces a new regime for accounting by charities, and includes measures to tighten control over professional fundraisers.

Whether or not an organization is deemed charitable in law depends on a huge corpus of accumulated case or judge-made law, and past court decisions. Historically, the preamble to the 1601 Statute of Charitable Uses was an important catalogue or index of purposes that are charitable, but the single most influential indicator has been Pemsel's case of 1891, when Lord MacNaghten gave the judicial seal of approval to a classification of charitable purposes put forward by Samuel Romilly in 1805:

> "Charity" in its legal sense comprises four principal divisions; trusts for the relief of poverty; trusts for the advancement of education; trusts for the advancement of religion; and trusts for other purposes beneficial to the community, not falling under any of the preceding heads. (*Income Tax Special Purposes Commissioners v. Pemsel [1891] AC 531*)

Organizations for the relief of poverty are the only ones capable of being charities if they benefit a small group of people, since the relief of poverty is assumed *ex hypothesi* to be of public benefit; otherwise, an organization's purpose(s) must

> be of actual benefit and it must benefit the public as a whole, or a sufficient section of the public ... The extent of public benefit may vary between different types of charity. It is not possible to define precisely what amounts to actual benefit or what forms a sufficient section of the public: cases must largely be considered on their merits. (Charity Commission, 1989:2–3)

In fact, in addition to the educational and religious establishments which have achieved charitable status under the second and third heads, a flexible and modern interpretation of the fourth head through an analogy to the preamble to the 1601 Act has allowed a huge variety of non-profit-distributing "public benefit" organizations to be legally admitted to the charitable sector. This includes health and social care agencies helping people or animals "in need," conservation and environmental bodies, organizations providing land and buildings "for public use," and organizations promoting racial harmony and equality of men with women in political and economic opportunity. Exclusive self-help groups and organizations deemed "too political" are, however, controversially, denied charitable status.

Also charitable in law are around 100,000 bodies which are not subject to the full regulatory powers of the Commission (Cmd 694, 1989, section 3.15). These are the so-called *exempted* charities, over which other government agencies exercise a supervisory role, and include universities and polytechnics, the Church Commissioners and the institutions they administer, and bodies registered with the Registry of Friendly Societies (see below), a small proportion of which have achieved charitable status. Other charities have been *excepted* from the duty to register, submit accounts and obtain consent from the Charity Commission to land transactions. These include Scout and Guide groups, religious trusts, and voluntary schools.

An important point to make, therefore, is that it is organizational substance rather than organizational form which dominates the legal position of charities: it is the pursuit of charitable purposes which earns charitable status, not the establishment of a particular organizational form or legal structure.

Although the framework of English charity law may at first sight seem somewhat rigid, it does in fact have a key strength in terms of its adaptability; its case law base means that "fossilization" can be avoided by the creative use of analogies: Lord Hailsham, the former Lord Chancellor, pointed out in 1980 that "the legal concept of charity [is] not static, but moving and changing." For this reason, the government decided not to change the existing approach in the recent Charities Act. Moreover, supporters of the *status quo* argue that the concept of activity "being for charity," as underpinned by trust law, is almost instinctively and universally understood by the general public. Charity is a constitutional privilege, giving citizens the freedom to join together in the public interest as defined by law, not by politicians, and in so doing at once having the protection of the Crown, the Courts, and the Charity Commission. In this context, the government's own assessment was that the present approach is preferable to the alternative of writing an actual definition into statute law, which "would be fraught with difficulty, and put at risk the flexibility of the present law, which is both its greatest strength and its most valuable feature" (Cmd 694, 1989, section 2.11).

In *Scotland*, where there is no statutory body directly equivalent to the Charity Commission, a rather narrower legal interpretation has evolved, with charity usually interpreted as meaning the relief of poverty, although the Scottish courts have recognized that a wider interpretation may often be necessary in connection with trust deeds. The lack of a supervisory body other than the Inland

Revenue, which prevents and detects tax abuse (see below), has been cause for concern for some time, and the *Law Reform (Miscellaneous Provisions) Scotland Act 1990* goes some way towards remedying the situation for the estimated 15,000 "Scottish charities." New measures implemented following the Act include the establishment of an index of these "recognized bodies" at the Scottish Inland Revenue open for public inspection, and the granting of supervisory and investigatory powers to the Lord Advocate, similar to those of the English Charity Commission (SCVO, 1991).

In *Northern Ireland*, the Department of Finance and Personnel has some supervisory powers, as a result of the *Charities Act (Northern Ireland) 1964*, but those powers are less extensive than those of the Commission in England and Wales, and there are apparently no immediate plans for fresh legislation.

In contradistinction to the legal establishment and regulation of charities, *tax privileges* accruing to charities are uniform across the UK. The English "definition" now applies everywhere, and the Inland Revenue grants reliefs or "tax expenditures" providing that it is satisfied that the funds have been applied exclusively for charitable purposes (Income and Corporation Taxes Act, 1988). These tax privileges mostly relate to direct taxation, including exemption from income, corporation, and capital gains taxes, mandatory relief of 80 per cent from the uniform business rate levied by local authorities, and various forms of tax-deductibility on both planned giving (covenants) and, more recently, one-off giving. Nevertheless, the overlap between the English "definition" and fiscal privilege is somewhat more complicated than it may appear, since an organization established as a charity in law may have its tax privileges withdrawn if it misapplies its income.[3]

Non-charitable voluntary organizations throughout the UK are not afforded the same constitutional protection as charities, and accordingly are not subject to the Charity Commission's powers, although the proposals for tighter controls over professional fundraisers in the Charities Act 1992 do apply to what are confusingly called "charitable institutions," which includes both charities and non-charities which raise funds for "charitable, benevolent or philanthropic purposes" (Driscoll and Phelps, 1992). As far as tax treatment is concerned, non-charity voluntary agencies may qualify for certain fiscal privileges, although not as automatic and comprehensive as those available to charities: "charitable status is not the only password to significant tax relief for institutions and donors engaging in philanthropy and the provision of social welfare" (Chesterman, 1979:253). For example, a body which is voluntary in the sense that "it is not a public body, but whose activities are carried on otherwise than for profit" (Local Government Act, 1972, section 137 (2D)) may get discretionary relief on local taxation, i.e. the uniform business rate; nonprofit-distributing scientific research associations are exempted from income and capital gains taxes; and hospitals, private schools, and housing associations which, for some reason, have not gained charitable status are still exempted from income tax as long as the relevant income is applied for charitable purposes only (Income and Corporation Taxes Act, 1988).

Legal structures

A number of legal structures are available to voluntary organizations, each with their own advantages and disadvantages, usually connected with the scale of the proposed activity and the amount and value of property which the body proposes to have.[4] The most common forms are the *trust*, the *unincorporated association*, and the *company limited by guarantee*. In the case of charities, as a direct consequence of underpinning English trust law principles, the governing boards are trustees, who must almost always remain unpaid, other than receiving legitimate expenses incurred in carrying out their duties, and must not personally materially benefit from the organization's activities, unless specifically authorized by the document originating or controlling the organization (which is rarely the case). This notion of unremunerated, "disinterested," even "altruistic," organizational management and control is possibly unique in Europe to the UK and the Republic of Ireland.

Neither the trust nor the unincorporated association have "legal personality;" therefore their property must be held by some individuals on the organization's behalf, often the trustees in the former case, and the members in the latter.[5] In the case of the trust, the organizations' founders are known as *settlors*, and the trustees who manage the property may be appointed or nominated in a way predetermined by the settlor(s). This structure is still in common usage amongst bodies formed today, particularly in the case of grantmaking organizations, and was also important as a vehicle for the individual philanthropy that characterized the Tudor period, during which the 1601 statute was enacted. The unincorporated association structure, by contrast, is usually adopted when the participation of a membership is desired, with the governing board – usually referred to as the management committee – democratically elected by the organization's membership, and trustees during their term of office.[6] This structure is significant amongst many new organizations operating with few financial resources (Chesterman, 1979:201).

The *company limited by guarantee* was first conceived in the *Companies Act 1862*, and differs from the two structures described above in being incorporated; that is, it has a separate personality recognized in law, and is therefore able to do most things that an individual can do, including purchasing, owning and selling property in its own right, suing and being sued in its own name, entering into contracts, being liable in tort, and being indicted and convicted for certain criminal offences. As with the unincorporated association, the governing boards of these organizations – which are usually referred to as Boards of Directors – are drawn from the organization's membership, and are trustees. Clearly, important incentives to adopt this structure include a desire to economize on transaction costs if an organization wishes to engage in contractual business agreements, and to gain the financial protection of limited liability with regard to business transactions. However, companies limited by guarantee are also regulated by UK company law and European company law directives, which might be regarded as restrictive in some circumstances. Writing in the late 1970s, one well-informed observer suggested that these "are not numerous but constitute an important segment of the newer and larger active charities" (Chesterman, 1979:201), and it seems likely that these have been the fastest-growing of the three forms during the 1980s, continuing the trend evident over the 1970s (Berman, 1983).

Other than through the limited company structure, voluntary-sector organizations may be incorporated by Royal Charter, ecclesiastical decree, or Act of Parliament, and some of these bodies, governed by "arcane and complex law" (Chesterman, 1979:203), sit uneasily on the government–voluntary sector boundary, although in the legal sense they are unambiguously in the charitable sector. The other two significant mainstream legal structures available to voluntary organizations are the *friendly society* and the *industrial and provident society*. These structures are far less common than the three principal forms cited, both for charities and for the wider voluntary sector; they are also adopted by some organizations which are excluded from the sector according to the structural–operational definition on the grounds that they are primarily businesses (see below). The friendly societies, as unincorporated mutual insurance associations, register with the Registry of Friendly Societies under the Friendly Societies Act, 1974, along with building societies, working men's clubs, some of the older forms of cooperative organizations, and a ragbag of others. This government registry has very limited powers compared to the Charity Commission, and also registers industrial and provident societies under the Industrial and Provident Societies Act, 1965. These bodies can be thought of as "quasi-corporations," being hybrids of the friendly society and limited company form, and are thus registered for the purpose of carrying on any industry, business, or trade, whether wholesale or retail, if either (1) the society is a *bona fide* cooperative society, or (2) in view of the fact that the business of the society is being, or is intended to be, conducted for the benefit of the community, there are special reasons why the society should be registered under the 1965 Act, rather than as a company under the Companies Act (Sections 1 (1), (2) of the Industrial and Provident Societies Act, 1965).

The State, society, and the voluntary sector

Before the first Elizabethan era, in which the 1601 Statute was enacted, the role of the State in the social arena was relatively minor; the informal sector and the Church were the key players. Social welfare functions were "essentially ... the province of the Church, with support from the customary obligations imposed on feudal lords and from the guilds. At a less formal level, personal almsgiving and the families of poor people endeavoured to fill the gaps" (Chesterman, 1979:13). It was only with the breakdown of feudalism and the reduction of the Church's power that the State and secular philanthropy came to the fore, particularly in the relief of poverty and provision of education, with the State beginning to facilitate voluntary endeavor through the development of the protective legal framework for charities which has remained a cornerstone of the sector's privileged position in law to this day.

Indeed, as we have already seen, from this period right up until the start of the twentieth century, the formal delivery of social services was dominated by the voluntary sector, with government provision, funded through local taxation, always the gap-filler. However, government policies were shifting: the state encouragement of philanthropy that had characterized the first part of the seventeenth century gave way to hostility and negligence from the judiciary and legislature for the last part of that century and for much of the next, as the high priority given to landlords' private property rights made it more difficult for property to be devoted to charitable purposes. In this period, the ruling classes were, in general, more repressive towards the poor, who were regarded as less of a threat as a result of a number of social and economic developments. However, Government policy again became more sympathetic to the poor and to the voluntary sector by the mid-nineteenth century, motivated by both genuine social concern and fear of social upheaval. Around this time, support for the sector came through legislation to establish a permanent Charity Commission to supervise the management of charitable trusts, the introduction of various technical legal privileges for them, and the initiation of certain tax expenditures, as charitable organizations were exempted from newly introduced forms of taxation, most noticeably income tax. Other than the expansion of legal and fiscal privilege for the sector, the highest profile example of cooperation between the State and the voluntary sector at this time was its understanding with the COS to operate in mutually exclusive spheres, with the COS ideologically supporting the Poor Law's distinction between the deserving and undeserving poor (Chesterman, 1979:45).

It was not until the early twentieth century that the State replaced voluntary organizations as the principal agents of formal social service provision. This was partly in response to the growing realization by a better-informed government of the scope and scale of *voluntary failures* – what we would now recognize as insufficiency, particularism, paternalism, and amateurism (Salamon, 1987) – in the face of rapidly growing social and individual needs.

This reversal of "market share" was a gradual process which reached its culmination in the Labor government's social legislation of the 1940s, achieving different rates of State penetration across the fields where voluntary agencies had previously dominated. The broadening of statutory responsibilities had begun with extensive grant funding of the sector by government, first in education in the late nineteenth century, and in the social welfare sector from 1914 onwards, but the end point resulting from the ensuing incremental encroachment was different for the four main areas of social provision.

As already noted, in the fields of health care, education, and social insurance the public sector almost completely took over both funding and production. Most voluntary-sector hospitals were unambiguously absorbed into the state sector. Many voluntary-sector schools became "maintained," retaining distinct religious identities and some autonomy, but nevertheless regarded then (as now) as state schools. In the field of social insurance, the friendly societies were excluded from the new arrangements, although Beveridge, the architect of the new system, had wanted them to administer the new state funds. In each of these "industries" or fields of activity, a small but significant number of providers survived fully outside the mainstream government system, funded mainly through private fees. By contrast, despite the perceived need for ever greater penetration of all-embracing State-run services, the voluntary sector continued to be a key player in most social care activities, particularly child care and care for elderly people (Knapp, 1989; Wistow *et al.*, 1994). A mixed economy of both funding and provision emerged over the post-war period, with voluntary sector bodies being used as agents of the State in fulfilling its new duties at local and national level, and also continuing to operate in mainstream areas where legislation had not mandated statutory responsibility.

Unsurprisingly, just as commentators – in government, and outside it, including those in the voluntary sector itself – had highlighted the limitations of voluntary action when voluntary agencies were the principal providers, so the deficiencies of the public sector, or *government failures*, became fully apparent once the welfare state apparatus had established the government sector as the dominant means of formally financing and providing social welfare. Initially, the assumption of government sector funding and provision seemed to be largely unchallenged across the political spectrum, with the voluntary sector seen as a "statutory supplementer" (Kramer, 1981) in its service-provision function. However, the voluntary sector's other functions, as discussed in the preceding section, were acknowledged, and hence the considerable government funding over the 1960s and 1970s of community development and self-help groups, which, by their very nature, could not be incorporated into the public sector, and the recognition of the key role of intermediary bodies in ensuring a healthy and vibrant voluntary sector (Wolfenden, 1978). The legislation passed at the start of this period (see above) further enhanced the State's protective legal framework for charitable organizations, although, in ensuing years, there was much controversy about the whole charitable law framework. Critics from the Left regarded it as having developed in such a way as to become inappropriately removed from its original "unifying purpose" of helping the poor and deprived (for example, see Gladstone, 1982; Gerard, 1983), and of being anti-working-class and perpetuating privilege. These commentators and others saw the Charity Commission's and the judiciary's interpretation of the core "public benefit" requirement, described above as inconsistent and too restrictive, particularly through "unfairly" subsidizing fee-paying schools and hospitals by allowing them charitable status, whilst stifling social change by denying it to those parts of the sector fulfilling key mutual aid and pressure group functions (Brenton, 1985; Gladstone, 1979; Whittaker, 1979).

Over the 1970s, an apparent consensus across the political parties seemed to be emerging both on the important roles of the voluntary sector in society, and on the need for effective partnership with the State to ensure healthy welfare pluralism. This view was vigorously endorsed by the Wolfenden Committee Report (1978), which emphasized the benefits to both sectors of pluralism and partnership, although the precise nature of the relationship was not clearly defined (Webb and Wistow, 1986), and some commentators drew attention to an imbalance of power, wherein the voluntary sector remained very much the junior, silent partner.

Moreover, Brenton (1985:139) detects "useful imprecisions and ambiguities" in the rhetoric of both the government and the opposition parties at the time, for the definition and coverage of the terms "voluntary action" and "voluntary sector" were implicitly being adjusted to emphasize the type of organization, or function of the sector, which happened to suit each proposed or actual policy initiative. She argues that the policy statements in support of the sector made by the moderate Labor government in the late 1970s, for example, verge on "wilful mystification" (Brenton, 1985:136) as it sought to rationalize freezing or reducing various forms of social expenditure with recession beginning to bite; indeed, she argues that its acceptance of pluralism in welfare service provision – particularly the encouragement of service provision from the middle-class, traditional, and "safe" wing of the voluntary sector – made it hard to distinguish from the left wing of the Conservative party.

From the radical Left, too, the voluntary failures and the irreconcilability of the sector with socialist objectives that had been stressed in the 1940s and 1950s were also conveniently put to one side. In this case it was the sector's capacity to enable "bottom up" radical social reform as a vehicle for participatory, decentralized social action which was highlighted. The new image of the sector was now represented by "the proliferation of self-organized community nurseries, disabled mutual aid groups, allotment societies, black supplementary schools, women's aid centres, gay counselling services, tenants' cooperatives, public transport campaigns, community bookshops, cyclists' action groups [wherein] lies a very old political tradition" (Worpole quoted in Brenton, 1985). This version of the voluntary sector – with its emphasis on the more radical elements of its development, mutual aid and pressure group functions, as opposed to its more traditional service-provision role – chimed with political goals, was to be the grass-roots mechanism which some left-wing Labor local authorities, and most prominently of all, the Greater London Council, were to attempt to utilize in confronting the Conservative government's centralization of power and loadshedding policies of the 1980s (Wolch, 1990).

Use of the voluntary sector as a strategic weapon in the political struggle between central and local government only partly explains local authority grantmaking to the sector during the 1980s; the familiar rationales of cost-effectiveness, flexibility and innovativeness, choice and specialization, for example, also motivated this tier of government, including moderate Labor and Conservative, as well as radical administrations (see, for example,

Judge and Smith, 1983; Knapp *et al.*, 1990). Central government, too, continued to justify increased support for the sector – most prominently via funding channelled though quangos, measures to facilitate and stimulate individual and corporate giving, and legislation to encourage contracting-out – on these apolitical grounds. Yet political factors were clearly at work here also, with the sector being used as a tool for centralizing power by bypassing local democratic control.

Many commentators cite the government's ideological desire for "privatization" as the key motivator of many of these policies, replacing public sector activity with nongovernmental activity wherever and whenever it could, and this was indeed a key policy objective of the Thatcher governments (McCarthy, 1989). Certainly, many policy statements made during the 1980s appeared to lump the informal and voluntary sectors together indiscriminately, and use the terms almost interchangeably with the word "volunteers," all during a time when state provision was being defined in residual terms for the first time since the early 1940s.

Into the 1990s, John Major's government continued to direct its attention towards the sector both with specific measures, through, for example, the charity legislation to which we have referred, the introduction of further measures to facilitate charitable giving, and more incidentally through the promotion of "quasi-markets" and the encouragement of contracting-out in fields where voluntary sector providers co-exist with other sectors (Le Grand, 1991; Wistow *et al.*, 1994). The explicit aim of injecting more competition within and for government has allowed both for-profit and voluntary-sector bodies to increase their shares in some industries. Most of these measures have been guardedly welcomed by the voluntary sector; government calls for improved partnership between the sectors, and for better accountability and enhanced efficiency (Home Office, 1990), pose challenges, offer opportunities, and threaten long-established relationships. However, there are very real fears that changes in the nature and mechanisms for government funding, in particular increased specificity through the replacement of grants with contracts, will threaten to undermine the autonomy of those organizations which receive these funds for their service provision function. It may also constrain the fulfilment of their other functions, including advocacy activities (Gutch *et al.*, 1990; Knapp and Kendall, 1991; Kendall and Knapp, 1996). There is also the concern that voluntary agencies, particularly small, local ones,[7] may be marginalized because central government fails to recognize their contributions and local authorities find it increasingly difficult to fund them from their declining resources.

Defining the voluntary sector

The UK voluntary sector includes a variety of legal and organizational forms, and has developed in response to a variety of needs, buffeted and encouraged by government and other relevant factors. There is no single or simple legal route to the definition or delimitation of voluntary organizations, nor can we easily fall back on tax codes or company law to furnish us with alternative concepts within the sector. Simon's (1987) utilization of Section 501 of the (US) Internal Revenue Code to distinguish four concentric "circles" to describe what he calls "the nonprofit world," for example, cannot be repeated with anything like the same precision for the UK. In these circumstances, it has been common for UK researchers either to concentrate on registered charities (see, for example, Posnett, 1993) or to build up a definition from component criteria which organizations should satisfy before being labelled as "voluntary" (see, for example, Hatch, 1980; Johnson, 1981; Brenton, 1985). The utilization of a similar "first principles" approach is therefore not merely appealing in the UK, but virtually obligatory if progress is to be made towards the description and analysis of a meaningful construct.

In this section, we discuss the relevance and interpretation of the structural–operational definition in the UK context. The structural–operational definition requires that, to be classified as belonging to the nonprofit or third sector, a body must possess the following characteristics: it must be a formal organization, self-governing, independent of government,[8] not profit-distributing, and voluntary.

Formal organization

All of the entities discussed above have formal character as organizations, ruling out of the study the huge set of informal activities of household and communities which are so important in some fields, particularly community development and social welfare. Public policy in the UK has recently paid more attention to this informal sector, for example in the *1990 National Health Service and Community Care Act*. Our research interest here, however, is in formal, structured entities, with a charter, constitution, or set of rules (thus including charitable trusts and unincorporated associations), perhaps formally registered with a public body (including the tax authorities) or with a local or national voluntary sector intermediary, and possibly incorporated under company law as a company limited by guarantee.

Independent of government and self-governing

The second and third requirements of the structural–operational definition are that a voluntary organization should be constitutionally or institutionally independent of government, and self-governing, that is with its own internal decision-making structures and not controlled by a for-profit or by government. Ben-Ner (1986) has argued that control by patrons (donors or clients) is the principal *raison d'être* for voluntary bodies, but many organizations are oligarchic, controlled by a "self-perpetuating board of directors." Hansmann (1980) calls these "entrepreneurial" as opposed to "mutual" bodies, which are controlled by patrons. These entrepreneurial bodies would stay within the structural–operational definition. One of the issues here is the *extent* of independence from government, and the essentially dynamic and changing nature of the relationship between government and organizations. For example, several charitable bodies exist which have been formed or incorporated by Acts of Parliament, and/or for which many of the trustees are government appointees, and/or which are fully funded by, or heavily reliant on, public money. Some of these agencies are consequently widely seen as government sector public bodies, including all but one of the universities, research and other "non-departmental public bodies" and quangos, maintained schools and the national museums; while others are regarded as voluntary, including many intermediary bodies, the Women's Royal Voluntary Service, Law Centres and Citizens' Advice Bureaux. In a legal sense, they are *all* completely separate from government, generally because of their charitable status. We should recall that together with the perpetuation of existence, the protection of assets from government was the primary benefit of charitable status, and pre-dated tax privileges by many centuries. Brenton (1985) and Wolch (1990) are among the many commentators who have expressed concern over the extent of state control over or "penetration of" the voluntary sector, via funding and otherwise. Wolch characterized the sector as evolving into the "Shadow State," a "para-state apparatus ... administered outside of traditional democratic politics" (1990:4). The empirical question is where to draw the line between independence and dependence. Ideally, we might want to look at the extent to which each borderline organization controls its own constitution (6, 1991), or to examine carefully the processes by which resource-allocation decisions are made in order to understand the dynamics of the relationship between organization and government.[9]

A very recent phenomenon in the UK, and one which may become increasingly important over the next few years, is the establishment of self-governing entities *within* the public sector. This builds on a general trend to increase the decision-making autonomy of many public bodies, and has been particularly noticeable with the proliferation of new "quasi-government agencies," particularly quangos and trading funds, designed to function at arm's length from government departments, thus avoiding direct political control. Although still responsible to Ministers, they operate mostly in a more commercially-orientated fashion than the bureaux which had previously discharged their functions (Parker and Hartley, 1991). Such trends towards autonomy inside the government sector have recently begun to affect the voluntary sector directly, as self-governing public bodies have been established to contest markets in key voluntary sector industries, including health, social services, and education. For example, National Health Service (NHS) trusts have been in existence since April 1991, operating independently of central government's district health authorities without actually leaving the public sector. The *new* grant-maintained schools which opt out of local authority control[10] are in a similar position, for they simply substitute central for local government as their paymaster. Curiously, however, the NHS trusts are not eligible for charitable status, but the grant-maintained schools are. Over time, these quasi-government entities may become quasi-*non*government entities, and could soon therefore arrive in the voluntary sector as defined in this study.

Not profit-distributing

The non-distribution constraint, to use Hansmann's (1980) terminology, is fundamental to most but not all definitions of the nonprofit sector: it bars a voluntary organization "from distributing its net earnings, if any, to individuals who exercise control over it, such as members, officers, directors, or trustees" (Hansmann, 1980:838). There can be no shareholders as such: profits can be earned, but must be ploughed back into the organization for investment purposes, to enable cross-subsidization, or to affect transfers to "noncontrolling persons" (Hansmann, 1987:27). The trustees of charitable bodies must remain disinterested and, under the legal restriction operating in the UK, this means unremunerated.[11] The non-distribution constraint rules out most cooperatives (including, for example, workers' cooperatives and agricultural cooperatives) and mutual benefit financial intermediaries, including some which have historically been regarded as part of the sector, such as building societies and some friendly societies, but whose commercial orientation is now so marked that they are sometimes hard to distinguish for users from private, for-profit bodies (see Kendall et al., 1992). Incidentally, many of these organizations would also fail to satisfy the voluntarism requirement (see below), whereas most voluntary hospitals and schools (usually charitable) and all housing associations (mostly not charitable) would meet it. In addition to applying any operating surplus to their missions, these organizations' governing boards must remain unremunerated, although they may be "commercial" in the sense that most of their income comes through fees paid by clients. Several modern types of mutual and cooperative organization, such as credit unions and some housing cooperatives, may be ruled out by the strict enforcement of this criterion, but are nevertheless intimately linked with some parts of the sector's activities and thus extremely hard to separate from them.

Voluntarism

The last criterion for an entity to be a voluntary organization is that it must benefit to a meaningful degree from philanthropy or voluntary citizen involvement. Even if 100 per cent of an organization's income came from government or from fees paid by clients, there might still be voluntarism in the form of gifts in kind or gifts of time from volunteers, either in the labor force or on the management committee. For the purposes of structural–operational definition, it is not necessary to require that voluntarism be motivated solely by altruism: enlightened self-interest, reciprocity, moral duty, and other motivations will do just as well. Participants, patrons, and staff, are not coerced into an activity or into membership; they make independent and autonomous choices to be involved.

Voluntarism is, of course, not the preserve of the voluntary sector, but it is an essential defining characteristic of the voluntary sector in the UK. This is instanced by those bodies with unremunerated governing boards (their trustees), the voluntarism of which is perhaps the single most important defining characteristic of the sector, and a key ingredient in nurturing trust and preserving the public's good will towards it (Nathan, 1990). Voluntarism, altruism or disinterestedness is also at the heart of charity law, though no "black letter rule expressed in terms of altruism has ever been formulated. There are simply cases which show that self-help and private profit prevent an organisation from qualifying as a charity because they deprive the organisation in question of an exclusively charitable nature" (Picarda, 1992:1).

It need hardly be said that, once again, we have a criterion which can be met, or violated, to varying degrees. Choosing the "right" degree is not straightforward. Where the voluntarism condition is clearly violated, while other criteria hold, and most of an organization's income comes from government, we have a quasi-nongovernmental body. If most or all income comes from fees and charges, and no resources are donated, some classifications would still see this as a voluntary organization; we would prefer to see an alternative classification. Hence, we would not regard the newly emerging bodies sometimes known as *not-for-profit agencies* in the UK, which are especially active in the social care area, as part of the sector. For the present, at least, they appear to satisfy all criteria except voluntarism and perhaps, by extension, the non-distribution constraint. This is because members of their management boards can be paid and may receive monetary payments linked to the health of the organization. If significant time or money donations were to be secured by these bodies at some point in the future, however, then they would fall within the structural–operational definition of the sector.

Conclusion

The five criteria referred to above together generate the structural–operational definition of the nonprofit sector. They have been shown to possess direct equivalents in the UK. We have also seen that the *extent* to which some of these apply – for in reality, most are to be found on a continuum rather than being simply met or not met in their entirety – in fact constitutes a key element in the present debate as to the actual or appropriate niche of the sector in the UK economy.

The criteria-based, first principles, approach to the definition of the voluntary sector has precedents in UK research, although the lists of requirements may not always have been the same. For example, Hatch (1980) identified three conditions for an entity to be in the voluntary sector – formal, independent of government and not profit-distributing – and Brenton (1985) included these same three conditions, plus self-governing (private) and public benefit. Johnson's (1981) four factors were independence from government, self-governing (private), not profit-distributing and receiving some of its income from voluntary donations. Knapp et al., (1987) and 6 (1991) suggest longer lists which, not surprisingly given that all studies are looking at basically the same set of entities, overlap considerably with the structural–operational definition. Thus, both the approach and the detail of the definition of nonprofit organizations in this study have solid precedents in the UK.

A potential criterion which has not been adopted by the structural–operational definition, but which, as we have seen, underpins the legal "definition" of *charity*, relates to the notion of "public benefit," and many commentators see this as an important characteristic of the voluntary sector. For example, Beveridge (1948) talked of "voluntary action for a public purpose – for social advance," and Robin Guthrie, the Chief Charity Commissioner, has argued that *charity* is "best defined as an action or gift of benefit to others" (1988:17). Indeed, Paton (1990) goes so far as to suggest that the very expression "voluntary sector," which he describes as "muddled, outdated, misleading and much else besides", should be rejected, and that we should instead start to think in terms of the "social economy" comprising "organisations oriented towards the provision of some kind of *common benefit or public good*" (1990:2; italics added). This property or orientation is usually linked implicitly to the voluntarism or non-distribution constraint through the "nonselfish or nonmaterialistic" behavior of those who are involved with the organization, most obviously through trustees and other volunteers. These organizations are seen as different because they are value-based, or because those who control them or work for them are characterized by levels of commitment, benevolence, altruism, or beneficence and solidarity (Gerard, 1983) which are not to be found in other sectors (for criticisms of this approach, see 6, 1991). Lord Simonds in the *Inland Revenue Commissioners v. Baddeley* Case (1955) referred to the public benefit purpose as "the most difficult of the many difficult problems in this branch of the law." As we have seen, the dividing line between primarily member-serving and primarily public-benefit organizations is an extremely controversial one.

In considering the definition and treatment of the UK voluntary sector, and providing an overview of the types of organization that populate it, what is clear above all else is the essentially *dynamic nature* of its juxtaposition to entities in other sectors and to "hybrids" on the borderline between sectors. Organizations can migrate from one sector to another over time, and also alter their function and type as a result of changing relationships with the other sectors. To understand these complex interactions, we require both an appreciation of the historical development of the sector, and of its currently changing relationship with the state – as legislator, regulator, funder, and provider.

Notes

1   The authors express their thanks to Marilyn Taylor for her considerable assistance in the preparation of the second section, and to

Geraint Thomas, Robin Guthrie, and Robert Venables for invaluable comments on the third and fifth sections. The paper has also benefited from comments by Helmut Anheier, David Forrest, and Adrian Longley.

2   These attempted to replace the COS as the center of gravity for much of the sector. The COS itself moved on from its role as an intermediary to becoming a social service specialist, and was later renamed the Family Welfare Association.

3   Tax privileges were first offered to Oxford and Cambridge Universities and Eton and Winchester Schools in the late fifteenth century, and extended to all charities three centuries later.

4   This is a separate issue from whether or not they hold charitable status or are part of the voluntary sector, as noted above.

5   There are, however, two instances when these bodies can have a separate legal identity. Firstly, they may be incorporated under Royal Charter (see below). Secondly, trustees of a trust or association may be incorporated under the *Charitable Trustees Incorporation Act 1872*, a procedure amended to be made more user-friendly by the Charities Act 1992. Also, even without incorporation, the position is necessarily different in relation to land, which can usually be vested in trustees.

6   A recent survey by the National Council of Voluntary Organisations found that three-quarters of management committee members do not realize that they are trustees, and certainly do not appreciate their liabilities.

7   This is particularly the case for community-based developmental, participatory, and campaigning groups, for whom public support is presently minimal and precarious in any case.

8   In the UK context, the expression "independent of government" rather than the word "private" is utilized for three reasons. First, since voluntary organizations with charitable status "operate in the public domain, and charity trustees are publicly accountable ... no charity is 'private', and even the founder of a charity cannot direct the charity to act without its trusts: it has an existence of its own, which [the Charity Commission] stand to protect" (Guthrie, 1991). Second, in English trust law, the term "private" is in fact used to describe trusts which are *not* charitable, where the interest under the trust is purely private – for example, a conventional will leaving money in trust to a relative – rather than when referring to a charitable trust whose beneficiaries are, by definition, the public at large. In the former case, the trust can be enforced by a private individual, whereas with the latter, this must usually be done via the Attorney General through what is known as a "relator" action. A third reason is that "private" is a shorthand term for "private" for-profit organizations.

9 Of course, the examination of these issues at the level of individual organizations is not possible in large-scale research enquiries with the focus described in this book. Instead, clear rules have to be made about how to treat broad groups of organizations. In our attempt to apply the structural–operational definition to the sector in the UK. Instead, organizations with charitable status – including those with government-appointed boards or chief executives and fully funded with state monies – were all initially assumed to be part of the UK voluntary sector (Kendall and Knapp, 1996).

10 They are not to be confused with the original maintained voluntary schools, which opted *in* to agreements with their local education authorities in the late 1940s. To confuse matters further, however, these latter bodies can, like the schools run directly by local authorities, replace local government with central government funding and also become grant-maintained.

11 The non-distribution criterion does not, of course, prevent an organization ploughing profits back into the improvement of conditions of employment, inflated salaries, opulent offices and other generous fringe benefits; but the limited evidence for the UK voluntary sector suggests this is uncommon (see, for example, Reward, 1992).

References

Ben-Ner, Avner (1986), "Nonprofit organizations: why do they exist in market economies?" in *The Economics of Nonprofit Institutions*, ed. Susan Rose-Ackerman. Oxford: Oxford University Press.

Berman, E.D. (1983) "Voluntary means business," *The Law Society Gazette: Charity and Appeals Directory 1984*, Supplement, 23 November 1983.

Beveridge, Lord (1948), *Voluntary Action: A Report on Methods of Social Advance*. London: Allen and Unwin.

Brenton, Maria (1985), *The Voluntary Sector in British Social Services*. Harlow: Longman.

Burnell, Peter (1991), *Charity, Politics and the Third World*. Brighton: Harvester Wheatsheaf.

Chanan, Gabriel (1991), *Taken for Granted: Community Activity and the Crisis of the Voluntary Sector*. London: Community Development Foundation Publications.

Charities: A Framework for the Future (1989), Cmd 694. London: HMSO.

Charity Commission (1989), *Starting a Charity*, Leaflet CC21. London: Charity Commission.

Charity Commission (1989), *Report of the Charity Commissioners for England and Wales for the Year 1990*. London: HMSO.

Chesterman, Michael (1979), *Charities, Trusts and Social Welfare*. London: Weidenfeld and Nicolson.

Driscoll, Lindsay and Bridget Phelps (1992), *The Charities Act 1992: A Guide for Charities and Other Voluntary Organizations*. London: National Council for Voluntary Organizations.

Gladstone, Francis (1979), *Voluntary Action in a Changing World*. London: Bedford Square Press.

Gladstone, Francis. *Charity Law and Social Justice*. London: Bedford Square Press.

Guthrie, Robin (1988), *Charity and the Nation*. London: Charities Aid Foundation.

Guthrie, Robin (1991), Personal communications to the authors.

Gutch, Richard, Christian Kunz and Ken Spencer (1990), *Partners or Agents?* London: National Council for Voluntary Organizations.

Handy, Charles (1988), *Understanding Voluntary Organizations*. Harmondsworth: Penguin.

Hansmann, Henry (1980), "The role of nonprofit enterprise." *Yale Law Journal*, 89:835–901.

Hansmann, Henry (1987), "Economic theories of nonprofit organization," in *The Nonprofit Sector: A Research Handbook*, ed. by W.W. Powell. New Haven: Yale University Press.

Hatch, Stephen (1980), *Outside the State*. London: Croom Helm.

Home Office (1990), *Efficiency Scrutiny of Government Funding of the Voluntary Sector*. London: HMSO.

Johnson, Norman (1981), *Voluntary Social Services*. Oxford: Martin Robertson.

Judge, Ken and Jillian Smith (1983), "Purchase of services in England." *Social Services Review*, 57: 209–233.

Kendall, Jeremy, Martin Knapp, Rob Paton and Alan Thomas (1992), "The 'social economy' in the UK," in *The Third Sector Cooperative, Mutual and Nonprofit Organisations*, ed. Jacques Defourny and José L. Monzón Campos. Brussels: De Boeck Université.

Kendall, Jeremy and Martin Knapp (1996), *The Voluntary Sector in the UK*. Manchester: Manchester University Press.

Knapp, Martin (1989), "Private and voluntary welfare," in *The New Politics of Welfare*, ed. Michael McCarthy. London: Macmillan.

Knapp, Martin and Jeremy Kendall (1991), "Policy issues for the UK voluntary sector in the 1990s." *Annals of Public and Cooperative Economics*, 62:711–732.

Knapp, Martin, Eileen Robertson and Corinne Thomason (1990), "Public money, voluntary action," *PSSRU Discussion Paper 500*. Unpublished report to the Home Office. University of Kent at Canterbury.

Knapp, Martin, Eileen Robertson and Corinne Thomason (1990), "Public money, voluntary action: whose welfare?" in *The Third Sector:*

Comparative Studies of Nonprofit Organizations, ed. Helmut Anheier and Wolfgang Seibel. Berlin: DeGruyter.

Kramer, Ralph M. (1981), *Voluntary Agencies in the Welfare State*. Berkeley: University of California Press.

Le Grand, Julian (1991), "Quasi-markets and social policy." *Economic Journal* 101:1256–1267.

McCarthy, Michael (ed.) (1989), *The New Politics of Welfare*. London: Macmillan.

Murray, G. J. (1969), *Voluntary Organizations and Social Welfare*. Glasgow: Oliver and Boyd.

Nathan, Lord (1952), *Report to the Committee on Law and Practice Relating to Charitable Trusts*. London: HMSO.

Nathan, Lord (1990), *Effectiveness and the Voluntary Sector*. London: NCVO.

Owen, David (1964), *English Philanthropy 1660-1960*. Cambridge, MA: Harvard University Press.

Parker, David and Keith Hartley (1991), "Organizational status and performance: the effects on employment." *Applied Economics*, 23:403–416.

Paton, Rob (1990), "The Emerging Social Economy." *Management Issues*, 3:2–7.

Picarda, Hubert (1992) "English charity law: vital and dispensable aspects." Paper presented at Charity Commissioners' seminar at Leeds Castle.

Posnett, John (1993) "The resources of registered charities in England and Wales – 1990–91," in *Researching the Voluntary Sector*, ed. Susan Saxon-Harrold and Jeremy Kendall. Tonbridge: Charities Aid Foundation.

Prochaska, Frank (1988), *The Voluntary Impulse: Philanthropy in Modern Britain*. London: Faber and Faber.

Reward Group (1992), *Charities 1991/92*. Stone, Staffordshire: The Reward Group.

Salamon, Lester (1987), "Partners in public service: the scope and theory of government–nonprofit relations," in *The Nonprofit Sector: A Research Handbook*, ed. by W. W. Powell. New Haven: Yale University Press.

SCVO (Scottish Council for Voluntary Organizations) (1991) "The Law Reform (Miscellaneous) (Scotland) Act 1990." Unpublished internal document. Edinburgh: SCVO.

Simon, John (1987), "The tax treatment of nonprofit organizations: a review of federal and state policies," in *The Nonprofit Sector: A Research Handbook*, ed. by W. W. Powell. New Haven: Yale University Press.

6, Perri (1991), *What is a Voluntary Organization? Defining the Voluntary and Non-profit Sectors*. London: NCVO.

Ware, Alan (ed.) (1989), *Charities and Government*. Manchester: Manchester University Press.

Webb, Sydney and Beatrice Webb (1912), *The Prevention of Destitution*.

London: Longman.

Webb, Adrian and Gerald Wistow 1986), *Planning, Need and Scarcity.* London: Allen & Unwin.

Whittaker, Ben (1979), "Time to reform the charity law?" *Voluntary Action,* 4.

Wistow, Gerald, Martin Knapp, Brian Hardy, and Caroline Allen (1994), *Social Care in a Mixed Economy.* Buckingham: Open University Press.

Wolch, Jennifer R. (1990), *The Shadow State: Government and Voluntary Sector in Transition.* New York: The Foundation Center.

Wolfenden Report (1978), *The Future of Voluntary Organizations: Report of the Wolfenden Committee.* London: Croom Helm, 1978.

Woodfield, Sir Philip, G. Binns, R. Hirst, and D. Neal (1987), *Efficiency Scrutiny of the Supervision of Charities.* London: HMSO.

Chapter 11

THE UNITED STATES

Lester M. Salamon

Introduction

Among the countries examined in this book, the United States has perhaps the most self-conscious and highly developed concept of a distinctive nonprofit sector. In fact, the existence, indeed the profusion, of nonprofit organizations has been one of the defining features of the American experience at least since the early 1800s, when Alexis de Tocqueville declared it to be the major factor explaining how America was able to avoid the dangers of tyranny and barbarism despite its highly individualistic culture. "In democratic countries the science of association is the mother of science," declared the perceptive Frenchman, "the progress of all the rest depends upon the progress it has made" (de Tocqueville, 1835 [1945]:116).

Yet there is a certain irony in America's reputation as the paragon of nonprofit action. For one thing, while nonprofit associations and organizations have a long history in America, the notion of a distinctive nonprofit sector sharing common characteristics is a relatively recent, and still not fully accepted, concept. In addition, American attitudes toward such organizations have historically exhibited a certain ambivalence. On the one hand, such organizations are prized for their celebration of individual initiative. On the other, however, they run foul of deep-seated populist sentiments against concentrated economic power and élitism.

Lacking a strong tradition of solidarity, either in the French sense of "fraternity" or the later Continental socialist sense of working-class consciousness, America's support for the nonprofit sector has actually been more problematic than current rhetoric might suggest. That the United States would develop a strong concept of an independent nonprofit sector was therefore by no means preordained. To be sure, such a concept finds support in traditional American values of individualism, hostility to centralized power, and separation of Church and State. However, these values proved perfectly consistent with a pervasive collaboration between the public and private sectors throughout the colonial period and the first century of the nation's existence. Not until the later nineteenth century, in fact, did the concept of a separate and distinct private nonprofit sector really emerge. It did so, moreover, as part of a broader effort that was then under way to establish an undisputed sphere of private business action unrestrained by the social and political demands being pressed through the State. In the process, the historic American practice of relying on voluntary organizations to meet community needs was transformed from a pragmatic necessity into a political ideology, which became, in the later nineteenth and early twentieth centuries, a rallying cry for conservative opposition to the extension of government social welfare protections and a rationalization for formerly unparalleled concentrations of wealth. While this ideology of voluntarism elevated the image of voluntary, nonprofit institutions in American life, however, it also created a powerful mythology that continues to obscure key facets of the way these institutions actually function.

Unraveling the true character of the nonprofit sector in the American setting thus turns out to be considerably more complex than is often assumed. To do justice to the topic, it is therefore necessary to look briefly at the historical and social context within which these organizations have developed, the legal framework that defines their basic structure, and the recent trends influencing their evolution. Only then will it be possible to assess the extent to which the "structural–operational definition" developed to examine these organizations in the context of comparative analysis, as outlined in Chapter 3 above, actually applies to the American case.

Background: Toward an ideology of voluntarism

Early ambivalence

That America would develop a powerful ideology of voluntarism as its distinctive contribution to the practice of social policy, and that this ideology would retain its vigor as a powerful basis for rearguard resistance to the extension of the modern welfare state, was hardly self-evident in the first hundred years of the nation's existence, or in the colonial era that preceded it. To be sure, a veritable profusion of associations made their appearance on the American scene early in the country's history. "We have societies for everything," James Walker, later President of Harvard College, thus reported ten years before Alexis de Tocqueville's historic visit. "Scarcely a month passes in which we are not called upon to join, or aid, some benevolent association" (Walker, 1825:241). Nor did this penchant for voluntary association dissipate as the century wore on. On the contrary, it seems to have grown in force (Bremner, 1980).

Several factors seem to have accounted for this phenomenon. One of these certainly was the deep-seated hostility to royal power and centralized state authority that the religious non-conformists who helped populate the American colonies brought with them when they fled the Old World. Hostile to state power, they were inclined to do things for themselves. This sentiment was reinforced, moreover, by the spirit of individualism that quickly took root in the seemingly boundless open spaces of the New World. In a sense, the formation of voluntary associations offered a compromise between the extremes of rampant individualism and dependence on monarchical power. It provided a way to confront common problems while still retaining a significant measure of individual initiative.

The arrival of large numbers of new immigrants in the middle and latter nineteenth century, moreover, added a further impetus to the formation of nonprofit associations: the impetus of communal identity and mutual aid. Nonprofit organizations formed along ethnic and religious lines provided vital mechanisms for newcomers to acclimatize themselves to the American scene and cope with the challenges of urbanization and industrialization that were newly overtaking American life (Bremner, 1956; Katz, 1986: 62–3). They did so, moreover, with a spirit of self-help and mutual aid that simultaneously built pride and self-respect.

Powerful though these factors may have been in encouraging the growth of voluntary organizations in eighteenth- and nineteenth-century America, however, it is easy to exaggerate their importance. For one thing, the impact of at least some of these sentiments on associational life was by no means wholly positive. Individualism, for example, can be quite corrosive of associational bonds. Alexis de Tocqueville, the Frenchman whose 1845 book, *Democracy in America*, first drew attention to the vital link between democracy and associations, himself recognized this when he acknowledged that "[u]nhappily, the same social condition [i.e. equality] that renders associations so necessary to democratic nations renders their formation more difficult among those nations than among all others" (de Tocqueville, 1835 [1945]:116). Individualism is thus something to be overcome in the formation of voluntary associations, not something to rely on.

What is more, individualism, hostility to centralized power, and ethnic identity were not the only impulses at work in early American culture. Side by side with these sentiments were strong currents of anti-corporatism, anti-élitism, and a penchant for popular control even of presumably private institutions that hardly encouraged the development of at least the more institutionalized portions of the charitable sector. On the contrary, as Peter Dobkin Hall has reminded us, private corporations and trusts were associated in colonial and post-Revolutionary America with the "corruptions of the Stuart monarchy and the Church of England" (Hall, 1987:3). Even esteemed educational institutions like Harvard College thus found themselves under attack as a consequence.[1] Democratic forces in many colonial and early state governments actively resisted efforts to incorporate eleemosynary or other institutions, and denied courts the equity powers needed to enforce trusts. Thus, New York State passed laws limiting the ability of charitable institutions to build up endowments, while Virginia enacted a statute transferring all property given for charitable purposes into the hands of county overseers for the poor rather than leaving it for private institutions to manage (Hall, 1987:4–5).

To an important degree, therefore, associations flourished in the American setting *despite*, rather than because of, the prevailing culture. What gave impetus to the formation of associations was not sentiment so much as pragmatism and necessity. Unlike what happened in Europe, society came into existence in America prior to the State. Americans therefore had to devise ways to provide themselves with essential services that other societies naturally relied on the State to supply. As James Walker explained:

Such is the distribution of property amongst us, and such the nature of our government, that individuals here can never hope to rival the splendid acts of princely munificence sometimes recorded of the old and immensely rich families of other countries; neither can we expect the same degree of legislative patronage. Much, therefore, of good that is effected elsewhere by private munificence, or royal and legislative patronage, can be effected here only by voluntary associations. It is idle to say of this, that it is not our best resource, for we have no other. (Walker, 1825)

Reflecting these pragmatic origins, early American nonprofit institutions lacked the purity that is now often ascribed to them. On the contrary, they blended public and private roles in ways that defy categorization. Private corporations were granted state charters on condition that they perform public functions and, often, provide for a degree of public control. Even many of the commercial corporations established during the colonial era and the first half-century after independence – such as banks, turnpike companies and railroads – were viewed as essentially *public* institutions (Hartz, 1948). In the case of eleemosynary institutions, such as colleges and hospitals, the sense of public purpose was even stronger. Such institutions were conceived to be part of the public sector, since they served essentially public purposes. Consistently with this, they were supported in important part by governmental subsidies, and often included public officials on their governing boards. Well into the mid-nineteenth century, for example, the Yale College board included the Governor of Connecticut and six members of the Connecticut legislature, and similar patterns were evident in other such institutions (Whitehead, 1973; Stevens, 1982).

As new nonprofit organizations surfaced to cope with the growing social and economic needs of the post-Civil War era, moreover, this widespread collaboration grew apace. A survey of seventeen private hospitals in 1889, for example, revealed that 12 to 13 percent of their income came from government (Stevens, 1982). This pattern was even more evident in the field of social services, where hundreds of mutual aid societies and children's agencies – many of them ethnically and religiously based – surfaced in the 1870s and 1880s. A study of 200 private organizations for orphan children and the friendless in New York in the late 1880s showed, for example, that twice as much of their support came from taxpayers in the form of government grants as from legacies, donations, and private contributions (Warner, 1894:337). Nor was this practice restricted to New York. On the contrary, a turn-of-the-century survey found that as of 1901 public subsidization of private charitable institutions was in evidence in all but two territories and four western states (Fetter, 1901/2:376).

In short, reliance on nonprofit organizations and associations was widely viewed as a necessity in nineteenth-century America, but not yet a virtue. Americans turned to associations in pragmatic fashion to address challenges they could not handle individually, but retained a healthy skepticism toward the institutional embodiments these associations took, denying them corporate status and restricting their ability to assemble self-perpetuating assets without a corresponding guarantee of their "public" character and dedication to public purposes. Instead of a rigidly demarcated nonprofit sphere, what existed instead was an easy-going blending of public and private action that nicely matched the twin sentiments of anti-statism and anti-corporatism then in vogue.

The advent of voluntarism as an ideology

Between the end of the Civil War and the Great Depression, however, a sharp shift occurred in this generally pragmatic attitude. Instead of a practical adaptation to the circumstances of non-statist America, reliance on charitable institutions was elevated into a high moral principle, and ultimately a political ideology. In the process, the widespread practice of government–nonprofit collaboration was overlaid by a pervasive paradigm of conflict, stressing the inherent tensions between the nonprofit sector and the State.

What accounted for this shift was the broader series of social, economic, and political changes that accompanied America's transformation from a rural–agrarian society into an urban–industrial one. Crucial to this transformation was the emergence of the joint stock company as a powerful instrument for amassing economic power and effecting change.[2] Armed with this instrument, business leaders proved able to accomplish prodigious feats that ultimately convinced them that they no longer needed the State to advance their economic goals. On the contrary, the State and the notions of "democratic capitalism" with which it was all too often associated at the time came to be seen as a definite hindrance to the promotion of business interests. Accordingly, it became imperative to liberate the corporate form from the public controls and expectations that had attended its use up until then. This, in turn, required the invention of a separate "private sector" sharply differentiated from the public sector and free of its democratic constraints (Hartz, 1948; Nielsen, 1979).

This project of invention dominated American political and economic discourse from the end of the Civil War to the end of the First World War. Most important for our purposes, moreover, it embraced not only the private *for-profit* sector, but also the private *nonprofit* one. Just as private business interests sought to banish government from its involvement in the economic sphere, so they sought to accomplish a similar goal in the field of charitable endeavor. Nonprofit organizations came to be defended not simply as useful supplements to public action, but as superior vehicles for meeting public needs. In pursuit of this agenda, new nonprofit organizations were formed in such fields as education, health, charity care, and the arts; and efforts were launched to free those already in existence from public influence and control (though rarely from public support). What is more, new doctrines were developed to justify separation between the two.

In the field of care for the poor, for example, a new doctrine of "scientific charity" emerged. According to this view, the root causes of poverty and distress lay in the bad habits and sloth of the poor. Because public agencies tend to provide aid too indiscriminately and unconditionally, they actually encourage pauperism. Private charity, by contrast, can deal with the root causes of pauperism by restricting assistance to the truly deserving and coupling it with the personalized moral suasion needed to induce the poor to overcome their vices (Bremner, 1980:32–3, 202–3; Katz, 1986:64–84). In the face of widespread economic dislocation resulting from rapid urbanization and industrialization in the later nineteenth and early twentieth century, therefore, charity advocates, armed with this doctrine, became ardent opponents of the extension of government poor relief. In the depths of the 1873 depression, for example, charity leader Louisa Lee Schuyler advised New York State officials to *reduce* the levels of public assistance outside of almshouses lest they encourage an inflow of paupers, and recommended that responsibility for coping with the needs of the poor be thrown instead "entirely on existing private charity" (Schuyler, 1873, quoted in Bremner, 1980). Similar arguments were used to terminate "outdoor" poor relief not only in New York City, but in Brooklyn, Buffalo, Indianapolis, Philadelphia, and Chicago as well (Bremner, 1980: 200).

Contributing to this new faith in the virtues of voluntarism and private charity, and to the concept of an inherent conflict between the nonprofit sector and the State that accompanied it, was a massive growth of personal fortunes and the propagation of a new "gospel of wealth" about what to do with the resulting riches. As articulated most forcefully by steelmaker-turned-philanthropist Andrew Carnegie, this gospel married Social Darwinism with Christian concepts of charity to make it a religious (and social) obligation on those whose natural superiority enabled them to amass great wealth to contribute this wealth to improve society (Carnegie, 1889). These developments made it possible to imagine that private charity might truly serve as a substitute for public action in providing for public needs, and a superior substitute at that.

How much the resulting set of ideas was motivated by sincere belief in the superiority of private voluntary institutions and private charitable effort as opposed to governmental assistance, and how much it was motivated by a desire to enforce work discipline, resist pressures for mandatory expansions of government social-welfare protections, and rationalize growing disparities of wealth is difficult to say. Very probably all of these factors were at work. What is clear, however, is that a powerful ideology of voluntarism took shape that posited an inherent conflict between the nonprofit sector and the State and put the nonprofit sector forward not as a supplement to the State but as an alternative to it. In the process, the ideal of voluntarism was thoroughly politicized, emerging by the later nineteenth century as the principal rallying-point for resistance to expanded public aid to cope with the growing poverty and misery that rapid urbanization and industrialization were creating. Not only did the ideology of voluntarism come to suffuse the contemporary policy debate, moreover; it was projected backward in time to create a fanciful image of historic separation between government and the nonprofit sector that could help justify the new view. Although the separation portrayed in this image finds little support in the historical record, it nevertheless quickly became part of national folklore, obscuring reality for decades to come (Nielsen, 1979: 25–49).

In short, the concept of a distinct nonprofit sector was a late-nineteenth-century invention in America, and one with powerful – and ultimately highly effective – political overtones. By creating a potent ideology of "voluntarism" and investing it with mythic status as the best and truest expression of the American character, conservative forces effectively held the State at bay for two generations, despite deteriorating social and economic conditions, and despite the clear inability of private philanthropy to live up to the expectations claimed for it. That this was possible is a tribute to the hold of the ideal of individualism and opportunity on the American psyche, to the harsh politics of ethnicity that impeded the development of a true workers' movement in America to challenge the hold of the prevailing economic powers-that-be, and to the reputation for corruption that unfortunately enveloped many public institutions during this period. Whatever the cause, by the early twentieth century the notion of voluntarism and the vast network of institutions it had nurtured had become a highly politicized and profoundly conservative force in America, "the great American substitute for social action and policy," as historian Roy Lubove has described it. "[V]oluntary institutions," notes Lubove, "failed to respond to mass needs, but thwarted government efforts to do so" (Lubove, 1968:2).

Myth v. reality in the Great Society era

Not until the Great Depression of the 1930s and the resulting Democratic electoral victory of 1932 was it possible to break the hold of this powerful social myth and establish a national system of basic social welfare protections. The resulting New Deal breakthrough, though significant, however, was far from complete, either programmatically or conceptually. Programmatically, the New Deal social protections left immense gaps both in coverage and in basic program design. Conceptually, the ideal of voluntarism remained firmly lodged in the pantheon of American symbols, available for resurrection when circumstances required.

When poverty was "rediscovered" in the 1960s, therefore, occasioning powerful new calls for federal involvement, the resulting response had to be largely indirect. Instead of establishing a system of direct federal assistance to supply the services considered necessary to allow individuals to break the cycle of poverty in which they were thought to be entrapped, the federal government was obliged to rely instead on state and local governments and private nonprofit groups. The era of the Great Society of the 1960s and 1970s was not, therefore, an era simply of massive expansion of the federal government, as it has come to be portrayed. Rather, what expanded was a pervasive partnership between government and the nonprofit sector, thus returning to a pattern with deep roots in the American past.[3] By the late 1970s, in fact, nonprofit organizations were delivering a larger share of *government-financed* human services than all levels of government combined, and government support had outdistanced the support these institutions received from private charitable donations by a factor of almost two to one (Salamon, 1987:99–117; Salamon, 1995). In the process, the American nonprofit sector underwent one of the most dramatic expansions in its history, growing substantially in both size and scope. This expansion took place, moreover, not *in spite of* the growth of government, as the "paradigm of conflict" would have us believe, but in large part *because of* it.

Nevertheless, so powerful has the continued hold of the ideology of voluntarism and its accompanying paradigm of partnership been on American thinking that this development largely escaped notice until relatively recently, and even then has been greeted with considerable suspicion.[4] One reason for this is that both those on the political Right and those on the political Left have had reason to downplay the reality of partnership and retreat to the paradigm of conflict instead.

For those on the Right, belief in an inherent conflict between government and the voluntary sector has remained a potent instrument for fending off further extensions of the modern welfare state. Indeed, this cultural icon gained a new lease on life as a result of the bureaucratic excesses of twentieth-century totalitarianism, which seemed to validate conservative warnings about the consequences that too great a reliance on the instrumentalities of the modern State would have on the survival of voluntary institutions (Nisbet, 1962). So strong was the straightjacket that this ideology fastened on conservative thinking, in fact, that a major project on "mediating structures" at the American Enterprise Institute in the mid-1970s could produce as its major recommendation the suggestion that government should make use of private nonprofit groups to deliver publicly financed social services without ever recognizing the massive extent to which the programs of the Great Society were already doing exactly this (Berger and Neuhaus, 1977).

But those on the political Left have had their own reasons to operate within the prevailing paradigm of conflict. With conservatives idealizing the voluntary sector and demonizing the State, liberals found it necessary to discredit voluntarism and private philanthropy in order to justify state involvement. This process was already well under way during the Progressive era at the turn of the century, as reformers attacked the practice of government subsidization of private charities not on grounds that it undermined the independence of charities, but on the grounds that it "gave over the defenseless to the care of the irresponsible" and squandered resources needed to establish a modern, public system of care (Warner, 1894:354). With Herbert Hoover championing voluntary action as the solution to the Great Depression, advocates of federal intervention intensified their attacks, thus effectively surrendering the symbols of voluntarism and nonprofit action to conservatives and accepting a paradigm that made it seem necessary to oppose the nonprofit sector in order to support an expansion of governmental aid. When the Great Society turned massively to nonprofit organizations to deliver new federally funded social service programs in the 1960s, therefore, few on the Left were willing to acknowledge, let alone defend, the resulting partnership, lest it inadvertently lend support to the conservative position about the virtues of voluntary action. Indeed, during the fifty years of liberal ascendancy, from the election of Franklin Delano Roosevelt in 1932 to the election of Ronald Reagan in 1980, the nonprofit sector essentially disappeared from the nation's policy discourse, as attention came to focus instead on the dramatic expansion of the State. Judging from either the public or the scholarly attention it attracted, one could easily have concluded that America's voluntary sector largely ceased to exist sometime around the early 1930s and had not been heard from since. Even the emergence during the 1960s and 1970s of a progressive new voluntarism in the form of consumer, environmental, civil rights, anti-war and related public interest movements hardly altered the widespread neglect to which the nonprofit sector *qua* sector was treated during this period. It thus remained possible for Ronald Reagan to reclaim the banner of voluntarism without contest in 1980 and ride to power promising to help the nonprofit sector by rescuing it from the harmful intrusions of the State.

In short, the nonprofit sector has come to be viewed in America through a powerful social myth. This myth idealizes the nonprofit sector and demonizes the State. In the process, it obscures central realities about each and denies the possibility of fruitful collaboration between the two. This myth has persisted, moreover, in the face of massive growth in cooperation between nonprofit organizations and government agencies at all levels. The result is an awkward duality in American thinking about the nonprofit sector and a lack of legitimization of one of the central features of modern American society. Not surprisingly, clear comprehension of this sector, even in America, has suffered as a consequence.

Types of nonprofit organizations

Terminology

Given the somewhat contested position of the nonprofit sector in American political history, it should come as no surprise that considerable disagreement exists about the appropriate terms to use to refer to the organizations that constitute it. Each of the many possible terms carries a bit of political baggage, because it highlights one facet of the operation of these organizations while throwing others into the shadows. Each is therefore at least partly misleading.

Nonprofit. Perhaps the most general of these terms, and the one that will be used here, is *nonprofit organization*. This term is probably the most neutral, since it emphasizes the most basic defining feature of this set of organizations: the fact that they do not exist to generate profits for their owners or directors. However, this term is also rather negative, identifying this set of organizations in terms of what they are *not*, rather than in terms of what they are. What is more, in a culture that measures success in terms of profitability, it somehow suggests failure. Finally, it is not, strictly speaking, accurate, since it falsely conveys the impression that these organizations cannot generate profits when in fact it is not the *generation* of profit but its *distribution* to owners or directors that is prohibited. A more precise rendering would therefore identify these organizations as *not-for-profit* rather than simply *nonprofit*.

Charity. A more popular term for referring to nonprofit organizations is *charities* or *charitable organizations*. This is the term encountered most often in the press and in popular accounts. Its great appeal is that it identifies this set of organizations with aid to the needy, which is the common definition of "charitable." In addition, it emphasizes the support these organizations receive from private donations. In both respects, however, this term is problematic. In the first place, as will become clear below, the term "charitable" has a special technical meaning derived from English common law that goes well beyond care for the needy. It embraces arts, culture, education and other activities as well that, while contributing to public welfare, do not necessarily target the poor. Using the term "charitable" to refer to this sector thus creates a false, if pleasing, image of what this sector really embraces. In addition, while private contributions are important to this set of organizations, they are hardly the only, or even the major, source of support. On both counts, therefore, the term *charitable* creates as many problems as it solves.

Voluntary. A third term sometimes used to refer to the range of organizations under consideration here is *voluntary organizations*. More common in the U.K. than in the U.S., this term emphasizes the important role that volunteers and voluntarism play in the life of these organizations. As such, it conveys the same positive image of the sector as does the term "charitable." However, this too is more a prescriptive than a descriptive term, since much of the activity of the organizations to which it is applied is actually carried out by paid staff, not volunteers.

Independent. The same is true about a fourth term increasingly used to refer to this set of organizations: *independent sector*. This term emphasizes the special role such organizations play as a counterpoise to the State and a vehicle for independent citizen involvement in social and political life. In practice, however, as we have seen, while the nonprofit sector does function outside the administrative structures of the State, it is hardly independent of the State. On the contrary, it is engaged in a widespread, and generally quite productive, partnership with government in a wide assortment of different spheres. Not *independent sector* but *interdependent sector* would therefore probably describe the reality of State–nonprofit relationships more accurately in the American context; but the term *independent sector* nevertheless still has great political attractiveness and prescriptive appeal.

Tax-exempt. Finally, the nonprofit sector is often referred to as the *tax-exempt sector* in the United States. This term is probably the most accurate in technical terms, since, as will become clear below, it is largely through the tax laws that these organizations have come to be legally defined in the United States. In particular, the federal tax code identifies some 26 different classes of organizations that are entitled to exemption from federal income taxation. The problem, however, is that the idiosyncrasies of American tax law make this a difficult term to use in cross-national work, since it does not really identify a conceptually coherent set of institutions.

Legal status

Given the ambiguities of the available terminology, it is useful to look a bit more closely at the legal treatment of nonprofit organizations in the American setting. This treatment is naturally shaped by certain underlying features of the U.S. legal structure, most notably its combination of a common law legal system with a written Constitution and its federal government structure, featuring a sharing of power between a national government and fifty state governments that have their own elected officials and their own sovereign authority. These circumstances make the legal position of the nonprofit sector in the United States far more complex and disjointed than the significant size and scope of this sector might suggest. No single body of law guarantees the existence of this set of institutions or defines its treatment in law. Nor is the right to form such organizations explicitly guaranteed. The closest one comes to an explicit guarantee of the right to form nonprofit organizations is in the First Amendment to the U.S. Constitution, which guarantees citizens the right to free speech and to assemble peaceably to petition the government. In addition, the national constitution prohibits government interference with religion, thereby implicitly granting religious organizations an inherent right to exist. Beyond this, nonprofit organizations are governed by a multitude of separate state and national laws relating separately to incorporation and taxation.

Unifying this somewhat disjointed set of legal provisions, however, is a deep-seated philosophic conviction that has developed over the course of U.S. history about the inherent right of Americans to form private associations and assemble private resources to pursue a wide variety of peaceful ends. This conviction, which reflects the deeply ingrained American aversion to concentrated governmental power, has been firmly enshrined in case law and in a variety of concrete legal provisions granting special tax and other advantages to such private organizations. Though not explicitly guaranteed in basic laws, therefore, the overwhelming sense enshrined in the history of legal development in the United States is that the formation of nonprofit organizations is a right inherently available to citizens rather than a privilege to be bestowed, or withheld, by governmental authorities.

Legal form

Reflecting this basic legal status, nonprofit organizations can take any of three different legal forms in the United States: (1) unincorporated associations: (2) corporations; or (3) trusts.

Unincorporated associations. Formally, any group of people can form themselves into an association and function as a nonprofit organization in the United States without any governmental approvals. As such, they can establish a bank account, accept contributions, and provide services. Assuming that they do not exist to distribute profits to their officers and directors, and that they adopt a set of basic rules spelling out the governance of their organization and the procedures that will be used to dispose of any assets upon dissolution, moreover, they can even claim exemption from the national income tax, and, by implication, from related state and local taxes as well. Beyond that, assuming that their purpose is "charitable" in the special meaning of the law, such unincorporated associations can even offer their donors deductions from tax obligations for contributions made to the organization. For much of the nation's history, in fact, nonprofit organizations functioned in precisely this way, as unincorporated associations operating as tax-exempt entities, but without official certification to this effect from the tax authorities. In fact, many academic and professional societies, as well as some clubs, continue to do so today.

Incorporated organizations. While nonprofit organizations are formally permitted to exist without incorporating, most such organizations in practice have sought corporate status in recent decades. The reason for this is that corporate status limits the liability that directors and officers bear for the acts of the organization. In addition, federal tax statutes stipulate that entities claiming tax-exempt status must pass an "organization test" to demonstrate that they are truly an organization and not a "formless aggregation of individuals," and incorporation is one convenient and reliable way of doing this. Finally, incorporation eases the way to securing an official certification of tax-exempt status, which provides added assurance to potential donors about the availability of tax deductions for their contributions.[5] For all these reasons, most of the more formal components of the American nonprofit sector – for example schools, colleges, universities, hospitals, museums, libraries, day care centers, social service agencies, and even advocacy groups – are thus likely to incorporate.

Corporation laws in the United States are the preserve of state governments. This means that the specific details of corporate structure and obligations differ from state to state. State corporation laws govern both nonprofit and for-profit corporations, moreover, though separate laws typically exist for the latter. The principal difference between the two relates to the allocation, or "inurement," of any profits derived from the operation of the organization. The for-profit corporation is operated for the benefit of its owners; any profits earned are privately inured, i.e. they are passed through to those who hold an ownership share in the corporation. Unlike the for-profit corporation, a nonprofit corporation is not permitted to distribute net earnings to those who control and/or financially support the organization. Rather, any such net earnings must be plowed back into the purposes pursued by the organization.

To incorporate under state laws, nonprofit organizations must generally file Articles of Incorporation and a set of Bylaws with the Attorney General of the state which is the organization's primary place of business. These documents spell out the purposes of the organization, indicate its adherence to the rules against private inurement, identify the incorporators and the organization's principal address, and detail the rules the organization will use to govern itself and dispose of any assets upon dissolution.

Trusts. Nonprofit organizations can also be *trusts.* A trust is essentially a body of assets dedicated to a particular purpose. Trusts are established by declarations of trust or trust agreements that place the assets in the care of a trustee. A trust is a common form of nonprofit organization where an entity is created out of the estate of a deceased person, where the assets in the estate are to be used for essentially charitable purposes in the special meaning of the law, and where the resulting entity has a single purpose (for example financing scholarships). Many foundations are established as trusts, as are most employee benefit funds and all political action committees. However, the trust form does not provide the shield against personal liability that the corporate form does.

Types of tax-exempt organizations

Although any organization that identifies a purpose other than that of distributing profits to owners or directors can normally qualify for nonprofit status under state law, a second, and somewhat more difficult, test of nonprofit status in the United States is the ability to pass muster in terms of the federal tax laws, which define a set of organizational purposes that qualify an organization for exemption from federal income taxes. Since these taxes are generally higher than state taxes, and since many states follow federal usage in their own tax treatment of nonprofit organizations, federal tax exemption has become the effectively operating defining feature of nonprofit status.

The definition of nonprofit status under federal tax law is fairly broad, however. This is so because the federal tax code stipulates more than 25 different classes of organizations that are exempted from federal income taxes, based on the purpose the organization pursues. Included here are organizations as diverse as title-holding companies, war veterans' organizations, and black lung trusts (see Table 11.1).

These various types of tax-exempt organizations can be grouped into two broad classes, however: (1) primarily *public-serving* organizations, also known as "charitable organizations"; and (2) primarily *member-serving* organizations. This distinction, which is based primarily on the purposes the organizations pursue, finds reflection in the way these two types of organizations are treated in the tax code. In particular, while both types of organizations are exempted from taxes on the organization's own income, all but one sub-class of the public-serving organizations are entitled as well to receive contributions from individuals, foundations, and corporations on which the donors can claim tax deductions. The principal rationale for this is that the activities in which these organizations are engaged, because they are principally of public benefit, are likely to relieve government of burdens it would otherwise have to bear. Collecting taxes on the contributions these organizations receive would thus be counterproductive. Generally speaking, among those most familiar with the nonprofit field, the term "nonprofit sector" is reserved for these public-serving organizations, whereas the broader term "tax-exempt sector" is used when both types are referred to.

Table 11.1

Types of tax-exempt organizations under Section 501(c) of the Internal Revenue Code

Tax Code Number	Type of tax-exempt organization
501(c)(1)	Corporations organized under an Act of Congress
501(c)(2)	Title-holding companies
501(c)(3)	Religious, charitable, scientific, literary, educational, public safety, etc.
501(c)(4)	Social welfare organizations
501(c)(5)	Labor, agricultural organizations
501(c)(6)	Business leagues
501(c)(7)	Social and recreational clubs
501(c)(8)	Fraternal beneficiary societies
501(c)(9)	Voluntary employees' beneficiary societies
501(c)(10)	Domestic fraternal beneficiary societies
501(c)(11)	Teachers' retirement funds
501(c)(12)	Benevolent life insurance associations
501(c)(13)	Cemetery companies
501(c)(14)	Credit unions
501(c)(15)	Mutual insurance companies
501(c)(16)	Corporations to finance crop operation
501(c)(17)	Supplemental unemployment benefit trusts
501(c)(18)	Employee-funded pension trusts
501(c)(19)	War veterans' organizations
501(c)(20)	Legal services organizations
501(c)(21)	Black lung trusts

Source: *Internal Revenue Service, Annual Report.*

Primarily public-serving organizations

Most of the primarily public-serving nonprofit organizations in the United States qualify for tax-exemption under one section of the Internal Revenue Code, Section 501(c)(3). They are therefore often referred to as "501 (c)(3) organizations."

Section 501(c)(3) of the U.S. Internal Revenue Code defines a broad set of purposes under which organizations can claim exemption from federal income taxes. Some of these purposes are enumerated in the law, while others are included by implication through the use of the term "charitable," derived from the English common law tradition. The enumerated purposes include relig- ious, scientific, educational, and literary purposes, testing for pub- lic safety, prevention of cruelty to animals, and fostering national or international amateur sports. The implied purposes embrace a much wider variety of activities that fit the English common law definition of "charitable," which has come to embrace at least four types of purposes: the relief of poverty, the advancement of edu- cation, the advancement of religion, and a catch-all "other pur- poses beneficial to the community."[6] Section 501(c)(3) thus covers an immense range of public-benefit organizations, indeed most of what in common parlance is thought of as the heart of the non- profit sector, including colleges, universities, hospitals, social ser- vice agencies, day care centers, nursing homes, environmental groups, civic associations, orchestras, museums, and many more.

Among these 501(c)(3) organizations, it is possible to distin- guish three major subgroups, as reflected in Figure 11.1.

Religious congregations. The first distinct type of charitable non- profit organization in the United States is the religious organiza- tion, or religious congregation. Promotion of religion is included as one of the enumerated purposes eligible for tax exemption under Section 501(c)(3) of the U.S. Internal Revenue Code, and is also one of the implied purposes covered by the term "charitable" in the English common law. However, because of the constitu- tional prohibition against governmental interference with religion in the United States, religious organizations – in the sense of orga- nizations engaged in the practice of religion – have a special status in U.S. law, including nonprofit law. In particular, such organiza- tions are exempted from the formal requirements to incorporate or to register for tax-exempt status. Rather, they are automatically considered to be tax-exempt charitable corporations, whether or not they formally incorporate or register. In addition, they are formally exempt from the requirement that other nonprofit organizations face to report annually on their finances. The one stipulation is that they truly be engaged in the practice of religion, which, under IRS rules, means that they must have some set of beliefs and some set of rituals.[7]

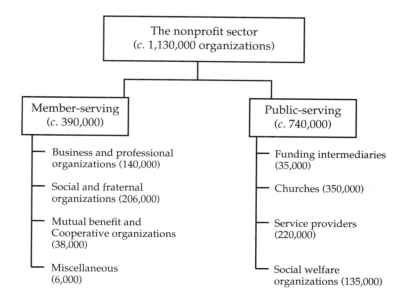

Figure 11.1 Major types of U.S. nonprofit organizations

Source: Adapted from Salamon (1992), p. 13. Data on member-serving
organizations from U.S. Internal Revenue Service, *Annual Report*,
1990. All data for 1989.

Foundations and other financial intermediaries. A second distinguishable subset of charitable or public-benefit nonprofit organizations are the numerous financial intermediaries that exist within this sector. What sets these organizations apart is not the purposes they pursue but the way they go about them. The principal function of the financial intermediary organizations is not to carry out programs or deliver services, like service organizations, but to channel financial resources to other organizations that do.

Included here are *federated funding organizations* like the United Way or the American Cancer Society, which raise money from the public to support a range of other organizations engaged in particular activities (for example providing social services, fighting cancer or heart disease, or promoting the arts). Also included, however, are private *foundations*, which distribute grants to other nonprofit organizations from pools of assets granted to them either by individuals (independent foundations) or corporations (corporate foundations).

Although foundations have long had a distinct function within the American nonprofit sector, they were generally not legally distinguished from other 501(c)(3) organizations until 1969, when the U.S. Congress imposed a variety of restrictions on these organizations in response to concerns that wealthy individuals were using the charitable foundation as a vehicle for evading inheritance taxes. The key distinguishing feature of foundations as defined in this law is that they receive their income and assets from a single source, unlike other charities, which receive income from multiple private and public sources.[8] Foundations so defined are prohibited from certain kinds of financial transactions that might constitute self-dealing, and are required to pay out a minimum of 5 percent of the value of their assets each year in grants or other "qualifying distributions."

Charitable service organizations. The balance of the 501(c)(3) public-benefit nonprofit sector consists of charitable service organizations, or "public charities", as they are formally identified in the law. Included here are private universities, schools, hospitals, clinics, orchestras, art galleries, museums, environmental groups, civic associations, social service agencies, day care centers, community development organizations, and many more – indeed, most of the organizations commonly thought of as making up the public-benefit portion of the nonprofit sector. These organizations deliver services, provide information, educate the public, advocate particular causes, provide management and financial assistance, and engage in dozens of other "charitable" activities.

Social welfare organizations. Aside from the three types of public-benefit nonprofit organizations identified above, a fourth type is authorized under section 501(c)(4) of the Internal Revenue Code. Known legally as "social welfare organizations," these organizations pursue purposes similar to those pursued by all charitable nonprofit organizations. However, they pursue them in a particular way – primarily by seeking to influence the legislative process. While such legislative "lobbying" is a permissible activity for all charitable service organizations, 501(c)(3) organizations are prohibited from devoting a "substantial" share of their energies to it, which has been interpreted to mean that they must so use no more than 20 percent of their expenditures. Charitable nonprofit organizations primarily engaged in such lobbying activities are therefore obliged to organize under a different section of the tax code. As such, their donors are not eligible to receive tax deductions on their contributions. The general concept here is that the State should not subsidize, even indirectly, efforts to influence its own policies.

Member-serving organizations

Beyond the primarily public-serving organizations classified under sections 501(c)(3) and 501(c)(4) of the Internal Revenue Code are a variety of essentially member-serving and related organizations that are also entitled to tax exemptions, but under other subsections of the tax code. Generally speaking, these organizations are vehicles through which individuals can pursue any of a number of common interests, whether social or economic. They thus contribute to social and civic life or promote mutuality. Because members already reap benefits from these organizations, however, contributions to them are not deductible in computing the members' own income tax obligations. Broadly speaking, four more or less distinct types of such member-serving organizations can be identified:

Business and professional organizations. In the first place, member-serving nonprofit organizations include a number of business and professional associations, such as business leagues, chambers of commerce, trade associations, and boards of trade (IRC §501(c)(6)), labor unions and agricultural groups (IRC §501(c)(5)), and local associations of employees (IRC §501(c)(4)). These organizations all exist to promote some common business or professional interest of their members.[9]

Social and fraternal organizations. A second type of member-serving organization is essentially *social* and *fraternal*, rather than business, in orientation. Included here are social and hobby clubs (IRC §501(c)(7)), homeowners' associations (IRC §528), fraternal beneficiary associations, fraternities and sororities, and veterans' associations.

Mutual benefit organizations. Organizations serving a *mutual or cooperative* purpose constitute a third class of tax-exempt member-serving organizations. Included here are group legal service organizations, teachers' retirement funds, black lung benefit trusts, mutual insurance companies (IRC §501(c)(15)), cemetery companies (IRC §501(c)(13)), credit unions (IRC §501(c)(14)), and farmers' cooperatives (IRC §521).

Miscellaneous. Finally, there are a variety of miscellaneous types of tax-exempt organizations. Included here are certain instrumentalities of the United States, title-holding companies, and political parties (IRC §527).

Basic dimensions

Because of the large number of unincorporated and unregistered nonprofit organizations in the United States, it is difficult to gauge the size of this sector with precision. In all likelihood the number of organizations exceeds 2 million. As reflected in Figure 11.1, just the organizations registered with the Internal Revenue Service, or eligible for registration as religious bodies, numbered over 1.1 million as of 1989.[10] Of these, the largest component by far are the public-serving organizations, which represent 65 percent of the total. Included here are approximately 350,000 churches, 220,000 charitable service organizations, 135,000 social welfare organizations, and almost 35,000 foundations and other financial intermediaries. The remaining 35 percent of the organizations are member-serving. This includes over 200,000 social and fraternal organizations, 140,000 business and professional organizations, and approximately 38,000 mutual benefit and cooperative organizations.

As Table 11.2 shows, these 1.1 million organizations represent a significant economic force in the United States. Taken together they had operating expenditures of close to $400 billion as of 1989. This is the equivalent of 7.4 percent of the American gross domestic product. Of this total, member-serving organizations accounted for approximately 16 percent and public-serving organizations for 84 percent. Clearly, the more numerous public-serving organizations also tend to be larger than the business, social, and mutual organizations that constitute the member-serving component of this sector. These figures would be even larger, moreover, if the volunteer input to this sector were considered.

Table 11.2

Current operating expenditures of U.S. nonprofit organizations, by type of organization, 1989

Type of organization	Amount ($ billion)	% of total
MEMBER-SERVING	62.0	16
PUBLIC-SERVING	327.1	84
Foundations	1.4	—
Religious	31.1	8
Health	165.2	42
Education/Research	76.9	20
Social and Legal	35.8	9
Civic and fraternal	10.2	3
Arts and Culture	6.4	2
International	—	—
TOTAL	389.1	100

Sources: *U.S. Bureau of Economic Analysis,* Survey of current business; *Hodgkinson* et. al., *1992.*

As Table 11.2 also shows, the largest component of the American nonprofit sector in terms of expenditures is the health component, especially private nonprofit hospitals. Just over half of all hospitals in the United States are private nonprofit institutions, and these tend to be huge institutions. Taken together, hospitals and other health providers account for over 40 percent of all nonprofit expenditures. Right behind the health subsector in terms of size is the education and research component of the nonprofit sector. Most important here are colleges and universities. Half of all higher education institutions in the United States are private nonprofit institutions, and although they tend to be smaller than the state colleges and universities, they nevertheless account for 20 percent of all nonprofit expenditures (Salamon, 1992: 60, 73).

Other components of the nonprofit sector are smaller in relative terms. Yet they nevertheless contribute significantly to the nation's social and economic life. Thus, the nonprofit sector includes virtually all the nation's symphony orchestras, 70 percent of its museums and art galleries, and two-thirds of its social service agencies (Salamon, 1992: 93, 84). So, too, virtually all the major social movements that animated American society during the 1960s, 1970s and 1980s emerged through the nonprofit sector. This includes the civil rights movement, the environmental movement, the consumer movement, the women's movement, the gay rights movement, and the conservative movement.

In short, whatever its history and whatever the neglect it has endured, the nonprofit sector remains a vital presence in American social and economic life. It functions, moreover, not simply as a symbol of a mythic golden age of voluntary action, but as a tangible presence delivering important services in a wide range of fields and a mechanism through which individuals and groups can exercise initiative in the pursuit of public and mutual purposes. Finally, it is not an isolated presence. Rather, nonprofit organizations interact extensively with both for-profit businesses and government at all levels in carrying out their public purposes.

Key issues

The significant place that nonprofit organizations hold in American life is by no means assured, however, despite the rich tradition such organizations embody. On the contrary, this sector has recently been coping with a variety of challenges that could well alter its historic position and role. Three of these challenges deserve particular attention here, because of the light they shed on some of the central dynamics affecting the evolution of the nonprofit sector's role in American society.

Relations with government

Perhaps the central challenge facing the American nonprofit sector at the present time involves the sector's relationship with the State. As we have seen, the tremendous growth that American nonprofit organizations experienced in the 1960s and 1970s was due in substantial part to the support they received from government. Constrained by continuing hostility to the expansion of the federal bureaucracy but facing new demands arising from the rediscovery of poverty and from the civil rights, disability rights, environmental, and consumer movements of the time, the federal government turned extensively to private, nonprofit organizations to help it respond, often stimulating the creation of nonprofit institutions where none existed. The upshot was a massive partnership between government at all levels and private nonprofit organizations that vastly extended the size and scope of nonprofit action. By the late 1970s, government assistance accounted for more than 30 percent of the overall operating revenues of nonprofit charitable service agencies; and in some fields, such as social services, it reached almost 50 percent. By comparison, private charitable giving by individuals, corporations, and foundations accounted for less than 20 percent (Salamon, 1992:26).

Important though government support became to the fiscal health and dynamism of the nonprofit sector, however, it remained somehow suspect and undervalued even within the sector. This was due in part to a gross lack of basic information about the scale that government support had attained. It was also due to the regulatory constraints and paperwork demands that government support brought with it. Most importantly, however, failure to appreciate the widespread pattern of government–nonprofit cooperation established in the 1960s and 1970s was caused by the continued hold of the ideology of voluntarism on American thinking about the nonprofit sector. With its stress on the inherent conflict between the nonprofit sector and the State, this doctrine failed to prepare observers to see the reality that developed before their eyes.

By the time Ronald Reagan assumed the presidency in 1981, there was still consequently little understanding or appreciation among political leaders or the public at large about the important role that nonprofit organizations were playing in the operation of the Great Society social programs of the 1960s and 1970s, or how crucial a role the partnership with government had become to the fiscal health of the country's nonprofit sector. What made this particularly troublesome, moreover, was the fact that this partnership, for all its contributions, also had serious operational problems that reflected the speed and lack of planning with which it had been constructed. Rather than address these problems, however, the Reagan Administration retreated to earlier conservative arguments, and proposed to help the nonprofit sector chiefly by getting government out of its way (Salamon, 1986). The result was to subject major components of the nation's nonprofit sector to significant fiscal strain. Outside the health field, in fact, federal support to nonprofit organizations declined by one-fourth in the early part of the decade, and did not return to its 1980 level until the early 1990s, by which time a new conservative tide was gaining strength to mount another attack on this crucial source of nonprofit dynamism and growth.

Far from a stable and valued relationship, therefore, the significant ties between the nonprofit sector and government remain highly contested in contemporary America, with considerable ambiguities on both sides. This has made it difficult for nonprofit organizations to hold their own in the face of a growing conservative tide. Indeed, nonprofit organizations have found themselves smothered in the conservatives' embrace, as right-wing defense of the nonprofit sector has come to be used as a rationale for eliminating the crucial support on which the nonprofit sector has come to depend.

Marketization and commercial competition[11]

One response that the nonprofit sector has made to the resulting strain has been to turn toward sources of income it can more reliably control. In practice, this has meant a dramatic increase in reliance on commercial sources of support, chiefly in the form of fees and charges for the sector's services. Between 1977 and 1989, for example, such commercial income accounted for most of the growth that the nonprofit sector experienced, not only in the fields of health and education, where it has traditionally held sway, but in the fields of social services and civic action as well (Salamon, 1993:24). In other words, while the nonprofit sector became somewhat less dependent on government during the decade of the 1980s, as conservatives hoped, it did not become more philanthropic; rather, it became more commercial.

As nonprofit organizations have turned more heavily toward "paying customers," however, they have found themselves in increasing competition with for-profit businesses. For-profit firms were attracted into the human service field during the 1960s and 1970s by the same growth of government spending that fueled the growth of the nonprofit sector. In addition, the target population for certain social and human services broadened considerably beyond the indigent, as women entered the workforce and lifespans lengthened, creating demands for day care, elder care, and related services. Since many of the new claimants for social services had resources to spend on them, market demand was created for many of these services, and for-profit as well as nonprofit firms moved to meet it. As of 1977, therefore, for-profit companies already accounted for 57 percent of the nation's day care centers, 23 percent of its other social service agencies, 10 percent of its long-term care hospitals, and 13 percent of its short-term hospitals (Salamon, 1993:21). During the later 1970s and the 1980s, however, the for-profit role in these fields exploded even further. Thus, while the number of nonprofit hospitals declined by 3 percent, the number of for-profit ones increased by 28 percent. In the rapidly growing field of home health, for-profits went from less than half of the establishments in 1977 to almost 70 percent in 1989. And similar developments were evident in other fields (Salamon, 1993:28–33).

The upshot of these developments has been to intensify the competition nonprofit organizations face not only from other nonprofits, but from for-profit organizations as well. Flushed out of their traditional role of providing care for the needy, in other words, nonprofit organizations are increasingly finding themselves engaged in difficult competition with for-profit firms in the commercial arenas in which they are consequently forced to operate.

Challenge to tax-exempt status

This situation has naturally begun to raise questions about the rationale for the tax-exempt status that nonprofit organizations enjoy. Echoes of these complaints began to surface in the early 1980s, when small business interests began challenging nonprofit entry into commercial business activities. Under U.S. law, nonprofit organizations are obliged to pay taxes on so-called "unrelated" business activities, i.e. business activities that are unrelated to the tax-exempt purpose of the organizations. Small business representatives charged, however, that the Internal Revenue Service was too lax in its administration of this Unrelated Business Income Tax (UBIT) requirement.

As competition has intensified between nonprofits and for-profits in the core fields of nonprofit activity, however, even more fundamental challenges have been raised to the whole concept of tax exemption. Local governments, in particular, have become increasingly aggressive in seeking tax revenues from nonprofit organizations in order to close revenue gaps that have grown increasingly serious at the local level. Such efforts are thus particularly in evidence in Pennsylvania, New York, New Hampshire, Oregon, Colorado, Maine, and Wisconsin. A recent study in Pennsylvania, for example, found that at least two-thirds of the state's counties are actively seeking taxes or payments in lieu of taxes from nonprofit organizations. In a particularly celebrated 1994 case, an Appeals Court in Pennsylvania overruled the more than 350 years of legal development that had firmly implanted the idea that education is an inherently "charitable" activity, and ruled that a private nonprofit college no longer qualified for charitable status under state law, because only a small fraction of its students were poor. These and other challenges suggest the confused state of popular understanding of the nonprofit sector in the United States and the extent to which popular support for charitable institutions has eroded.

U.S. nonprofit organizations in comparative context

Given the distinctive history and complex legal structure of the nonprofit sector in the United States, it should be clear that the American definition of the nonprofit sector is in important respects historically, rather than conceptually, determined. Certain types of organizations have been granted tax-exempt status that might not qualify for this status if a strict conceptual standard were enforced. What is more, legal definitions do not line up well with popular conceptions. Thus most people identify the nonprofit sector with "charity" in the sense of assistance to the needy, when in fact the legally defined "charitable" portion of this sector extends well beyond that. One of the great potential advantages of a common definition is that it will make it possible to correct for some of the idiosyncracies of local usage and formulate a conceptually more defensible concept of what this sector should embrace.

To what extent, then, does the structural–operational definition of the nonprofit sector developed for cross-national comparative purposes, as outlined in Chapter 3 above, fit the American case?

What facets of the U.S. nonprofit scene does this definition adequately handle and what facets does it overlook or obscure? How adequate, therefore, is this definition for analyzing the American case and comparing it to the situations elsewhere?

To answer these questions, we examine each of the five basic dimensions of the structural–operational definition detailed in Chapter 3 and assess how well it applies to the U.S. nonprofit scene. As will become clear, the general conclusion that flows from this analysis is that the nonprofit sector demarcated by this definition fits American realities quite well, though it includes some elements that fall beyond what most popular accounts would include in this sector.

Formal

The first criterion of the nonprofit sector identified in the structural–operational definition is that the entities included be in some sense "formal" or "structured." This is to differentiate the nonprofit sector from mere *ad hoc* collections of individuals or informal family groupings.

Generally speaking, this criterion applies quite well to the American setting, so long as "formal" is not interpreted to mean "officially registered" with any governmental body. As we have seen, the formation of nonprofit organizations is considered to be a basic right in America, not a privilege that is granted or withheld by governmental authorities. Organizations can thus come into being and function effectively as nonprofit entities without securing the approval of any governmental body, and thousands, perhaps millions, of them do. Even the tax exemption available to such organizations when they are engaged in any of a wide variety of exempt activities is not viewed as something that is "granted" by the tax authorities. Rather, the function of the Internal Revenue Service is merely to "recognize" the organization's entitlement to the exemption (Hopkins, 1987: 616). Organizations therefore do not have to apply to the IRS for tax-exempt status. So long as they fit the purposes stipulated in law they can operate as if they are exempt until they are challenged. However, IRS regulations stipulate that eligibility for tax-exempt status is restricted to *organizations* and is not available to "formless aggregations of individuals" (U.S. Internal Revenue Service [n.d.]

IRM 7751). In practice, this means that the entity must have an organizing instrument, some governing rules, and regularly chosen officers. In short, the organizational requirement of the structural–operational definition fits the American requirements quite well: permitting unregistered and unincorporated entities but stipulating that they nevertheless have some organizational reality to them.

Private

The second stipulation in the structural–operational definition is that the entities considered part of the nonprofit sector be organizationally and structurally separate from the State. Here, again, so long as "private" and "nongovernmental" are not interpreted to exclude organizations receiving significant financial support from the public sector, this condition fits all but one class of American tax-exempt organizations – namely, §501(c)(1) organizations formed under an Act of Congress. Beyond this, nonprofit organizations in the United States are governed by private boards of directors and are considered part of the private sector. Indeed, as we have seen, separating the nonprofit sector from the public sector was a major thrust of national political struggle from the late nineteenth through to the early twentieth centuries, and nonprofit organizations jealously guard their "independence" from state organs.

In practice, however, while organizationally and structurally separate from government, nonprofit organizations are heavily influenced by government policies. For one thing, as we have seen, government support to the nonprofit sector has historically been quite extensive in the United States, and it has grown massively in the period since 1960. Inevitably, this has brought significant elements of the nonprofit sector within the orbit of government programs and exposed them to the rhythms and requirements that government funding inevitably entails. In some cases, in fact, government has stimulated the creation of wholly new nonprofit corporations. This was the case, for example, with the hundreds of local Community Action Agencies created in the 1960s as part of the federal government's War on Poverty. Elsewhere, nonprofit organizations operating with public funds have found themselves bound by government regulations pertaining to equal opportunity, handicapped accessibility, environmental protection, workplace safety, protection of human subjects, and sexual harassment. Some analysts have bewailed this circumstance as an undue intrusion of government control that has undermined the basic character of the nonprofit sector (Smith and Lipsky, 1993). Most empirical assessments indicate, however, that nonprofit organizations have managed the trade-offs involved in receipt of government support reasonably well and have managed to retain a considerable degree of discretion and autonomy in the process (deHoog, 1985; Salamon, 1995). What is most important for our purposes here, however, is that the structural–operational definition, by defining the nonprofit sector in terms of its basic *structure* rather than in terms of its *sources of support*, accommodates the American realities quite well.

Non-profit-distributing

The *non-profit-distributing* criterion of the structural–operational definition also fits the American circumstances reasonably well. As we have seen, the "private inurement" test is a fundamental basis for a grant of a nonprofit corporate charter under state corporation laws. Even for unincorporated organizations, however, the federal tax laws stipulate that, to be exempt from federal income taxes, an organization must be operated in such a way that "no part of ... [its] earnings inures to the benefit of" the organization's officers or directors; and the organization's founding documents must stipulate this. More generally, the tax laws specify that the entity must be organized exclusively to carry out one of the specific purposes articulated in the law as entitling it to tax exemption, though "exclusively" here has come to mean "principally." To the extent that business activities or the generation of profits are a principal purpose of an organization, therefore, the organization would disqualify itself for tax-exempt status.

It is worth noting here that the term "non-profit-distributing" in the structural–operational definition is more precise than the term "nonprofit" often used to refer to this set of organizations in the United States. "Nonprofit" suggests that these organizations do not, or are not permitted to, earn profits in the sense of an excess of receipts over expenditures. In fact, however, U.S. nonprofit organizations are permitted to earn profits, and many do. Indeed, under U.S. law, nonprofit organizations are even permitted to operate businesses that are unrelated to the tax-exempt purposes of the organizations. Three conditions attend these business activities, however: first, any profits generated from such businesses are taxed at the same rate as are profits from any for-profit business; second, the net profits after taxes must be used only to promote the tax-exempt purpose of the organization and not be distributed to the organization's officers or directors; and third, the business cannot be the principal purpose of the organization.

Certain practical problems nevertheless attend the application of this non-profit-distribution condition. One of these has to do with the distribution of profits not in the form of dividends but in the form of salaries and other benefits. Although U.S. law limits nonprofit compensation to levels considered "reasonable and customary," this is a slippery standard that has caused difficulties in practical application.

Even more difficult is the treatment of the entire class of member-serving organizations. As noted above, numerous such organizations are included within the U.S. tax-exempt sector even though they are operated principally for the benefit of their members. U.S. law gets around this by stipulating that the benefits must accrue to particular individuals by virtue of their position in the organization in order to be considered a violation of the non-profit-distributing restriction. Many organizations that would fail to fit the popular conception of a nonprofit organization, which carries with it the sense of general public benefit, nevertheless thus qualify as nonprofit organizations in legal terms. Under the non-profit-distributing condition of the comparative definition, at least some of these would be excluded – particularly mutual benefit organizations and cooperatives that are essentially engaged in business activities. However, business and professional associations would be included, even though they fall outside the circle of 501(c)(3) charitable organizations that most people have in mind when they think of nonprofit organizations in the U.S.

Self-governing

The provision in the structural–operational definition restricting the concept of the nonprofit sector to organizations that have their own internal mechanism for self-government fits the American case extremely well. As noted earlier, one of the basic requirements for tax-exempt status in the United States is that the entity pass an "organizational test." Central to this is a showing that the organization has developed a set of formal procedures for its own internal governance, including designation of governing bodies and methods for selecting trustees, choosing officers, and disposing of assets upon the organization's dissolution. Although no prohibitions exist about placing government officials on the boards of nonprofit organizations, this practice is nowhere near as common now as it was in the first hundred years of the nation's existence, and, in any event, does not commonly convey control over the organization's internal decision-making to public authorities, as is the case in some other countries (for instance Japan).

Voluntary

The fifth key requirement in the structural–operational definition is that the organizations included in the nonprofit sector embody some meaningful degree of voluntary involvement. This criterion works along with the non-profit-distributing requirement in the definition as a proxy for the concept of "public benefit," which is extremely difficult to define cross-nationally. The general thrust of the argument is that if organizations are able to attract volunteers and to operate without the promise of distributing profits, they must have some public purpose attraction to them.

"Voluntary" as used here has two different meanings, however: first, that volunteers be involved in the operation of the organization, either as members of the board or as personnel assisting the organization in carrying out its mission; and second, that participation in the organization not be coerced or mandatory.

Generally speaking, both of these meanings fit the American case. However, there are important caveats to enter with respect to both.

So far as volunteer involvement is concerned, voluntarism is a highly regarded value in American society, and volunteer activity is widespread. Thus, according to recent surveys, over half (54 percent) of Americans over the age of 18 reported volunteering, and about two-thirds of this volunteer activity went to support tax-exempt organizations (Hodgkinson *et al.*, 1992:65, 71).

Impressive though these numbers are, however, they must be

approached with a degree of caution. In the first place, notwith-standing the value attached to voluntarism in American culture and the myth of voluntarism that has come to surround the non-profit sector, there is no formal requirement that nonprofit organi-zations be operated exclusively, or even chiefly, by volunteers. By custom, the boards of such organizations are normally volunteers; but it is legally permissible to compensate even board members for their work. As the U.S. Tax Court put it: "[The law] places no duty on individuals operating charitable organizations to donate their services; they are entitled to reasonable compensation" (World Family Corporation v. Commissioner, 1983). More gener-ally, organizations are free to utilize or not utilize volunteers, and it is quite common even for charitable organizations to operate entirely with paid staffs. One of the major criticisms of the growth of government funding, in fact, is that it diminished the reliance of organizations on volunteers and made it possible – in some cases necessary – for them to engage professional staff. Perhaps reflect-ing this, volunteer input is hardly distributed evenly within the American nonprofit sector. On the contrary, well over 40 percent of all volunteer time is dedicated to religious organizations. By contrast, health and educational organizations, which account for 44 percent and 22 percent of all paid employees, respectively, absorb only 11 percent and 9 percent of all volunteer time (Hodgkinson *et al.*, 1992:120). The American nonprofit sector thus contains at least two relatively distinct sets of organizations, one of which is still heavily volunteer-based, and the other of which makes relatively modest use of volunteers except for a thin stra-tum of volunteer board members at the top. Since the struc-tural–operational definition requires only that there be at least some meaningful degree of volunteer involvement, even if only at the board level, most charitable nonprofits and a significant portion of the balance of the tax-exempt sector probably meet the definition. However, in the minds of many this is a rather attenu-ated definition of volunteer participation.

With respect to the other meaning of voluntary – that is, non-mandatory – the situation is more complicated. At least some types of tax-exempt organizations have compulsory membership. This is the case, for example, with labor unions in cases where a "union shop" has been established, or with professional associa-tions that perform licensing functions for the profession. Such organizations would probably be excluded from popular conceptions of the nonprofit sector in the United States anyway, however, even though they are formally tax-exempt. American usage would thus be consistent with what the structural–operational definition prescribes.

Summary

In short, the structural–operational definition of the nonprofit sector described earlier works relatively well in demarcating a distinctive set of organizations from among the welter of purposes identified as tax-exempt in American law. The nonprofit sector so defined relates well to popular conceptions of this set of organizations, moreover. The principal deviation from common usage is the inclusion of most of the member-serving organizations within the nonprofit sector. This runs counter to the legal treatment, which draws a sharp distinction between "charitable" organizations, which operate for general public benefit, and all other nonprofit organizations, which serve a variety of collective, but more narrowly focused, group purposes. It also runs counter to popular conceptions, which tend to restrict the concept of the nonprofit sector to a subset even of the formally "charitable" organizations (namely, those serving the poor or supported mostly by charitable contributions). This popular conception is probably excessively narrow, but most Americans would probably find the sector delineated by the structural–operational definition a bit too broad. Though broad, however, it is certainly workable within the legal parameters applicable in the United States.

Conclusion

Voluntarism and nonprofit action are thus firmly rooted in American tradition. In the absence of a capable State, Americans early developed a habit of self-reliance and a penchant for voluntary association to meet common needs. This habit was reinforced by a strong ethos of individualism and by a deep-seated philosophical hostility to centralized government. At the same time, it was tempered by anti-corporatist sentiments and by suspicion of undue concentrations of economic power as well. During much of the colonial era and the first hundred years of the nation's existence, these competing impulses were reconciled by forming hundreds of associations, but then requiring that these associations pursue public ends and work hand-in-hand with public authorities, often with the aid of publicly generated revenues.

Towards the end of the nineteenth century, however, the easygoing pattern of government–nonprofit cooperation that had characterized the country's early years was challenged by a new orthodoxy stressing the virtues of voluntarism as an *alternative* to the State in meeting human needs. This orthodoxy politicized the idea of the nonprofit sector and created a powerful social myth that has obscured clear thinking about the actual operation and role of the nonprofit sector in American life ever since.

Against this backdrop, a careful re-examination of the nature of the American nonprofit sector is very much in order. Such a re-examination can usefully be undertaken in comparative terms, moreover, to get outside the sterile ideological perspective from which this topic is often approached. For this to be possible, however, it is essential to begin with a clear understanding of what this sector embraces and how it is defined. Hopefully the discussion here will provide a useful step towards this goal.

Notes

1 Protests were thus lodged at town meetings in Massachusetts during debates over the ratification of the Constitution about the practice of providing public grants to Harvard College on grounds that Harvard provided insufficient information on its use of these funds and was unresponsive to public needs in its educational philosophy (see Nielsen, 1979:33).

2 A joint stock company is a legal entity created by state charter and empowered to enter into contracts and act as an economic person, thus shielding its investors from personal risk for the entity's activities.

3 For a broader discussion of the practice of "third-party government," of which the government–nonprofit partnership is a part, see Salamon, 1981: 255–75.

4 Not until 1981 was a full accounting of the extent of government support of private nonprofit organizations developed (see Salamon and Abramson, 1981).

5 Formal evidence of tax-exempt status is also a virtual necessity to

secure foundation grants, since foundations are required by law to pay out a minimum share of their asset value each year to such eligible tax-exempt organizations.

6 For additional elaboration on the English common law definition of "charitable," see Chapter 10 by Kendall and Knapp above.

7 Although churches, synagogues, mosques and other religious bodies are not formally required to register as tax-exempt organizations with the Internal Revenue Service, many nevertheless voluntarily choose to do so for many of the same reasons that other nonprofit organizations do – to secure clear assurance of their charitable status and to provide protection against personal liability for directors and officers.

8 In addition to the two types of foundations mentioned here there are at least two other types: first, *operating foundations*, which deliver services directly in addition to making grants; and *community foundations*, which are grantmaking institutions supported not by a single donor but by a number of donors in a particular community who choose to leave their bequests to a common community institution for the promotion of charitable objectives. Community foundations have considerably more favorable tax status than the independent foundations.

9 To the extent that an organization exists to promote a particular business, as opposed to the common interests of a type of business, it would be classified as a for-profit organization and not entitled to tax-exempt status. Similarly, some professional associations can qualify for charitable status where they are principally engaged in activities that serve a broad public interest rather than primarily the interests of the members of the profession. Thus bar associations and medical societies are commonly classified as business leagues by the Internal Revenue Service, whereas organizations representing economists, historians or other learned professions can often qualify for 501(c)(3) charitable status.

10 Because of the special position of religious organizations in American law, the exact number of registered nonprofit organizations is difficult to determine. This is so because some religious congregations register with the Internal Revenue Service even though they are not required to. The 1.1 million figure recorded here is thus a net figure that takes account of the estimated proportion of the churches listed in the *Yearbook of American and Canadian Churches* that are already included in Internal Revenue Service listings of 501(c)(3) organizations. No reasonable estimate exists of the number of unregistered and unincorporated nonprofit organizations.

11 This section draws heavily on Salamon, 1993:16–34.

Bibliography

Berger, Peter and John Neuhaus (1977), *To Empower People: The Role of Mediating Structures in Public Policy*. Washington: The American Enterprise Institute for Public Policy.

Bremner, Robert (1956), *From the Depths: The Discovery of Poverty in the United States*. New York: Basic Books, Inc.

Bremner, Robert H. (1980), *The Public Good: Philanthropy and Welfare in the Civil War Era*. New York: Alfred A. Knopf.

Carnegie, Andrew (1889), "Wealth," *North American Review*, 148:653–64.

deHoog, Ruth (1985), "Human service contracting: environmental, behavioral, and organizational conditions," *Administration and Society*, 16:427–54.

de Tocqueville, Alexis (1845), *Democracy in America*. The Henry Reeve text as revised by Francis Bowen. New York: Alfred A. Knopf, 1945, Vol. II.

Fetter, Frank (1901–2), "The Subsidizing of Private Charities," *American Journal of Sociology*:371–6.

Hall, Peter Dobkin (1987), "A Historical Overview of the Private Nonprofit Sector," in Walter W. Powell (ed.), *The Nonprofit Sector: A Research Handbook*, pp. 3–26. New Haven: Yale University Press.

Hartz, Louis (1948), *Economic Policy and Democratic Thought: Pennsylvania 1776–1860*. Cambridge, MA: Harvard University Press.

Hodgkinson, Virginia A., Murray S. Weitzman, Christopher M. Toppe, and Stephen M. Noga (1992), *Nonprofit Almanac, 1992–93: Dimensions of the Independent Sector*. San Francisco: Jossey-Bass Publishers.

Hopkins, Bruce (1987), *The Law of Tax-Exempt Organizations*, 5th edn. New York: Wiley.

Katz, Michael (1986), *In the Shadow of the Poorhouse: A Social History of Welfare in America*. New York: Basic Books, Inc.

Lubove, Roy (1968), *The Struggle for Social Security*. Cambridge, MA: Harvard University Press.

Nielsen, Waldemar (1979), *The Endangered Sector*. New York: Columbia University Press.

Nisbet, Robert (1962), *Power and Community*, 2nd edn. New York: Oxford University Press.

Powell, Walter W. (1987), *The Nonprofit Sector. A Research Handbook*. New Haven: Yale University Press.

Salamon, Lester M. (1981), "Rethinking public management: third-party government and the changing forms of public action," *Public Policy*, 28:255–75.

Salamon, Lester M. (1986), "The nonprofit sector: the lost opportunity," in John Palmer and Isabel Sawhill (eds), *The Reagan Record*, pp. 261–86. Cambridge, MA: Ballinger Publishing Co.

Salamon, Lester M. (1987), "Partners in public service: the scope and theory of government–nonprofit relations." In Powell, 1987, pp. 99–117.

Salamon, Lester M. (1992), *America's Nonprofit Sector: A Primer*. New York: The Foundation Center.

Salamon, Lester M. (1993), "The marketization of welfare: changing non-profit and for-profit roles, in the American welfare state," *Social Service Review*, 67(1):16–39.

Salamon, Lester M. (1995), *Partners in Public Service: Government–Nonprofit Relations in the Modern Welfare State*. Baltimore: Johns Hopkins University Press.

Salamon, Lester M. and Alan J. Abramson (1981), *The Federal Budget and the Nonprofit Sector*. Washington: The Urban Institute Press.

Schuyler, Louisa Lee (1876), 'Outdoor Relief in New York County,' in New York State Board of Charities, *Nineth Annual Report, 1874–75*. Albany: New York State Board of Charities. Quoted in Bremner, 1980:200.

Smith, Steven Rathgeb and Michael Lipsky (1993), *Nonprofits for Hire: The Welfare State in the Age of Contracting*. Cambridge, MA: Harvard University Press.

Stevens, Rosemary (1982), "A poor sort of memory: voluntary hospitals and government before the depression," *Millbank Fund Quarterly/Health and Society*, 60(4).

U.S. Bureau of Economic Analysis (1991), *Survey of Current Business*. Washington: U.S. Government Printing Office.

U.S. Internal Revenue Service (1990), *Annual Report*. Washington: Internal Revenue Service.

U.S. Internal Revenue Service (various years), *Exempt Organizations Handbook*, IRM 7751, quoted in Hopkins, 1987:612.

Walker, James (1825), "Associations for benevolent purposes," *Christian Examiner*, II. In Bremner, 1980.

Warner, Amos (1894), *American Charities: A Study in Philanthropy and Economics*. New York: Thomas Y. Crowell.

Whitehead, John S. (1973), *The Separation of College and State: Columbia, Dartmouth, Harvard, and Yale, 1776–1876*. New Haven: Yale University Press.

World Family Corporation v. Commissioner, 81 T.C. 958 (1983), quoted in Hopkins 1987.

Part III

DEFINING THE NONPROFIT SECTOR IN DEVELOPING SOCIETIES

Nonprofit organizations are by no means restricted to the developed societies of Europe, North America, and Japan. Anthropologists have long pointed out the rich tapestry of indigenous voluntary associations in Africa and Asia; historians have described the long history of charitable organizations in Latin America; and students of Islam and other religions have emphasized the strong philanthropic traditions present in nonWestern societies, even though such traditions may take different cultural expressions and institutional forms.

Despite the growing awareness of such philanthropic traditions outside the Western world, little is known about the nonprofit sector in the developing countries in a systematic way. In recent years, nongovernmental organizations, or NGOs, have emerged as important actors in the field of humanitarian assistance and development cooperation, domestically as well as internationally. The full range of nonprofit organizations in developing countries, however, includes a much wider spectrum of organizations that are typically not regarded as NGOs. Examples are village associations in Africa, caste associations in India, charitable trusts in the Arab world, and local community organizations in Latin America.

In this respect, the following chapters take a broader look at the universe of nonprofit institutions in a wide assortment of developing countries (Brazil, Ghana, Egypt, India, and Thailand). They go beyond a description of NGOs and examine the role of traditional and modern as well as indigenous and Western types of nonprofit organizations in developing countries. Although the countries covered in this part share some of the characteristics typical of developing societies, they vary in a number of other relevant dimensions. Thus, they represent every major geographic region (South America, Africa, the Middle East, South Asia, and Southeast Asia), as well as most of the major world religions (Christianity, Islam, Hinduism, Confucianism, and Buddhism). As a consequence, immense variations exist in the overall contours and dynamics of the nonprofit sector in the five countries examined in this study.

At the same time, certain striking similarities are also apparent in the structure and character of nonprofit activities in these countries. One is the prominent role of NGOs in developmental and humanitarian assistance, but also in the field of advocacy and human rights. Some NGOs are Western-based development agencies transplanted to developing societies to promote social and economic change. Increasingly, however, this term has come to be used to depict domestic organizations as well.

A second common characteristic of nonprofit activity is the generally higher level of politicization of this sector in developing countries. While traditions of independent political action outside the State are hardly new, they are often less accepted and taken for granted in the developing world, in part because democratic forms and styles of government are less institutionalized. As a consequence, political authorities often look with heightened suspicion at the potential challenge that independent groups can pose to state power. The level of tension between the State and the nonprofit sector is therefore more pronounced in these settings than it is in the developed countries.

Increasingly, however, governments, the United Nations, and other multi-lateral organizations like the World Bank are coming to recognize the tremendous potential nonprofit organizations have both for ensuring democracy and for promoting the goals of development. Particularly in countries where state institutions are weak or mistrusted, nonprofit organizations have the capacity to reach out to a wider population and engage citizens directly in the process of change. Understanding these organizations and the role they play in their societies has therefore never been more important than at present.

Chapter 12

BRAZIL

Leilah Landim[1]

Introduction

The idea that nonprofit organizations, as a group, form a "sector" is not commonly found in Brazilian sociological and economic thought. The substantial internal diversification of such a sector there would not constitute one history, but rather several specific and differentiated ones. Nonetheless, the concept of "nonprofit" is recently gaining visibility in Brazil. The redefinition of the role of the State, the advance of market-oriented policies, the issues of political empowerment, participatory and institutional democracy, pluralism, and ethnic and cultural identity are the themes at the center of the agenda for the 1990s. The non-profit formula is caught up in the ferment of these issues, and finds a place among the various positions within the academic and political debates which are developing in the country. The formula is being increasingly evoked, as it points to special possibilities for re-drawing the frontiers between the public and the private spheres.

Political debates focus mainly on the role of non-profit organizations *vis-à-vis* other sectors of Brazilian society, especially the State, and on their ability to solve pressing social problems, especially poverty. Some of the debated topics include the role of non-profit organizations in mobilizing material resources, their functions as agents, extensions, or substitutes of the State, their capacity to influence public policy, their effective competence and their potential for alleviating poverty, and their contribution to the democratization, maintenance, and manifestation of ethnic identity, indigenous cultures, and "forgotten" values of altruism and social solidarity, as well as their relationships to organized religion and political parties. The issues are diverse, reflecting not only different lines of thought in political and sociological debates, but also, above all, the very internal diversity of the universe of so-called nonprofit organizations.

This chapter intends to contribute to our understanding of nonprofit organizations in Brazil – a set of organizations on which little research has accumulated and for which few quantitative data are available. Our objective is basically to describe the principal terms and concepts used in Brazil to indicate what is understood here as "the nonprofit sector" – including the general features of the country's legislation that deals with this sector. This description seeks a general vision of the types of organizations contained in this universe, as well as the forms with which they are defined and classified in the Brazilian context, taking into consideration, for comparative purposes, the core definition of the nonprofit sector suggested by Salamon and Anheier (1992).

Historical background: State, Church, and society in Brazil

The history of voluntary associations in Brazil is linked with the colonial origins of the Brazilian State. The two pillars of Portuguese colonization were the plantation system and a close relationship between the colonial government and the Roman Catholic Church.

The institution of plantation – the "big house," slave quarters, chapel, cane fields, sugar mill, and accommodation for free servants and other residents – was a closed world ruled by patriarchy. Under this system, the social and economic position of freemen was dependent on personal relationships with the landlord. This dependency created a system of clientelism – vertical, reciprocal alliances of individuals exchanging loyalty and services for protection and favors. Such a system did not provide fertile ground for the emergence of autonomous voluntary associations to provide public-interest services, such as those that emerged in the North American colonies (Gurin and Van Til, 1990).

In that context, the Roman Catholic Church, closely integrated with the government, played a fundamental role in organizing civil society. Its uncontested prominent role lasted for four centuries until the proclamation of the Republic in 1889. Catholicism was the official religion of the State. A governance system for priests, vested in the political power (in Portuguese, the *padroado*), by which the Papacy had conceded to the Portuguese Crown direct control over the Church in Brazil, was in full force. Religious rituals, such as baptism, matrimony, and funerals, were the prerequisite for the individual's social recognition. To be Catholic was indispensable for the exercise of citizenship. The Church and its institutions, oratories, chapels, confraternities, religious fraternal organizations, parishes, and dioceses, formed the public forum for social life. They functioned "as civil registry, schools, instances of conflict resolution between individuals and between families, as centers for parties and leisure, and even as mutual aid societies and social and medical assistance societies" (Ribeiro de Oliveira, 1985).

However, the Catholic Church was weakened by the State protectorate system, and it was "popular Catholicism," stemming from the medieval Iberian tradition of patron saints, devotions, feasts, and *Confrarias* – religious societies of lay people – that played an important role in the development of philanthropy and voluntary associations. The *Confrarias*, generally formed on the local collective initiative, sometimes despite formal government prohibitions, provided important social services to the communities such as financial and medical assistance in times of crisis, and the organization of leisure, funeral services, or refuges for beggars (Bruneau, 1974). These associations were recognized by ecclesiastical and civil law. Their statutes had to have royal and ecclesiastical approval, which recognized them as legally constituted organizations, not dependent on ecclesiastical authority for their internal governance or business (Azzi, 1968; 1969; Bruneau, 1974; Hoornaert, 1974; 1977; Beozzo, 1977). Drawing from this tradition, the *Irmandades da Misericordia* (Brotherhood of Mercy) were among the first to establish Brazilian hospitals, hostels, and asylums known as *Santas Casas* (Holy Houses). These establishments were supported, in a large part, by donations from the well-to-do members of colonial society.

Throughout the nineteenth century the symbiosis between the Catholic Church and the State was weakened. The State adopted an increasingly secular stance, and began to assume the provision of public services previously left to the Church. After proclamation of the Republic, the Church–State separation was institutionalized definitively in the 1891 Constitution. Among other measures, the Constitution prohibits government from providing financial assistance to religious cults. As a result, the Catholic Church, suddenly without constitutionally-grounded political support, reformed itself as a clerical body in direct cooperation with Rome, and established new links to the population and institutions from which it derived parts of its resources. In this phase, the establishment of schools, hospitals, and charities of all types was a strategic move by the Churches to gain access to the population.

Constitutionally guaranteed religious freedom and immigration facilitated influences of other denominations and religions during that period. Denominations such as Anglicans, Lutherans, Congregationalists, Presbyterians, Methodists, Baptists, and Pentecostals were instrumental in founding schools and universities designed primarily for the middle class. Like their Catholic counterparts, these educational institutions registered as nonprofit bodies. Less conspicuous religious groups, like the Spiritists and the Afro-Brazilian religions – frequently persecuted by the authorities – also developed during that time. They established significant ties with the urban poor and other marginalized groups which did not participate in the formal sector of the economy. Although these marginalized networks frequently initiated various social work projects, little is known about their role, dimensions, and membership.

Another form of voluntary association that developed during the early nineteenth century was numerous Masonic lodges, many of which were clandestine. Dominated by British influences, they attracted social élites, and played various roles ranging from literary to scientific and openly political, as these organizations were frequently instrumental in starting regional revolts. This organizational form provided institutional mechanisms for the élites through which they identified themselves with the European centers.

The abolitionist movement during the late nineteenth century gave rise to numerous associations attracting a wide variety of urban classes, such as students, academics, professionals, industrial workers, traders, business people, and the military. The most prominent examples include *Caixas Emancipacionistas* (Emancipationist Savings Banks), set up to finance the abolition campaigns, and *Clubes* and *Associações Abolicionistas* organizing marches, rallies, and support for runaway slaves. There were also clandestine groups like the *Caifazes* in São Paulo, and an umbrella group *Conferedação Abolicionista*.

By the end of the nineteenth century, voluntary associations gained considerable prominence in Brazil. At that time, mutual-aid societies multiplied in the urban industrial centers. They were "European imports" brought by the waves of immigrants who constituted the first labor pool for Brazil's emerging industries (Simão, 1966; Rodrigues, 1967). Following the European example, the first mutual aid societies were initially formed by the well-to-do citizens, but the trend soon reached lower income groups in the form of labor unions. Soon, many sectors of the urban population gradually organized around interest groups. In 1878, a representative was sent from Rio de Janeiro to the First Congress of International Welfare in Paris. By that time, the new mutual-aid societies (which, unlike the traditional *Irmandades*, offered services only to their members) formed a growing type of voluntary associations. They provided their members with medical and pharmaceutical care, and assistance in case of illness, unemployment, disability, or death. As these organizations began to attract more workers, they became politicized under the leadership of European immigrants, chiefly anarcho-syndicalists from Italy and Spain. Groups linked to the middle class also began to develop, such as the *Associação Brasiliera de Imprensa* (Brazilian Press Association) established in 1908, and the *Associação Central Brasiliera de Cirurgies Dentistas* (Central Brazilian Association of Dental Surgeons) established in 1911, as well as employers' associations which followed the example of the *Associação Comercial do Rio de Janeiro* (Rio de Janeiro Trade Association) established in 1834.

In short, from the final decade of the nineteenth century onward, voluntary associations proliferated in major cities throughout the country. Their profile gradually shifted from being religious or local groups to being groups organized around wider political and professional interests at the regional and national levels. As the militancy of the trade unions increased, so did their repression by the State. The attitudes of the government toward the unions are epitomized by the following statement made by the President of the Republic: "Social issues are a case for the police." To deal with the so-called "union problem" during the 1930s, the government implemented authoritarian, paternalistic policies designed to provide universal social security on the one hand, and to regulate and control labor unions on the other. Social security was organized on a job category basis, and administered by several *Institutos de Aposentadoria e Pensões* (Retirement and Pension Institutes) which, although formally not state agencies, depended on government recognition and were administered by presidential appointees under rules laid down by the Ministry of Labor, Industry, and Trade.

Private social security arrangements, like the *Caixas de Aposentadoria e Pensão* (Retirement and Pension Savings Banks), were successively replaced by retirement plans politically and administratively controlled by the government. Since these organizations commanded significant funds, they became instruments of power and channels for the exchange of favors between the government and trade unions.

Despite the domination of public life by the State, there was also some room left for a private nonprofit sector which, to be sure, was closely aligned with the State. The legal basis of their cooperation was the 1935 law establishing the *Declaração de Utilidade Pública*, a Presidential prerogative to grant a nongovernmental organization the designation of "public interest." In 1938, the government established the *Conselho Nacional de Serviço Social* (National Social Service Council – NSSC) under the Ministry of Education. Organizations registered with the NSSC are entitled to receive government subsidies. The eligibility criteria for public interest designation include a wide array of activities, from social welfare and health services to child care and education, and to promotion of occupational safety.

Also founded during that period was the *Legião Brasiliera de Assistencia* (Brazilian League for Social Assistance), responsible for providing care for particularly vulnerable groups like young children, expectant and nursing mothers, and the elderly. The position of the League's president is reserved, by statute, for the First Lady of the Republic. Its patrimony comprises both private donations and public funds. To ensure private–public cooperation, the League is prohibited from service delivery, which is left exclusively to private nonprofit organizations under the agreement with the League. In practice, however, the League has always provided service directly. The League was also frequently used as a prime channel for the central government's clientelist policies, providing an institutional vehicle for "charity" by society ladies and state governors' wives.

This period is also characterized by a new alliance between the Roman Catholic Church and the State, as religious organizations were seen by the latter as an important tool in maintaining social order. Religious schools, hospitals, and other social projects received tax exemptions and government funding. Another important group in this universe of philanthropic initiatives is immigrant and foreign organizations, like German, French, and North American schools or major hospitals like *Beneficiencia Portuguesa*, the *Hospital Sirio e Libanes*, or the *Hospital Espanhol*.

The general government policy of that period, however, was selective support of organizations linked to either the apparatus of production or organized religion, while excluding the vast majority of the popular associativist movement. Although a great number of civil associations, both left- and right-wing, sprang up during the 1930s, most of them were suffocated by the authoritarian regime installed in 1937. Examples of such associations include the 180,000-member strong fascist *Ação Integralista Brasileira* (Brazilian Integralist Action), the 70,000-member democratic and anti-imperialist *Aliança Nacional Libertadora* (National Liberation Alliance), the *Liga de Defensa da Cultura Popular* (League in Defense of Popular Culture), the *União Feminina do Brasil* (Women's Union of Brazil), the *Comite Contra a Guerra Imperialista e a Reação Fascista* (Committee Against the Imperialist War and the Fascist Reaction), and the *Sociedade Amigos da Russia* (Friends of Russia Society).

The associativist movement was also an important force counteracting the authoritarian tendencies within the Brazilian government. The *União Nacional de Estudantes* (National Student Union – NSU), set up in 1937 as a part of the scheme controlled by forces loyal to President Vargas, became in the fifties one of the most important organizations struggling for democracy and reform. In late 1950, the NSU set up *Centros Populares de Cultura* (Popular Culture Centers) which were engaged in theater, cinema, poetry, and popular literacy training. Their activities were partially funded by the Ministry of Education and Culture.

In the democratic period of the fifties, Church-based organizations, like the *Serviço de Assistencia Rural* (Rural Assistance Service) and the *Serviço de Orientação Rural de Pernambuco* (Pernambuco Rural Orientation Service), supported by North American development agencies to counter the influence of Marxist groups, were active in community development and leadership training projects. At the same time, the lay movement linked to *Ação Catolica* (Catholic Action) were forming progressive, left-wing groups within the Roman Catholic Church (DeKadt, 1970; Souza, 1984).

After the end of the 1937–45 dictatorship, there was intense activity on the part of civil society which gave a leading role to nonprofit organizations. The aims of these organizations varied from economic and political action and lobbying, to civil rights promotion, to community development, and to culture, research, and education. They were permeated by the ideological debates and political forces in confrontation at the time, but generally acting either through or in collaboration with government agencies.

The 1964 military coup in reaction to the "trade union republic" and the possible social revolution buried both the "populist pact" and the power structure created in the 1930s. A new authoritarian era began under the military government, leading the country into the sphere of control of international capital. The new government centralized and reformed education, health, social welfare, social security, and housing services, bringing them under a single political and financial administration. To end the labor union participation in the now-unified social security system, the government instituted sweeping privatization, applying the logic of the market to the placement of public funds.

In the course of this privatization, the business sector grew, while the non-profit sector remained stagnant. This is especially true in the health field, where the social security system contracted services out to private organizations, encouraging the growth of for-profit hospitals and out-patient enterprises and the development of the pharmaceutical and equipment industries. Moreover, the Ministry of Education and Culture pressed for the privatization of education. The privatization affected educational establishments at all levels, but predominantly higher education. Grossly insufficient government supervision and absence of public control mechanisms, however, led to considerable mismanagement of these "nonprofit" establishments, which functioned in a business-like manner and generated considerable fortunes for their directors. In fact, in some cases the nonprofit status was a mere artifice for disguising private concerns (Ribeiro, 1992).

In general, the authoritarian policies of the military government deprived the associativist movements of their traditional channels of participation in the public sphere: political parties, trade unions, and government agencies. The only organizational framework left relatively intact was the Catholic Church. Although the Catholic hierarchy supported the military coup of 1964, this situation radically changed three years later as an aftermath of the political persecutions and tortures suffered by religious activists. Beginning in the 1970s, the most influential bishops of the National Conference of Bishops of Brazil (CNBB) openly expressed their support for human rights and civil liberties. The Church also gave its open support to workers' and peasants' struggles through the creation of new workers' organizations and opened its facilities – schools, churches, community houses, etc. – for the creation and functioning of grass-roots initiatives and organizations of all types. The support of the Church for social movements was particularly important, since it was the only institution which, after the military coup, could maintain its structure practically untouched – at a time when universities, unions, political parties, and other civic organizations were, in large part, curtailed by the military regime.

During that period, the so-called "People's Church," a radical wing of the Church inspired by Latin American "Liberation Theology," became active among urban and rural populations. Perhaps the most visible result of these activities is the Christian Base Communities (CEB) spread throughout the country. Their number is estimated between 80,000 and 100,000. The CEBs formed a social base for the emergence of political leaders, social movements, and various popular organizations.

After the end of military rule, Brazil witnessed a boom in civil associations. Although official statistics on this process are not available, there has been a considerable growth of activities in both traditional and new areas of voluntary activism. These more recent associations that grew up under the military regime are distant from, and even in open opposition to, the State, and remain close to the "popular Church" and left-wing groups in general.

They frequently shun business and government support, and seek support among international nongovernment sources, mainly the so-called nongovernmental organizations (NGOs).

NGOs form a distinct category in the Brazilian nonprofit universe, mingling Christianity and Marxism, militancy and professionalism. They were born in the seventies, with a strong influence of Marxist and Christian ideologies. During the eighties, they passed through a diversification of conceptions, themes, and activities, which range from popular movements to AIDS-related projects, to environmental protection, and to problems concerning women, ethnic minorities, street children, etc. The size of this newly developed sector is difficult to assess owing to its flexible boundaries, but according to one estimate it comprises about 3,000 organizations (Landim, 1992).

To summarize, the nonprofit universe in Brazil is as diverse as the religious, social, and political forces that led to its formation. There are three themes, however, that underlie this development. The first theme is the prominent role of Catholicism in both popularizing the idea of philanthropy and providing the organizational framework for traditional as well as contemporary associations. The second theme is the historically strong role of the State in creating and shaping a significant part of the nonprofit sector in Brazil. And the third theme is the politicization of many associations which reflect the diverse interests of the many different segments of Brazilian society.

Major terms used to describe nonprofit organizations in Brazil

Any attempt to classify nonprofit organizations in Brazil encounters several difficulties. First, the term "nonprofit sector" itself has not yet gained currency in sociological and economic literature, or even in everyday language. Second, research on that topic is rather rare, compared to what is done in other countries. We can, however, group existing terms that refer to nonprofit organizations into five broad categories:

- civil societies or nonprofit organizations,
- associations,

332

- philanthropic or charitable organizations,
- nongovernmental organizations (NGO), and
- foundations.

It is important to remember, however, that these categories are descriptive, and not mutually exclusive. Thus, some types of organizations belong to more than one category.

Civil societies or nonprofit organizations

These terms, recently gaining more public recognition, are perhaps the most general and ideologically the most "neutral." They designate any private organization which is noncommercial in objectives and behavior. Above all, this expression suggests a judicial reference. It is used frequently in "technical" contexts, when the legal stature of the organization is in play.

As part of the Roman Law tradition, the Brazilian legal system is codified through a body of written laws based on a set of abstract principles which form the legal doctrine. The Brazilian Civil Code distinguishes between legal corporations according to the following categories: internal public law corporations (Federal, Federated States, Municipal, Federal District, and Autarchies) and external public law corporations (e.g., embassies); and private law corporations. Nonprofit organizations are formally recognized in Article 16 of the Brazilian Civil Code (Law no. 3107, January 1, 1916) regarding private law corporations.

According to Article 16, private law corporations include:

- Commercial organizations; and
- Civil, religious, charitable, ethical, scientific, or literary societies, public-interest associations, and foundations.

The distinction between commercial and other types of private law corporations is based on the type of organizational goals. Organizations with non-economic, "ideal" ends are included in the second category, whereas those pursuing economic ends are commercial organizations and are governed by the Commercial Code.[2]

The difference between associations and foundations is based primarily on the legal status of the "agency" of the members or administration. Associations are characterized by a "governing agency," as members or administrators can make a wide range of decisions, including those pertaining to organizational goals and rules. By contrast, the "agency" of foundations is restricted. Organizational goals and rules are set forth by the founders (either individuals or the State), and neither members nor the administration can change them.

Any of the nonprofit organizations may be designated as a public-interest entity by the State. These are nonprofit organizations, including foundations, that pursue public interests, formally recognized as such by appropriate State agencies. Thus while the Civil Code provides for the establishment of nonprofit organizations independent of the public or private commercial interest pursued by the founders, the State officially recognizes a smaller group of public-interest organizations acting for the common good.

All nonprofit organizations, however, are eligible to apply for tax exemptions, as regulated by the Federal Constitution and Tax Code. Article 150 of the Federal Constitution sets forth limitations on the power to tax, declaring, in reference to nonprofit organizations: "Without prejudice to other guarantees to which the taxpayer is entitled, the Central Government, States, the Federal District and municipalities are hereby prohibited from: ... VI. – Levying taxes on: ... assets, revenues, or services rendered by political parties including their foundations, workers' unions, and nonprofit educational and social welfare institutions, when all legal requirements are complied with." It has subsequently been established that these prohibitions apply solely to assets, revenues, and services related to the essential aims of the organization in question.

In accordance with Articles 126 and 130 of the Income Tax Regulations, these organizations, referred to as "educational and social welfare institutions, societies and foundations of a philanthropic, beneficent, charitable, scientific, cultural, instructive, literary, recreational, or sports-related nature, and associations and unions," are not required to submit a declaration of income when the necessary conditions are met.

These conditions are stated in the provisions of Article 130 of the Income Tax Regulations: "Non-remuneration of directors; non-distribution of profits of any type whatsoever; application of all funds for maintenance and development of corporate objectives; maintenance of full accounts of revenues and expenses, and respecting conventions that ensure accuracy; and provision of information required by law to tax assessors or to collect withheld income tax."[3] These organizations are obliged to present annual Declarations of Exemption of Income Tax for Law Corporations to the Federal Tax Bureau.

Associations

As in many other countries within the tradition of Roman Law, "association" designates organizations based on contracts freely established among individuals to exercise common activities or defend common interests. In Brazil, the term association is virtually synonymous with "nonprofit." Beyond its legal definition, it denotes primarily membership organizations, comprising a variety of forms and activities ranging from recreational and sports-related clubs to cultural and artistic associations, and to labor unions.

The incorporation of associations begins with the filing of the articles of incorporation with the Registration Office for Corporations. Registration requires the publication of abstracts of the organization's bylaws, minutes of the founding meeting, a list of the organization's directors, and a list of its founding associates in the government bulletin, *Diario Oficial* (Official Daily), in accordance with Article 114 of the Public Registration Law (Law 6015/73).

Foreign nonprofit corporations that wish to operate in Brazil must comply with the legal procedures set forth in Article 11, paragraph 1, of the Introductory Law to the Civil Code, which states: "Organizations intended to operate in the public interest, such as societies and foundations, shall comply with the law of the State in which they are founded. They may not have affiliates, agencies or establishments in Brazil until their articles of association have been duly approved by the Brazilian government, and shall be subject to Brazilian laws."

In terms of legal limitations imposed by the law for the creation of associations, Article 5 of the current Federal Constitution[4] establishes "total freedom of association for licit purposes, with groups of a paramilitary nature prohibited." It also states that the creation of associations does not depend on authorization, and that the government is prohibited from interfering in their operation. The Constitution and the Law of Public Registries prohibits registration of articles of incorporation when they are illegal, immoral, or contrary to public or social order. The operation of such associations may be disbanded through the initiative of any citizen or the government. They may also be suspended temporarily by the President of the Republic, should they be carrying out an activity that is illicit or contrary to public order.

Although the term association has a legal definition similar to that of other countries based on the Roman Law tradition, the term also carries context-specific connotations. In Brazil, the term association frequently suggests organized civil society in opposition to the State. This "anti-government" connotation gained weight especially in the last 20 years, beginning in the era of the military regime. In a period in which important social organizations and interest groups, such as parties and unions, were closed down or allowed to operate only under the close supervision of the government, associations became the vehicle for the many groups and social movements seeking some form of political participation, and the promotion of specific social and economic interests. Such initiatives were often organized parallel to, and against, the State, or as part of larger movements pressing their demands upon the government. Only in exceptional areas, however, did some form of cooperation between government and association emerge.

A good example, and one which certainly contributed significantly to the social visibility of the term, is the neighborhood associations or residents' associations which were spreading through the poorest areas of the cities during this period, and which today have a nationally organized structure. These associations are, in fact, articulations of numerous other initiatives, bringing together local groups such as "groups of sellers' and buyers' clubs," "youth groups," "mothers' clubs," "production groups," and "community groups" with diverse objectives and formats. The terms "group," "club," and "nucleus" indicate a greater informality. They would be "small associations" or "pre-associations," many of which are not registered.

There are few official statistical data available on associations in Brazil (Paula, 1991). Research recently conducted by Santos (1990) refers to associations created between 1920 and 1986, based on the Registry of Law Corporations of the city of Sao Paulo. The study found a growing organizational diversification, as 68.2 percent of these organizations were created in the last 16 years, and new areas of activities have been added. Among these, community associations are the most recent type, with 97.6 percent of these associations created between 1970 and 1986. They exemplify the set of diversified locally-grounded initiatives mentioned above. During the 1970s and 1980s, many organizations in this field were connected with the "popular" wing of the Church. This cooperation did not endanger the autonomy of the community associations, which are of a secular nature. Similarly, 90.5 percent of residents' associations were created in the same period. Thus, associations have grown both in number and in scope.

Similar results were obtained for the city of Rio de Janeiro between 1946 and 1987 (Santos, 1990). In this case, 65 percent of the associations were created between 1971 and 1987. Moreover, we find that 90.7 percent of all community associations and 85.3 percent of residents' associations were created in this period. Though the data are region-specific, the pattern may be cautiously generalized to the country's largest cities. Furthermore, the symbolic effect of what occurs in Rio de Janeiro and Sao Paulo is remarkable, and will increase the visibility of the nonprofit sector as a whole.

Despite its limitations, Santos' study provides interesting indications of the importance of professional associations. For example, a list of the 15 most recently created types of associations in Sao Paulo includes professional associations for health workers, lawyers, teachers, artists, doctors, non-manual and manual workers, and civil servants. In a society such as Brazil, and especially for the authoritarian period much of Santos' data reports on, the creation of this type of association often assumed political proportions, and went beyond the concerns of specific interest groups. The borders between the political and the economic in Brazil are particularly fluid and movable. These observations apply also to the so-called "class associations," like unions, which multiplied significantly in recent decades, taking up a struggle of a particularly political character in a long-lasting defense of their autonomy. By law, they had been linked to the Ministry of Justice since 1930, a structure modified only after the Constitution of 1988.

Philanthropic, beneficent or charity-related organizations

These types of organizations tend to be oriented to clients, recipients, and other third parties in providing social assistance (shelters, orphanages, drop-in centers for indigents, distribution of clothing and food, etc.), or social services in the areas of health and education.

Philanthropic organizations and associations have the same legal status. Both are grouped in the Civil Code as nonprofit organizations or associations, constituted through registration in the Registration Office for Corporations. Their legal recognition as organizations in the public interest depends on the same mechanisms as are applied in the case of any other type of association or foundation. However, philanthropic organizations have greater facility in qualifying for certain benefits than associations, as they have a more clearly and frequently pronounced public character of collective benefit. Furthermore, the Federal Constitution establishes that organizations related to education can receive governmental support if they are classified as "community, confessional or philanthropic schools, as defined in the law" (Article 213), as can organizations providing social assistance (Article 195).

Independent of legal dispositions, the distinction between philanthropic organizations and other associations is based on values such as altruism, good will, and service to the community which the former invoke. These values set philanthropic organizations apart from the political ideas that "associations" frequently connote and bring them closer to the Church and religious groups. Within this universe, one finds the numerous initiatives and charities which are spread throughout the social fabric without high visibility, attending to the immediate needs of the poorest and most marginalized sectors of the population.

All private establishments of higher education in Brazil are legally defined as nonprofit organizations. The majority of secondary schools are religious. Unfortunately, it is not possible to obtain precise data on schools because "nonprofit" establishments are not identified separately. Instead, the principal division is between public and private institutions (Cunha, 1985).[5] That is, despite a large number of educational organizations officially registered as nonprofit, this status has little relevance, since private for-profit and nonprofit schools are considered as something indistinguishable. Those who prefer public over private education tend to view nonprofit schools as fraudulent and as instruments of favoritism, since the private schools function in fact like for-profit businesses. Similar tendencies have been observed in the health sector, where larger nonprofit hospitals are becoming increasingly like for-profit businesses.

Finally, corporate philanthropy is difficult to evaluate in terms of its role and effective weight in Brazil. In any event, it is an area which has had little visibility in public opinion, and which has found little or no interest in the academic community. Nevertheless, significant changes have begun to occur in this situation during the last two or three years, when new corporate institutions have begun to appear in the arena of nonprofit private action for public benefit. In Brazilian society, an example is the recent creation of the *GIFE – Grupo de Institutos e Fundacões Empresariais* (Group of Corporate Institutes and Foundations), a new kind of association of philanthropic institutions in the Brazilian context.

Nongovernmental organizations

Until recently, the term NGO was rarely used in Brazil. However, within the last five or six years, NGO has become an increasingly prominent term. NGOs make it to the headlines of newspapers, become the subjects of academic debates and theses, and arise as recognized actors on the political and social scene. Evidently, NGO is not a juridical term. It has connotations which are quite political; these do not, however, suggest that it is linked with any particular political ideology.

NGOs have expanded both in numbers and the space they occupy in public discourse. Many new organizations have come into existence over the last 15 or 20 years, and without being political parties, Churches, para-government agencies, or universities themselves, they are doing work which is political, pastoral, or "public" in character, without being called such. The adoption of NGO as a cognitive category of self-identification for these new organizations indicates a process of the creation and recent recognition of a common identity. The roots of this trend are in the "Centers of Popular Education" or "Centers for Consulting and Support to the Popular Movements." They were born and flourished at the height of the dictatorship, with their "backs to the State" and "under the shadow of the Church." They grouped together activists with a middle-class background, both religious and nonreligious, intellectuals seeking alternatives to academia, ex-militants from traditional leftist groups, and the "'68 genera-tion." This diverse set of constituencies, endowed with a set of ideas clustering around the "participation" and "organization" of the poorest segment of the population, developed and imple-mented numerous activities at the grass-roots level across the country within a general perspective of the structural transforma-tion of society from below.

With the process of democratization, these organizations diver-sified and became more visible and secularized. They embarked on a course of institutionalization and professionalization; many became NGOs. The vagueness and ambiguity of the term NGO proved functional for designating a group of initiatives which by themselves are quite heterogeneous and fluid. These organiza-tions are dedicated to a variety of issues, such as popular move-ments, women, race, street kids, indigenous issues, ecology, and AIDS. The local NGOs were joined by a transnational group of organizations; their funds come from international development agencies, some of which are NGOs themselves in their country of origin.

"NGO", as is the case with "association", indicates an organiza-tional commitment to civil society, social movements, and social transformation. On the other hand, NGOs are distinct from associ-ations in the sense that they are rarely membership-based and pri-marily oriented to serve third parties. They are also distinct from philanthropic organizations – and this is taken as a point of honor by the NGOs – because they do not set out to exercise any type of charitable practice, the idea of which would be contrary to their aim of the construction of autonomy, equality, and participation among popular groups. The values of welfare and charity (in Portuguese, *assistencialismo*) are rejected by the NGO community.

Foundations

This is fundamentally a legal concept. As has already been men-tioned, foundations constitute a type of corporation whose internal structure is the result of someone's having provided funds for a specific purpose. Pursuant to the Civil Code (Articles 24 and following), a foundation is created by its founder, through a public document or will that allocates property for a specified purpose, stating, if desired, the manner in which it is to be administered. It is the founder's responsibility to name someone to set up the statutes of the foundation. In the event that the founder does not do this, it becomes the responsibility of the Public Ministry, and they must be approved by a judge within six months. The supervisory agency for foundations is the Public Ministry of the state in which they are located (Article 16 of the Civil Code), whose responsibility it is to verify that all the clauses listed in the founding act are observed, that the foundation's funds are sufficient for reaching its proposed goals, and to approve the determination of the foundation's arrangements for functioning.

There are significant numbers of foundations instituted by government agencies at the federal, state, and municipal levels. A legal debate about the public or private nature of foundations developed as the autocratic State began to replace private founders and set aside part of its assets for public-interest objectives. Are such foundations public or private law corporations? Might not the public nature of the founder and the public good character of objectives alter the legal essence of what is legally and predominantly a private corporation? This ambiguity between public and private poses problems for the inclusion of public law foundations into the set of private nonprofit organizations in Brazil. Foundations created and controlled by state agencies do, in fact, represent para-state agencies and should be excluded from the nonprofit sector.

Public-interest designation

As noted earlier, civil societies, associations, foundations, and NGOs may qualify for the status of "public-interest civil association," as defined in the civil code. Legally, the term refers to any nonprofit organization that, in the view of the government, undertakes activities in the public interest at large. Public-interest civil associations receive state benefits that go beyond tax exemption:

- exemption from employer contributions to social security;
- option to receive donations from the federal government and state agencies;
- charitable deduction status, allowing donors the right to deduct their contributions from taxable income – deductions are limited to 10 percent of gross income for individuals, and 5 percent of gross profits for corporations (Articles 79 and 246 of Income

Tax Regulations);
- option to receive revenue from the proceeds of federal lotteries;
- option to hold raffles authorized by the Ministry of Finance; and
- exemption from monthly deposits to the Severance Payment Fund (unemployment compensation).

The original law governing public interest associations (Law 91) was passed in 1935. As might be expected, for much of the statute's history, personal networks and favors played a deciding role in obtaining the much sought-after designation. In an attempt to eliminate favoritism, a less subjective process was instituted through a new Directive issued by the National Secretary of Citizen's Rights and Justice on 13 June 1990 (Ministry of Justice, 1990). Eligibility is dependent on the organization's ability to provide services without regard to race, creed, color, or political conviction of actual or potential clients, and without a profit motive (Ministry of Justice, 1990).

To be eligible for public interest designation by the President of the Republic, nonprofit organizations must provide services needed by the community, such as social welfare, medical care, scientific research, and educational and cultural services (Ministry of Justice, 1990:5). Not eligible are religious institutions, except for Church-related organizations that are separately incorporated, animal protection groups (rationalized on the grounds that they do not serve human beings), and some scholarly societies. Further, board members and managers of public interest associations may receive no remuneration for their services. Nor may any income in excess of expenses be distributed to members and founders. Finally, qualifying organizations must have been in existence for at least three years prior to their application; this existence must be evidenced by detailed reports and financial statements.

Because religious organizations constitute a significant part of Brazil's nonprofit sector, their exclusion from public interest status merits some discussion. Basically, the exclusion is based on the Constitutional principle of separation of Church and State (Article 19 of the Federal Constitution). The law prohibits any and all levels of government from "establishing or subsidizing religious sects or churches, inhibiting their operations, and maintaining with them any relationship based on dependence or unity, except as established by law, collaborations in the public interest" – an exception that allows the designation for Church-related organizations. An explanation for the principle of Church–State separation, as applied to the public interest status of religious bodies, is contained in the June 1990 Directive by the Ministry of Justice mentioned above. According to the Directive, conferring this status on religious associations would imply that the state is "furthering the cause of the religious congregation, which it is prohibited from doing."

Separately incorporated religious organizations and subsidiaries in the field of social, educational, or health services, however, are eligible for public interest status provided they "abstain from religious promotion, for otherwise their services would be nothing but a tool for indoctrination" (Ministry of Justice, 1990). Examples of acceptable subsidiaries include public charity hospitals, child care centers, and teaching centers founded by the Spiritist, Evangelical, or Catholic churches. Critics have argued that this exception does lead to the possibility of indirectly favoring one or another religious group or Church – a repeat of the Brazilian experience with Catholicism. Notwithstanding the general religious exclusion from public interest status, the Constitution does grant religious groups the same kind of tax exemption offered other nonprofits (Article 150, Section VI).

Defining the nonprofit sector

In general, the various types of nonprofit organizations in Brazil correspond to elements of the structural–operational definition suggested by Salamon and Anheier (1992). The following section examines the applicability of the key elements of that definition for the Brazilian nonprofit sector.

Formal. This requirement is met by the provisions of the Civil Code that require any association that wishes to register to publish its bylaws, minutes of the founding meeting, and a list of its directors. These requirements are essential for applying for tax-exempt status and public interest designation. Foundations and foreign nonprofits face even more stringent regulations. On the other hand, there are organizations that do not wish to register. These will be discussed as borderline cases.

Private. As already observed, the term "association" in Brazil is almost synonymous with "nonprofit;" it also implies an organization based on a contract freely established among individuals to exercise common activities or defend common interests; government interference in the operations of associations is constitutionally prohibited. On the one hand, private associations are legally distinguished from government agencies and foundations set up to provide social services. On the other hand, the government sponsorship and control of many nonprofit organizations is not uncommon and varies under different regimes. Some borderline cases will be discussed below.

Self-governing. The governing bodies of associations have the power of making a wide array of decisions regarding all aspects of the association's structure and operations. However, the power of the governing bodies of foundations is restricted by law from changing the foundation's goals and rules set forth by the founders.

Non-profit-distributing. This requirement is stipulated by the Income Tax Regulation as a condition for tax-exempt status. Tax-exempt organizations are explicitly prohibited from distributing profits of any kind and required by law to use all funds for maintenance and development of the organization's formal objectives.

Voluntary. This requirement is met by the constitutional guarantee of the Freedom of Association (Article 5 of the Brazilian Constitution). Citizens are free to establish and join any association, except those set for illegal purposes. This implies that they are also free not to join any organization if they wish so.

It is useful to discuss two types of organizations in Brazil that present borderline cases: organizations that have not been formally registered with the government, and government-created foundations. Non-registered groups, recognized in the draft Civil Code revision as "*de facto* or irregular," may be borderline cases because, technically, they have no official legal status, although the law imposes certain requirements on them. Government-sponsored foundations should not be characterized as private, but as para-governmental. Their decision-making functions and internal operations are subordinate to government agencies. It should be noted, however, that governmental sponsorship alone is insufficient to deny an organization nonprofit status. The case of unions is illustrative here. During the 1930s, under the inspiration of the autocratic Carta del Lavoro, unions were forced to adopt an organizational structure based on vertical, corporate lines, linking them to the Ministry of Labor. In 1988, however, following a 20-year struggle for autonomy from the State, they were granted independence by the Constitution. Undeniably, unions today would represent nonprofit organizations, as they are affiliated with the independent workers' movement and other social movements.

Member-serving vs. public-serving

Associations, a major component of Brazil's nonprofit sector, are organizations that tend to serve both their own members and the general public. Comprising and representing segments of the population often fiercely at odds with the State, associations tend to be intensely political, and may be organized explicitly to bring about social changes to improve the lot of large segments of the public. To these associations, the distinction between member interests and public interests may have little practical meaning. In the context of an authoritarian State like Brazil, the political nature of associations is perhaps inevitable.[6] The 1970s were marked by frequent confrontations between the federal government and associations representing professionals, residents, workers, and others. Often the demands of the latter went no further than that the government put its laws, rules, and regulations into practice.

Even for some groups that are purely cultural or recreational, the distinction between public- and member-serving tends to fade. Carnival-related clubs and societies, for example, tend to identify themselves as "Black organizations," joining various ethnic and racial movements. Many of yesterday's social clubs are today's NGOs. Finally, the move from "club" to "NGO" changes the meaning of the "voluntary" criterion. For NGOs, voluntarism is associated primarily with the boards of directors, whereas their staff is becoming increasingly professional. In fact, NGOs have evolved into a veritable labor market attractive to certain groups of middle-class intellectuals.

In general, however, much of the polarization between civil society and the State has lessened in recent years. This is a consequence both of the return of a democratic order and of the increasing diversity among associations themselves. But this has not diminished the significance of this group of organizations. As exemplified by the *Ordem dos Advogados do Brasil* (Brazilian Bar Association), associations have become important in the democratization of the country and in the struggle for human rights.

Conclusion

Politically, socially, and economically, the Brazilian nonprofit sector is fragmented and heterogeneous. Its numerous organizations are extremely varied, and differ significantly from each other in terms of the roles they play in Brazilian society. Legally, the sector has acquired more coherence in recent years, given the laws and legal definitions applicable to nonprofit organizations. But even here, the law is not always applied consistently; and sometimes legal stipulations are not applied at all.

At the very least, the sector's borders are hazy. Distinctions often fade between religious and secular, business and nonprofit, political and civil. Nonprofit and for-profit hospitals are sometimes indistinguishable from each other, at least from the perspective of patients. The same would apply to schools and universities from the perspective of students. In some cases, unclear and fluid borders contribute to the negative public image of some nonprofit organizations, which are seen as illicit enterprises, profiteering from public resources particularly in areas where no public policies and programs serve the population. The privatization of public funds, personal favoritism (*clientelismo*), nepotism, selective application of the law, absence of government supervision – all these may mar the image of nonprofit organizations in Brazil. In fact, the role of these organizations in the traditional context of favoritism continues to be debated in Brazil.

It is no coincidence that the 1990 Directive of the Ministry of Justice sought to clarify the terms under which nonprofit organizations become eligible for the designation of "public utility," which, as we have seen, confers significant state benefits. The Directive intends to reverse "the phase previous to the enactment of the Law [1935], in which, [to use] the expression of then-President Prudente de Morais Filho, 'the declaration of public utility for associations has something quite similar to the concession of patents by the National Guard – a means of pleasing political friends'" (Ministry of Justice, 1990:5). Whether negatively or positively viewed, however, nonprofit organizations have pushed to center stage the issues of democratization of State and society, of the necessity for profound institutional reforms, and the creation of a genuine public sphere in Brazil. Nonprofit organizations are increasing in size and scope, and are more visible today than at any time in Brazil's history. Analysis of Brazilian society, which traditionally focused only on businesses and the public sector, must now take into account the nonprofit sector as a significant social and political actor.

Notes

1 The author would like to thank Eriberto Marin for his collaboration with the legal research for this chapter, and the Project Directors, Wojciech Sokolowski and Nathan Weber, for helpful comments and suggestions on earlier drafts.

2 This terminology has recently begun to be debated in an ongoing legal revision of the Civil Code (1972). According to the new version, only the term *association* (together, naturally, with *foundation*) comes into consideration for referring to nonprofit organizations, with *civil society* reserved for those with economic ends (Article 52). The central argument is that of the necessity of greater precision in terminology in order to limit abuses in the obtaining of benefits by organizations not entitled to such. In the Code currently in place, however, two expressions are used interchangeably – *civil association* and *civil society* – to indicate nonprofit organizations. See Bevilacqua (1959); Reale (1972); Custodio (1979).

3 Their eligibility to receive government subsidies or donations from private sources through tax deductions will be discussed in greater detail in the section on *public-interest* organizations.

4 The current Brazilian Constitution was promulgated in October 1988. The one prior to it had been promulgated in 1967, at the height of the military regime. Democratic institutionalization was only fully reestablished in December 1989, with direct elections for the presidency of the Republic. Nevertheless, the Brazilian legal system is still in a transitional phase. Although the regulation of the organization, rights, and liberties of some nonprofit organizations were liberalized in the new Constitution, several articles and laws of the legislation in question were revoked.

5 Historically, this debate in Brazil was cloaked in a dispute between the Church and the proponents of public education, with the former institution being the great defender of the application of public resources

to private education for several decades. More recently, the "progressive" wing of the Church has come to defend public education.

6 One rural leader who sparked a wide movement of peasant leagues, and who was wont to carry the Civil Code under his arm wherever he went, observed that in Brazil, implementation of the Code is a revolutionary act.

References

Azzi, Riolando (1986), *Os seminários e as vocaçes religiosas no Brasil* [Seminarians and Religious Vocations in Brazil]. Rio de Janeiro: CERIS/CNBB.

Azzi, Riolando (1969), *Os leigos na vida religiosa do Brasil* [The Laity in the Religious Life of Brazil]. Rio de Janeiro: CERIS/CNBB.

Beozzo, Jose Oscar (1977), "Irmandades, santuários e caplinhas" [Religious Fraternities, Sanctuaries and Chapels]. *Revista Eclesiástica Brasileira* [Brazilian Ecclesiastic Review], vol. XXXVIII, no. 148. Rio de Janeiro: CERIS.

Bevilacqua, Clovis (1959), *Código Civil Comentado* [Civil Code with Commentaries], vol. 1. *Teoria Geral do Direito Civil* [General Theory of Civl Right]. Rio de Janeiro: Editora Rio.

Bruneau, Thomas (1974), *O catolicismo brasileiro em época de transiço* [Brazilian Catholicism in Transition]. São Paulo: Loyola.

Cunha, Luiz Antonio (ed.) (1985), *Escola Publica, Escola Particular e a democratizaço do ensino* [Public School, Private School and the Democratization of Teaching]. São Paulo: Cortez.

Custódio, Helita Barreira (1979), *Associaçes e Fundaçes de Utilidade Publica* [Public Utility Associations and Foundations]. São Paulo: Revista dos Tribunais.

DeKadt, Emmanuel (1970), *Catholic Radicals in Brazil*. London: Oxford University Press.

Gurin, Maurice and Jon Von Til (1990), "Philanthropy in its historical context," in *Critical Issues in American Philanthropy*. San Francisco: Jossey-Bass.

Hoornaert, Eduardo (1974), *Formação do catolicismo brasileiro – 1550–1800* [The Formation of Brazilian Catholicism – 1550–1800]. Petropolis: Vozes (3rd edn: 1991).

Hoornaert, Eduardo (ed.) (1977), *História Geral da Igreja na América Latina* [The General History of the Church in Latin America]. Rio de Janeiro: Vozes.

Landim, Leilah (1992), "What is an NGO?" Paper presented at the Third International Conference of Research on Voluntary and Nonprofit

Organizations, February 1992, at the Indianapolis Conference Center. Mimeographed.

Ministry of Justice (1990), *Entidade de Utilidade Publica Federal: Manual para Requerimento* [Federal Public Utility: A Requirements Manual]. Brasilia: The Ministry.

Paula, Sergio Goes (1991), *Fontes e dados estatísticos sobre as organizaçes privadas sem fins lucrativos no Brasil* [Statistical Sources and Data on Private Nonprofit Organizations]. Mimeographed. Rio de Janeiro.

Reale, Miguel (1972), *Exposiço de Motivos do Código Civil* [Exposition on Motives in the Civil Code]. São Paulo: Saraiva.

Ribeiro, Gloria (1992), Director of the ANDES (National Association of Professors). Interview in January 1992.

Ribeiro de Oliveira, Pedro (1985), *Religio e Dominaço de Classe* [Religion and Class Domination]. Rio de Janeiro: Vozes.

Rodrigues, L. M. (ed.) (1967), *Conflito Industrial e movimento sindical brasileiro* [Industrial Conflict and Union Movement in Brazil]. São Paulo: Difusão Européia do Livro.

Salamon, Lester M. and Helmut K. Anheier (1992), "Defining the nonprofit sector I: the question of definitions," *Voluntas*, 3(2):125–151. (See also Chapter 3 in this volume.)

Santos, Wanderley Guilherme (1990), *Publico e privado no sistema brasileiro* [Public and Private in the Brazilian System]. Mimeographed. Rio de Janeiro.

Simão, A. (1966), *O sindicato e o Estado. Suas relaçoes na formaçao do proletariado de São Paulo* [Unions and State. Their Relationships in Building a Working Class in São Paulo]. São Paulo: USP, Dominus.

Souza, Luiz Alberto G. (1984), *Os Estudantes Católicos e a Política* [Catholic Students and Politics]. Petrópolis: Vozes.

Chapter 13

EGYPT

Amani Kandil

Introduction

The nonprofit sector in Egypt today reflects three fundamental characteristics of the nation's social order: a State apparatus intensely distrustful of civil society; a political economy that underwent dramatic changes during the past four decades; and an Islamic movement that is progressively supplanting the State itself in the delivery of many public services. This chapter discusses the way the Egyptian nonprofit sector is defined and conceptualized in the context of these three characteristics.

State distrust of civil society began a few years after the 1952 revolution. Before that time, nonprofit organizations (NPO) had been very active in Egyptian political, economic, and intellectual movements, from as far back as the second decade of the 1800s. Associations and private foundations were allowed to carry on their operations autonomously under civil law well into the present century. But in 1956, the State enacted its first association law, establishing the principle of State guardianship over NPOs.

Eight years later, in 1964, the State increased its control of the nonprofit sector with the enactment of Law 32, which restricted the establishment of associations, subjected many of their activities to close scrutiny by the State, and even authorized the public authorities to disband NPOs at will. Enacted during the consolidation of Nasser's single-party system, the law remains in effect today.

During the 1970s, under Sadat, the government's attitude toward nonprofit organizations changed to a kind of open-door policy, although without any change in Law 32. Thus, government policies were no longer congruent with past legislation that remained in effect. While the State may increasingly recognize the advantages of nonprofit organizations in the delivery of services to people it is no longer able to reach, it is, at the same time, not willing to give up its tight legal and political control of the nonprofit sector as such. As a consequence, state policy today is often contradictory, with regard to both the nonprofit sector and the private or business sector.

The political economy of Egypt has witnessed deep changes during the last four decades. Demographic factors are one important cause in this respect. The population increased by more than half between 1960 and 1976, from 26 million to 40.5 million. By 1986, it had leapt almost another fifth to 48 million. Throughout, the annual rate of growth has been increasing.

Accompanying this significant population growth was an increase in the rate of urbanization. In 1986, nearly half (43.9 percent) of Egypt's population lived in urban areas, largely in the cities of Cairo and Alexandria. This makes Egypt one of the most highly urbanized countries in the world, and the social and economic implications of this concentration are apparent if we consider how rapid urbanization has been: from 17.2 percent in 1907 and 38 percent in 1960 (CAPMAS, 1986; Morkus 1988:18–22).

The population explosion and the concomitant urbanization generated enormous social problems which the State has found increasingly difficult, if not impossible, to solve. Per capita public spending for health, education, housing, and social welfare has decreased markedly during the past decade in both relative and absolute terms. Health allocations, for example, have dropped from 4 percent of gross national income at the start of the 1980s to 1.5 percent in 1989. Education expenditures declined from 5 percent of gross national income to 3 percent during the same period. Housing and unemployment present other serious problems. Official estimates in 1986 showed joblessness at 14 percent; unemployment among university graduates was a crushing 38 percent (Annual Conference on Economic Problems, 1990).

As we will see below, these developments have led to the emergence of new types of nonprofit organizations, accompanying the traditional organizations subject to Law 32. The new groups include civic companies with no special tax privileges, and organizations operating without *de facto* legal status.

The role of the Islamic movement in Egypt has grown during the last decade. It is important to note the increased presence of Islamic organizations within the nonprofit sector. Many of the services that were previously provided by public agencies, schools, and hospitals are now delivered by Islamic nonprofit organizations. The State, with its dwindling resource bases, could not compete with the grass-roots efficiency of an organized religious movement in reaching the poor or providing public education and health services.

Any understanding of the effectiveness of Islam as a service provider requires at least a brief overview of its historical role in the culture, economy, and politics of Egypt. Religious associations were numerous during the latter part of the nineteenth century. They functioned both as social centers and political entities, becoming even more politically active with the deterioration of the Ottoman Empire and the ensuing British occupation, which began in 1882.

To the Egyptian élite and the growing nationalist movement at that time, Islam and Coptic Christianity faced threats from three sources: British occupation; foreign religious missions; and ethnic or religious minorities of Greeks, Turks, Armenians, French, and Jews. The minorities were governed by their own laws – a privilege granted by the government – and were active in their own organizations and associations. Some of the Christian associations were supported by Western religious missions. The flourishing Islamic and Coptic organizations in Egypt were a consequence of facing these threats. Mobilizing efficiently at local levels, the religious nonprofit organizations quickly addressed the daily needs of the population, as well as its spiritual needs.

In part because of the sensitivity of Islam as a national issue, and in part because the State itself is limited in its own capabilities, religious associations are relatively independent and self-governing. In recent decades, however, the relationship between the State and the religious associations has become increasingly complex and ambiguous. Two examples of the sometimes contradictory relationship between the State and organized Islam may prove instructive.

A traditional Islamic nonprofit activity is *Al Wakf*, a system of bequests of properties that generate income for charitable purposes. The administration of *Al Wakf* funds, historically a province of Islamic organizations, was taken over by the government in the

1950s. The negative effect of the introduction of a governmental control mechanism was a significant drop in bequests and funds donated. This drop motivated the government to encourage, once again, the nonprofit administration of *Al Wakf* based on Islamic principles.

Al Zakat, or charitable tithing, is another Islamic philanthropic tradition; indeed, it is one of the five basic elements or pillars of Islam, the others being prayer, fasting, pilgrimage, and the belief in one God.[1] Islam mandates a 2.5 percent tithe on income, the proceeds of which are to benefit the poor. In 1971, the State established the Nasser Bank of Social Work, funded largely by *Zakat* deposits made through a network of thousands of mosques. The mosques, not the State, continue to administer *Zakat* successfully. This experience demonstrates the effectiveness of Egyptian operations based on religious motivations, and shows also how the State succeeds in mobilizing funds via religious institutions through the application of Islamic principles.

Historical note

The Egyptian nonprofit sector has evolved through four major periods: from the nineteenth century to the First World War; from the end of the First World War until 1952 – which may be referred to as the sector's golden years; from the 1952 revolution through to 1974; and from 1974 to the present.

From the nineteenth century to the First World War

The first Egyptian nonprofit organization was established in Alexandria in 1821 by Greek minorities. Almost four decades later, in 1859, a group of Egyptian intellectuals founded the Egypt Institute for the purpose of studying the nation's history. Other associations followed, including organizations devoted to the study of culture (1868) and geography (1875), established by Egyptian nationals who had studied in the West.

In terms of Islamic nonprofit organizations, only two had existed prior to the British occupation in 1882. One was philanthropic (1879), and the other, founded in 1878 in Alexandria, was part of the national Islamic movement. The occupation, however, sparked a virtual nonprofit movement, particularly in the area of religion. In effect, the occupation awakened what had been a dormant national consciousness. Both Moslems and Copts sought to establish organizations to promote education, culture, religion, and social work.

Factors other than the British occupation also contributed to the growth of NPOs, religious and otherwise, during this period. Various ethnic and religious minorities established their own professional and trade associations and labor unions. According to one account, minorities comprised a third of the Alexandrian population by 1846, following a decade in which their numbers had doubled (Abdel-Malek, 1983:80–81).

The period prior to the First World War was characterized by religious competition, which encouraged the development of nonprofit organizations in Egypt. Concentrating their activities in education, foreign missionary societies set up nonprofit schools and religious missions, largely in an effort to encourage the Egyptian Orthodox population to embrace Protestantism or Catholicism. In response, Egyptian Moslems and Copts moved to establish their own schools and religious associations.

From the First World War to the 1952 revolution

More than twenty religious associations were established during the 1920s, headquartered in Cairo and with branches in various "governates" or local governments. The better known among them still exist today, such as the Moslem Brothers, the Christian Youth Association, the Islamic Youth Association, and the Sharia Islamic Association.

The Islamic Youth Association (1927) and the Moslem Brothers (1928) marked a turning-point in the Egyptian nonprofit sector. Both were highly popular, well organized, and had branches in various Arab countries, including Palestine, Iraq, and Syria. They had a profound effect on Arab politics both inside and outside Egypt. Within the country, their political takeoff point was the presentation of a formal opinion criticizing the 1923 secular constitution. Outside Egypt, at the Yaffa conference in Palestine, they issued a warning to Moslems on the dangers posed by Western missionary societies and spoke on events of particular importance to Palestine (El Berchi, 1980:492–496).

Another association formed during this era, the *Miser El Phata Association*, became one of the important political parties active in what has been called the Liberal Era of 1923 to 1952. Still other associations were established, dedicated to such issues as women's emancipation, cultural development, and various national questions. The development of these organizations reflected, in part, a growing political and intellectual debate on Egyptian identity: whether Egypt should retain its traditional Islamic identity, or establish itself as a modern nation-state. Proponents of each position created their own nonprofit organizations to further their interests.

In sum, the key formative events of the Egyptian nonprofit sector during this "golden era" included the 1923 constitution, the 1936 agreement on Egyptian independence from Great Britain, conflicts over Egypt's cultural and national identity, and the problem of Palestine.

From 1952 to 1974

The most important factors relevant to the nonprofit sector during this period were the 1952 revolution, the new regime's social policies, the role of the public sector, the one-party system, and the State's domination of civic life in general. Together, these developments served to weaken rather than strengthen the sector. In particular, Law 32, enacted in 1964, precipitated a serious decline in the number of nonprofit organizations from its high point of around 5,000 in the mid-1950s. Although the number eventually began to rise, it did so at a sharply reduced rate.

As a consequence of the State's economic policy, no business associations were allowed to form, nor was the establishment of professional interest groups encouraged. Four professional groups, however, did come into existence (there had been nine prior to 1952), but their activities were strictly limited. State social policy prevented the organization of human rights groups; politically, it outlawed any form of oppositional activity.

From 1974 to the present

The adoption of a liberal economic policy, and a multi-party system – albeit one with various restrictions, such as a ban on the establishment of any religious parties – paved the way for a revitalization of the nonprofit sector. For example, notwithstanding the fact that the restrictive Law 32 is still in effect, nonprofit associations and private foundations numbered around 12,800 in 1989 (Ministry of Social Affairs, 1989).

Professional groups now enjoy considerable freedom. Some of them, including associations of engineers, doctors, and lawyers, even engage in political and socio-economic activities. New types of nonprofit business associations have come into existence, and have been very active in lobbying for business sector demands. Still, many if not most associations remain limited in their legal activities, and State efforts to disband various groups have not ceased. This is particularly the case with political associations and labor groups like the Suez Canal Guide Society.

Major types of nonprofit organizations

Seven types of organizations, each governed by different laws, constitute the Egyptian nonprofit sector. These include associations and private foundations, regulated by Law 32; professional groups, regulated by some twenty distinct laws; business organizations; nonprofit foreign foundations; advocacy organizations; Islamic *Wakf* and Christian charities; and clubs and youth centers.

The legal definitions, treatments, and privileges of these types differ markedly from one type to another. This disparity in legal treatment underscores two key aspects of the Egyptian nonprofit sector: its lack of homogeneity and its absence of a clear defining concept guiding its operations. To the State, of course, the nonprofit sector is simply and clearly conceived: it consists of associations and foundations governed by Law 32. But in reality, the sector is far broader. A number of informal terms are now in circulation, employed mainly by the Egyptian academics and business élites. These include *indigenous sector, national organizations, nongovernmental organizations,* and *civil society institutions.* Such terminology connotes voluntary and professional activities, which, depending on citizen initiative, are oriented to political issues and social problems.

Associations and private foundations governed by Law 32

Nonprofit organizations subject to the provisions of Law 32 include both those serving their own members primarily, such as community-based social clubs and closed membership clubs (for example, Greek associations), and those providing services to the public. Nonprofit organizations are engaged in social services for the poor, the aged, women, youth, etc., and in cultural and intellectual activities, science, family planning, international friendship, prisoners' protection, social advocacy, and community development. In general, organizations subject to Law 32 face severe restrictions, which will be discussed below. According to official announcements, by 1993 these organizations had reached 15,000 in number, a fact which reveals changes in government attitudes.

To obtain legal status under this law, associations in this category must consist of at least ten people, and may not pursue profits (Article 1, Law 32). According to Article 2 of Law 32, foundations governed by the law must provide funds for religious, scientific, social welfare, or public benefit goals. Some of these foundations and associations are the outgrowth of *Al Wakf* donations or Christian charities. In general, they enjoy tax deductions and are eligible for public subsidies. At an average of $200 annually per organization, however, these subsidies are largely symbolic. Almost a third of the organizations receive this amount. The associations also receive benefits in the form of personnel paid by the State. This is important, given scarce resources and a limited number of volunteers.

Through Presidential decree, some associations are declared and treated as quasi-public authorities. They supervise various State projects and are supported by the Ministry of Social Welfare, which often pays their employees and provides expert technical assistance. The government assumes that labor inputs on the part of nonprofit organizations are minimal. In fact the Ministry of Social Affairs includes in its personnel statistics employment in nonprofit organizations. In general, however, it is difficult to estimate the degree of independence and self-governance in these associations and foundations.

Professional groups

There were 22 nonprofit professional groups active in Egypt in

1988. The fact that each is subject to a separate law governing its objectives, structure, and responsibilities indicates both the complexity of this part of the nonprofit sector in legal terms and the apparent difficulty of the State in dealing with special interest groups.

Labor unions are similar to professional associations in terms of seeking to protect their members. But they have a different relationship to the State: whereas professional groups are entirely self-governing, unions may not be. To the extent that internal self-government is a characteristic of nonprofit organizations, Egyptian labor unions can be said to operate on the margins or borderline of the nation's nonprofit sector.

The nonprofit status of both unions and professional groups qualifies them for direct and indirect state subsidies: budgetary allocations, tax exemption, deductible tariffs, a 25 percent reduction on the cost of equipment and transportation, and a 50 percent reduction on the cost of water and electricity consumption.

Two recent trends mark the activities of professional groups: economically, they engage in efforts to circumvent the restrictions on profit-making and politically they have moved closer to involvements with political opposition. Legally, professional groups are prohibited from seeking a profit. For example, they may not invest capital in the stock market, but are obliged to place it in State banks. Nevertheless, during the 1980s, some of the groups established and invested in private market companies. This trend is currently under debate in Egypt; it reflects a growing disparity between legality and reality.

Politically, professional groups are increasingly siding with opposition political parties in demanding various, usually democratic, reforms. Participation may take the form of joining ad hoc committees established by the parties or simply attending public meetings. This political trend is a consequence of two factors: the ban on religious political parties and the growing influence of the Islamic movement within the professional groups. The Moslem Brothers, for example, have joined professional groups as an alternative to specific parties and have been highly successful in mobilizing support under the slogan "Islam is the answer." Owing to the increasing presence of the Islamic movement, more and more professional groups have begun to offer social services in the areas of housing, unemployment, education, and health (Kandil, 1989a).

Business groups

Traditional business associations, such as chambers of commerce and industry, tended not to be self-governing. Like labor unions, these groups may best be placed on the periphery of the nonprofit sector. More recently, however, business groups have become far more independent and better financed. Six new types of such groups are now located in Cairo, Alexandria, and other cities. Having evolved during the late 1970s as a result of the government's open-door policy, they tend to represent socially homogeneous populations and to command considerable wealth. The largest, announced in 1977, is the Egyptian Business Men's Society, which became active in 1981. Another is the American Chamber of Cairo, which secured its legal status through Presidential decree. Others were established as branches of commercial chambers.

These groups are almost entirely oriented towards economic policy and have proven themselves effective lobbyists, particularly in support of the State's economic liberalization program. (Since 1974, Egyptian economic policy has moved away from central planning and towards greater reliance on market mechanisms.) Outside of addressing their own economic interests, however, business groups tend to refrain from political activity (Kandil, 1989b:6-7).

Foreign foundations

About 20 foreign foundations now operate in Egypt, many as branches of international bodies. Some are active in culture and scientific areas, others in social work. Some operate as hybrid foundation–associations, funding various projects as well as providing their own services. Among the better-known foreign groups are the Ford Foundation, Caritas, CARE, Catholic Relief Services, and the Population Council.

The legal status and privileges of these organizations are not uniform. Much depends on whether they are governed by the Ministry of Foreign Affairs or the Ministry of Social Affairs. The former provides greater privileges to the foundations. Perhaps the most salient factor about these foreign foundations is their efforts on behalf of Egyptian associations and a large number of small development projects. In many cases, the aim of foreign foundations is to broaden private sector economic activities.

Advocacy organizations

Many of the organizations supporting human rights are nonprofit organizations in a *de facto* sense, but are not recognized as such under any law. Nor do they receive tax benefits or privileges afforded other nonprofit organizations. In 1984, a group of Arab intellectuals established the Organization for Arab Human Rights, in Cyprus, with an Egyptian branch established several years later. The parent group, which is now based in Cairo with branches in Arab and Western countries and which has its own charter, addresses human rights abuses in various Arab states and communicates regularly with foreign governments, the United Nations, and worldwide organizations like Amnesty International. So far the Egyptian branch, known as the Egyptian Organization for Human Rights, has not been prevented by the government from carrying on its activities.

Islamic *Wakf* and Christian charities

Al Wakf is a system under which some form of capital – usually land or real estate, but lately money as well – is allocated by the owner for charitable purposes. Income, generated by the *Al Wakf* property and traditionally administered by Islamic organizations, is earmarked for schools, hospitals, and the like.

In 1953 the State assumed jurisdiction over *Al Wakf* allocations through the Ministry of *Al Awkaf*. In 1957, Law 152 conferred upon the State the right to substitute money for land. This law was an outgrowth of the 1952 revolutionary government's new agrarian policy. Subsequent legislation, such as Law 264 of 1960 which concerns Coptic charities, established government control over *Copt Wakf* (Christian charities), but restrictions were significantly less severe than those for the Islamic system.

The nationalization of Islamic and Coptic hospitals in the 1960s extended the State's involvement in the *Al Wakf* system. In effect, the State became a mediator between donor and donee – between the "will" of *Al Wakf* and the beneficiaries, or areas of allocation. The effect of this mediation was negative; *Al Wakf* allocations dropped significantly.

A distrustful State generates a distrustful society. As *Al Wakf* allocations decreased, new types of philanthropy were born far from the State's hands. The most important were investments in private Islamic banks, the proceeds of which were allocated to the poor, to other private associations, or for philanthropic work in general. The best example of this in Egypt is the *Islamic Phisel Bank*.

Clubs and youth centers

Another category of NPOs in Egypt is clubs and youth centers acting under the supervision of the "High Supreme Council For Youth and Sports." They are, according to law, NPOs aimed at serving the young and developing their interests in sports. There were 931 clubs in 1992, and youth centers were estimated in 1993 to number over 3,900. There is an imbalance in the distribution of these organizations between urban and rural areas, particularly in the case of youth centers, which are oriented toward poor people. Members and beneficiaries from these organizations are about 1 million, a limited number compared with the total population of Egypt.

The State, Islam, and civil society

Severe legal constraints faced by Egyptian associations and foundations reflect the efforts of the State to dominate not only the voluntary or nonprofit sector, but civil society in general. But as with many such efforts, they have proven only partially successful. Indirectly, and perhaps ironically, the distrustful State has served to strengthen at least one broadly-based form of opposition: the Islamic movement.

Restrictive provisions of Law 32

Enacted in 1964, Law 32 remains in effect today, almost three decades later. It imposes numerous constraints on both the establishment and the activities of nonprofit associations and foundations. Restrictions on the creation of new groups are imposed for four broad reasons: "national security," preservation of the nation's general political system, support for social morals, and opposition to the revival of previously dissolved associations. This last justification is used against the re-establishment of the outlawed Islamic Brothers Association, which had been, and still is, the strongest informal association in Egypt. These restrictions allow the government wide latitude both in preventing associations from arising (Article 12), and in dissolving those already in existence (Article 57).

Concerning associational activities, the government exercises control through several key provisions. Various ministries have the right to check the documents and records of organizations to "make sure of their conformity to laws and to the association's [own] regulations" (Article 27). The Ministry of Social Affairs has the right to appoint a temporary board of directors when it deems necessary. Public agencies may prevent an association from affiliating with an international organization or even from participating in joint endeavors. Further, these agencies may prohibit the receipt of any financial support from foreign individuals or organizations (Article 23).

The appropriate authority – usually the Ministry of Social Affairs – may suspend any internal organizational decision that it deems in opposition to either Law 32, or any other law, or to Egyptian morals in general (Article 33). And finally, state authorities may terminate the "material and legal entity" of associations. This last power was authorized to override a provision in the Egyptian Civil Code that, until 1956, prohibited the dissolution of associations by administrative means.

Clearly, these restrictions reveal the government's political apprehensions. For in practice, the State apparatus interferes with internal association activities mainly when the groups function as centers of political opposition. Several years ago, for example, Islamic leaders, upon election to the boards of University Professors' Clubs, began to engage in oppositional politics. Deciding that such activities were against the nation's general and national system, the Ministry of Social Affairs moved to dissolve the boards.

Islamic penetration of civil society

As previously mentioned, laws against the establishment of religious political parties have contributed to the efforts by Islamic activists to enter the nonprofit sector, through which they attempt to realize goals which would otherwise appear political. Notwithstanding the restrictions established by Law 32 – or perhaps because of them – a high percentage of nonprofit organizations subject to this Law are Islamic associations, formally registered as providing cultural and social services.

A survey undertaken as part of the Johns Hopkins Comparative Nonprofit Sector Project revealed that 34 percent of Egyptian nonprofit organizations operating under Law 32 are Islamic and that 9 percent are Coptic (Kandil, 1991). The Coptic figure is high in comparison to the Copts' share of the population in the country, in which they numbered nearly seven million out of a total population of 56 million in 1989. Both Islamic and Coptic groups are highly active, efficient, and well-funded. Islamic associations are considered a symbol of "popular Islam," active not only in religion and social welfare, but among professional groups as well. In effect, Islam has succeeded in mobilizing both the lower and the middle classes. For its part, the State has found it difficult to disband these nonprofit organizations or even to confront them effectively.

Defining the Egyptian nonprofit sector

To what extent does the Egyptian nonprofit sector conform to the "structural–operational definition" introduced by Salamon and Anheier (1992)? By and large, the definition is applicable to Egypt. But there are notable differences, particularly in the case of organizational administration. It is therefore useful to explore those areas where Egyptian nonprofits do not meet, or only partially meet, that definition, and then to review organizations that qualify as borderline cases.

Shared public-private administration and operations

The structural–operational definition portrays nonprofit organizations as self-governing and private, that is, not subject to the decisive control of any outside entity, nor functioning as a unit of the State. Under Egyptian Law 32, the Ministry of Social Affairs has the authority to supervise numerous internal operations of many organizations, including disbanding them, disallowing their decisions, or replacing their boards. This authority is not *pro forma*; it has been exercised on many occasions. The State also exercises control through the subsidies it gives to some nonprofit organizations, either in the form of funds or by appointing state employees from the Ministry of Social Affairs to serve on the staff of nonprofit organizations.

Further, some associations and foundations are granted the legal status of "public benefit authorities," empowered to administer various State projects. To that extent, they can be considered functionally incorporated into the state. Organizations that administer *Al Wakf* are typical in this regard; notwithstanding their philanthropic purpose, many clearly lack self-administration in any meaningful sense.

Professional groups enjoy greater freedom, since they are not subject to Law 32, but they, too, are subject to indirect government control. For example, the government seeks to influence professional associations by supporting the election of candidates close to the ruling National Party for office on governing boards.

Of course, unofficial organizations also exist in Egypt. Lacking legal status, they operate underground or through religious bodies such as mosques and churches, providing public services. Extremely limited information is available concerning these groups' organizational structures, sections, leaders, or sources of funding. They are viable, however, as can be seen from their social output.

Voluntarism

The structural–operational definition requires nonprofit organizations to utilize "some meaningful degree of voluntary involvement," through either the use of voluntary labor or the donated services of a board of directors. Some Egyptian nonprofits were established by the State, such as the Egyptian Association for Population Studies, which has become the General Association for Family Planning and which plays a major role in implementing the State's population policies. As a result of dominant state involvement, voluntary participation has been discouraged.

Borderline institutions

Organizations that fall on the borderline of the Egyptian nonprofit sector include cooperatives, religious social service providers known as *Sufi Tarika*, some types of hospitals and research centers, and the *Social Nasser Bank*. We will discuss each in turn.

Cooperatives. Consumer, producer, and housing cooperatives in Egypt provide needed social services but are allowed to distribute some profit to their members. Consumer groups tend to serve those on the lower levels of the economy, often providing basic commodities. Producer cooperatives serve artisans, providing loans or otherwise meeting their production needs. In both cases, they serve both their own members and the disadvantaged. Housing cooperatives can be considered borderline cases to the extent they provide low-cost shelter.

All three cooperative types enjoy special privileges such as tax deductions, subsidies from the State and local councils, and priority in obtaining loans from public banks (see Article 15 of the Law on Cooperative Societies of 1956, and Article 66 of the Law on Housing Cooperatives of 1981). At least 15 percent of their earnings in excess of expenses must be spent on the provision of social services. In terms of profit, 10 percent of their income above expenses may be distributed to board members. Further, among these groups, the notion of voluntary work is often absent. In fact, some cooperatives have completely changed their nature from borderline organizations to for-profit entities.

Sufi groups. If cooperatives are considered secular borderline organizations, they have a religious counterpart in Egypt as well. An amalgam of philosophic and Islamic tenets, Sufism is a way of life designed, according to its followers, to achieve security and happiness. It began in the second century of Islam's founding as a special "way to God." Far from the luxuries of everyday life, Sufis immersed themselves completely in prayer and the performance of philanthropic deeds.

Sufism attracts millions of supporters in Egypt and other Arab countries. It functions effectively as a form of social solidarity among Moslems. Today, some 61 *Tarika*, or way of life groups, financed by wealthy members, are engaged in a host of social service and other nonprofit activities (El Gohari, 1983:335–349). Their meetings and special celebrations are authorized by Presidential decree, which means they are not subject to Law 32. They receive a fair amount of indirect political support.

Religious and private hospitals. Many hospitals in Egypt have been established by religious associations, either Moslem or Coptic, and some continue to receive contributions from either *Al*

Wakf or Christian charities. Since 1960, 40 hospitals have been nationalized under Presidential Decree 135. They are under the umbrella of a special health authority, the Treatment Foundation, a quasi-public body controlled by the government. Although the nationalized hospitals are under the supervision of the Ministry of Health, they are independently managed. Further, their profits are reinvested in upgrading health services or are used to finance free medical care for those in need.

Research centers. Several recently-established research centers, such as the Arab Union Research Center, adopt cultural and national objectives and channel most of their earnings towards the development of their services. Nevertheless, in Egypt they are registered under the Companies Law, which officially places them within the boundaries of private enterprises.

Social Nasser Bank. Lastly, the Social Nasser Bank, too, represents a borderline organization. Established by the State in 1971 to support social services, it depends mainly on *Zakat*, or Islamic charity. The donations, obtained through thousands of committees in Egypt's mosques, are then deposited in the bank. The committees, incidentally, are legally registered, but the *Zakat* is administered by the mosques, not the State. The Nasser Bank is an interesting example of how the State and nonprofit organizations cooperate to allocate *Zakat* funds for the benefit of the poor.

Conclusion

Major developments in the political economy of Egypt related to the precarious position of the secular State in an Islamic culture form the backdrop of the country's nonprofit sector. The three main features of this political economy include a State intensely distrustful of civil society, radical changes in public policies over the past few decades, and an Islamic movement successful in substituting its own social services for those of the government. Three related challenges face the sector in the coming era.

The first challenge relates to the relationship between the State and the nonprofit sector. The Egyptian State is in a position where financial weakness and a shrinking resource base no longer allow the government to play the role it designed for itself in the 1950s and 1960s. And while the State withdraws from many responsibilities in many social and economic areas, it has so far failed to put policies in place that would allow other providers to compensate for shortfalls in public sector provision. The State remains distrustful and leaves legislation in effect, in particular Law 32, that is detrimental to the development of the nonprofit sector. Thus both the State and the nonprofit sector may be unable to pursue and implement decentralization and liberalization policies unless stifling legal restrictions on the various types of nonprofit organizations are lifted. This dilemma entails the second challenge. The nonprofit sector must find a broader base in society at a time when public confidence in many modern institutions has decreased and may even drop further. Thus the Egyptian nonprofit sector finds itself a double hostage to the State: while being distrusted and restricted by the State itself, the decline in the public legitimacy enjoyed by the secular State apparatus reflects back on large parts of the nonprofit sector itself. It is within this context that the full implications of the third challenge, the Islamic movement, come to light. Islamic activism may well spur a politicization of Christian groups. This will in turn affect large parts of the nonprofit sector itself, given its high proportion of both Islamic and Christian Coptic organizations. The challenge to the nonprofit sector is whether it will be able to develop at arm's length from the State while remaining free of divisive religious conflict.

Notes

1   *Sadakat*, or personal voluntary giving, is also an Islamic tradition. However, it is not religiously obligatory.

References

Abdel-Malek, Anwar (1993), *Egypt Revival*. Cairo: Egyptian Public Organization for Books.

Annual Conference on Economic Problems (1990), *Unemployment in Egypt*. Cairo: Faculty of Economic and Political Science, 1990.

CAPMAS (1986), *Population and Development in Egypt*. Cairo: National Census.

El Berchi, Tarek (1980), *Moslems and Copts in the Context of National Community*. Cairo: Egyptian Public Organization for Books.

El Gohari, Abdel Hadi (1983), *Sociology*. Cairo: Nahdet el Charque Library.

Kandil, Amani (1989a), "Islamic movements and professional groups." *Kadia Fakria*, 8:12–28.

Kandil, Amani (1989b), "Business association and politics." Paper presented at the Third Conference of Political Science. Cairo University.

Kandil, Amani (1991), "A profile of the nonprofit sector in Egypt." Mimeographed. Baltimore: The Johns Hopkins Institute for Policy Studies.

Ministry of Social Affairs (1989), *Annual Report on Social Indicators*. Cairo: Publications of the Ministry of Social Affairs.

Morkus, Widad (1988), *Egypt's Population: An Analytic Review*. Cairo: Arab Center for Studies.

Salamon, Lester M. and Helmut K. Anheier (1992), "In search of the nonprofit sector I: the question of definitions." *Voluntas*, 3(2) (1992):125–151. (See also Chapter 3 in this volume.)

Chapter 14

GHANA

Lawrence Atingdui[1]

Introduction

Ghana is a highly instructive case study for cross-national research on the emergence and potential role of the nonprofit sector in developing countries. The country's nonprofit sector is constituted by several overlapping components that include very different types of organizations. Among the major components are associations rooted in traditional African society and cultural practices, Christian and Islamic institutions, and organizations that are part of the massive and prolonged impact of the West. In short, Ghana's nonprofit sector offers a rich diversity of indigenous and Western, traditional and modern types of organizations. The complex path of Ghana's uneven economic and political course since independence has certainly contributed to the diversity of organizations in the country's nonprofit sector. In addition to traditional forms of organizing that date back well into precolonial times, Ghana's nonprofit sector today includes indigenous grass-roots organizations, government-sponsored community development organizations, Church-related and Islamic welfare organizations, international development and relief organizations, professional and business associations, local craft unions, market women's associations, migrant groups, and village associations, to mention a few.

In contrast to many other African countries, most voluntary organizations faced relatively few restrictions, and relationships with governments were generally neutral, if not cooperative, particularly in the fields of health, social services, and education. The only exceptions to this are political and advocacy groups, such as the Ghana Bar Association, the Trade Union Congress (TUC), and the National Union of Ghana Students (NUGS), which frequently voiced their opposition to government policies. Throughout Ghana's postcolonial history, the fate of such advocacy organizations was closely tied to the changing fortunes of the country's political system, and their relationship with the government fluctuated between co-optation and support on one hand, and distrust and repression on the other. Only in recent years have government and advocacy groups been able to forge the beginnings of a new relationship that seems to go beyond the patterns characteristic of previous decades.

Ghana has always been in the forefront of economic and political developments in Africa. It was the first sub-Saharan country to achieve independence from British colonial rule in 1957, and, until the mid-1980s, no other African country had experienced such persistent political instability and so many regime changes (Schaum, 1982; Gyimah-Boadi, 1994). Ghana's independence opened a new chapter in the country's ambitious course toward economic development. The ideological direction of this program, however, changed repeatedly over time and included pro-market, Pan-African, and socialist as well as autocratic and democratic ideologies. Nor has the course always brought the country closer to greater economic prosperity and social stability. On the contrary, despite Ghana's immense economic potential, the highest level of educational attainment in Africa, and rich and diverse natural resources, the country was unable to generate sustained economic development for most of its first three post-independence decades. Combined with worsening terms of trade, that situation ultimately brought about a long period of economic decline and political instability between the 1960s and the mid-1980s, manifested by low or negative economic growth rates, declining investments, a fall in public savings, and rapid inflation (Kay, 1972; Apter, 1972; Rathbone, 1978; Huq, 1989).

Ghana was also one of the first African countries to implement a far-reaching economic recovery program (World Bank, 1984; Hutchful, 1985), starting in 1983 under an autocratic military regime, and continuing after 1992, under a democratically elected government. Aided by the International Monetary Fund, the World Bank, and various bilateral donor agencies, this reform has come to be perceived as a prime exemplar of "structural adjustment programs," the hallmark of economic policies in many developing countries in the 1990s. Among other changes, the reforms aimed at down-sizing and redefining the role of government in economic affairs. These reforms reversed the decade-long decline of Ghana's economy: whereas industrial output declined by 1 percent annually between 1970 and 1980, it has expanded by 4 percent annually between 1980 and 1992 (World Bank, 1994:164). Similarly, agricultural production either stagnated or declined slightly for much of the 1970s, and has shown an average growth of 3.4 percent since then (World Bank, 1994). The reforms also implied a shift away from direct governmental intervention and controls toward increased reliance on the market and the private sector, including nonprofit or nongovernmental organizations. Indeed, the reforms gave increasing prominence to the nonprofit sector and brought it to the forefront of policy concerns in the 1990s.

Ghana's organizational diversity provides ample opportunities for studying social, political, and economic forces that shape the emergence of the nonprofit sector in developing nations. However, that diversity also creates terminological complexity. The local terminology used to refer to nonprofit organizations is quite blurred, and includes significant overlaps and inconsistencies among terms. For instance, the popular term NGO, or nongovernmental organization, is usually employed as a very broad, virtually all-encompassing, term to refer to almost all types of private nonprofit, even quasi-State, organizations (Anang, 1994). The term PVO, or private voluntary organization, borrowed from American usage, is used interchangeably with NGO, but does not include quasi-public agencies, whereas yet another term, VOLU or voluntary organizations, refers to local development associations funded by international donor agencies and the Ghana National Trust Fund.

A study of the nonprofit sector in Ghana must, therefore, begin with a systematic inventory of the concepts used to denote the various types of nonprofit organizations that exist in the country. This is followed by a brief account of the historical development of the sector, a description of some of the major laws dealing with the nonprofit sector, and a discussion of the relationship between the State and the nonprofit sector in Ghana. The final section examines how the structural–operational definition of the nonprofit sector

(Salamon and Anheier, 1992) applies to the situation in Ghana, and concludes with a brief discussion of current issues and trends.

Terminology and classification

The terms most frequently used to depict organizations generally covered under the rubric of the nonprofit sector include: *traditional associations, community-based organizations, religious, church-related or charitable institutions, voluntary organizations* (VOLU), *private voluntary organizations* (PVOs), *and nongovernmental organizations* (NGOs). As mentioned before, the various terms are often used interchangeably, and much overlap exists among them. This, however, should be no great surprise. Institutions in Ghana, as in most African countries, are emerging and consolidating, and the nonprofit sector, like government and business, is still being shaped. This is part of a long-term process of institutional development that involves combinations of indigenous, international, secular, and religious, as well as public and private elements that may lead to outcomes different from the experience in other regions of the world.

One local effort to classify Ghana's nonprofit organizations was made at a 1990 conference of nongovernmental organizations in Accra. That classification groups nonprofit organizations primarily according to their relations with funding agencies and other overseas institutions, and includes the following categories:

- local grass-roots organizations without external affiliations to donor agencies or parent institutions;
- national organizations without such external affiliations;
- international organizations operating locally; and
- national affiliates of international organizations.

This classification can be useful for addressing practical aspects of nonprofit activities, such as geographic area of operations, access to funding opportunities, or ties with political institutions and international networks. However, its usefulness for comparative analysis may be rather limited, since it tends to lump together organizations established during different historical periods, and originating in different types of social and political institutions, such as organized religion, the government, or international philanthropy.

In Ghana, as in any other country, the various types of voluntary organizations are the typical products of distinct historical periods. Many traditional institutions existed well before Western influences and urbanization. Church-related organizations emerged largely in the early part of this century from missionary societies, often in close cooperation with the colonial administration. Community-based organizations have generally emerged from the town and village development programs of the late 1950s and early 1960s. Many government-sponsored organizations emerged in the 1960s as a result of public social welfare efforts that tried to focus on community development by encouraging popular participation at the local level. By the late 1970s, in the face of growing economic and social problems (rapid urbanization, unemployment and growing population pressures, and deep recession), the State became increasingly unable to meet the welfare needs of the population, and demands began to shift toward private voluntary associations and nongovernmental organizations.

The diversity of Ghana's nonprofit sector notwithstanding, the various types of nonprofit organizations seem to reflect three types, each indicative of broad historical and ideological currents:

- First, there are traditional types, grounded in institutions indigenous to Ghanaian society and culture. This type also includes community-based organizations (CBOs). Although they developed relatively recently in Ghana's history, they nonetheless make a strong connection between their mission and *modus operandi* and the country's traditions and cultures.
- Second, there are religious organizations, based on the world-views and missions advanced by the major monotheistic religions, especially Christianity and Islam. Religion-related groups gained salience during the colonial period, and have been an important element of Ghana's nonprofit sector ever since.
- Third, there are modern organizations, based on the principle of separation between the public and the private sphere, and subject to formal–rational rules and regulations. This type of organization was established during the colonial and postcolonial periods, by either governments or quasi-governmental entities, to address the needs of various economic and social development programs.

We will discuss each type in turn.

Traditional associations and Community-Based Organizations (CBOs)

This type represents the various forms of organizations rooted in traditional African social structures, and includes self-help groups, village associations, and mutual aid societies. At times, to varying degrees, and often in cooperation with missionary societies and Church-related organizations, they embarked upon the construction of schools, hospitals, feeder roads, market stalls, postal agencies, sanitary structures, etc. According to the *Annual Reports of the Department of Social Welfare* dating back to the 1960s, these traditional organizations have been instrumental in providing assistance to the poor or the community at large. These indigenous associations reflect the ethnic and cultural heritage of Ghana and serve a variety of purposes, from the social and economic to the religious and cultural. They are typically membership-based associations, and rarely formally registered.

The variety of groups in this category can be typified by three organizations: the *Asafo Company*, the *Susu* group, and the migrant association. The *Asafo Company* originated in Anomabo, a small town in the coastal area of the country's Western Region. Qualifications for membership in the *Asafo Company* tend to be framed in terms of the traditional criteria of lineage and age, and offices are distributed according to ascribed status (De Graft Johnson, 1971). Principally, the company's activities include seasonal agricultural work, for example planting, weeding and harvesting, and communal labor such as roads and wells, including welfare and the maintenance of cultural practices. For example, the *Asafo Company* has a musical band that performs at important social functions like funerals, marriages, or the enstoolment of chiefs. In other traditional settings, they had responsibility for the defense of the community.

The West African *susu* is an indigenous form of credit and savings association. Typically founded along ethnic, neighborhood, or trade lines, *susus* are funded by regular member contributions to a common pool, which is disbursed to members on either a rotating or a non-rotating basis. While funds are usually distributed to members, they may also be used to grant loans to people outside the association. The origins of such savings associations lie in the demands of the village-based economy, which required people to assume relatively large but irregular expenditures such as the payment of dowries or educational expenses for children (Anheier, 1987). In recent years, the objectives of *susus* have shifted to meet the demands placed on the population by the modern urban economy. Today, they are particularly common among local traders, craftsmen, and others who find it difficult to gain access to banks and other financial institutions. As a consequence, *susus* are more frequent and more developed in urban than rural areas of Ghana.

Voluntary associations among Ghanaian migrants, while largely a product of the early and mid-twentieth century, are nonetheless deeply rooted in traditional African cultures. Already by the 1950s only half of the population living in Accra (330,000) was born locally – a phenomenon not uncommon in other cities such as Kumasi and Sekondi-Takoradi. Many migrants found jobs in the expanding industrial economy; and by 1953, nearly 60 percent of all households in Accra and other coastal cities had wage incomes, and migrant families represented nearly half of them. For anthropologists like Little (1965), voluntary associations provided the link between the traditional, rural society of origin, and the modern, urban surroundings: "Belonging, in his rural home, to a compact group of kinsmen and neighbors, he has been used to a highly personal set of relationships. He knows of no other way of communal living than this and so to organize similar practices of mutuality is for him a spontaneous adjustment to his environment. Nor in view of the strangeness of his surroundings is it surprising that the migrant often prefers to remain as far as possible in the company of previous associates" (Little, 1965:24). Voluntary associations are seen as a response to the urban condition, and rather than weakening traditional forms of culture and sociability, they seemed to maintain them,[2] at least temporarily.

The majority of nonprofit organizations in Ghana today are community-based organizations that are, to varying degrees, rooted in traditional local institutions. These organizations have emerged over time from village or town committees. Their operations are limited to specific geographical areas and ethnic groups, and they are usually led by indigenous local elites. Like the traditional organizations from which they emerged, they are rarely registered. The activities of these organizations cover a wide range of efforts, including water and sanitation projects, health care, agriculture and food distribution, and, lately, environmental protection. These organizations are likely to play an increasingly pivotal role in Ghana's future economic development (see below).

Religious and church-related organizations

This category of organizations encompasses mainly charitable groups affiliated with two worldwide religions, Christianity and Islam. This sets them apart from the numerous indigenous religious institutions related to the numerous African cults and religious belief systems. In recent years, the number of syncretic cults that combine traditional African and Christian beliefs has increased significantly.

The first Christian mission was founded on the Gold Coast in 1482 by the Portuguese. Perhaps the most significant of them was the Evangelical Missionary Society of Basel, Switzerland (the Basel Mission) established on the Gold Coast in 1828. The mission had a profound impact on the different tribal groups living in the coastal area, especially in terms of education, practical skills, and social mobility (Miller, 1994). More missionary societies and Church-related organizations followed as the British colonial administration began to establish itself in the country.

Today, the best known Christian charities operating in Ghana are Catholic Relief Services, the National Christian Council of Ghana, the Presbyterian Relief Society (the legacy of the Basel Mission), the Evangelical Lutheran Church of Ghana, the Charitable Mutual Society of the New Pentecostal Church, and organizations related to the Methodist and the Anglican Churches, as well as groups linked to the growing number of African churches that merge elements of Christianity with traditional African religions. These charities provide services in such areas as education, health care, and emergency relief, and increasingly provide development assistance.

Islamic organizations are primarily active in the northern part of the country. These include the Muslim Koran Study Association, the Ahmaddiya Muslim Movement, and the Ghana Muslim Representative Council. These associations provide services similar to those delivered by their Christian counterparts, but place more emphasis on holistic human development, by seeking to integrate spiritual and economic needs. However, the Islamic organizations tend to be more politicized and fragmented, and overall they offer relatively fewer services when compared to Christian organizations.

In the Ghanaian context, the term *charitable organization* defines local, national, or international organizations that offer temporary relief and social assistance. Those organizations, many of which are Church-related or offshoots of missionary societies, help victims of natural disasters (floods, fire, or famine), refugees and war victims, and individuals in need of special assistance, such as orphans, the elderly, and the mentally or physically handicapped. They focus on meeting immediate emergency needs through direct action such as the distribution of food, the fielding of health teams, and the provision of shelter.

Private voluntary organizations and non-governmental organizations

The terms "private voluntary organization" (PVO) and "non-governmental organization" (NGO) are used interchangeably. These two terms were not well established in Ghana until the early 1980s. Today, the term NGOs is used to denote a broad spectrum of nonprofit and local organizations. Their objectives are diverse and include private development assistance groups as well as relief agencies and social service and health providers (see Anang, 1994). In addition, some NGOs represent economic and other special interests – craft guilds, chambers of commerce, professional associations, recreation clubs, youth associations, environmental groups, and trade unions, among others, that go beyond the concept of development assistance as such.

The related term "voluntary organization" (VOLU) originated in the 1970s from the work of foreign relief agencies. During the 1980s the term was also associated with students working in various community development projects as volunteers. Unlike charitable organizations, such voluntary associations aim at creating more permanent institutional structures to facilitate economic development; they offer technical assistance in the building of schools, hospitals, clinics, roads, and agricultural infrastructure.

VOLUs usually select remote villages for their activities, although their head offices are often in urban areas, and their revenues come primarily from international donors. Today, however, the usage of the term VOLU is limited to the Voluntary Work Camp Association of Ghana, and is less frequently used to refer to other types of voluntary activities.

The variety and number of associations grouped under the terms NGO, PVO, and VOLU make their classification very difficult. One criterion is that of origin. Many associations have their origins outside Ghana and were introduced either by international organizations, like the US-based World Vision and European NGOs, or by members of the local élite educated abroad, as is the case for the Rotary Club. The influential Ghana Trade Union Congress (TUC), although not considered a typical NGO, was established by union officials from the United Kingdom. The services of the union movement were requested and financed by the colonial government, even though the TUC's structure, regulation, and leadership style have changed since independence. Today, the TUC is an umbrella group coordinating 17 other union groups whose activities are built around specific labor-related issues.

In 1981, the Christian Council of Ghana, a coalition of fourteen Protestant Churches operating in Ghana, formed an umbrella group under the name of Ghana Association of Private Voluntary Organizations in Development (GAPVOD). GAPVOD has a diverse membership mix of international NGOs, local service-providing agencies, and some community-based organizations. Since 1987, GAPVOD's membership has increased with the appearance of numerous new indigenous NGOs, in part owing to a newly developed interest among multilateral donors in working with NGOs and GAPVOD's own interest in mobilizing local institutions to join its ranks. Today, GAPVOD membership is around 70 organizations.

Historical background

The pre-colonial and colonial periods

Before the arrival of Europeans, numerous tribes lived in the Gold Coast area of West Africa that later became Ghana. The region was dominated politically by the Ashanti and Fanti branches of the Akans, who had created well-defined governments and states. European settlements in the Gold Coast date back to 1471 and were typically linked to commerce and the slave trade. During the first three-quarters of the nineteenth century, all European settlements came under the British administration. The consolidation of British power in Ghana proceeded in two major steps. First, the coastal area was made a Crown Colony in 1874. Then, in 1901, the Ashanti Confederacy was declared a conquered colony and the Northern Territories were made a protectorate. As in other Crown Colonies, the coastal area had a legislative council. The Ashanti and Northern Territories were directly under the responsibility of the British Governor, with no legislative councils.

The British colonial policy of indirect rule was characterized by the use of indigenous institutions as agencies for continuous and decentralized administration (Rattray, 1955 [1923], 1956 [1929]; Seidman, 1968). The intended effect of these policies was the preservation of traditional social life, using the native chiefs as agents of the colonial administration, and reserving custodial powers for the colonial authorities. Another objective of indirect rule was the establishment of a common system of law for the entire Gold Coast colony.

During the period of indirect rule, the Gold Coast became the scene of increased economic activity. For much of the colonial period, this economic momentum facilitated the establishment and growth of indigenous voluntary associations such as the Asafo Native Affairs Group, founded in 1909; the Aborigines Rights Protection Society of 1913; the Co-operative Societies of Ghana, created in 1927; the Ayobulo Society of the North; the Islamic societies among the northern Dagombas; and the various *susu* savings associations and trade unions in the growing urban areas.

This period also saw the establishment and growing recognition of religious societies, both Christian and Muslim, and their charitable branches. Prominent examples were the Northern German Mission to Ghana of 1852, the Fanti Mission of 1887, the Basel Mission, and the Presbyterian and Catholic Missions (De Graft Johnson, 1971, vol. 17). Religious groups and missionary societies established their own schools, hospitals, and agricultural societies throughout the country, often in collaboration with the colonial administration, but typically with little government assistance and interference.

The relative economic prosperity that characterized Ghana's colonial period (1891–1957) was probably a unique phenomenon in tropical Africa in terms of its scale and duration, although disparities existed between the more developed southern parts of the country and its northern regions. During these six decades, Ghana became the biggest exporter of cocoa in the world and the second largest gold exporter in Africa.

The independence period

Ghana became independent on 6 March, 1957 – the first African nation to gain independence. The high hopes of the independence era soon gave way to disillusionment, and the country's history for the next 25 years is characterized by political and economic instability.

Political transformations. The Gold Coast was given a new constitution in December 1950, following an overwhelming victory by Nkrumah's Convention People's Party (CPP) in the 1951 first general election for the new Legislative Assembly. Nkrumah became prime minister in March 1952 and remained in power until February 1966. Between 1952 and 1957, discontent began to take root in the CPP. In 1954, the Northern People's Party was established to protect and advance the interest of the North. Of significant advantage to the CPP were numerous rivalries between local chiefdoms, that had been left intact by British indirect rule. Because of these local and regional political frictions, Nkrumah faced no united opposition from traditional authorities. A protest party formed in the Ashanti region in 1954 also failed to halt Nkrumah's political rise. In addition, the well-organized CPP managed to exploit local rivalries in the Ashanti–Brong–Ahafo regions. The various opposition parties came together at the end of 1957 to form the United Party (UP) under Busia. The UP obtained most of its support from the Ashanti area, where cocoa farmers felt exploited by a State-dominated cocoa marketing system.

Amidst growing political discontent, Nkrumah crushed all opposition, with the aim of introducing his ideals of "African

Socialism" and Pan-Africanism (Jones 1976), and assumed an autocratic style of government. In 1964, Ghana became a one-party State, with the CPP as the ruling political party.

By the early and mid-1960s, the political and economic situation in Ghana became increasingly difficult. Politics turned more violent as financial and economic problems grew. Dissatisfaction became apparent through clashes that occurred among the army, the CPP, and the judiciary. In February 1966, conspiracy finally turned into rebellion and Nkrumah was overthrown by the army and the police while on a visit to the People's Republic of China.

The coup leaders established the National Liberation Council (NLC), led by General Ankrah, and took a number of measures to reverse the economic decline. They also brought charges against CPP officials and freed many political prisoners. However, as a result of discontent within the NLC, Ankrah was forced to resign in 1969. His successor Afrifa promised a return to civilian rule and introduced a new constitution. Elections, held in August 1969, to form a new National Assembly, resulted in a tremendous victory for Busia's Progress Party (PP). Busia became Prime Minister in September 1969.

The following years continued to be characterized by economic and political problems, and resulted in a military coup and the formation of the National Redemption Council in January 1972. The new leader, General Acheampong, abolished the constitution of the Second Republic, banned all political parties, and appointed new officials to key government institutions. In October 1975, all political power was transferred to a newly established Supreme Military Council (SMC), with General Acheampong as the head of state. Like previous military leaders, Acheampong proposed a referendum to return to a civilian government. However, poor economic performance and a general loss of political legitimacy again resulted in civil unrest.

In July 1978, Acheampong's deputy, Akuffo, assumed power in a palace coup. He freed political leaders, set up a Constituent Assembly, and declared that a civilian government would be in power no later than July 1979. Akuffo lifted the six-year ban on political parties, and 16 political parties registered. However, only 14 days prior to the scheduled elections, another coup was staged by the junior ranks of the armed forces led by Flight Lieutenant Jerry Rawlings.

Rawlings's main concern was to punish former military leaders for their economic policies, so aptly summarized by Acheampong's slogan for his previous economic recovery program, "Make War on the Economy." Rawlings established an Armed Forces Revolutionary Council (AFRC) and began a crackdown on economic racketeers and corruption at all levels. Former heads of state Acheampong, Akuffo, and Afrifa and six other senior army officials were tried for corruption and executed.

Return to civilian rule was postponed until September 1979. Elections resulted in a government coalition, with Limann as President. The government took some measures to halt a continuing economic decline and to restore public order. Growing political difficulties in the governing coalition, however, implied very limited efficacy in dealing with growing economic problems. Once more, on 31 December 1981, Rawlings took power in a military coup and established a Provisional National Defense Council (PNDC) with himself as chairman. The PNDC abolished existing political institutions and the constitution, and established People's Defense Committees (PDC), to introduce elements of popular participation into an otherwise rigid military government.

After a short period of populist support, discontent with Rawlings's economic policies began to surface. Several attempted military coups and serious student riots marked Rawlings's first years in office. Ghana's economy hit bottom in 1983, and further problems were caused by the mass expulsion of Ghanaian workers from Nigeria.

Rawlings's government subscribed to an IMF recovery package whose three main ingredients were free-market policies, structural adjustments, and externally financed private and public investments. Beginning in 1983, the PNDC introduced a number of unpopular measures relating to exchange rates, wage, salary and price structures, public sector employment, State-owned enterprises, and the export industry.

In 1992, the country returned to a democratic form of government with the election of Rawlings as President, and adopted a democratic constitution in 1993. This constitution guarantees basic individual freedoms and the right of associations, and brings to a close nearly three decades of often tumultuous political history that saw such rights often threatened, if not abandoned.

Social and economic transformations. At the time of independence in 1957, Ghana inherited a colonial economy that was largely agricultural, export-oriented, and deficient in technical and managerial human capital. The main aim of the Nkrumah government was to improve the overall quality of life for all Ghanaians. To this end, and as part of its overall public policy, the government devised a series of National Development Plans.

The plans included steps to establish and support "local development communities" as part of a reform of the public sector (Austin, 1964; Sady, 1960). These policies were made in the general post-Second-World-War spirit of economic reconstruction and planning and inspired by the ideals of Nkrumah's African Socialism. The Second Development Plan encouraged the formation of development communities and the reorganization of traditional associations in accordance with the Plan's social and economic objectives. The Plan shifted the implementation of many development initiatives to local government to take advantage of closer ties with communities and associations in an effort to built civic responsibility in the rural areas. Unfortunately, key aspects and assumptions of the various plans did not reflect the country's economic constraints as well as potentials at that time.

The government's development policy during the independence period was one of continuity and growth for the emergent nonprofit sector. For example, before independence, a government memorandum of 19 September 1949 stressed two objectives for the promotion of local development committees (du Sautoy, 1958): first, the committees were to reach out to local voluntary organizations and to encourage self-help initiatives; second, they were asked to mobilize not only the representatives of formal organizations but also informal groups, and (at least initially) irrespective of their political and religious affiliations. Both the CPP and the development committees operated, in principle, on the notion of popular participation. This was implicit in the CPP's ideology of local self-reliance and national self-government.

The development committees and the nonprofit sector cooperated on a voluntary basis in providing education, health, and other essential services to the people of Ghana. Between 1957 and 1972, they cooperated in more than 2,236 projects. The projects included construction of schools, community centers, and halls, rest houses, dams, wells and health clinics and posts, feeder roads, bridges, postal agencies, lorry parks, latrines etc. Some of the religious organizations used foreign assistance funds to provide electricity in the areas in which they operated. According to Catholic Relief Services, nearly 900 projects were under construction and over 1,000 were in the planning stage at the end of 1962. Yet these activities could not stop Ghana's economic decline between 1960 and 1985, and they were soon overshadowed by financial and political difficulties.

Clearly, Ghana's political and economic problems fed upon one another, forming a vicious cycle seen in many African countries in recent decades: poor economic performance leads to a loss of political legitimacy, which, in turn, results in political instability and regime change and so on. Since Nkrumah's regime, Ghana's economic policies have always lacked coherence. State interventionism (the *de facto* result of African Socialism) was replaced by a privatization campaign under the next government, only to be reversed by the following government. Ghana's economic structure became a peculiar and contradictory product resulting from state intervention and state retreat policies – none of them implemented and carried through in a coherent and coordinated way.

Ghana's GNP declined in real terms at an average of 2.1 percent per year between 1965 and 1983. From independence to 1982, the real average per capita income dropped by 1 percent each year. Indeed, before economic restructuring in 1981–1982, the budget deficit accounted for 157 percent of state income. The industrial output index fell from 100 in 1977 to 63.3 in 1981. Capacity utilization in assembler-type industries remained below 25 percent for a number of years. After 25 years of economic decline, which left an over-expanded public sector, a ruined export economy, huge excess capacities in industrial enterprises, a three-digit inflation rate, and an extremely over-valued currency, Ghana embarked on a difficult road to recovery (see Boateng, 1979, on inflation; Twum-Baah, 1983, on labor underutilization; Ewusi, 1984, on poverty; World Bank, 1994, and Hutchful, 1985, on various adjustment policies).

Cooperation between government and the nonprofit sector continued throughout this period, despite political instability and ill-fated socio-economic policies, but the relationship was often disrupted by regime changes and the impact of changing policy directions. The Churches and missionary societies, which had cooperated with the colonial administration and the subsequent governments alike, were among the first to document the sharp erosion of social welfare conditions. In 1967, the Annual Report of the Social Welfare Department stressed that charitable and voluntary associations had contributed immensely to general well-being in Ghana since the pre-independence era. Churches and charities continued to be among the leading providers of emergency relief, health, and education. They implemented government programs and complemented governmental efforts to meet increasing social welfare needs. During this prolonged crisis, the cooperative relationship between the State and nonprofit organizations continued until the early 1980s.

The period of 1983–1990 constitutes an important turning-point in the development of the nonprofit sector in Ghana, owing to the massive reorganization of the country's public and private sectors. As a consequence of this restructuring, Ghana's economic and financial performance improved substantially, even though a number of structural and institutional constraints remained. This improvement occurred in the context of political stability secured by a dictatorial regime, at the expense of personal freedom, human rights, and free speech. Importantly, PNDC Law 221 of 1981 banned all religious and Church-related organizations, and required them to reapply for registration under close government scrutiny (see below).

Despite this brief period of government crack-down on the nonprofit sector, the 1980s and 1990s saw significant growth in the scale of charitable, relief, and development activities carried out by nonprofit organizations. The Catholic, Presbyterian, Anglican, and Methodist Churches were particularly active at local levels during this period. The expansion of multilateral and bilateral development assistance funds available to Ghana after 1983 encouraged the presence of many foreign nongovernmental organizations in the country. Finally, the formation of umbrella groups for nonprofit organizations such as GAPVOD complemented the general expansion of the nonprofit sector during the period of structural adjustment.

Since the late 1980s, two factors have exerted a significant impact on the size and role of the nonprofit sector in Ghana. First, there was a dramatic increase in international development assistance to Ghana. Between 1989 and 1990, the official development grants jumped from 5 percent to 8 percent of the country's GDP

(Table 14.1). More importantly, a greater share of that assistance was directed to the service sector of the economy, where most of Ghana's nonprofit organizations are concentrated. As Table 14.2 shows, the total value of financing commitments to education, technical assistance, social and health services, and sanitation more than doubled between 1988 and 1991.

Table 14.1

Net Official Development Aid (ODA) to Ghana, 1988–91 ($million)

	1988		1989		1990		1991	
		of which		of which		of which		of which
	Total ODA	in grants:	Total ODA	in grants:	Total ODA	in grants:	Total ODA	in grants:
Bilateral	249.1	188.2	354.1	216.3	266[a]	468.7[a]	460.2[a]	505[a]
Multilateral	328.2	42.4	363.4	51.5	297.4	42.1	425.5	47
Total net flow	577.3	230.6	717.6	267.8	563.4	510.8	885.7	552
As % of GDP	11	4	14	5	9	8	13	8

Sources: OECD, *Geographical Distribution of Financial Flows to Developing Countries, 1988/1991* World Bank, *World Tables*

[a] Net total (ODA) is smaller than disbursed grant amounts due to the negative loan balances in 1990 and 1991.

Table 14.2

Official development financing commitments to Ghana, by purpose, 1988–91 (millions US $)

	1988	1989	1990	1991
Education, social and health services, sanitation	62.70	117.05	139.90	155.00
Programme assistance, debts reorganization	58.79	103.55	73.83	286.13
Agriculture	39.19	72.03	19.43	29.81
Manufacturing, trade, and other	231.22	157.57	155.44	125.16
Total	391.90	450.20	388.60	596.10

Source: OECD, *Geographical Distribution of Financial Flows to Developing Countries, 1988/1991*

The second factor was the government policy, adopted in the late 1980s, to encourage rural development and to intensify efforts to aid the poorest population groups as well as those most adversely affected by the structural adjustment program. That policy led to an increase in public outlays for education, health, and social welfare services from 2.4 percent of GDP in 1983 to 5.8 percent of GDP in 1989, and from 29.1 percent of total government expenditure in 1983 to 41.7 percent in 1989.

Although it is uncertain, at this point, how much of those funds were actually received by nonprofit organizations, a dramatic increase in resource availability may well have created unprecedented opportunities and incentives for nonprofit organizations. Consequently, the number of nonprofit organizations, including development committees registered at the Department of Social Welfare, has substantially increased to over 700 since the inception of the Economic Recovery Program.

Finally, the third phase of the Economic Recovery Program focuses on poverty alleviation through the development of private sector initiatives that include nonprofit organizations. As part of this policy, and for the first time in more than a decade, government–nonprofit sector relations are being discussed openly through several public policy fora and meetings. More recently, the government, with the active cooperation of nonprofit organizations, developed new programs relating to population policy formulations, poverty reduction, promotion of science and technology, and private sector building initiatives.

Laws regulating the nonprofit sector

Within the general policy of indirect rule, British law was introduced to the Gold Coast rather selectively, primarily to mitigate conflicts between the colonists and the native population. One consequence was the existence of a dual legal system: one governing relationships among the local population, and another one governing the relationship between the colonial administration and the natives. Furthermore, the law introduced to Africa was much different from that existing in Great Britain. While British law at home contained provisions restricting property rights under the imperatives of the welfare state, such restrictions were generally absent from the law introduced to the colonies (Due, 1963; Seidman, 1968).

The independence and the imperatives of economic development created an urgent need for a coherent legal system capable of regulating relations among individuals and modern social, economic, and political institutions. Neither the colonial nor the customary African law alone was adequate for that end. The development of the legal system in Ghana can be viewed as a continuous effort to develop a modern legal system drawing from these two distinctive legal traditions.

The first laws regulating voluntary associations in Ghana were promulgated as a result of the increased presence of missionary societies and other religious and Church-related organizations during the late colonial period. A 1947 ordinance[3] made the first provisions on how nonprofit organizations were to be treated in the law and how such organizations were to be formally recognized and registered in administrative terms. The ordinance regulated export taxes (the most important source of revenue in Ghana at the time) and stated that the Catholic, Anglican, and Presbyterian churches were the only religious bodies to be exempted from paying duties on imported items (Cox-George, 1974).

When income taxation was first introduced to Ghana in 1943, based on the 1922 Income Tax Ordinance, it laid down provisions to fund nonprofit activities. The activities to be financed from tax revenues included education, medical care, social welfare, and the general improvement and extension of the judicial system.

After gaining independence, the Nkrumah government introduced a series of fiscal measures, including the passage of the "Non-Profit Making Taxation Ordinance" (Income Tax Ordinances, 1960, 1961), which broadened the funding provisions from the colonial period. The new law exempted from taxation the income of ecclesiastical or charitable organizations, indigenous institutions and friendly societies, the Christian Council of Churches, the Muslim Council, the Red Cross and social welfare organizations, as well as nonprofit sporting and recreational establishments (Income Tax Amendments 1974–75 to 1977–78; Supreme Military Council Decree 116).

The Trustees (Incorporation) Act of 1962 re-enacted and extended to all of Ghana the law enabling trustees of voluntary associations and bodies established for any religious, educational, literacy, scientific, sports, social, or charitable purpose to be incorporated, to hold land, and to have perpetual succession.

In 1966 after Nkrumah's fall, the National Liberation Council passed new tax legislation exempting from duties goods imported by religious organizations, charitable societies, cooperatives and public trusts established under section 3 (1) of the 1963 Act. The Income Tax Decree of 1975 and the Supreme Military Council Decree 5 and its amendments recognized nonprofit organizations of a "public character" and exempted their income from taxation in as far as such incomes were not derived from business activities.

However, after the 1982 coup, the legal position of missionary societies, religious bodies, and other types of nonprofit organizations was nullified by the laws promulgated by the Provisional National Defence Council (PNDC). Specifically, the PNDC Law 221 stipulated that no person should fund or establish any association for a religious purpose unless such activities were in accordance with the provisions established by the PNDC. The failure to obtain the authorization or to comply with the PNDC guidelines could have resulted in criminal prosecution of the offenders and the dissolution of the organization (PNDC Law 221 of 1981).

In fact, Law 221 required all missionary societies, religious bodies, and various other types of nonprofit organizations to reapply for registration and official recognition. They were also expected to apply to the PNDC Secretariat and the National Revenue Secretariat for tax exemptions on any imported goods. These policy measures resulted in a series of challenges between Church leaders and the government. However, by the mid-1980s the nonprofit sector was on a solid expansion course as the military government realized, under pressure from international funding agencies, that the presence of nongovernmental organizations constituted a much needed ingredient in its efforts at social and economic development, particularly at the local level.

Consequently, as part of the third phase of the structural adjustment program in the 1990s (see above), the government adopted programs to foster social development; and as part of this policy change, the government began to take greater account of the nonprofit sector as well. Moreover, the process of democratization in general, and the adoption of the new Constitution in 1992, fully established the right to freedom of associations, and many of the restrictive PNDC regulations were dropped. The new Constitution in fact nullified the PNDC Law 221 and related legislation.

Today, a new law is in the process of being formulated to regulate nonprofit organizations and NGOs in particular. This law seeks to establish a National Advisory Council for Non-

Governmental Organizations. The Council is to provide a regulatory framework to guide the operations of nonprofit organizations in Ghana. The establishment of the council is a compromise between the nonprofit organizations, which attempt to protect their autonomy, and the Department of Social Welfare, which is charged with overseeing the nonprofit sector.

Tax exemptions. The Personal Income Tax Ordinance of 1961 guarantees tax-deductibility of contributions to charitable organizations recognized by the 1947 Legislative Assembly Ordinance. Under the current law, all organizations classified as nonprofit receive similar tax treatment. Tax exemptions were less of a problem, when they were first introduced. Most nonprofits were donative charities that received a substantial portion of their income in the form of donations, and provided either public goods or aid to the poor through religious bodies, thus offering a substantial rationale for public support.

The Company Investment Act of 1963, amended in 1985 by the National Investment Code, made specific provisions allowing tax deductions and exemptions from custom import duties for corporations and certain individuals. The scope of these exemptions has been extended (PNDC Law 224 of 1989) to nonprofit as well as commercial organizations providing either nursing and hospital care or services for the elderly and the handicapped.

Today, tax exemptions for nonprofit organizations follow a specific set of procedures and rules. International organizations must sign an agreement with the government, in which any such tax concessions are specifically stated. For local nonprofit organizations, no such specific agreements are required. However, exemption is not automatic, but granted on a case-by-case basis in a complex procedure that involves various committees, such as Customs and Excise, the Overseas Gift Committee of the Department of Social Welfare, and finally, the National Revenue Secretariat and the Ministry of Finance and Economic Planning.

Relationship between the state and the nonprofit sector

One of the key issues emerging from recent work on African societies by a number of social scientists has been the recognition that distinctions such as "indigenous" and "western," "tradition-al" and "modern," and "religious" and "secular" are of little value in countries like Ghana (Sandberg, 1994; Bratton, 1994; Anheier 1994). To understand how the nonprofit sector in Ghana devel-oped we need to examine the history of the relationship between the nonprofit sector and the State. This relationship evolved grad-ually from mutual co-existence and independence during the colonial period to a brief period of conflict with the PNDC regime and now to recognition, and even partial incorporation, by the State and the international donor community.

The mutual relationship between State and private nonprofit organizations, first established during the colonial period, was maintained by the nationalist government after independence as part of a move toward nation-building and political development in Ghana Naturally, independence came with many demands: schools, health services, safe drinking water, roads, and employ-ment opportunities. To address all those needs, the government obviously needed partners, and such partners could be found locally among the nonprofit institutions, especially those estab-lished and run by Christian missionary societies. Nkrumah saw the operations and missions of nonprofit organizations as being consistent with his socialist philosophy under the motto "Progress for all ... Work and Happiness." He recognized their innovative potential for promoting social change, and advocated the concept of "good partnership" in the development of Ghana.

Under the policy of coexistence, Nkrumah's government active-ly encouraged the establishment of new types of nonprofit institu-tions. Modeled to some extent after Soviet prototypes, organizations such as the Ghana Young Pioneer Movement and the Workers' Brigade operated alongside Church-related youth organizations, the Boy Scouts, the Life Brigade, the Red Cross and the YMCA. However, for political reasons, the Ghana Young Pioneer Movement and the Workers' Brigade became the most prominent groups. Other nonprofit organizations could pursue their objectives, but they did not enjoy the same level of govern-ment support. However, their independence from the govern-ment enhanced their capability to foster national unity and integration as well as the stability of the CPP regime (Gyimah-Boadi, 1994).

The relationship between the State and those nonprofit institutions that voiced their opposition to the political regime or criticized government policies deteriorated during the prolonged social and political crisis between 1966 and 1991 (Gyimah-Boadi, 1994), particularly for the Ghana Bar Associaton, the TUC, and student associations. Although no significant policy changes took place until the early 1980s and the introduction of Law 221, the relationship between State and nonprofit sector was increasingly characterized by economic austerity. While the various governments did not have the same views about the ideals and functions of nonprofit organizations as Nkrumah did, they nonetheless continued to support them politically and through the tax exemptions first introduced by the Nkrumah government.

In contrast, the Revolutionary Government of the PNDC which took over power in 1981 came with new policies under the philosophy of "Accountability and Probity." Nonprofit organizations and business enterprises, alongside well-known Ghanaian individuals, were brand-marked as exploiters of the masses, i.e. the ordinary citizen. As we have seen, PNDC Law 221 suspended some of the previous laws and ordered a review of many nonprofit organizations.

By the mid-1980s, the relationship between the State and nonprofits began to change. Following a general depoliticization, in which an organization's economic role was more important than its political one, government official policy moved dramatically from political radicalism to economic realism. Under this new policy approach, voluntary organizations, social services agencies, social development groups, cultural societies, nonprofit health care providers, etc., were encouraged to assume duties that had previously been seen as exclusive domains of the State (PNDC Policy Options, 1984–86). With the support of international donors, NGOs were encouraged to link up with local organizations, and to be active in rural development and income-generating activities to ensure sustainability of their programs.

Ghana's adjustment efforts since 1983 have resulted in an overall favorable economic and financial performance. The 1983–91 period saw a strong influx of foreign assistance in many forms not only to the State but also to the nonprofit sector, i.e. to NGOs through Programs and Actions to Mitigate the Social Cost of Adjustment (PAMSCAD) and other sectoral programs (see Tables 14.1 and 14.2).

Four areas currently constitute the central focus of PAMSCAD policies:

- the organization of community projects, in which rural communities are expected to mobilize their own resources in a general self-help effort;
- the provisions of basic human services in health, education, shelter, and potable water;
- job-creation programs, such as labor-intensive projects, and credit schemes for small-scale enterprises and farmers; and
- human capital sustenance and development, which includes retraining of retrenched civil servants.

In all of these PAMSCAD areas, the government recognizes nonprofit organizations as major partners in its development efforts. This policy has been clearly stated in several policy documents, especially in *Vision 2020* as recently announced by President Rawlings to the Parliament, drawing up major policy goals for the next 25 years. Representatives of nonprofit organizations are also serving on several ministerial advisory boards and other policy committees of the government and development agencies in Ghana. To buttress this policy change, the ministerial responsibility for the nonprofit sector, which hitherto had been changing from one ministry to another, is now permanently placed under the Ministry of Employment and Social Welfare.

The key challenges facing Ghana's nonprofit sector include the consolidation of coordinating bodies among nonprofit organizations, the establishment of a government–nonprofit sector relationship that acknowledges the sector's independence, the introduction of endowed foundations at the local level, and the improvement of managerial and technical skills among the staff of nonprofit organizations.

Definition of the non-profit sector

As we have seen, Ghana's institutional landscape is populated by a number of different types of nonprofit organizations – an organizational diversity reflected in a terminological hodgepodge. This section evaluates how well the structural–operational definition suggested by Salamon and Anheier (1992) fits Ghana's institutional environment. The structural–operational definition stipulates that nonprofit entities are defined as: formal, private, nonprofit distributing, self-governing, and voluntary. We will briefly look at those criteria which may prove problematic in the case of Ghana.

Formal. In the narrow, legalistic sense, a nonprofit organization must have its own bylaws and the requisite information about these must be approved by the Department of Social Welfare (Preamble for Nongovernmental Organizations, Department of Social Welfare, 1989). The current requirement is that the Department of Social Welfare must provide a standard format for the registration and recognition of all national nonprofits in Ghana. Registration requirements include indigenous leadership and meaningful objectives which cover social services, education, the national health service, and other non-commercial activities. In addition to these requirements, nonprofits must register with the Registrar General's Department as a company limited by guarantee.

Non-Ghanaian nonprofit organizations may be exempted from those requirements under the terms of an agreement that can be reached between the Ghana government and the NGO applying for nonprofit status. In some cases there may be no such agreement, but the organization's area of operation may fit into the government's priorities, for example rural water supply and health services. All agreements have to be channeled through the Department of Social Welfare, which reviews the application and makes a recommendation to the Ministry of Mobilization for approval. Such agreements with international nonprofit organizations also specify the nature of tax exemptions and import duty rebates.

Most religious and "Western" organizations meet the criterion of "formal." As to the indigenous organizations, most of them can be considered borderline cases. The traditional associations, such as Asafo companies, emerge from a need within the community to help out individual members. The *susu* can be regarded as informal financial institutions or credit co-operatives that offer financial services to their members at little or no interest. Village associations are at the local government level and are often formed to deal with the governing and administration of community projects. Trade and farmers' unions are organized around the economic interest of people following similar trades and crafts. All those organizations may have little formal structure and are rarely registered.

Private. The distinction between private and government-operated entities continues to be substantially blurred in Ghana. Some of the most visible nonprofit organizations in the country, for example, the Committee for the Defence of the Revolution or the 31st December Women's Association, have been established and supported by the government, or serve as a link between local communities and government agencies (Gyimah-Boadi, 1994). Other examples of such organizations include the TUC, the Ghana Co-operative Societies, and the Council on Women and Development. They were all established by the government as the vehicles of public policy. However, those organizations may only partially meet the private character criterion, since some of their officials are appointed by the government.

Several factors contribute to blurring the still unsettled and weakly defined boundaries between the government and the private sector. One is Ghana's colonial past, particularly British indirect rule, which relied on the traditional indigenous institutions to carry out the policies of the colonial authorities. Another one is the Soviet and Chinese influences promoting a one-sector model, in which the boundaries between the government and the economy are blurred. Similarly, Islamic influences also promote a "one-sector model" blurring the boundaries between religion and the State. Yet another factor is Ghana's political turmoil and dependence on foreign assistance that rendered private entities the most reliable agents distributing foreign government aid. Moreover, international relief organizations and charitable institutions operating in Ghana, although nominally private, frequently serve as channels to distribute development aid provided by foreign governments (Anang, 1994). Recent legislation, however, establishes a "private legal sphere" to the nonprofit sector that goes beyond past laws and policy practices.

Prohibition of profit distribution. Any nonprofit organization that distributes profit to its members will lose tax-exempt status. The NLC Decree 114, Section II (1967) provides a clear core definition which among other things requires that to be classified as belonging to the voluntary or nonprofit sector for tax-exemption purposes, the organizations must fall into one of the specified groups.

Nonprofit schools, day care nurseries, missionary health centers, and social clubs really fall into these categories. By definition, nonprofit entities are not expected to engage in market transactions for profit. Failure to adhere to this will lead to the withdrawal of subsidies and reduction in subventions.

Some difficulty in applying this criterion stems from the ambiguity of the term "profit." If we focus on the output of an activity, "profit" denotes any surplus resulting from that activity. If, on the other hand, we focus on the intended purpose of an activity, "profit" obtains only when the participants engage in an activity solely to maximize their monetary gain, as opposed to an engagement whose purpose is to provide some collective benefit.

From the "output" perspective, consumer or producer cooperatives aim at creating surplus for their members, and thus ought to be classified as for-profit entities. From the "purpose" perspective, however, those cooperatives can aim at providing some collective benefit (for example a better utilization of tools, transportation, or irrigation) that could not be obtained by individuals. Another aim of cooperatives is to serve as a vehicle for instituting political and institutional changes, often initiated by governments (Anheier, 1987). In either case, the main motivation behind cooperative action (be it "from below" or "from above") is the achievement of some collective utility, rather than favorable cost–benefit ratios guaranteeing "profitability."

For those reasons, consumer and producer cooperatives should be considered for-profit inasmuch as those organizations provide mainly tangible benefits to their members. On the other hand, organizations established to obtain some collective benefit, including political or institutional transformation of the country, meet the prohibition of profit-distribution criterion, because the intended beneficiary is the general public rather than a narrowly defined group of actors.

To summarize, the application of the structural–operational definition to characterize Ghana's nonprofit institutions allows us to discern interesting relationships between the operations of nonprofit organizations and their economic and political context:

- The formal character appears characteristic of nonprofit-government relationships in the developed but not in the developing countries; Ghana's government frequently set up or relied upon informal indigenous organizations as the means for solving local problems or acting as vehicles of its policies.

- The prohibition of profit distribution is meaningful in societies with well-established market institutions; in the developing countries that rely, for a large part, on the informal economy, it is rather difficult to distinguish between organizations set up primarily to generate surplus (or "profit") for their members, and those delivering public goods and services for local communities (Anheier, 1987).
- The private character (i.e., independence from the government) is also context-specific; Western charities may be independent from their governments in their native countries, but become vehicles of their own governments' foreign aid policies in the developing countries.

Conclusion

We can conclude that Ghana's nonprofit sector is, for the most part, a product of Western influences interacting with indigenous institutions. The colonial administration exercised its authority through collaboration with local institutions which, in turn, were strengthened through that collaboration and survived to the post-colonial era. Those institutions became the backbone of Ghana's rural development policies. The second type of foreign influences leaving their mark on Ghana's institutional landscape are represented by Christianity and Islam. Islam has been present in this part of West Africa since medieval times, but Christianity gained the upper hand as a result of British colonial domination. During that time, Christian charities established their influences in the Gold Coast. That influence continued after Ghana gained independence, because religious charities became vehicles for distributing foreign assistance. Finally, the third type of foreign institutional influences comes from secular organizations providing aid to Ghana. As in the case of Christian charities and indigenous institutions, their position is strengthened by foreign government policies governing the distribution of development assistance.

Yet it would be wrong to view Ghana's nonprofit sector as merely a foreign implant. As we have seen, different institutions developed as a result of, and often in response to, the process of integration of Ghana in the world economy. While Ghana's position in that system was not always on the most advantageous terms, that process was the driving force that stimulated the development of Ghana's nonprofit sector, promoting its isomorphism to various institutional forms found in the developed nations.

Another lesson we can learn from the development of Ghana's nonprofit sector is the key role of the government in that process. As Ghana's postcolonial experience shows, various nonprofit institutions emerged as a direct or indirect result of government policies. While the role of nonprofits varied from social and political mobilization, to policy implementation, to addressing the most urgent needs of rural communities, government support was crucial for the establishment and continued existence of those organizations.

The complexity of Ghana's governance and regulatory environment suggests that the government will continue to be a key player in further development of the nonprofit sector. Even with freedom of association granted, government still keeps a very close eye on NGOs. Given the past ambiguity of the government–nonprofit relationship, this may also suggest that NGOs in African nations are much more dependent on government policies, both national and international, than their counterparts in developed countries.

Notes

1 This chapter was written by Helmut Anheier and Wojciech Sokolowski based, in part, on a draft outline and related material submitted by Dr Lawrence Atingdui shortly before his untimely death in September 1993. We are grateful to Dr Emmanuel Laryea for his many useful comments and suggestions on a previous draft.

2 Little (1965, p. 27) estimates that close to 17,000 persons belonged to such associations in the late 1950s in Accra alone. The largest associations had about 2,000 members, but most had fewer than 50.

3 Laws passed in the British colonies prior to independence were known as ordinances, as were laws passed in Britain if they applied to the entire empire.

References

Anang, Frederick T. (1994), "Evaluating the role and impact of foreign NGOs in Ghana," in *The Changing Politics of Nongovernmental Organizations and African States*, ed. Eve Sandberg, pp. 101–120. Westport: Praeger.

Anheier, Helmut K. (1987), "Indigenous voluntary associations, nonprofits, and development in Africa," in *The Nonprofit Sector: A Research Handbook*, ed. W.W. Powell. New Haven: Yale University Press.

Anheier, Helmut K. (1994), "Nongovernmental organizations and institutional development in Africa: a comparative analysis," in *The Changing Politics of Nongovernmental Organizations and African States*, ed. Eve Sandberg, pp. 139–168. Westport: Praeger.

Apter, David E. (1972), *Ghana in Transition*, 2nd edn. Princeton, NJ: Princeton University Press.

Austin, Dennis (1964), *Politics in Ghana*. London: Oxford University Press.

Boateng, E. Oti (1979), "Inflation in Ghana: problems and prospects." *Institute of Statistical, Social and Economic Research Discussion Paper*, no. 4. Legon: University of Ghana.

Bratton, Michael (1994), "Nongovernmental organizations in Africa: can they influence public policy?" in *The Changing Politics of Nongovernmental Organizations and African States*, ed. Eve Sandberg, pp. 33–58. Westport: Praeger.

Cox-George, N.A. (1974), *Studies in Finance and Development – The Gold Coast (Ghana) Experience 1914–1950*. London: Dobson.

De Graft Johnson, J.W. (1971), *Towards Nationhood in West Africa; Thoughts of Young Africa Addressed to Young Britain*. London: Cass.

Due, John F. (1963) *Taxation and Economic Development in Tropical Africa*. Cambridge, MA: Massachusetts Institute of Technology Press.

du Sautoy, Peter (1958), *Community Development in Ghana*. London: Oxford University Press.

Ewusi, Kodwo (1984), "Dimensions and characteristics of rural poverty in Ghana." *ISSER Technical Publication*, no. 43. Legon: University of Ghana.

Gyimah-Boadi, E. (1994), "Associational life, civil society, and democratization in Ghana," in *Civil Society and the State in Africa*, ed. John W. Haberson, Donald Rothchild, and Naomi Chazan, pp. 125–148. Boulder: Lynne Rienner Publishers.

Huq, M.M. (1989), *The Economy of Ghana*. Basingstoke: Macmillan Press.

Hutchful, E. (1985), "IMF adjustment policies in Ghana since 1966." *African Development*, 1/2:122–136.

Jones, Trevor (1976), *Ghana's First Republic, 1960–1966*. London: Methuen.

Kay, Geoffrey B. (1972), *The Political Economy of Colonialism in Ghana*.

Cambridge: Cambridge University Press.

Little, Kenneth (1965), *West African Urbanization: A Study of Voluntary Associations in Social Change*. Cambridge: Cambridge University Press.

Miller, Jon (1994), *The Social Control of Religious Zeal: A Study of Organizational Contradictions*. New Brunswick: Rutgers University Press.

OECD (1991), *Geographical Distribution of Financial Flows to Developing Countries, 1988/1991*. Paris: OECD.

Rathbone, R. (1978), "Ghana," in *West African States: Failure and Promise*, ed. J. Dunn, pp. 22–36. Cambridge: Cambridge University Press.

Rattray, Robert S. (1955 [1923], *Ashanti*. Kumasi: Basel Mission Book Depot.

Rattray, Robert S. (1956 [1929]), *Ashanti Law and Constitution*. London: Oxford University Press.

Sady, J. (1960), "Community development and local government." *Journal of African Administration*, 11(4):179–186.

Salamon, Lester M. and Helmut K. Anheier (1992), "In search of the nonprofit sector I: the question of definitions." *Voluntas*, 3(2):125–151.

Sandberg, Eve (ed.) (1994), *The Changing Politics of Nongovernmental Organizations and African States*. Westport: Praeger.

Schaum, F. (1982), "Ghana," in *Handbuch der Dritten Welt* (Band 4), ed. D. Nohlen and F. Nuscheler, pp. 172–194. Hamburg: Hoffmann and Campe.

Seidman, Robert B. (1968), "Law and economic development in independent, English-speaking, sub-Saharan Africa," in *Africa and Law*, ed. Thomas W. Hutchinson, pp. 3–74. Madison: The University of Wisconsin Press.

Twum-Baah, K.A. (1983), "Some indicators of labor underutilization in Ghana." *ISSER Discussion Paper*, no. 12. Legon: University of Ghana.

World Bank (1984), *Ghana: Policies and Program for Adjustment*. Washington: World Bank.

World Bank (1994), *World Tables*. Baltimore: Johns Hopkins University Press.

Chapter 15

INDIA

Siddhartha Sen

Introduction

India's complexity as a country lies in its religious, political, ethnic, social, and cultural diversity, as well as in its long history of civilization.[1] Therefore, defining the nonprofit sector in India is a difficult task because no single underlying theme or pattern can characterize the development of the nonprofit sector. Hence, this chapter uses a historical perspective as an analytical tool to describe definitions – both conceptual and legal – that are then related to the structural–operational definition of the nonprofit sector suggested by Salamon and Anheier (1992). The sector and the various terms used to describe it are analyzed in the context of the broader political economy at various periods of history to uncover underlying themes that are useful to understand its present and past role.

It is useful to divide the development of modern voluntarism[2] and the Indian nonprofit sector into four periods: the middle to late colonial period (1810s to 1947); the early post-independence period (1947 to the late 1950s); the period between 1960 and 1980; and the more recent past since then. Each period is characterized by a number of distinct themes or patterns that are important to understand the development of the nonprofit sector in India:

- The dominant themes of the late colonial period included patronage received by the Church-based nonprofit organizations (NPO) to intervene in the social and religious life of the indigenous population; demands made on the colonial State by the Hindu élite for social and religious reform; socio-religious movements and organizations formed by other religions; ethnic movements; introduction of a political content in voluntary work by the turn of the century; and emergence of new forms of communal, religious, and separatist movements and organizations.

- The salient pattern in the early post-independence period was the emergence of a large number of Gandhian NPOs. This is attributable to the initiative taken by the newly independent Indian State to promote NPOs in development work. It can also be viewed as an alternative reward given to the followers of the Gandhian movement who did not or could not join the government. The period is also characterized by the existence of religion-based NPOs (both Christian and non-Christian) primarily involved in relief work.
- Many new trends appeared in the 1960s and 1970s, of which the most distinct were the emergence of "welfare-oriented" NPOs in the 1960s and "empowerment-oriented" NPOs in the 1970s.[3] The emergence of both groups is related to the socio-economic and political context of India at that time and is discussed in detail in the next section of the chapter.
- The patterns of the 1980s and 1990s are the formation of non-governmental organizations (NGOs)[4] and the resurgence of separatist, fundamentalist, and ethnic movements and organizations. These new trends are also related to the political and economic forces in the country during this period of history and are discussed later in detail.

Historical development[5]

Voluntarism has long been an integral part of Indian society, dating back to 1,500 BC when it was mentioned in the *Rig Veda*.[6] Voluntarism was the main source of welfare and development except for those few empires with a well-developed public welfare system.[7] The role of the political regimes was mainly restricted to promoting the moral, aesthetic, and spiritual progress of the civilization, in addition to enduring exploitation by the monarch, the aristocracy, and government officials. Naturally, voluntarism played an important role in the social and economic development of the civilization. It operated in the fields of education, medicine, and cultural promotion, and in crises such as droughts, floods, epidemics, foreign invasions, and pillaging by robbers and criminals. The disadvantaged and the poor were taken care of by social mechanisms outside the State – through the joint family, caste, solidarity of colleagues, guilds, and individual religious philanthropy. The joint family was, perhaps, the largest source of social security and support in times of distress, followed by caste solidarity, individual philanthropy, religious philanthropy, and trade guilds. Individual and religious philanthropy were interrelated. The relationship between individual philanthropy and religion is explained by the mandates regarding charity laid down by the predominant religions – Hinduism and Islam – as well as other religions: Buddhism, Jainism, Zoroastrianism (Dadrawala, 1991), and Sikhism.

The middle to late colonial period (1810s–1947): The era of church, national bourgeoisie, Gandhian philanthropy, and separatist movements

The first voluntary efforts in social development were initiated by Christian missionaries in the early 1810s (Pande, 1967; Terry, 1983; Baig, 1985; Bhattacharya, 1987; Inamder, 1987; Tandon, 1988). Although their principal objective was propagating Christianity, they started to build schools, colleges, dispensaries, and orphanages around the 1810s and 1820s (Natarajan, 1962; Singh, 1968). Parallel to their efforts in the urban areas, Christian missionaries formed rural colonies from the 1860s until the 1940s, with an emphasis on modernization and, to a certain extent, empowerment (Pande, 1967; Terry, 1983). The modernization efforts focused on self-help, and the establishment of cooperative credit societies, health care, and training facilities, whereas the empowerment component consisted of adult literacy classes and the establishment of *panchayats* (local village councils) to solve local problems.

Toward the middle to late 1820s, that example was emulated by the modern Indian élite, who became social reformers. Local middle-class Hindus in Bengal, especially in Calcutta, who studied in the missionary schools and were influenced by Western thought, began similar efforts from the middle1820s under the leadership of the social reformer Raja Ram Mohan Roy (Natarajan, 1962). Besides building schools, colleges, dispensaries, and hospitals, the national bourgeoisie was also concerned with social reform, especially the abolition of child marriage and polygamy, the improvement of the social status of women, the promotion of women's education, and remarriage of widows. By the 1840s this form of voluntarism had spread to western India, around Bombay (Singh, 1968) and by the end of the century had taken deep roots in Indian society (Inamder, 1987; Natarajan, 1962; Seth, 1982; Singh, 1968). From the 1870s, institutions such as *the Brahmo Samaj*[8], *Arya Samaj*, *Ramkrishna* Mission, *Satyahodhak Samaj*, and Indian National Social Conference began to emerge from these social movements (PRIA, 1991). According to our assessment, the most important organizational offshoot of the nineteenth-century reform movement and subsequent national consciousness was the establishment of the Indian National Congress, in 1885. Liberal-minded British officials and businessmen assisted the modern Indian élite in establishing the Congress which became the official platform for expressing growing national consciousness (Kochanek, 1974; D'Cruz, 1988; PRIA, 1991).

Socio-religious movements and organizations were also formed by other religious and ethnic groups during this period. For example, two religious movements, the *Nirankari* and the *Namdhari*, emerged among the Sikhs in the 1860s and 1870s.[9] Although both movements had little impact upon the masses, the followers of such movements started social reform organizations, such as *Singh Sabha* in 1873 in Amritsar.[10] Although the primary objectives of the first *Sabha* were purely sacramental, later *Singh Sabhas* established schools, colleges, orphanages, Sikh archives, and Sikh historical societies.

The three main Islamic movements of the late 1800s, the *Deoband*, *Firangi Mahal*, and *Aligargh* movements,[11] emerged for three main reasons: to protect Islamic interests from the Western-educated Hindus, who were rapidly gaining indigenous élite status; as a reaction to Christian missionary criticism of Islam; and as a response to British cultural and political hegemony. Started as educational movements with a strong commitment of loyalty towards the British, they acquired a political content at a later phase, leading to the formation in 1886 of the Muhammadan Educational Conference to discuss the problems of Indian Muslims and promote national brotherhood among them. The Muslim League was launched in 1906 at the annual meeting of the

Educational Conference in Dacca. The League's objective was to lobby for Muslim political rights. Initially the League's intention was to maintain the integration of India, and members considered the organization as a parallel organization to the "Hindu" Congress. From 1937 onward, the League changed its role and was instrumental in the formation of Pakistan. Other institutions that emerged from these movements include *Jamiat-al-Ansar*, *Majlis-a-Islahm*, and *Anjuman-e-Khuddam-e-ka'aba*.

Ethnic movements such as the Tribal[12] movements are even older than the philanthropy and social reform movements of the nineteenth-century Hindu Indian élite and their Sikh and Muslim counterparts.[13] The most well-known among these are periodic tribal uprising in the Jharkhand region against the non-tribal immigrants (known as *dikus* among the tribes) and British colonizers. The earliest uprising can be traced back to 1780. The subsequent well-known uprisings until the end of the ninteenth century include the *Bumiji* and *Kurmi* revolts of 1798–99; the *Kol Vlgulan* (rebellion) during 1831–32; the *Santal Hul* rebellion of 1855; the *Sardar Larai* uprising during 1875–95; and the *Birsha Munda* uprising during 1895–1900. Most of these movements were generally violent and were centered around the issues of exploitation and alienation of the tribals by the non-tribals and the British. Specifically, the issues included tribal alienation from land and forests; exploitation and torture of tribal women; religious hegemony imposed by the Hindus and Christian missionaries on tribal religion; and a desire for tribal autonomy. Movements led by Christian missionaries began to appear in the late eighteenth century. The nature of the movements began to change by the early twentieth century with a greater emphasis on social reform and the economic amelioration of tribal life. These movements were led by Christian missionaries and students, and a number of institutions had begun to emerge from these movements by this time. Many of these were cooperative societies aimed at liberating tribals from the clutches of moneylenders.

The desire to overcome the urban missionary bias led to the formation of a new organization – *Kishan Sabha* – in 1931. This organization's success was limited because its programs were not suitable for the entire region. By 1937, many of these organizations assumed the role of political parties as they contested the elections. The electoral setback of the tribal candidates in 1937 saw a change in the attitude of tribal leaders and an attempt was made to bridge the gap between Christian and non-Christian tribes. As a result, an organization called *Adivasi Mahasabha* was formed in 1938. The *Mahasabha* started placing demands for a separate State soon after its formation. The organization did not mature into a political party until 1946, when it contested general elections. The *Mahasabha* was routed in the elections, and two tribal organizations that contributed to its defeat were the *Adim Jati Seva Mandal* and *Sanatan Adivasi Mahasabha*. Such fragmentation and co-optation by ruling parties led to the dilution of the demand for a separate State on the eve of independence.

The 1870s also saw the emergence of dormant caste associations (Rudolph and Rudolph, 1967; Verma, 1979) such as *Kurmi Mahasabha*[14] and *Nadar Mahajan Sangam*.[15] These associations were formed mainly by the élite of lower castes to promote their social and political mobility.

The middle to late 1800s saw the emergence of business associations to protect indigenous and British industrial and commercial interests.[16] The Calcutta Chamber of Commerce was formed in 1834, followed by the formation of Madras and Bombay Chambers of Commerce in 1836. European trading houses[17] were the principal members of these Chambers and, as such, represented the interests and opinions of European commerce and industry. The example was followed by Indians who formed their own associations 50 years later. The Bengal National Chamber, organized in 1887, was the first Indian chamber. Very soon a host of other chambers were formed by Indians to represent their own business and trading interests. Some of these associations were formed to represent the business interests of particular castes or ethnic and religious groups. Indian associations, however, began to have a stronger voice after the First World War, when the Indian industrialists began to make more demands on the colonial State. For example, the Federation of Indian Chambers of Commerce and Industry (FICCI) is an apex body that was set up in 1927 to promote Indian business and industrial interests. The FICCI and some of its members were also supportive of the Congress in their national liberation movement and even supported the Congress financially. FICCI was set up seven years after the formation of a British and European apex body – the Associated Chambers of Commerce. The organization continued to represent British and other foreign business interests until the late 1960s, when it was "Indianized" because of pressure from a group of Bombay industrialists. Today the association mainly represents Indian business interests and is known as Associated Chambers of Commerce and Industry of India (ASSOCHAM).

Nascent forms of trade unions began to appear in the late 1800s. The Bombay Millhands Association was established in Bombay in 1890 by mill workers. Although the association did not have a constitution, formal memberships, or funds, it organized meetings and represented workers' demands to the viceroy and various committees. More formal forms of trade unions began to appear at the turn of the century (Vaidya, 1985).

In the late 1800s, the English formed a number of organizations for the promotion of professions, arts, culture, and research.[18] Typical examples include the Calcutta Phrenological Society, the Society for Promotion of Industrial Arts, the Bombay Branch of the Royal Asiatic Society, and the Bombay Natural History Society. The membership in these organizations was often restricted to Europeans only.

The voluntary movement received the maximum impetus and incentive from Gandhi, who believed that voluntary action was the only path to India's development. Gandhi's concept of development included all aspects of life: social, political, economic, cultural, and spiritual (Chaturvedi, 1987). His notion of rural development was constructing self-supporting, self-governing, and self-reliant village communities where everyone's needs were satisfied and everyone lived in harmony and cooperation. To achieve this goal, Gandhi introduced a "constructive program" to achieve egalitarianism in Indian society by introducing basic education and sanitation, and by eradicating "untouchability."[19] Besides rural development, Gandhi called upon volunteers of the Congress Party to participate in India's independence movement. The volunteers in turn cooperated with Gandhi in mobilizing the masses to achieve political autonomy from the British through passive resistance.

The first effort of mass mobilization of the Muslims began with the *Khilafat*[20] movement (1919-1924) to unite the fragmented Muslim community by using religious and cultural symbols – mainly the *Khalifa* and the *Khilafat*.[21] Although there was a variety of motivations among the leadership, the section that was making an effort to mobilize the community endeavored to assemble a Pan-Indian Muslim constituency for Muslim participation in the Indian Nationalist movement. The most important organizational offshoots of the movement were the Bombay *Khilafat* Committee, the All-India *Khilafat* Committee, and a religio-political institution, the *Jamiat al-Ulama-e-Hind* – an all-India organization of the *ulama*.[22]

The Hindu–Muslim *entente* and the alliance of the Westernized Muslim leadership, *ulama*, and Hindu leadership during the *Khilafat* movement was short-lived. By 1924, the movement collapsed, and new forms of communal and religious movements and organizations began to appear along with the Nationalist movement led by Gandhi and the Congress. The most important of these were the Hindu *Suddhi* (re-conversion to Hinduism) and *Sangahtan* (unification) movements and the Muslim *Tabligh* (propagation) and *Tanjim* (organization) movements.[23]

The *Suddhi* movement was launched by the *Arya Samaj* in response to the Muslim conversion that was taking place in the early 1920s. Its aims were to proselytize fallen Hindus (recently converted Hindus) and borderline Muslims (those that retained many Hindu customs) and to abolish untouchability by converting to *Arya Samaj* tenets. The *Sangahtan* movement aimed at unifying the Hindu community with a political self-consciousness. The organization which nourished the movement was the All-India Hindu *Mahasabha*. This organization also nourished the growth of a fundamentalist Hindu organization, *Rashtriya Swayam Sevak Sangh* (RSS), the National Corps of Volunteers.

The Muslim *Tabligh* and *Tanjim* movements and their organizational offshoots were a part of a reaction to the Hindu right-wing movements and organizations. This called for an organization of Muslim volunteer corps, charitable institutions, and even Muslim banks. The most important organizational offshoot of these movements is the *Tablighi Jamat*, founded in 1926. Today there are thousands of followers and missions of *Tablighi Jamat* all over the world, although no formal membership counting or registration has been undertaken.[24]

The Sikhs also started similar movements at the turn of the century. The organizations that nourished these movements and those that emerged from them include the *Chief Khalsa Diwan*, the *Shiromani Gurdwara Prabandhak* Committee (SGPC), and the *Akali Dal*.[25]

Underlying themes. In addition to the various types of voluntarism discussed, five major themes characterize the period: patronage received by the Church-based NPOs to intervene in the social and religious life of the indigenous population; demands made on the colonial State by the Hindu élite for social and religious reform; socio-religious movements and organizations formed by other religious and ethnic groups; introduction of a political content within voluntary work by the turn of the century; and emergence of new forms of communal, religious, and separatist movements and organizations.[26] The Church-based NPOs received patronage from the colonial State to intervene in the social and religious life of the indigenous population. Such intervention was, perhaps, a blessing in disguise. The local élite in Bengal who studied in schools and colleges established by the missionaries started the social reform movements which subsequently became associated with anti-colonial resistance. The indigenous NPOs were formed to make demands on the State for issue-based social and religious reform. The major shift in the organization of voluntary work was through Gandhi's voluntarism. It emphasized empowerment and transformation of society and acquired a political context, instead of the issue-based voluntarism of the nineteenth century. Other themes include the demands made by various classes on the colonial State and the promotion of professions, arts, culture, and research by the European élite. Demands were made by various classes to further their social, political, or economic interests, as exhibited by the formation of business and caste associations. The promotion of professions, arts, culture, and research by the European élite was a result of the leisure time available to this class combined with their interest in such activities.

The early post-independence period (1947 to the late 1950s): the era of religion-based and Gandhian NPOs

Two types of NPOs were predominant in this period of history: Gandhian NPOs and religion-based NPOs (including both Christian and non-Christian NPOs). Concurrent with these trends, older types of NPOs continued to exist in the sector.

The primary activities of the Gandhian NPOs in this period were development and empowerment, while those of religion-based NPOs were welfare and empowerment. During this period, Gandhian NPOs were also requested to train government officials employed in development projects. For example, the Ministry of Community Development involved Gandhian NPOs to organize and conduct training programs for its extension workers. Another example is the training of health workers undertaken by Gandhian NPOs at the request of the Ministry of Health (Muttalib, 1987; Tandon, 1988). The development orientation of Gandhian NPOs was reflected in their principal projects, which included promotion of agricultural and animal husbandry programs, *Khadi* (hand-woven cloth) and village industries, cooperative dairies, poultry and fishery units, etc. The empowerment orientation is reflected in the establishment of educational institutions.

The welfare component of most religion-based NPOs in this period is reflected in their effort to provide relief for refugees and flood and famine victims, and provision of health and nutrition services for the poor. The empowerment component is reflected in their educational activities.

The primary motive of the religion-based NPOs was religious philanthropy, while that of the post-independence Gandhians that formed NPOs was to ensure a secure financial future (Sethi, 1988).[27] Kothari (1986) writes that Gandhi's constructive program was continued by NPOs headed by Gandhians with financial assistance from the State. He suggests that Gandhians who did not or could not join the ruling party or the government worked closely with the government to set up handicrafts and village industries, rural development agencies, credit cooperatives, and educational institutions.

Underlying themes. The emergence of a large number of Gandhian NPOs is, perhaps, attributable to the initiative taken by the newly independent Indian State in promoting NPOs in development work. For example, the government took the initiative to form the Central Social Welfare Board (CSWB) in 1953 to promote and fund NPOs, setting aside 30 million rupees (approximate 1990 value = 410 million rupees or US $22 million) for funding them (Paul Chowdhury, 1987; Inamder, 1987). Paul Chowdhury states that planners under the leadership of Jawarharlal Nehru and voluntary social worker Durgabai Deshmuk felt that social work should be left to the voluntary sector, with the State providing technical and financial support. In the following year, the CSWB created the State Social Welfare Advisory Boards (SSWAB) for the purpose of strengthening existing NPOs and establishing new ones in the project areas that did not yet have them (Jagganadham, 1987). The CSWB was the first instance when the NPOs began to obtain access to funds for implementing projects. According to Chaturvedi (1987), the creation of CSWB and the SSWABs gave a new lease on life to the stagnating Gandhian NPOs. Seth and Sethi (1991) view the close relationship and dependence of the Gandhian NPOs on the State as the demise of a vibrant sector of Gandhian organizations. It can, however, be seen as an alternative reward given to the Gandhians who did not or could not join the party that they helped to gain State power.

The 1960s and 1970s: increased differentiation

The types of NPOs that existed in this period include: welfare-oriented NPOs; indigenous NGOs formed by international NGOs and welfare wings of churches (WCO); NGOs formed by the middle-class professionals; NPOs known as non-party political formations or action groups; community-based organizations (CBOs) formed by the poor with help from other types of NPOs or the local government; corporate philanthropy; and developmental NGOs formed by the Indian government. Concurrent with these newer trends, the older types of NPOs continued to exist in the sector.

The welfare-oriented NPOs that emerged in the 1960s and to a certain extent in the early 1970s were mainly involved in providing relief to victims of disasters such as famines, floods, and cyclones. Indigenous NPOs formed in the mid-1960s by international NGOs were primarily development-oriented with an element of empowerment. The NGOs formed by the middle-class professionals in the late 1960s and early 1970s were capable of a high degree of specialization in development work, while including empowerment. The NPOs known as action groups or non-party-political formations began to emerge in the late 1960s, and their numbers began to grow after the mid-1970s.[28] The primary emphasis of these NPOs was empowerment, although some of them mixed empowerment with development. CBOs that were formed in the early and mid-1970s undertook various developmental and empowerment-oriented projects. Corporate philanthropy consisted of development programs in rural areas (Franda,

1983; Terry, 1983). The NGOs formed by the government were also development-oriented (Franda, 1983; Kothari, 1986).

The founders of NPOs in the 1960s and 1970s had different motivations. The welfare-oriented NPOs and NGOs formed by the middle class and action groups were probably products of the socio-economic and political conditions of this period. These are discussed in detail in the next subsection. International NGOs formed Indian NGOs out of a compassion for the poor in the developing world. CBOs were formed by the poor, who felt a need to serve their community, often with outside intervention from the local state or NPO assistance. Corporate philanthropy emerged because of tax incentives provided by the State, while the state-sponsored NGOs were formed to develop appropriate technology.

Underlying themes. The emergence of a large number of the welfare-oriented NPOs in the 1960s and to a certain extent the early 1970s is attributable to two factors (Franda, 1983; Terry, 1983; Fernandes, 1986). First, there was a need for relief work because of the regular occurrence of disasters such as famines, floods, and cyclones in this period of Indian history. The need for relief work was further exacerbated by the Bangladesh War, in 1971, which led to a massive influx of refugees into India. Second, Western funding for relief work increased considerably during this period of history.

Emergence of NGOs in the late 1960s and early 1970s was conceivably due to the lack of jobs among the educated youth (for good analyses of a lack of jobs, see Kaul, 1972; Sharma and Apte, 1976), as well as growing dissatisfaction with the existing institutional arrangements in India. The action groups that emerged at that time were formed by six groups of people:

- educated middle-class and lower-middle-class youth, dissatisfied with the model of development adopted by the State and with the politics of leftist parties.
- officials of existing NPOs who were involved in the modernization projects in the 1960s, but who became disillusioned because such projects had little effect in alleviating poverty.
- younger followers of the *Sarvodaya* movement, which focused on voluntary redistribution of land (Ostergaard and Currell, 1971; Franda, 1983). The movement reached its peak in the mid-1970s, but lost its momentum in the late 1970s. The younger followers who formed these groups were disillusioned not only

with the disintegration of the movement, but also with the factional infighting within the party (Janata Party) that they had helped to win the 1977 elections.

- former members of the Naxalite movement, which disintegrated in the early 1970s. The Naxalite movement was a revolutionary Maoist-Leninist armed movement started in the late 1960s. Mrs Gandhi's administration was able to suppress the movement with the help of the army and police by the mid-1970s. Most Naxalites were jailed or imprisoned, while some went underground. The Janata government, however, released all of these political prisoners. Some of these released prisoners and other ex-Naxalites, disillusioned with the fragmentation of their movement, formed action groups.

- New Left academics influenced by Western Marxist thought during this period of time. These intellectuals mainly formed documentation and research centers. These centers provided advice and training to the action groups working with the poor, undertook participatory research, and documented the experiences of action groups.

- Indian Christians influenced by liberation theology. Most of these groups were also involved in research, documentation, and publication, besides working with the poor and training other action groups.

The 1980s and 1990s: the predominance of NGOs and the era of separatist, fundamentalist, and ethnic movements and organizations

Although the predominant organizational form was the NGO, the period saw the resurgence of separatist, fundamentalist, and ethnic movements (e.g., the Sikh movement, the Kashmiri movement, the Nepali movement, the Naga movement, the Jharkhand movement, and the Hindu fundamentalist movement) and organizations that were either their offshoots or the ones that nourished them.

Underlying themes

NGOs. The emergence of NGOs as the predominant form of NPO is mainly attributable to the government's stricter control of the sector and promotion of "apolitical NPOs," the disintegration of the action groups, and the professionalization of the NPO sector, offering viable employment opportunities for young professionals. Among the above factors, we discuss the government's stricter control of the sector and promotion of "apolitical NPOs" in detail.

The government's control of the nonprofit sector began to increase when the Janata Party went out of power in 1980 and the Congress Party (Indira) was reelected. Sympathetic Indian scholars and NPO officials have often claimed that the new government appointed a major commission of inquiry, the Kudal Commission, in retaliation against the support given to Jayaprakash Narayan by the NPOs (Fernandes, 1986; Jain, 1986). The commission was set up to inquire about the working of the Gandhi Peace Foundation, an umbrella organization of NPOs. The commission made allegations about missing funds against 945 Gandhian NPOs. B. Roy (1988) claims that the Kudal Commission was a result of a conflict between two sets of Gandhians. The commission was dissolved in 1986–87 when a younger group of NGO officials were successful in their campaign to end the commission.

A section of Indian academia and NPO officials also claim that, besides the creation of the Kudal Commission, the Indian State has instituted other policies to increase its control on the NPO sector (Fernandes, 1986; Jain, 1986; Kothari, 1986; J. Sen, 1986; Tandon, 1986). The Foreign Contributions (Regulation) Act of 1976, the Financial Act of 1983, removal of tax exemptions from all income-generating activities of NPOs, a proposed National Council and State Councils for rural voluntary agencies in 1986, and a Code of Ethics for NPOs joining those councils are seen as the State's increased control on the NPO sector.

The Foreign Contributions (Regulation) Act (FCRA) of 1976 was enacted in the Parliament to maintain surveillance of NPOs that received foreign funds (Fernandes, 1986). An amendment was passed in 1985 making it obligatory for all NPOs receiving foreign funds to register themselves with the home ministry, get a Foreign Contributions account number, receive all donations into that account, and notify the ministry of the number. The Act empowers the State to ban any organization from receiving foreign contributions, should the state consider the organization to be a political instead of a neutral NPO. According to a government official, the Act was introduced to keep surveillance on fundamentally religious, separatist, and extremist groups that were receiving foreign

414

funds. It is to be noted that, much to the dissatisfaction of the NGO subsector, the government has been reluctant to make changes in the FCRA.[29] NGO leaders have argued for liberalization of the FCRA on the grounds that liberalization has been taking place in all other sectors of the Indian economy, including the relaxation of the Foreign Exchange Regulation Act (FERA) of 1973. They have also requested that the government reconsider the income tax acts governing NPOs and moving the FRCA section from the home to the finance ministry to reduce bureaucratic hurdles.

The Financial Act of 1983 limits the funds that NPOs may receive from industries. This Act removed income tax exemptions that were previously given to industries for donations to rural development projects undertaken by NPOs (Kothari, 1986). Around the same time, all tax exemptions from income-generating activities of NPOs were also removed. It is claimed that the Financial Act of 1983 resulted in a reduction in the industrial philanthropy which was active in the 1970s, although there is no evidence to substantiate this claim. In fact, Dadrawala (1992) refers to a 1981 study which indicated that 600 industrial houses had contributed Rs 1.5 billion (approximate 1990 value = Rs 3 billion or US $170 million) for rural development in that year. Dadrawala also refers to a 1984 Ford Foundation study of a sample of 36 companies in Bombay, which found that they had spent Rs 85.6 million (approximate 1990 value = Rs 135 million or US $7.5 million) on their own developmental projects and donations to other agencies. Finally, he points out that a workshop on "Corporate Social Accountability in India" held in May 1989 estimated that the annual contribution by business was Rs 4 billion (approximate 1990 value = Rs 4.316 billion or US $239 million).

The National and State Councils for rural NPOs was a proposed umbrella organization that such NPOs could join (Kothari, 1986). The Code of Ethics consisted of 19 rules by which NPOs joining the council had to abide (Deshpande, 1986). The proposed Council(s) and Code of Ethics were, however, not adopted, owing to initiatives and lobbying undertaken by certain NPO officials. (It should be noted that the Council(s) and Code of Ethics were proposed by a prominent NGO official who was an adviser on NPOs to the central government at that time.) This very success indicates that the claim made by the NPO sector that the State has increased its control over the sector is an overstatement.

The Congress Party government did not withhold support for non-political NPOs. This is evident from several factors. First, by the late 1980s NPOs could acquire more financial resources directly from the Indian government and para-governmental bodies such as the Council for Advancement of People's Action and Rural Technology (CAPART) (Tandon, 1988). Second, central government funding is available to NPOs working in the fields of providing drinking water, preventing deforestation, social and economic advancement for women and children, health care, adult education and literacy, and rural housing. Third, the seventh five-year plan set aside 2.5 billion rupees (approximate 1990 value = 3.8 billion rupees or US $200 million) for NPOs (Sethi, 1988). Fourth, the eighth five-year plan calls for increased participation of NPOs in improving the delivery of social services and in ensuring people's participation for micro-level planning (Government of India, 1992). Fifth, the new Draft National Housing Policy (NHP)[30] of 1992 encourages NPOs to get actively involved in provision of housing for the poor – a relatively uncommon field of NGO activity (Ministry of Urban Development, 1992). Clearly, the Congress Party (Indira) that ruled India throughout the 1980s was supportive of NPOs as long as they adhered to development.

This is also true for the Rao administration – another Congress Party (Indira) government – which came to power in June 1991.[31] In addition to the special role envisioned for NGOs in the eighth five-year plan, the Planning Commission organized a two-day convention over March 7–8, 1994, to bring about a collaborative relationship between NGOs and the government. The meeting was attended by the Prime Minister, the Vice Chairman of the Planning Commission, senior ministers and secretaries of the government of India, and several NGO leaders. The dialogue resulted in a framework for agreement of principles, procedures, and strategies to strengthen the collaboration between the governmental and non-governmental sector in the country. The willingness of the two sectors in translating into action the framework for the agreement is yet to be seen.

The fieldwork also revealed that empowerment that was not radical in nature was also tolerated by the Congress governments. The only type of voluntarism disapproved of by the Congress governments was the use of the voluntary sector by opposition parties or extremist groups to carry out political objectives. The government has not, however, been able to control such activities, because organizations close to or affiliated with political parties continue to register as NPOs and use the funds to promote partisan gains.[32]

Separatist movements. In this section, we discuss Sikh separatism, Kashmiri separatism, and Hindu fundamentalism as illustrative examples of separatist and fundamentalist movements.

The origins of Sikh separatism date back to the pre-independence period, when the Sikhs demanded a separate state.[33] Although a formal memorandum demanding a Sikh majority state was presented by the Sikh members of the Punjab Legislative Assembly to the Constituent Assembly, which was framing the Indian Constitution, the demand was rejected. By 1952 the *Akali Dal* launched a campaign for a separate state on linguistic lines, taking advantage of similar demands that were being placed in other parts of the country at that time. However, after years of agitation and campaigning, the Indian Cabinet accepted the *Akali* proposal in 1966. Subsequently, the predominantly Hindu and Hindi-speaking southern areas were formed into a new state, Haryana, while other Hindi-speaking parts were merged into the neighboring state of Himachal Pradesh. Encouraged by this success, *Akali Dal* passed another resolution in 1983 that bolstered further separatist demands. In 1981, Sikh fundamentalists launched a "holy war" against the central government that ended in the seizure of the Golden Temple, a Sikh shrine in the Punjab state, by the Indian army in 1984. This seizure and the massacre of Sikhs after Mrs Gandhi's assassination further exacerbated Sikh fundamentalism and caused the revival of several traditional Sikh institutions such as the *Sarbat Khalas* (a general gathering of the Sikhs called by the *jathedar* (manager) of the Golden Temple). There were a number of fundamentalist and extremist groups in Punjab until recently. Many of them had links with organizations such as the All-India Sikh Students Federation, but were organized under their own names, such as the Khalistan Commando Force or the Bhindranwale Tigers. The Punjab situation is relatively under control now, but this was after a decade of violence in which about 25,000 people died (Gautam, 1993).

Kashmir, accessed to India out of a Pakistani threat of invasion, has always maintained a separatist tendency.[34] The death of the charismatic leader Sheikh Abdullah in 1982 created a further political vacuum which was filled by fundamentalist organizations such as *Jammat i Islami*. The situation was further exacerbated by the rigging of the 1987 state elections by Congress. The coalition government that came to power after the election lacked popular legitimacy, increasing Kashmiri distrust against the center. As a result, grievances could only be voiced through separatism. There are three main umbrella groups that are involved in insurgency in Kashmir. The first is composed of pro-Pakistani Islamic fundamentalists. Some of the organizations allied to this group are *Jammat i Islami*, the Muslim Students Federation, *Hezb-i-Islami*, and *Islami-Jammiat-Tulba*. The second group is linked to the Jammu and Kashmir Liberation Front (JKLF). Some of the organizations allied to this group are *Mahaz-i-Azadi*, the Kashmir Students Liberation Front, and the Kashmir *Muzahidden* Liberation Front. This group and its organizations demand a separate nation-state. The third group, which is also pro-Pakistani, is mainly represented by an organization known as the Jammu and Kashmir People's League. The Kashmiri uprising has continued and the militancy has increased over the past few years. Recently, many of the disorganized militant bands have been transformed to fully-fledged guerilla groups with help from Afghan *Muzahids* (Baweja, 1993).

The recent surge of Hindu fundamentalism has been led by the BJP, which came to the forefront of politics after the 1989 elections. The 1980s also saw a resurgence and flourishing of Hindu fundamentalist organizations. For example, the membership of RSS grew by 80 percent between 1979 and 1989. In the early 1990s, there were 2.7 million RSS volunteers in the country (Ghimire, 1992). Other groups that came to notice during this period include the Great Hindu Assembly, the National Defence Committee, *Bajrang Dal*, The Forum for Hindu Awakening, and *Vishwa Hindu Parisad*. Most of these groups gain their support and encouragement from parties like BJP or *Shiv Sena* or older organizations such as RSS. Even at the time of preparing this chapter, many of these groups were instigating communal violence over a controversial Mosque in Ayodhya. The mosque was built by Babar, the Mogul emperor, on a site that is claimed to be the birthplace of the Hindu god, Ram. The fundamentalists led by BJP have been trying to tear down the mosque and build a temple since the early 1980s. They were successful on 6 December 1992, when a 300,000-strong mob destroyed the mosque. The demolition of the mosque saw the worst violence in India since partition in 1947, with over 1,700 people dead, and over 5,500 injured (Thakur, 1993).

Terms and concepts: conceptual and legal

This section discusses first the conceptual definitions and then the legal definitions, in order to illustrate the differences between the two.

Conceptual definitions

According to the literature (Seth, 1982; Franda, 1983; Sethi, 1984; Sethi and Kothari, 1984; D. Roy, 1984; Fernandes and Lobo, 1986; Jain, 1986; Kothari, 1986; PRIA, 1987; Seth and Sethi, 1991) and my observations and interviews (from May 1988 to June 1988; June 1992 to August 1992; and July 1994 to August 1994), the terms used to refer to the NPOs in India are: voluntary associations; voluntary organizations; voluntary agencies; philanthropic organizations; welfare organizations; action groups; non-party political groups; non-party political formations; social action groups; people's groups; women's organizations; non-party, nongovernmental organizations; subaltern organizations; nongovernmental organizations; government-organized NGOs; Church organizations; Christian groups; religious groups; and CBOs). The most commonly used acronym in India is VOLAG (Voluntary Agency), which is unique to India. Terms that seem common in other countries, such as nonprofit sector, charitable sector, independent sector, tax-exempt sector, associational sector or *économie sociale* (see Salamon and Anheier, 1992), are uncommon in India. The sector is generally referred to as the voluntary sector or the nongovernmental sector.[35]

"Voluntary associations" and related terms are traditional "Indian English" terms. In Hindi, the national language, NPOs are referred to as *Seshcha Sevi Sangasthas/ Sanghatanas*.[36] Such terms as action groups; non-party political groups; non-party political formations; social action groups; non-party, nongovernmental organizations; subaltern organizations; and government-organized NGOs have been coined by Indian scholars and individuals involved in the sector (Seth, 1982; Sethi, 1984; Sethi and Kothari,

1984; D. Roy, 1984; Fernandes and Lobo, 1986; Jain, 1986; Kothari, 1986; Seth and Sethi, 1991).

With the exception of the term "government-organized NGOs" (which was coined to describe NPOs formed by the government for developmental purposes, e.g. the National Dairy Development Board and CAPART), all the above terms refer to empowerment-oriented NPOs that emerged from the 1960s onwards. It was argued that these groups had the potential to bring about socialist transformation in India, outside a Communist-Party-centered revolution. Subsequently, a section of Indian academia and NPO officials (refer to the citations above) coined such terms as action groups; non-party political groups; non-party political formations; social action groups; non-party, nongovernmental organizations; and subaltern organizations. Among these, the term non-party political formations (NPPF) was used most frequently because it symbolized the notion that socialist change could be brought about without a party.

The view was challenged by the Communist Party of India – Marxist (see Karat, 1984; A. Roy, 1985) on the grounds of the Doctrine of the Vanguard Party.[37] This had substantial implications for the treatment of NPPFs, which were viewed as expressions of false consciousness.

The term NGO is a "catch-all" phrase which fails to capture the wide array of institutions which share common features with such organizations (see Salamon and Anheier, 1992, in this context). NGOs are generally formed by professionals from the middle class to serve the poor, and have salaried employees (Padron, 1987; May, 1989). As pointed out by Salamon and Anheier (1992) the term NGO has changed over time. Today, NGOs are defined as humanitarian organizations and are recognized as having "NGO status" by intergovernmental organizations such as the United Nations (UN) or European Community (EC), by NGOs in developed countries, or by national governments (Borghese, 1987; May, 1989). It is, however, difficult to single out Indian NGOs because there is no accepted mechanism for recognizing whether or not a particular organization has NGO status. Generally, large and medium-sized developmental and empowerment-oriented NPOs which receive foreign funds are categorized as NGOs in India. NPOs formed by the government also fall under this category. Officials of many of these NPOs would, however, like to be classified as action groups, non-party political formations or voluntary agencies. According to a popular NGO – the Society for Participatory Research in Asia – the term "NGO" is a negative and non-explanatory label because it includes private sector formations, development corporations, welfare boards, etc. According to this NGO, the term "voluntary development organizations" should be used rather than NGO to define developmental organizations. There is no general consensus about the time of emergence of the term in India.[38]

The terms Church organizations, Christian groups, religious groups, and CBOs are also found in the literature. The Church organizations are generally the welfare wing of Churches which have a legal status. Christian groups refer either to WCOs or to action groups formed by Christians. The word religious groups includes more traditional religious NPOs such as the Ramakrishna Mission as well as radical Hindu groups such as the *Ananda Marg*. CBOs are defined as organizations formed by members of the low-income community, most of whom offer their services voluntarily, although it is becoming increasingly common to have salaried employees.

There is a considerable difference between the legal and conceptual definitions of the sector in India. Although other types of organizations (for example a religious trust, a business association, or a cultural association) can classify as legal nonprofit entities, Indian academia and officials of the above types of organizations do not consider such organizations as NPOs. There seems to be a general consensus that in order to qualify as a "voluntary organization," an organization must be development-oriented. All other types of NPOs are seen as serving narrow interests of particular social classes, narrow causes, or even self-interests. For example, religious trusts are seen as serving narrow religious interests and not viewed as voluntary organizations.[39] Private schools and hospitals with a nonprofit status[40] are not seen as a part of the voluntary sector because they serve narrow interests. It is also claimed that such institutions are used as vehicles to get tax benefits for the élite who own them. To use another example, business associations such as the ASSOCHAM and FICCI are not seen as voluntary organizations because they serve the interests of the industrialists.

Legal definitions

Legally, five types of NPOs have a nonprofit status in India.[41] These are: a society registered under the Societies Registration Act of 1860; a trust registered under the Indian Trusts Act of 1882; a cooperative under the Cooperatives Societies Act of 1904; a trade union under the Trade Union Act of 1926; and a company under Section 25 of the Companies Act of 1956. The following sections discuss these acts in detail.

The Societies Registration Act(s)

The Central Act of 1860 was to enable the registration of literary, scientific, and charitable societies. Later on amendments were made to the Act by various states, to broaden the types of organizations that could be registered under the Act.[42] In Bihar, for example, promotion of industry and agriculture has been added to allow organizations that undertake these activities to register under the Act. To cite another example, in Uttar Pradesh, organizations that promote *Khadi*, village industry, and rural development can also register under the Act. Although the types of NPOs that can register under the act vary from state to state, generally the types of organizations that can register under the act include development/empowerment-oriented NPOs; clubs; cultural and literary societies; professional associations; educational institutions; and scientific and medical institutions.[43]

According to the main provisions of the Act, seven persons who subscribe to a Memorandum of Association can register a society.[44] A set of rules and regulations governing the society must also be filed with the Registrar of Societies.[45] The Registrar ensures that the various provisions of the act have been met with and that no other society is registered with a similar name before granting a certificate of registration. According to the central Act, a society is required to submit a list of the members of the managing body after the annual general meeting. The rules of each state may have additional requirements. The membership of a society is open to those who subscribe to its aims and objectives. A fee may be charged for membership. A society can sue and be sued. The liability of its members is, however, limited, because no judgement can be enforced against their private assets.

Two advantages of a society are its democratic organizational nature and flexibility in making amendments to rules and regulations. The democratic organizational nature arises from a society's periodical election of a governing body accountable to its general members.[46] The flexibility arises from its capacity to change rules as an internal process.[47] The Act was initially formulated for societies providing services to beneficiaries who were not members, creating problems for modern-day organizations. Modern NPOs' beneficiaries are often themselves society members, which leads to legal complications. For example, the Registrars in the state of Andhra Pradesh and the Union territory of Delhi have been lobbying for a declaration that the activities of a society should not benefit its members. Another problem is payment of salaries to society members who work as staff. Although payment of salaries to society members has been accepted by Registrars of most states and Union territories, some states such as Tamil Nadu do not allow this. Another problem arising from members working as staff is the possible loss of tax-exemption status under the Income Tax Act of 1961.[48]

The Trust Act(s)

There are two basic types of trusts in India – public and private.[49] Although there is no central law for forming public trusts, such institutions can be registered under the Registration Act. A private trust is governed by the Indian Trust Act of 1882. The law provides for creating a trust to manage property for private, religious, public, and charitable use.[50] According to the Act, the trustees are required to manage the trust and are liable for breach of trust. The private property and assets of trustees can be confiscated to recover loss or a breach of trust. Trustees cannot withdraw from their responsibilities unless they resign or retire. They are not allowed to use the trust for their private personal profit or benefit, but can charge expenses for managing a trust. The act also allows the trust to approach the court to seek information about the management and functioning of the trust. A trust receives almost the same status as a society under the Income Tax Act of 1961. Most trusts are religious, charitable, communal, and educational,[51] although some development- and empowerment-oriented NPOs have used the Act to form organizations.

Other legislation governing trusts in India includes the

Charitable Endowments Act of 1890; the Charitable and Religious Trust Act of 1920; Section 92 of the Code of Civil Procedure; and the Official Trustee Act of 1913. The Charitable Endowments Act of 1890 provides for vesting and administration of property held by the trust for charitable purposes and appointing an officer of the government for the purposes of managing and administering the property of the trust. The Charitable and Religious Trusts Act of 1920 provides for the administration of such trusts; approaching the court to seek advice on managing the trust; and auditing and examining the trust under Section 92 of the Code of Civil Procedure. Section 92 of the Code of Civil Procedure covers several aspects related to breach of trust. These include appointment and removal of a trustee; vesting of property in a trust; directing the trustee to deliver the possession of any property; directing accounts and enquiries, etc. The law also allows alteration of the original purpose of a religious or charitable trust. The Official Trustee Act of 1913 outlines the rights and obligations of trustees.

In addition to the above laws, there is a Bombay Public Trust Act of 1950 applicable to the states of Maharashtra and Gujarat. Under this Act, a public trust is defined as a trust either for religious or charitable purposes, or for both, and includes religious or charitable societies registered under the Societies Registration Act of 1860. In Maharashtra and Gujarat, a registered society created for a charitable purpose must also register under the Bombay Public Trust Act, making the procedure bureaucratic.

Except for the Bombay Trust Act, the Indian Trust Act has three advantages: it is extremely flexible and government interference is minimal; it does not specify the number of trustees; and the mode of creating the legal entity is very simple. There are three problems associated with a trust. First, a trustee cannot enjoy any benefits from the trust, causing problems for trustees who become staff members. Second, the closed nature of the organizational structure does not allow the removal of an appointed member. Third, the liabilities of the trustees require careful management.

The Cooperative Act(s)

The first Cooperative Act was introduced in 1904 and has been subsequently modified in several states since then. Each state and Union territory has its own laws, and institutions registered as cooperatives are expected to abide by these laws. Generally, the government has more control over the cooperatives. In some states, the registrar's office has the right to conduct elections, audit accounts through its own department, inspect and conduct enquiries, dissolve elected committees, nominate its own officials, etc.[52]

The Delhi Cooperative Societies Act of 1972 serves as a good illustrative example, because several provisions are similar to those in other states. According to the Act, an organization formed with the objective of promoting the economic interests of its members may be registered as a cooperative, provided it adheres to cooperative principles. These principles include voluntary membership, a democratic system, limited interest, equitable distribution, cooperative education, and mutual cooperation. Voluntary membership implies that membership should be available to anyone who is willing to accept it, irrespective of that person's social, political, and religious beliefs or racial origins. A democratic system is defined as one in which the administrators are elected or appointed democratically and all members participate in decision-making. Limited interest implies that share capital should receive a strictly limited rate of interest, if any. Equitable distribution implies that economic results should be shared equally among all members. The cooperative education requirement mandates that education about principles and techniques of cooperation should be provided to members, officers, and employees and to the general population. Mutual cooperation is defined as cooperation with other cooperatives at local, national, and international levels.

In order to form such an organization, ten persons from different families need to make an application. The general body of the cooperative is the final authority in managing the institution. Annual auditing, general meetings, and accounting are required. Regular election of committees is also a required legal aspect. Any change in the bylaws of a cooperative must be filed with the Registrar, and prior permission must be obtained to make these changes. According to the Act, a cooperative society can transfer its liabilities and assets to other such societies or divide itself into two or more societies. The Registrar and two-thirds of the members of the cooperative must, however, approve of such a decision. At the same time the Registrar has the power to direct amalgamation, division, or re-organization of a cooperative in the public interest. Agricultural cooperatives must reserve half of the membership for scheduled castes.[53] In cooperatives where central government shares capital, up to one-third of the persons in the managing committee can be nominated by the government. The Registrar has also the right to supersede elected committees, order fresh elections, or appoint one or more administrators who are paid remunerations from the funds of the committee. The Act limits net yearly profit to 5 percent, which must be utilized for a cooperative's educational purposes. Finally, the Act prohibits a cooperative from providing loans to persons other than its members.

The main disadvantage of cooperatives is the excessive governmental control. It has been claimed that the government has used cooperative societies to catch votes, as well as for sources of funds for party workers. The rural élite has also been able to control such societies. Some empowerment-oriented NPOs have, however, creatively used the law for registration.

The Trade Union Act

The Trade Union Act of 1926 provides for registration of trade unions. The Act defines a trade union as a temporary or permanent institution, formed for regulating the relations between workers and employers, between workers, or between employers. The Act also allows for a federation of two or more unions. Under the Act, any seven persons can apply to register a trade union. Any person above the age of 15 may become a trade union member. Every application must be made with a copy of the rules and regulations (constitution and bylaws) of the trade union. This includes names, occupations, and addresses of the members making the application; the address of the head office; the name of the trade union; and the titles, names, ages, addresses, and occupations of the officers of the trade union. In addition, the constitution and bylaws should include the objectives, purposes for which general funds will be applied, adequate facilities which need to be inspected by officials and members for inspection, admission of ordinary members, their membership fee, the number of non-worker officials on the executive committee,[54] the conditions under which members are entitled to benefits, the manner in which the members of the executive committee and other officials are appointed and removed, safe custody of the funds, annual audit and adequate facilities to inspect account books by officials and the members, and the manner in which the trade union may be dissolved. A registered trade union is required to submit to the Registrar annual income and expenditure statements; and any changes in constitution, bylaws, and appointments of officials or addresses of the union.

A trade union is different from other types of legal NPOs in two distinct ways. First, the general fund of a trade union may be used for remunerating its staff, legal procedures, and educational activities, and for the welfare of its members. Second, a trade union may legally have separate funds for promoting the civil and political interests of its members. The trade union may receive funds from its members for the above purposes, but a member who does not contribute to the political fund may not be excluded from any benefits. No legal proceedings can be held against any trade union, or its officers or members, for any action taken to further a trade dispute.

The greatest advantage of a trade union is its capacity for collective bargaining. The second advantage is that it can employ staff. The main disadvantage of a trade union is that it can receive foreign funds only after prior approval of the central government under the Foreign Contributions (Regulations) Act. Generally, trade unions are highly politicized institutions in India and belong to a political party. There are of course certain exceptions among the states. For example, the state of Maharashtra has a long history of "apolitical" trade unions. Some NGOs have, however, used the law in a skillful fashion to register.

Section 25 of the Companies Act of 1956

Although the Companies Act of 1956 was intended for profit-making entities, it is possible to obtain nonprofit status under Section 25 of this Act. A company may obtain nonprofit status if it fulfills the following conditions: the Memorandum of Association of the company makes it expressly nonprofit; the income of the company is solely applied for promotion of charitable objectives; and the members do not get any dividends or other profits. Such companies are known as charitable companies and can hold property for charitable purposes. In such cases, this must be stated in the

427

Memorandum of Association and the central government has to grant a license. The registration procedure for a company is elaborate and requires the submission of a printed Memorandum of Association and Articles of the Association to the Register of Companies. Such companies can have directors who are the trustees. They can manage the company and get reimbursement for management, but cannot accept remuneration or share a profit, which creates problems in employing staff. Another disadvantage is the cumbersome and bureaucratic reporting procedure under the Act. There seems to be little advantage in registering as an NPO under the Act, although some business associations do resort to it.

Tax laws regarding NPOs and donations to NPOs[55]

Laws regarding charitable giving and the nonprofit status of organizations are covered under sections 10, 11, 12, 13 and 80G of the Income Tax Act of 1961. Section 80G specifies that any donation paid to an organization which has an 80G exemption gives the donor the benefit of a 50 percent tax deduction on the donated amount.[56] To qualify for deductions, donations must not be less than Rs 250 (approximate 1990 value = Rs 2,300 or US $128).[57] The maximum amount that can be donated to a charitable organization cannot be more than Rs 500,000 (approximate 1990 value = Rs 4.5 million or US $250,000) or 10 percent of the total income of the organization (whichever is less). Clearly, organizations with an 80G exemption are likely to attract most donations. To get an 80G exemption, organizations must secure tax-exemption status under the mandates laid down by Sections 10 to 13 of the Income Tax Act of 1961. According to these sections, voluntary organizations are defined as "religious and charitable" organizations (PRIA, 1990:163). These two types of organizations are further sub-classified into organizations that are totally exempt from income tax and those that can acquire income tax exemptions. Organizations that are totally exempt from income tax are:

- scientific/research associations;
- universities/colleges or other educational institutions existing solely for educational purposes;
- hospitals or any medical institutes existing solely for medical treatment of suffering persons and not for profit;

- any associations or organizations existing solely for the encouragement of games such as cricket, hockey, football, etc; and
- any such organization existing solely for the protection or encouragement of *khadi* and village industries (which should be registered with the *khadi* and village Industries Commission) (PRIA, 1990:163).

The law further states that "such organizations are totally exempted from income tax if they continue working on their objectives and utilize their income for those objects only" (PRIA, 1990:163).

Organizations that are not included in the preceding list, but are "charitable" in nature can acquire the exemption. Under Section 2 (15) of the Income Tax Act of 1961 the term "charitable purpose" includes "relief of the poor, education, medical relief, and advancement of any other object of public utility not involving the carrying on of any activity for profit" (PRIA, 1990:164). Each of these concepts is defined below.

Relief of the poor. NPOs that are generally working to help the poor can qualify for this status. Relief of the poor includes providing food, getting them married, and giving them gifts. Gifts for the relief of the poor can take three forms: direct distribution of money; indirect distribution of money through establishment of institutions such as a home for the destitute; and supporting NPOs that are helping the poor. To qualify for tax exemption, the NPOs that receive support must be public in nature.

Education. Education is defined as "systematic instruction, schooling, or training given to the young in preparation for the work of life" (PRIA, 1990:164). Thus, mainly institutions such as schools, colleges, and universities can acquire this status. Other activities that qualify as educational include vocational training, providing scholarships, running libraries, and non-formal schools.

Medical relief. Any organization that is formed with the objective of providing medical relief, nursing, and medical facilities for the poor can qualify under this status. The organization can at the same time cater to needs of other social classes, provided that this does not affect the "charitability" of the organization. The services offered, however, must be available to the general public.

General public utility. The concept of general public utility is an open one and difficult to define. It includes any activity that is carried out for the benefit of the public in general and not strictly for any particular group of people. For example, digging wells and ponds, construction or maintenance of community centers, or establishment of cultural societies will fall under the realm of public utility. In addition, organizations must fulfil the following conditions to acquire exemptions:

- property from which income is generated should be held under a trust;
- property should belong to a charitable organization;
- trusts formed after 1 April, 1962 cannot be for the benefit of any particular caste or community, or utilize any part of their income for the benefit of the trustees;
- the part of the income that is entitled to exemption must be used and/or accumulated for charitable purposes;
- accumulated income can be applied only in India;
- incomes of trusts involved in business activity are calculated on the basis of Section 11 (4A) of the Income Tax Act of 1961;[58]
- trusts that want income tax exemption should register under Section 12 (A) with the Income Tax commissioner within one year of their formation;
- trusts that have an annual income of Rs 25,000 (approximate 1990 value = Rs 230,000 or US $12,000) and above should have an annual audit;
- trusts are required to invest their accumulated income with nationalized banks or government undertaking; and
- trusts are required to apply 75 percent of their total income of the year for charitable purposes during the same year.[59]

Applying the structural–operational definition

As pointed out by Salamon and Anheier (1992), the structural–operational definition avoids many of the pitfalls of other types of definitions (for example, the legal or the economic definition). This is especially true for India because of the long and complex history of NPOs, and differences between the various legal and conceptual definitions. The following section examines the usefulness of each of the five key features of the structural–operational definitions and their applicability in the Indian context.

Formal. The criterion of formal organization is useful in India because of the "looseness" of definitions in India. From this viewpoint, the earliest institutions that took the premodern organizational form were the guilds of the precolonial period. If we apply this criterion, the organizations (for example, the *Brahmo Samaj, Arya Samaj, Ramkrishna* Mission, *Satyahodhak Samaj,* and Indian National Social Conference) that emerged from the voluntaristic efforts of the eighteenth-century Hindu élite can be included in the nonprofit sector. Similarly, organizations that emerged from other socio-religious movements (for example, the *Singh Sabhas, Jamiat-al-Ansar,* or *Anjuman-e-Khuddam-e-Ka'aba*) fall under the sector. The constructive work organizations or *ashrams* that emerged from Gandhian voluntarism at the turn of the century can also be placed in the category of the nonprofit sector. By similar logic, we can include organizational offshoots of more recent social movements – tribal movements, women's movements, environmental movements, Jayaprakash's movement, the Naxalite movement, the Sikh and the Kashmiri movements – in the nonprofit sector (for example, Khalistan Commando Force, the Bhindranwale Tigers, *Mahaz-i-Azadi,* or the Kashmiri Students' Liberation Front). We can also include organizations that nourished such movements (for example, the *Gurdwara,* the SGPC, the *Chief Khalsa Diwan,* or the *Jammat-i-Islami*).

Another important feature of this particular criterion is that it allows for the inclusion of business associations, professional associations, associations for the promotion of arts and culture, and even fundamental religio-political organizations under the NPO category, though these would otherwise be excluded from the sector given conceptual definitions in India. The problem has been discussed by Salmon and Anheier (1992), who point out that the structural–operational definition allows us to capture a wider array of organizations which share common features with development-oriented NGOs. As we shall see, employing the "voluntary" criterion also allows us to increase the array of NPOs under the sector.

Private. This criterion is also important in India because the government has formed and financed NGOs for developmental purposes, the National Dairy Development Board and CAPART being typical examples. Often the boards of directors for such NPOs include government officials. For our purposes, such institutions should be treated outside the nonprofit sector to the extent that they are created, financed, and controlled by the nation-state, but included, to the extent that they are self-governing. In this way, these are quite similar to "para-state" institutions in Britain. The cooperatives will also be another borderline case because of the government's strong financial and administrative control over the sector. As discussed earlier, according to the Delhi Cooperative Societies Act (which is similar to Acts in other states and Union territories), cooperatives in which the central government shares capital may have up to one-third of their managing committees nominated by the government. The borderline nature of cooperatives is further illustrated in the discussion on the "self-governing" criterion.

Self-governing. This concept is useful because it helps us single out types of NPOs that are borderline cases, i.e., cooperatives and trade unions. Once again the Delhi Cooperative Societies Act serves as a good example. In this case, the Registrar, a government official, has the power to amalgamate, divide, or re-organize a cooperative in the public interest. In cooperatives where central government contributes to the share capital, the Registrar also has the right to supersede elected committees, order fresh elections, or appoint one or more administrators who are paid remunerations from the funds of the committee. Finally, the Act requires that agricultural cooperatives must reserve half of the membership for the scheduled castes, thereby violating the "self-governing" criterion. Similarly, most unions follow the mandates of a party and are not self-governing from this point of view, making them borderline cases. Again if we were to apply the analytical scheme applied by Salamon and Anheier (1992) in their effort to analyze the applicability of the structural–operational definition in Brazil, we would have to include trade unions in this sector, given the "highly charged political atmosphere" in a developing society and because they help build a civil society outside the central state.[60]

Non-profit-distributing. The tax system and the removal of all income-generating activities of NPOs in India clearly demonstrates that the government has virtually ensured that NPOs are non-profit-distributing (see the subsections "Legal definitions" and "Tax laws regarding NPOs and donations to NPOs"). In this way, in contrast to what happens in many developing countries, most community-based development organizations are not able to distribute profits to their constituents.[61] Again, the very laws which have imposed strict control also have their loopholes, which create borderline cases. As NPO officials have often complained, the élite often form educational, research, or similar organizations to get tax benefits. Thus such organizations exist for "indirect profit motives," making them borderline cases.

Voluntary. This concept is useful in India because of the various types of NPOs that exist in the country. Thus, business organizations, associations for arts, culture, and professions, religio-political organizations, and so on can be termed NPOs. Although many scholars and NPO officials are reluctant to include such organizations within the sector, the structural–operational definition allows us to capture a wider array of organizations which share common features with development-oriented NGOs. At the same time we have to be cautious, and consider institutions created by the élite for tax benefits as borderline cases, because hidden motives lie behind the voluntary nature of such NPOs.

In summary, the nonprofit sector in India includes religio-political institutions, institutions that have emerged from or nourished social movements, NGOs, CBOs, welfare wings of religious organizations, business associations, cultural associations, scientific associations, associations for promotion of sports or arts, caste associations, and traditional voluntary agencies, according to the structural–operational definition. By implication it excludes social and political movements and political parties. Borderline cases include cooperatives, trade unions, government-organized NPOs, and NPOs formed by the rich to get tax benefits.

Conclusion

Clearly, the conceptual and legal definitions vary considerably in India. Such a difference in definitions is explained by the long history of the political and social context of the sector. Although modern organizational forms began to emerge around the 1870s in the form of reform institutions such the *Brahmo Samaj* or the *Arya Samaj*, an element of political and social content remained even in these institutions, because they emerged from social movements of the eighteenth century. Despite the recent reduction of political context, the notion of voluntarism is essentially romantic. It is not perceived as an organizational effort, but rather as a self-initiative and social commitment. It is not uncommon for scholars in India to classify social movements – tribal movements, women's movements, environmental movements – as part of the voluntary sector. Thus, we see the objection to even the word "sector" in India among scholars and NPO officials. This is in direct contrast with the perception of the nation-states which sees the voluntary sector as a partner in its developmental effort.[62] The structural–operational definition, however, allows us to distinguish between borderline cases and NPOs. It also allows us to include a wider array of organizations in the sector. Clearly, the structural–operational definition is useful in making cross-national comparisons, which neither the legal nor the conceptual definitions permit. To use Salamon and Anheier's (1992) terms, it helps us overcome the "terminological tangle" or "amorphousness" of the definitions employed in depicting the sector.

In summary, the discussion presented here suggests that the Indian central State leaves additional available space for the formation of a civil society outside the State institutions. One factor that facilitates the formation of civil society outside the Indian State is the presence of a free press. The Indian State, however, is not a monolithic entity. As has been shown in this chapter, regional variations can be observed in terms of laws and regulations regarding NPOs. Finally, we want to conclude with a comment on the failure of that State to separate itself, as well as politics, from religion. Although this failure has allowed a civil society to grow up outside it, especially among minorities, it has also fuelled fundamentalism, as exhibited by the recent resurgence of Hindu fundamentalism and the Kashmiri and Sikh separatism.

Notes

1   The first settled cultures can be dated back to the end of the fourth millennium (Basham, 1968).

2   Note that there is a need to distinguish between the term "NPO" and terms such as "voluntarism," "philanthropy", or "charity." The term NPO refers to organizations, whereas the other terms refer to individual efforts or collective social efforts, although they exhibited some organizational permanence (see Salamon and Anheier (1992) for clarification of this concept).

3   The terms "empowerment," "modernization," and "welfare" are often used in this chapter to describe various types of NPOs. They are

derived from the literature which identifies three types of NPOs in terms of their project orientation (see Brodhead, 1987; Drabek, 1987; Elliot, 1987; Landim, 1987; Korten, 1987). Three types of NPOs are defined using project orientation, as the principal variable. First, there are NPOs with a welfare orientation, which provide famine or flood relief, child sponsorship, etc. Second, there are NPOs with a modernization or developmental orientation. These NPOs support development projects that enable the poor to provide for their own basic needs. Third, there are NPOs with an empowerment or conscientization orientation. These NPOs see poverty as the result of political process and are committed to train communities to enter these processes to bring about social change. It is not uncommon to have more than one orientation within the same NPO.

4 The term NGO is defined in a later section of this chapter.

5 This section draws from an earlier publication by the author (S. Sen, 1992). For other historical accounts, see for example: Baig, 1985; Inamder, 1987; Seth, 1982; Tandon, 1988; Seth and Sethi, 1991; PRIA, 1991.

6 Ancient Aryan religious scripture composed between 1,500 B.C. and 1,000 B.C. Although the first settled cultures can be dated back to the end of the fourth millennium, the earliest history of voluntarism can be traced back only to the *Rig Veda* (see Dadrawala, 1991). Since the nature of philanthropy did not change with the advent of the Muslims around the late 1100s, the entire period can be classified as the precolonial period. Although the period starts around 1,500 B.C., it is likely that voluntarism became more widespread with the emergence of republics and kingdoms after 600 B.C. The description of the precolonial period is based on Inamder's (1987) work, and to a certain extent on the general history of India (see Basham, 1968; Thapar, 1968; and Spear, 1961), unless otherwise stated.

7 Among the Hindu empires these were the Maurya Empire (*c.* 324 B.C. to 183 B.C.) and the Gupta Empire (*c.* A.D. 320 to A.D. 550). The Muslim rulers formed empires with a lesser degree of social welfare. The two major exceptions were the benevolent regimes of Shersha (*c.* A.D. 1537 to A.D. 1544) and Akbar (*c.* A.D. 1544 to A.D. 1605), which saw the existence of government welfareism. In this context, note that Shersha did not establish his rule over a large section of the subcontinent until A.D. 1539.

8 The word *Samaj* means an association where people abide by certain unwritten rules, beliefs, and norms of human behavior. In this context, note that Raja Ram Mohan Roy had formed the *Atmiya Sabha* (the word Sabha means a gathering of "men" to discuss and debate on issues) as early as 1815 in Calcutta. The *Sabha* later allied with the Christian Unitarians and formed the Unitarian Committee in 1821.

The eroding Hindu base led to the establishment of *Brahmin Sabha* in 1828, which subsequently became the *Brahmo Samaj*. Other examples of *Sabhas* and *Samajs* formed in this period include the *Manohar Dharam Sabha* of Gujarat, *Paramhans Sabha*, *Prathana Sabha*, *Kalyanonnayak Samaj*, and the *Hindu Dharm Sabha* in Maharashtra.

9   Discussion on Sikh associations and Sikh movements in the entire chapter is based on Juergensmeyer (1979), Kapur (1986), and Madan (1991), unless otherwise stated.

10 The tenth *guru* instructed all the true male followers to adopt a common surname, Singh (lion), to avoid caste distinction and establish solidarity among the followers.

11 Discussion on Islamic movements and institutions in the entire chapter is based on the work of Rashid (1977), Minault (1982), Jalal (1985), D'Cruz (1988), Hasan (1990), and Ahmad (1991), unless otherwise stated.

12 Tribes are the indigenous population of India. Among others these include the Mundas, Santals, Hos, Gonds, Bhils, and Oraons. Although most of them have been Hinduized or converted to Christianity, they originally had their own religion which emphasized nature worship, especially of the forests which provided them with their subsistence livelihood.

13 See on this point, Ghosh (1991).

14 The word *Mahasabha* means a grand gathering of "men."

15 The word *Sangam* means association.

16 This section is based on the work of Rungta (1970), Kochanek (1974), an interview, and brochures (FICCI, 1988; ASSOCHAM, n.d.), unless otherwise stated.

17 The trading houses were private British partnership concerns dealing with various types of trades and businesses: indigo and coastal trade, ship and house-owning, farming, manufacturing, banking, bill-brokering, etc. It is to be noted, however, that some Indian firms joined the Calcutta Chamber of Commerce. The Bombay chamber was a joint endeavor of British and Parsi trading companies.

18 Based on Ray (1984) as cited in Bhattacharya (1987), Ellsworth (1991), interviews, and brochures (Bombay Natural History Society, 1983; Bombay Branch of the Royal Asiatic Society, 1954).

19 In traditional Hindu culture and religion, the members of the higher castes would not touch those of the lower castes or eat food prepared or touched by the lower castes, as they were considered "untouchables."

20 The word *Khilafat* means the line of succession to the Prophet Muhammad.

21 *Khalifa* is the successor to the Prophet Muhammad as the head of the Muslim Community.

22 The word *ulama* includes Muslim theologians, jurists, and religious teachers.

23 Discussions on Hindu religious movements and organizations in the entire chapter are based on Minault (1982), D'Cruz (1988), and Gold (1991), unless otherwise stated.

24 Although the *Tablighi Jamat* has generally been classified as a grass-roots movement, we contend that there is some organizational character and permanence exhibited by the movement's local organizations.

25 A fundamentalist organization which subsequently became a political party.

26 Also see Seth and Sethi (1991) in this context.

27 There were, of course, exceptions. Many Gandhians formed NPOs on the basis of Gandhian ideology.

28 Discussions on action groups in this entire chapter are based on Baxi (1986); Fernandes (1981, 1983, 1985, 1986); Fernandes and Lobo (1986); Sethi (1984); Sethi and Kothari (1984); Volken (1985); Karat (1984); D. Roy (1984); and interviews with NPO officials, unless otherwise stated.

29 This section is based on interviews with NGO officials and an NGO newsletter *VANI* (1993).

30 There were several drafts of this policy, of which the latest one available to the author is the 1992 draft.

31 This section is based on interviews with NGO officials and an NGO newsletter *VANI* (1994).

32 Forming NPOs to promote partisan gains is very common among two parties: the Bharatiya Janata Party (BJP) and the Communist Party of India (Marxist) (CPI(M)).

33 Note that here the word "state" refers to political and territorial units. India is divided into political and territorial units known as states and Union territories. There are 22 such states and nine Union territories in India. Whenever lower-cased in this chapter, the term will refer to these political and territorial units.

34 The discussion on Kashmir is based on D'Cruz (1988), Ahmad (1991), Thomas (1992), and Ganguly (1992).

35 Some scholars and NPO officials even find the word "sector" to be objectionable and refer to the sector as a social movement.

36 The words *Seshcha Sevi* mean voluntary, while the words *Sangasthas* and *Sanghatanas* mean organization.

37 According to that doctrine, the working class has a false consciousness resulting from influences of bourgeois cultural and political institutions. Because of that, the role of the party is similar to that of a therapist – it is supposed to assist the working class in attaining true class-consciousness.

38 According to interviews, the dates varied from the 1950s to the 1980s

39 With the exception of welfare wings of churches or Hindu religiou organizations such as the Ram Krishna Mission which mix welfar with development in their project orientation.

40 Note that not all schools and hospitals have a nonprofit status.

41 The legal description draws on PRIA (1987, 1989, 1990), unless other wise stated. Note that some NPOs register under the Partnership Ac of 1932. This act does not give an organization a nonprofit status, bu the rates of taxation are low. Under the Income Tax Act of 1961, th taxable income of a partnership firm is between 3 percent and 24 per cent of its business profit.

42 Most of the State Acts are structured around the Central Act and con tain the same provisions. The major difference is in terms of addi tional sections, additional rules, and constraints that have bee brought about by different states and Union territories.

43 Government-sponsored NPOs have also been registered under th Act. Typical examples are CAPART, the National Labor Institute and the National Dairy Development Board.

44 The Memorandum of Association should include: the name of th society; its objectives; and the names, addresses, and occupations o those members subscribing to it and those who are the members o its governing body. The members of the governing body are als entrusted with the management of the society.

45 These rules and regulations should contain the name and address o the registered office of the society; manner, criteria, and procedur for enrolling and removing various categories of members; rights obligations, and period of membership for the members; criteria manner, and procedure of forming the governing body; manner i which meetings are conducted; notice period for such meetings; des ignation, manner of election, and removal of its office holders; th powers and rights of members; procedure for conducting the annua general body meetings or special meetings; accounts and audit pro cedures; manner in which the objectives, rules, and regulations of th society can be changed; and other provisions that are required b state act.

46 Although the law allows for democratization, the author contend from his observations that this democratic process is not applicabl to certain NPOs, especially NGOs which have a charismatic leader.

47 In some states (for example, Karnataka, Madhya Pradesh, Tami Nadu, and West Bengal), the Registrar of Societies can amend th rules of a society.

48 Although this is not a general rule, some income tax officers view society as a taxable one, if most of the members of the governin body are also paid staff.

49   Trusts are synonymous with foundations.

50   The Act states that a trust is "an obligation annexed to the ownership of property, and arising out of a confidence reposed in and accepted by the owner, or declared and accepted by him, for the benefit of another or of another and the owner" (PRIA, 1987:8). The person who declares the "confidence" is the author of the trust, while the person who accepts the "confidence" is called the trustee.

51   See Dadrawala (1991). See also Consumer Education and Research Center (1991). "Educational trusts" includes research institutions and those that fund such institutions or education in general. Communal trusts are formed for the benefit of a particular community or caste.

52   See also Reddy (1986).

53   Lower castes in India.

54   At least half of the executive committee must be workers.

55   This section is based on PRIA (1990).

56   The benefit of section 80G goes to the donor and not to the NPO, unless it gets an 80G exemption.

57   Although all rupee figures have been converted to 1990 values, the government has not built in inflation and increased these figures to present values.

58   According to section 11 (4A), no tax exemption is available to any charitable trust unless it fulfills the following conditions (PRIA, 1990:167): "the business is carried on by a Trust for public religious purposes and the business consists of printing or publication of books or is a kind notified by the government, or; the business is carried on by the institution wholly for charitable purposes and the work in connection with business is mainly carried on by the beneficiaries of the institution; and separate books of accounts are maintained by the trust." The above conditions were imposed in 1983. It should be noted that if an NPO is publishing educational books and other printed material related to its work and making a profit, it will be taxed. Religious publications are, however, exempted from tax.

59   If a trust is unable to apply 75 percent of its total income for charitable purposes, then the balance can be set aside for specified application within the next ten years under section 11(12) of the Income Tax Act. A notice should, however, be sent to the income tax officer on Form 10 of the Income Tax Act within four months or by 30 June, whichever is later. Errors on Form 10 may lead to taxation at the rate of 62.25 percent.

60   In this context, note that the Indian central state leaves more space for civil society to form outside it. This is discussed in detail in the concluding section.

61   There are of course a few exceptions, such as the Self-Employed Women's Association (SEWA) in Ahmedabad. This NGO has skill-

fully worked around the law to distribute profits to its constituent members. It has simultaneously registered as a trade union and a cooperative. The trade union is used as an association of women's workers for empowering them and the cooperative for economically gainful projects.

62 Note that, like that of many scholars and officials of the development-oriented subsector, the central State's definition is also narrow. But interestingly enough, it has created laws that allow for the existence of a wider variety of NPOs.

References

Ahmad, Mumtaz (1991), "Islamic fundamentalism in South Asia: the Jamaat-i-Islami and the Tablighi Jamaat of South Asia," in *Fundamentalisms Observed*, ed. E. Marty Martin and R. Scott Appleby. Chicago: University of Chicago Press.

ASSOCHAM (Associated Chambers of Commerce and Industry of India) (n.d.), *What is it? What does it do?* New Delhi: ASSOCHAM.

Baig, Tara A. (1985), "Voluntary action: retrospect and prospect." *Mainstream*, 23:11–15.

Basham, A.L. (1968), *The Wonder that was India: A Survey of the History and Culture of the Indian Subcontinent before the coming of Muslims*. 3rd edn. New York: Taplinger Publishing Company.

Baweja, Harinder (1993), "Kashmir: increasting intensity." *India Today* (15 September 1993):26–28.

Baxi, Upendra (1986), "Activism at crossroads with signposts." *Social Action*, 36:378–389.

Bhattacharya, Mohit (1987), "Voluntary associations, development and the state." *The Indian Journal of Public Administration*, 33:383–394.

Bombay Branch of the Royal Asiatic Society (1954), *Sardha-Satabdi Celebrations* (150th Anniversary). Bombay: Bombay Branch of the Royal Asiatic Society.

Bombay Natural History Society (1983), *Hornbill* (Centenary Issue). Bombay: Bombay Natural History Society,.

Borghese, E. (1987), '*Third World development: the role of non-governmental organizations.*' *OECD Observer* 145:10–13.

Brodhead, Tim (1987), "NGOs: in one year out the other?" *World Development*,15 (Supplement): 1–6.

Chaturvedi, H.R. (1987), "Role of voluntary organizations in rural development." *The Indian Journal of Public Administration*, 33:533–546.

Consumer Education and Research Centre (1991), *A Directory of Philanthropic Organisations in Ahmedabad*. Ahmedebad: Consumer

Education and Research Centre.

Dadrawala, Noshir H. (1991), *Handbook on Administration of Trusts*. Bombay: Centre for Advancement of Philanthropy.

Dadrawala, Noshir H. (1992), *The Art of Fund Raising*. Bombay: Centre for Advancement of Philanthropy.

D'Cruz, Emil (1988), "Indian secularism: a fragile myth". New Delhi: Indian Social Institute, Mimeograph.

Deshpande, V. D. (1986), "Code of conduct for rural voluntary agencies." *Economic and Political Weekly*, 21:1304–1306.

Drabek, Anne G. (1987), "Development alternatives: the challenge for NGOs – an overview of the issues." *World Development*, 15 (Supplement):ix–xv.

Elliot, Charles (1987), "Some aspects of relations between the North and the South in the NGO sector." *World Development*, 15 (Supplement): 57–68.

Ellsworth, Edward W. (1991), *Science and Social Science Research in India, 1780-1880: The Role of Anglo-Indian Associations and Government*. New York: Greenwood Press.

Fernandes, Walter (1981), "Nature of people's participation in development: role of voluntary organizations," in *Participatory Research and Evaluation: Experiments in Research as a Process of Liberation*, ed. Walter Fernandes and Rajesh Tandon. New Delhi: Indian Social Institute.

Fernandes, Walter (1983), "Post-conciliar social awareness in the Indian Church." *Vidyajyoti*, 47:279–291.

Fernandes, Walter (1985), "External support for social action groups: the role of macro organizations," in *Social Activists and People's Movements*, ed. Walter Fernandes. New Delhi: Indian Social Social Institute, 1985.

Fernandes, Walter (1986), "The National NGO Convention: voluntarism, the state and struggle for change." *Social Action*, 36:431–441.

Fernandes, Walter, and R.G. Lobo (1986), "Social action groups and search for alternatives," in *Inequality, its Bases and Search for Solutions*, ed. Walter Fernandes. New Delhi: Indian Social Institute.

FICCI (Federation of Indian Chambers of Commerce and Industry) (1988), FICCI. New Delhi: FICCI.

Franda, M. (1983), *Voluntary Associations and Local Development: The Janata Phase*. New Delhi: Young Asia Publishers.

Ganguly, Sumit (1992), "The prospects of war and peace in Kashmir," in *Perspectives on Kashmir: The Roots of Conflict in South Asia*, ed. Raju G.C. Thomas. Boulder, CO: Westview Press.

Gautam, Akhil (1993), "Punjab: peace seems to have returned." *India Abroad* (11 June, 1993):8.

Ghimire, Yubaraj (1992), "Rashtriya Swayamsevak Sangh: altrustic expansion." *India Today* (31 July 1992):27.

Ghosh, Arunabha (1991), "Proving the Jharkand question." *Economic and*

Political Weekly, 26:1173–1181.

Gold, Daniel (1991), "Organized Hinduisms: From Vedic truth to Hindu nation," in *Fundamentalisms Observed*, ed. E. Martin Marty and R. Scott Appleby. Chicago: University of Chicago Press.

Government of India (1992), *Eighth Five Year Plan, 1992–1997, Vol. 1*. New Delhi: Government of India, Planning Commission.

Hasan, Mushirul (1990), "Adjustment and accommodation: Indian Muslims after Partition." *Social Action* 40: 241–258.

Inamder, N.R. (1987), "Role of voluntarism in development." *The Indian Journal of Public Administration*, 33:420–432.

Jagannadham, V. (1987), "Voluntary agencies and social welfare." *The Indian Journal of Public Administration*, 33: 482–491.

Jain, L.C. (1986), "Debates in the voluntary sector: some reflections." *Social Action*, 36:404–416.

Jalal, Ayesha (1985), *The Sole Spokesman: Jinnah, the Muslim League and Demand for Pakistan*. Cambridge: Cambridge University Press.

Juergensmeyer, Mark (1979), "The forgotten tradition: Sikhism in the study of world religions," in *Sikh Studies: Comparative Perspectives on a Changing Tradition*, ed. Mark Juergensmeyer and N. Gerald Barrier. Berkeley: Berkeley Religious Studies Series, Graduate Theological Union.

Kapur, Rajiv A. (1986), *Sikh Separatism: The Politics of Faith*. London: Allen and Unwin.

Karat, Prakash (1984), "Action groups/voluntary organizations: a factor in imperialist strategy." *The Marxist*, 2:51–63.

Kaul, J.N. (1972), "Development of Indian higher education." *Economic and Political Weekly*, 7:1645–1652.

Kochanek, Stanley A. (1974), *Business and Politics in India*. Berkeley: University of California Press.

Korten, David C. (1987), "Third generation NGO strategies: a key to people centred development." *World Development*, 15 (Supplement):145–160.

Kothari, Rajni (1986), "NGOs, the State and world capitalism." *Economic and Political Weekly*, 21:2177–2182.

Madan, T.N. (1991), "The double-edged sword: fundamentalism and the Sikh religious tradition," in *Fundamentalisms Observed*, ed. E. Marty Martin and R. Scott Appleby. Chicago: University of Chicago Press.

May, R. (ed.) (1989), "The emerging role of nongovernmental organizations in shelter and urban development," in *The Urbanization Revolution: Planning a New Agenda for Human Settlements*. New York: Plenum Press.

Minault, Gail (1982), *The Khilafat Movement: Religious Symbolism and Political Mobilization in India*. New York: Columbia University Press.

Ministry of Urban Development (1992), *Draft Housing Policy*. New Delhi: Ministry of Urban Development, Government of India.

Muttalib, M.A. (1987), "Voluntarism and development: theoretical perspectives." *The Indian Journal of Public Administration*, 33:399–419.

Natarajan, S. (1962), *A Century of Social Reform in India*. New York: Asia Publishing House.

Ostergaard, G. and M. Currell. (1971), *The Gentle Anarchists: A Study of the Leaders of the Sarvodaya Movement for Non-violent Revolution in India*. Oxford: Oxford University Press.

Padron, Mario (1987), "Non-governmental development organizations: from development aid to development cooperation." *World Development*, 15 (Supplement):69–77.

Pande, Vindhyeshwari Prasad (1967), *Village Community Projects in India*. London: Asia Publishers.

Paul Chowdhury, D. (1987), "Critical appraisal of voluntary effort in social welfare and development since Independence." *The Indian Journal of Public Administration*, 33:492–500.

PRIA (The Society for Participatory Research in Asia) (1987), *Forms of Organisation: Square Pegs in Round Holes*. New Delhi: PRIA.

PRIA (The Society for Participatory Research in Asia) (1989), *Management of Voluntary Organisations*. New Delhi: PRIA.

PRIA (The Society for Participatory Research in Asia) (1990), *Manual on Financial Management and Accounts Keeping*. New Delhi: PRIA.

PRIA (The Society for Participatory Research in Asia) (1991), *Voluntary Development Organizations in India: A Study of History, Roles, and Future Challenges*. New Delhi: PRIA.

Rashid, Abdur M. (1977), *Islam in the Indo-Pakistan Subcontinent: An Analytical Study of Islamic Movements*. Lahore: National Book Foundation.

Ray, N.R. (ed.) (1984), *Public Associations in India*. Calcutta: Institute of Historical Studies.

Reddy, Rama (1986), "The cooperative sector and governmental control." *Social Action*, 36:370–403.

Roy, Ajit (1985), "Activist groups: fundamental issues," in *Social Activists and People's Movements*, ed. Walter Fernandes. New Delhi: Indian Social Institute.

Roy, Bunker (1988), "Voluntary agencies twenty years from now." *Mainstream*, 26:17–19.

Roy, Dunu (1984), "Between dogma and debate," in *The Non-Party Political Process: Uncertain Alternatives*, ed. Harsh Sethi and Smithu Kothari. New Delhi: United Nations Research Institute for Social Development/ Lokayan.

Rudolph, Lloyd I. and Susanne H. Rudolph (1967), *The Modernity of Tradition: Political Development in India*. Chicago: University of Chicago Press.

Rungta, Radhe S. (1970), *The Rise of Business Corporations in India:*

1851–1900. Cambridge: Cambridge University Press.

Salamon, Lester M. and Helmut K. Anheier (1992), "In search of the non-profit sector I: the question of definitions." *Voluntas*, 3(2):125–151. (See also Chapter 3 in this volume.)

Sen, Jai (1986), "On antivoluntarism: the PADI Committee proposals for protection and regulation of voluntary organizations." *Lokayan Bulletin*, 4:8–36.

Sen, Siddhartha (1992), "Non-profit organizations in India: historical development and common patterns." *Voluntas*, 3:175–193.

Seth, D.L. (1982), "Movements." *Seminar*, 278:42–52.

Seth, D.L. and Harsh Sethi (1991), "The NGO sector in India: historical context and current discourse." *Voluntas*, 2:49–68.

Sethi, Harsh (1984), "Redefinitions: groups in new politics of transformations." *Economic and Political Weekly*, 19:305–316.

Sethi, Harsh (1988), "Trends within." *Seminar*, 348:21–24.

Sethi, Harsh and Smithu Kothari (eds) (1984), *The Non-Party Political Process: Uncertain Alternatives.* New Delhi: United Nations Research Institute for Social Development/Lokayan.

Sharma, G.D. and M.D. Apte (1976), "Graduate unemployment in India." *Economic and Political Weekly*, 11:915–925.

Singh, R.S. (1968) *Nationalism and Social Reform in India: 1885 to 1920.* New Delhi: Ranjit Printers and Publishers.

Spear, Percival (1961), *India: A Modern History.* Ann Arbor: University of Michigan Press.

Tandon, Rajesh (1986), "Regulating NGOs: new moves." *Lokayan Bulletin*, 4:37–42.

Tandon, Rajesh (1988), "Growing stateism." *Seminar*, 348:16–21.

Terry, A. (1983), *Catalysts of Development: Voluntary Agencies in India.* West Hartford: Kumarian Press.

Thakur, Ramesh (1993), "Ayodhya and the politics of India's secularism: a double-standards discourse." *Asian Survey*, 33:645–664.

Thapar, Romilla (1968), *A History of India: Vol. 1.* Baltimore: Penguin Books.

Thomas, Raju G.C. (ed.) (1992), "Reflections on the Kashmir problem," in *Perspectives on Kashmir: The Roots of Conflict in South Asia.* Boulder, CO: Westview Press.

Vaidya, Shanta A. (1985), *Trade Union Organizations in Maharashtra: A Study of Trade Unions in Maharshtra State.* Bombay: Research and Training Programme (Hind Mazdoor Sabha) and Manibehn Kara Institute.

VANI (Voluntary Action Network India) (1993), *Vani News* (October):2.

VANI (Voluntary Action Network India) (1994), *Vani News* (April):1–2.

Verma, K.K. (1979), *Changing Role of Caste Associations.* New Delhi: National Publishing House.

Volken, Henry, (1985), "Action groups: beginning or end of a dream," in *Social Activists and People's Movements*, ed. Walter Fernandes. New Delhi: Indian Social Institute.

Chapter 16

THAILAND

Amara Pongsapich

Introduction

Thailand's nonprofit sector, long viewed by the country's various military governments as a potential if not actual competitor for power, is increasingly recognized as essential to the nation's economic and social development efforts. The distrust of the State and the wariness of its administration have by no means disappeared, as many grass-roots development and advocacy organizations continue to be suspected of harboring communist or other political sentiments that the State deems hostile. Nevertheless, recent long-range plans issued by the government openly call for cooperation with a wide array of nonprofit organizations, including those active in rural development.

The nonprofit sector in Thailand, as in many other countries, has its origins in religion. From its earliest times, Buddhism has been a significant source of philanthropy and social service, and remains so today. Buddhism, however, has also served as a source of political stability, which is why its treatment under various regimes has been notably different from that accorded other nonprofits. During the post-Second World War era, non-religious organizations came to the fore, particularly advocacy and development groups. In spite of periods of suppression, such groups continue to grow in number and type of activity.

This chapter offers an overview of the history of Thailand in relation to the evolution of its nonprofit organizations, describes the types of Thai nonprofit organizations, and summarizes relations among the State, Thai society, and the nonprofit sector.

446

Historical note

Philanthropy in Thailand has a very long tradition. To witness rows of Thai monks begging for food from citizens who give alms every morning is to observe a ritual dating back to the dawn of Buddhism in the country. Buddhism established the foundations of philanthropy, and with it the nonprofit sector. From the earliest times, monks and their monasteries provided refuge for the needy and the sick; their schools offered education to the public, and their precincts were used for communal activities in all localities.

The role of Buddhism, however, went beyond a general ministering to the population's social needs. A thirteenth-century stone inscription attributed to King Ramkamhaeng during the *Sukothai* era reads: "He who is troubled may ring the doorbell of the palace, and the king shall come out to decide the case himself." The king was seen as the fountain of justice and the guarantor of human dignity (Muntarbhorn, 1991). Later, during the *Ayuthaya* period, the Hindu–Buddhist concept of a divine king was incorporated into Thai ruling ideology, helping to legitimize the throne. Merit-making and philanthropic giving became a part of everyday Buddhist life. The king and the populace adhered to the same belief. Well into the twentieth century, religion served to maintain cultural and political stability. This function was rewarded by the monarchy during the 1900s. Relations between the throne and the religious hierarchy, *sangha*,[1] were mediated by Buddhist religious and philanthropic institutions. This influence remained in effect far beyond the 1932 coup which supplanted the monarchy by a nominal "democracy." Indeed, long after the Second World War, the nation's leaders would identify Thailand as a homogeneous, Buddhist country.

Notwithstanding its importance, Buddhism was but one of several forces accounting for the establishment of a Thai philanthropic and nonprofit sector. Other contributing factors included Christian missionaries in the nineteenth century, the indirect influence of British and French colonialism in Asia, fear of Communism in the post-Second World War era, and student activism in the 1970s.

Christian missionaries and Western influences

Missionaries from the West came with the intention of bringing change which would lead to religious conversion. The first

Catholic missionary arrived in Thailand in 1567–1568 from Portugal, followed by the Spaniards and the French. In 1662 there were approximately 200 Catholics in the country, most of whom were non-Thais. The first mission was officially established in 1669. A hospital and a youth group were also established in that same year. This period was considered unsuccessful, however, because few Thais were converted and philanthropic activities introduced by Catholic missionaries were not integrated into Thai society.

Although Thailand was never colonized, it came under the economic and cultural influence of Western European nations. Both King Rama IV (1851–1868) and King Rama V (1868–1910) sent their sons to the West to learn about different ways of life in order to bring change to the country. Catholic missionaries became more successful during the reign of King Rama IV, who initiated the modernization process and opened the country to liberal policies.

Eventually, the Catholic mission was officially recognized as a legal body with the right to land ownership. Two types of land were classified for possible missionary ownership – specifically, land to be used for churches, schools, and housing for priests; and land to be used as a communal compound by Christians for residence and income-generating activities. This permission to own land led to the expansion of church, school, and hospital activities. The French-operated Assumption College was opened in 1885 (Khumthaweeporn, 1990). Philanthropic activities of the Catholic missions certainly helped in gaining converts during the second phase of Catholic activities in Thailand.

After the Second World War the Catholic Church faced the difficulty of being recognized and accepted by the public. The Church realized the need to reform and, instead of putting emphasis on faith, it started viewing religion as a vehicle to solve social problems. It became a prerequisite for developmental workers to learn local culture and indigenous knowledge as important criteria to be integrated with the Catholic concept of salvation. Subsequently, the organizational structure of the Catholic Mission in Thailand, as is the case in other countries of the world, was revised, with an emphasis on cooperation at the regional level.

Protestant missionaries first arrived in Thailand in 1828, more than 200 years after the Catholics. The first, exploratory, phase was classified as being between 1828 and 1878, when King Rama

V announced freedom of religious belief in the country. The London Missionary Society, established in Bangkok, identified the Chinese in Bangkok as the first "target group" to be approached.

The British Protestant groups were followed by American denominations, such as the Baptists and Presbyterians, whose missions were instrumental in the establishment of clinics to treat the deadly diseases of the time. The missionaries of the American Presbyterian Church also helped bring about many innovations, including the country's first newspaper, the *Bangkok Recorder*, for upper-class Bangkok readers, and established the Bangkok Christian Boys' School (Khumthaweeporn, 1990). Between 1878 and 1934, Thai nationals became involved in Protestant organization because of the nationalistic movement after the First World War and the fear of Communism after the Russian Revolution. Unlike the Catholic Mission, the Protestant Mission expanded their proselytizing activities in the form of preaching; but like the Catholics, they built hospitals, schools, churches, and leprosy centers, and worked with minority groups other than the Chinese, with whom they had already established a close relationship.

The contemporary phase of Protestant missionary activity started with the establishment of the Church of Christ of Thailand, which became a fully independent and autonomous body in 1957 after the dissolution of the American Baptist Mission. Another Protestant denomination, the Seventh Day Adventists of Thailand, built a large Mission Hospital and a school.

Toward the end of the nineteenth century, Thailand, although never colonized, became a political buffer zone between the expanding empires of Britain in the west and France in the east. The pressure modernized philanthropy in the sense that secular forms of charity emerged within the Thai upper class. In 1885, for example, women of the royal family, seeking medical care and supplies for wounded soldiers, successfully petitioned King Rama V to establish the *Sapa Unalom Daeng* – the forerunner of the Thai Red Cross. Traveling throughout Western Europe during the same era, King Rama V decided that European institutions should be imported to Thailand to contribute to the country's modernization (Muntarbhorn, 1991). Following this idea, his successor, King Rama VI (1910–1925), established the Thai Boy Scouts. By the turn of the century, other nonprofit organizations emerged, many of which provided a variety of social services. Among them was the

Samakhom Satri Thai Haeng Sayam (Women's City Club), formally established by the female editor of a daily women's newspaper, *Ying Thai*, in the offices of a labor organization (Skroebanek, 1983:33).

Ethnic minorities

Although the Thai rulers and government officials tend to portray Thailand as a homogenous society, ethnic minorities constitute about one-fifth of the Thai population. The largest ethnic minority are the Chinese, who, during the period 1917–1966, made up about 10–13 percent of the entire population (Skinner, 1957). That figure is now much lower, however, because of the assimilation process taking place.

Since these minority groups were often excluded from mainstream society, they maintained their own associations to protect their interests. These associations evolved from the so-called "secret societies" which proliferated in the nineteenth century. Although many of these societies were viewed by the government as mere gangs of robbers, they did provide assistance and protection to certain groups of people. In the late nineteenth and early twentieth centuries, some of those secret societies became inactive, whereas others transformed into legitimate mutual-aid and language associations, serving the needs of occupational groups and new immigrants. Among the more important functions of these associations were providing social welfare and mutual aid, expanding Chinese education, and providing religious and burial services for the Chinese immigrants.

Another welfare organization which became prominent in Bangkok by the early 1920s was the *Pao-te Shan-t'ang*, recognized as a benevolent society in Bangkok. Based on highly eclectic (Confucian, Buddhist, and Taoist) religious precepts, its major activities were collecting and burying corpses found on the streets and unclaimed dead from the *T'ien-hua* Hospital, providing free coffins and burial to destitute families, maintaining a free cemetery on the outskirts of town, and organizing relief to victims of fires and floods.

Among the language associations, the Cantonese Association was the most advanced. It founded a cemetery in 1884 and a clinic in 1903. Between 1927 and 1938, major community associations, such as the Chamber of Commerce and the language associations, substantially reorganized in response to the increased pressure put on the Chinese by the Thai government. The *Hakka*[2] Association was the first to reorganize. A new constitution was drawn up in 1927, membership was regularized, and the Association was registered.

The Chinese Chamber of Commerce also underwent significant changes during this period. In the year 1932–1933, it organized relief for the Shanghai war refugees, arranged for an exhibition in Bangkok of Chinese products, mediated in the rickshaw-pullers' strike, arranged for the return to China of girls abducted to Bangkok for prostitution, assumed full responsibility to the Thai government for several hundred Chinese immigrants detained for their failure to meet immigration requirements and eventually secured their legal entry, and founded and operated the biggest and best Chinese middle school in the country. In 1933, the Chamber tightened its organization according to a new constitution, which provided that the full membership elect an executive committee of 15 members and a supervisory committee of seven, and for the election by the committee members of the chairman, secretary, and treasurer.

The status of the Chinese and the inter-ethnic relations depended largely on government policies. During the *Phibun* Regime, when the government adopted nationalism and anti-foreigner policies, ethnic conflicts were highly visible. Later, Thai–Chinese relations gradually improved. After 1980, when the Communist Party of Thailand was officially abolished, the Thai–Chinese ethnic relations became quite cordial, as the government no longer viewed Chinese associations as a threat to national security. Today clan and speech-group associations have only the social function of providing an opportunity for people of the same clan or speech-group to meet.[3]

The Second World War era

With the proliferation of diverse types within the nonprofit sector, associations were ordered to register with the government under the National Cultural Act in 1942, in an effort to ensure state control over a growing and potentially threatening sector. After the Second World War, the philanthropic nature of Buddhism was viewed by the government as a barrier to an encroaching communist ideology. Buddhist philanthropic institutions were promoted by the State, while other organizations and associations were closely controlled (although not prohibited). As in the pre-coup era, the politically stabilizing role of Buddhist philanthropy was recognized and rewarded by the government.

In 1962, an organization known as the *Thera* Association was revived to monitor and supervise Buddhist activities and institutions. Through the *Thera* Association, whose members are nominated from high-ranking monks, the military dictatorship (1960–1973) continued its policy of tolerating only those activities that were philanthropic.

Other nonprofit organizations, not necessarily Buddhist, also emerged during the period from the mid-1940s through to the mid-1970s, with varied purposes and roles. One example was the housewives' groups, typified by the Women's Cultural Club. This club was established in 1943 by the Prime Minister's First Lady. Its objectives were to promote cultural and social activities among its members, and to provide welfare for the needy. By 1956, it had branches in virtually every province of the country, each headed by the provincial governor's wife. The group has since been reorganized as the National Council of Women in Thailand.

Organizations based on school alumni and vocations also came into existence during this period, as did upper-class business associations promoting economic development, and various social clubs. Many of the latter, including international organizations like the Rotary, Lions, and Sontas, are now national networks, with branches in most or all of the provinces. Religious organizations also operated with provincial branches.

Student activism

During the 1960s, when the country was under military rule, students were not politically active. Some, however, found viable outlets for their socio-political leanings in rural summer camps. Working in these settings enabled many youths from the upper and middle classes to familiarize themselves with the realities of rural poverty and wide economic disparity.

After the student *coup d'etat* on 14 October, 1973, nongovernmental organizations (NGOs) emerged to promote social development from a humanitarian perspective – as opposed to the government-sponsored development plan since 1961, which, in the view of NGOs, benefited the wealthy more than the poor. Most of the new organizations, however, did not formally register as nonprofit. Called public interest nongovernment organizations (PINGO), they demanded radical reforms to stop the alleged transfer of national resources from the poorer to the wealthier sectors of Thai society. But the rise of the left-wing movement generated a right-wing counter-movement, which in turn led to the overthrow of the democratically elected government in 1976. Toward the end of the decade, many grass-roots nonprofit organizations found themselves branded as Communist, and their supporters as Communist agents or sympathizers.

Consequently, the turn of the decade marked a very low period for development activities among NGOs. Student and grass-roots groups were suppressed. The only nonprofits tolerated were those representing the upper classes. Many younger people fled to the jungle to join the Communist Party of Thailand, which offered an alternative vision of economic development.

The present era

This suppression of nongovernmental and nonprofit activity lasted until the latter part of the 1980s. After the fall of the Communist Party of Thailand (CPT) in the 1980s, the Thai government granted an amnesty for all Thai citizens who had fled to the jungle to return home (known as Policy 66/1980). At that time, unregistered groups began to revive their activities, and new groups formed, slowly assuming an increasingly active role in the development of Thai society. Today, most of the public-oriented organizations devoted to development were founded during the late 1980s. They are not registered, and their membership reflects the middle class – a sharp contrast to earlier philanthropic organizations, which represented the nation's economic élite.

International support

Since the fall of Saigon and Phnom Penh in 1975, Thailand has experienced an influx of Vietnamese, Laotian, and Cambodian refugees, most of whom have been placed in refugee camps just inside the Thai border. This situation has influenced the composition of the Thai nonprofit sector, as numerous international organizations have joined with the United Nations High Commissioner for Refugees to offer assistance. Most of these groups are non-Thai, and form a distinct category of nonprofit organizations.

Today, the nonprofit sector in Thailand receives support from a variety of international organizations which can be grouped into two major categories. The first category consists of organizations affiliated with the United Nations, such as UNICEF, UNESCO, UNIFEM, WHO, and UNIFPA. They support projects aimed mainly at benefiting women and children, the promotion of health and family planning, rural development, and the protection of the environment. The second category consists predominantly of private German, British, Scandinavian, Australian, and U.S. organizations and foundations, such as the Friedrich-Naumann-Foundation, the Friedrich-Ebert-Foundation, the Konrad-Adenauer-Foundation, *Terre des Hommes*, the Ford Foundation, the Rockefeller Foundation, CARE International, OXFAM, Save the Children Fund, Redd Barna, and Christian Aid, providing financial support to projects according to their specific funding areas, such as rural development, labor issues, and the development of local self-governance. There is little coordination among the activities of these organizations in Thailand.

Major types of nonprofit organizations

Legally, only three types of nonprofit organizations are recognized and registered by the Thai government: associations, labor unions and federations, and foundations. Other terms exist, such as councils and leagues, but to acquire legal status they must register under one of the three legally acceptable terms. All registered nonprofits are nonpolitical; they must, in fact, declare themselves nonpolitical under their written statement of objectives. Political parties are, on the other hand, registered separately and, of course, allowed to have political objectives.

Unregistered organizations, including development and religious groups, may or may not be recognized by the government, but do relate to Thailand's nonprofit sector, as either component or borderline entities.

Legally registered NPOs

Associations

Foundations and associations are governed by the civil code, a body of law based heavily on the European Roman law system (Muntarbhorn, 1991). The code, technically known as the Civil and Commercial Code, specifies the legal purpose and method of governance for nonprofit organizations. Under Sections 78–109: "A contract of association is a contract whereby several persons agree to unite for a common undertaking other than that of sharing profits. Every association must have regulations and must be registered."

Different types of associations are registered with different government agencies. These include general nonprofit associations, commercial associations, cremation associations, and employers' associations.

General nonprofit associations include organizations whose objectives are not specialized. General associations established for cultural and social purposes may register with the National Cultural Commission in Bangkok, or the provincial governor's office in other provinces. All associations, general or otherwise, must have real memberships, and their boards of directors must be elected from among those memberships. They must hold at least one annual meeting to which all members are invited. Further, the agenda for this meeting must include an election of the board, presentation of an annual report, an annual budget, and a statement of expenditures certified by a qualified accountant (which must later be submitted to the National Cultural Commission). Internal regulations must be clearly identified and must include organizational objectives, membership qualifications, fees, and bylaws pertaining to association activities, such as board electoral procedures. In 1989, the total number of general nonprofit associations (excluding cremation, commercial, and employers organizations) registered after 1942 was 8,404.

Commercial associations include organizations whose objectives are not profit-sharing, but whose membership derives from commercial enterprises. Examples include import–export groups and commodity sales groups. They are registered with the Department of Internal Trade, Ministry of Commerce. They differ from other organizations in that they operate for the interest of members rather than for the public. Commercial associations in Thailand in 1989 numbered 373.

Cremation associations are, in fact, viewed as welfare organizations, attending to the basic needs of people in matters of death and cremation. Buddhist theology, for example, prescribes ceremonies for the proper care of the bodies of the deceased. Joining a cremation association is one way to assure that the rituals are followed correctly. Cremation associations are registered with the Department of Public Welfare, Ministry of Labor and Social Welfare.[4] A separate type of cremation association is composed of customers of the Bank of Agriculture and Agricultural Cooperatives. These groups were established as an organizing mechanism in rural areas, where the Bank conducted extensive services. Eventually, the Bank itself agreed to incorporate cremation associations as part of its normal business activities – a strategy to attract rural customers. At the end of 1989, registered cremation associations totaled 2,773.

Employers' associations, technically established to promote good worker–employer relations and to protect employers' rights and benefits, in fact serve as a mechanism through which business owners counter the power of unions. Based on strict industry lines, the groups register with the Department of Labor. Registration requirements include a founding membership of no less than 30 employers within the same industry; and internal regulations governing membership qualifications and fees, financial management, procedures for the cessation of operations, and strategies for approving agreements on employment conditions. Employer associations themselves can combine in federations (see below).

Labor groups

Unions, like employers' associations, exist technically to promote good relations between employers and employees, but in fact represent the interests of employees when negotiating with employers. Membership consists of employees in a single company, or in several companies within an industry. To register with the Labor Department as a labor union, ten employees designate themselves as founders. Registration requirements include a formal name for the union, a statement of objectives, location, membership qualifications, fees, rights, and obligations. In addition, unions must promulgate regulations governing financial matters, strikes and negotiations with employers, annual meetings, and elections of administrative directors.

Federations can be established by both employer associations and labor unions, which must also be registered with the Department of Labor. Acceptance into a federation must be voted on and approved by more than half of either the union's or the association's members, and the federation's board must represent the membership. Regulations governing the delegates to these meetings are developed by the federations themselves.

Councils are umbrella associations designed to promote education and labor relations activities. They comprise either labor unions and federations, or employer associations and federations. Council formation requires no less than five employer groups, and fifteen labor groups. Laws applicable to both employer and labor organizations apply to the councils.

Foundations

Nonprofit organizations engaged in public welfare activities in their own private capacity for charitable, religious, scientific, literary, or other purposes are defined as foundations under Section 110 of the Civil and Commercial Code. Traditionally, foundations are established in honor of distinguished Thai citizens to provide welfare and relief assistance to the indigenous populations, as well as to promote education, culture, and preservation of the cultural heritage. More recently, foundations are being established for environmental protection and economic development as well.

Applications to establish foundations are submitted to the National Cultural Commission in Bangkok, or to provincial governors' offices elsewhere. Following an initial approval, founders must secure police approval of documents containing a profile of the foundation, its objectives, location, and other data. Collateral of at least US $8,000 must be deposited in a foundation bank account. Upon registration, foundations must submit minutes of board meetings and personal biographies of the directors. Qualifications of directors and managers, meeting schedules, and annual reports are also subject to government regulations. However, the management has broad powers, including the power to change the foundation's original mission.

Foundations derive their revenues primarily from individual donations and/or fundraising drives. They are prohibited from engaging in profit-making activities. In general, the government does not provide any funds for foundations, nor does the business sector become involved in foundation activities. Usually, when a well-known business person dies, a foundation may be established in his or her memory. In 1989, there were 2,966 foundations registered in Thailand. Almost half (1,278) of them focused on funding cultural and educational activities.

Other NPOs

Unregistered groups

In addition to the types of organizations mentioned above, unregistered nonprofit groups organize for specific purposes but do not retain legal standing. Such organizations are known as project or working groups, units, and forums. They tend to be small, and are dedicated to public welfare, community development, and campaign advocacy issues such as human rights, the environment, and cultural promotion. They may, on occasion, combine under umbrella councils or coordinating committees. A 1986 survey of developmental NGOs revealed that most of these groups tend to be found near colleges and universities. The issues they address appeal to young people, who are apparently more willing to work for the public interest, and are easy to recruit.

Grass-roots organizations and advocacy groups usually do not register with government agencies, often because of burdensome endowment or membership requirements. Beyond development and advocacy groups, various unregistered centers and institutions in Thailand operate action projects and/or research programs. Many religious organizations are also unregistered. Every village has a temple or *wat* engaged in religious philanthropic activities. Traditionally, young boys lived at *wats* if they were poor, or if they sought education – the monks there serving both as teachers and healers. Fundraising is carried out at least once a year in a *pha pa* or *kathin* – the annual religious ceremony of presenting robes to Buddhist monks in different monasteries.

In general, unregistered groups operate as unregistered associations, except they need not report to any authority. Many developmental groups prefer not to register because they need not report to anyone. The National Cultural Commission, which registers associations and foundations, has neither the authority nor the manpower to monitor unregistered groups, and thus cannot initiate any actions against those who do not register.

Umbrella organizations

Umbrella organizations, both registered and unregistered, also form part of the Thai nonprofit sector. Calling themselves councils and leagues, some register as associations with the National Cultural Commission in Bangkok or with provincial government offices. Table 16.1 shows a list of the major umbrella groups established and registered as associations during the past half century.

Umbrella groups that do not register are those that coordinate a variety of types of organizations working on particular projects. Technically, they are defined as either coordinating or working committees/groups. Among the unregistered coordinating groups, the best-known is the National Coordinating Committee of Non-Government Organizations for Rural Development (NGO-CORD). Total membership, including its regional subcommittees, encompasses 220 organizations. Other unregistered coordinating groups are, for example, associations active on behalf of children, women, primary health, human rights, slum improvement, and environmental protection. Each such body coordinates between ten and 20 organizations.

The environmental groups, which have been organizing annual Environmental Conferences for the past four years, are expanding, consisting of over 30 organizations in 1992.

Tax treatment

Tax exemption for registered nonprofit associations and foundations is granted by the Ministry of Finance. To qualify for tax-exempt status, an organization must apply for the status, it must be in existence for more than three years, and its books must be endorsed by a certified accountant during that period. Salaries paid to employees are not exempt. Donations to registered non-profits are tax-deductible, upon the consent of the Ministry, but only up to 1 percent of earnings or profits. Donations are tax-deductible only when made to qualified organizations granted the tax-exemption status by the Ministry of Finance.

Maintenance of registered status, and therefore of tax exemption and deductibility, is dependent on submission of annual reports, minutes of meetings, and budgets. It is also dependent on the avoidance of political activity. In 1991, under an announced policy of promoting the nonprofit sector, the interim government established a committee to review much of the legislation governing nonprofits, and recommended tax incentives for the nonprofit sector.

Table 16.1

Major umbrella groups in Thailand

Council	Year of Registration
Hindu Dharma Sabha Bangkok	1943
Council of Church of Christ Association of Thailand	1943
The Netherlands Chamber of Commerce in Thailand	1955
Board of Trade	1955
Council of Buddhist Propagation Foundation	1955
National Council of Women in Thailand	1956
National Council on Social Welfare of Thailand	1959
National Council of Young Buddhists Association	1960
Spiritual Assembly of the Baha'is of Bangkok	1963
The Foundation of the Church of Christ in Thailand	1965
Research Officer Association of the Territorial Defense Department	1966
League of Foundations	1967
The Congress of Parents' and Teachers' Associations of Thailand	1972
National Council for Child and Youth Development	1985
League of Associations	1986
Council of International Popular Culture Association of Thailand	1989
Senior Citizens Council of Thailand	1989
Council of Catholic Education (Thailand)	1989
Council of Science and Technology Associations of Thailand	1989

Society, the State, and the nonprofit sector

Government and Buddhism

Buddhism is not only a religion, but also a major force unifying Thai society. With adherents among 95 percent of the Thai population, it is integral to the nation's culture, and enjoys a special relationship to the State. For example, despite the refusal of the government to declare Buddhism a state religion, Buddhist organizations are subject mainly to their own laws, under the administration of a religious body known as the *Thera* Association. When King Rama V introduced administrative reforms during the late nineteenth century, he promulgated the *Sangha* Act providing for separate administration of Buddhist institutions. The Act was revised in 1941, almost a decade after the democratic reform was instituted. In essence, the revisions provided for the adherence of the hierarchical Buddhist structure to the political and administrative structures of the secular State.

In 1959, a new military dictatorship seized power, and the *Sangha* Act was revised yet again in 1962. This time, the *Sangha* structure was altered to confer authority upon the Supreme Patriarch and the *Thera* Association, whose members are nominated from high-ranking monks to monitor all activities carried on by *Theravada* monks. The *Thera* Association has the authority to order Buddhist institutions to cease operation on religious and moral grounds. Institutions opposing the *Thera's* orders must secure legal recognition from the State.

In general, Buddhist fundraising is governed by religious rather than state authority. Religious donations to temples, in the spirit of "making merit" for a better future, are managed by monks and temple committees. However, foundations established in honor of a particular monk or individual to dispense funds must adhere to state regulations monitored by the National Cultural Commission.

Cultural diversity

Until the Second World War, the government viewed Thailand as an ethnically homogeneous country inhabited only by the Thai people. The non-Thai ethnic minorities were outside the Thai social structure. They lived as separate groups, but intermixed with the Thai, having free cultural and economic exchanges. Among lowland groups, cultural borrowing, adoption, and assimilation were accepted and even welcomed.

Nationalism in Thailand is a recent phenomenon. The question of ethnic differences became important after the formation of a nation-state. Nationalism was reinforced by King Rama VI's anti-Chinese policies. Thus, in modern times, Thai society has been vigorously indoctrinated with nationalistic sentiments that were supposed to serve as a "psychological foundation" for the Thai (Dhiravegin, 1985:3). After the reign of Rama VI, the government started the process of democratization. However, the constitutional government that came to power after the 1932 *coup d'état* shifted its priorities away from the questions of ethnicity and nationality.

Nationalism re-emerged during the Second World War under the *Phibun* regimes (1938–1944 and 1948–1960). Prime Minister Phibun Songkhram adopted segregation and discrimination policies toward non-Thai ethnic minorities and changed the name of the country from Siam to Thailand. The word "Thai" became an important national symbol. Legally, the Thai are defined as those holding Thai nationality and, rather loosely defined, Thai ethnicity. "Thai-ness" also strongly implies Buddhist religion and Siamese culture. From that standpoint, a "true" Thai is perceived as one who is of Siamese origin and practices Buddhism. All those who do not simultaneously fall into both categories (for example ethnic minorities, Muslims, etc.) are automatically perceived as "non-Thai" (Suthasasna, 1985:31–32).

Historical studies of the status of Chinese minorities in Thailand indicate that it changed over time, depending on both government policies and Chinese attitudes toward those policies. Under the *Phibun* regimes, ethnic conflicts were quite intense, but afterwards Thai-Chinese relations gradually improved. After the official dissolution of the Communist party of Thailand in 1980, these relations became quite cordial. As a consequence, the appeal of clan associations and language associations became limited to people of the same clan or dialect. The adoption of market-oriented development policies by the government had a positive impact on Chinese participation. Rather than organizing clan and language associations, the Chinese established their own commercial and trade associations, which became prominent and influential elements of the development process in the country. Other ethnic groups have not been as successful as the Chinese. Minorities in some rural areas are still marginalized, both economically and socially. They have not been able to organize themselves, largely because small groups remain isolated from one another in the mountain terrain, and outside organizing efforts have not yet reached that part of the country.

Another factor that had an effect on ethnic minority organizations is the influence of Catholic and Protestant missionaries. The Catholic missionaries, who were the first to come to Thailand, started working with the Thai people, but were not successful in converting them to Catholicism. By contrast, the Protestants started working with ethnic minorities, both the Chinese and the *Karen* inhabiting the mountain area. The marginal role of these groups in Thai society, and the social and moral support they received from the missionaries, became important factors in converting them to Protestantism.

International organizations came to Thailand to promote economic development and, after 1975, to work with refugees. Although they initially used mostly European and American volunteers, the international NGOs later became focused on projects at the grass-roots level. Local Thai NGOs seeking financial support and mutual collaboration also learned to work with international organizations. Since the government did not support the nonprofit sector, international nonprofit organizations provided a substantial contribution to the development of the Thai nonprofit sector.

Government and other religions

Traditionally, non-Buddhist religious organizations were allowed considerable freedom in Thailand, in terms of their internal organization and the activities of their personnel. But after the fall of Saigon and Phnom Penh in 1975 the government's fear of Communism generated widespread suspicion not only of advocacy and economic development nonprofits, but of foreign religious institutions and foreign nationals, or expatriates, operating within the country. In 1981, the Department of Religious Affairs – with which all churches, temples, mosques, and other houses of worship must be registered – tightened its policy regarding expatriate missionaries. Basically, it restricted distribution of its "letters of recommendation" sought by missionaries who wished to extend their visas – letters which were influential with Thai immigration officials.

By 1983, however, another arm of the State, the Department of Public Welfare, declared a policy of cooperation with foreign volunteers who asked to serve as social workers in Thailand. The Department of Public Welfare announced its own regulations governing the issuance of "letters of recommendation," after the Department of Religious Affairs embarked upon more restrictive criteria for the extension of visas. As a result, the Public Welfare Department provides support for members of foreign voluntary agencies lawfully engaged in public welfare activities. The notion of "foreign volunteers" is understood broadly as any alien-working for a voluntary agency without pay, except for a food allowance, medical care, and transportation.

Students, NGOs, and urban development policy

In 1980, the military offered an amnesty to students and activists who had fled to the jungle in the wake of the 1976 right-wing takeover of the government. Many nonprofit organizations which had operated on a grass-roots level were reactivated, particularly those involved in rural development and in advocacy. As a result of the political thaw during the late 1980s, many non-registered groups reviewed their activities and many new groups were formed. These organizations assumed an important role in the development of Thai society.

Unlike the earlier organizations, composed mainly of members with an upper-class background, the newly established NGOs attracted primarily the middle class, student activists, and unemployed college graduates. These organizations constitute the majority of the NGOs working predominantly in rural areas. A few work in urban settlements and carry out advocacy work. Most of these NGOs are unregistered.

The development of modern grass-roots NGOs was affected by two conditions. First, the problems associated with economic development created a need to understand the plight of the poor and help them to become economically independent. Second, many activists came to the conclusion that the efforts of the government agencies might not be sufficient to provide solutions to social problems. Despite improving relations, tensions between these NGOs and the government remained high throughout the 1980s. The government suspected many nonprofits – in particular, grass-roots groups – of using a legitimate organizational form as a front to carry out anti-State political activities. In addition, some associations and social clubs were suspected of engaging in gambling or other illegal behavior. Still other groups have been charged with using their tax-exemption privileges to import equipment for profit-oriented purposes.

Only recently has this tension and mutual suspicion begun to abate. An example of the improvement in government–nonprofit relations is the establishment of a Joint Coordination Committee (JCC), through which government functionaries and representatives of development-oriented NGOs and volunteer groups meet. The Committee, in turn, sets up regional NGO–CORD subcommittees active in environmental and developmental issues.

In its Sixth and Seventh National Development Plans (1986–1990 and 1991–1995), the government formally acknowledged the role of NGOs in rural development. Among other things, the Plans promote the establishment of local groups to carry out developmental activities. Previously, the only areas allowed for nongovernmental organizations were for-profit business and investment.

Two factors accounting for the change in the government's policy are widening disparities in wealth resulting from rapid economic development, and a consequent increase in state expenditures. As in other parts of the world, the Thai government has expressed a determination to reduce its budget. The 1991 interim government, consisting largely of appointed technocrats, announced a policy of loosening controls throughout the nonprofit sector. Other announced measures include the liberalization of registration procedures, and the revision of tax laws to spur increasing nonprofit activity.

Defining the Thai nonprofit sector

The Thai nonprofit sector comprises associations and foundations engaged in philanthropy, economic and social development, health and social services, advocacy, and cultural and recreational activities. In general, these organizations meet the criteria of the structural–operational definition of the nonprofit sector suggested by Salamon and Anheier (1992). That is, they are formally organized (whether or not registered), they are separate from the government and operate primarily or largely for the public at large, they do not distribute income in excess of expenses (profits) among their own members, they are self-governing, and they include a meaningful degree of voluntarism. Several types of Thai organizations, however, are not so easily classified:

- A small but rapidly growing number of grass-roots groups, currently active in broad-scale economic and social development, including skills training, certainly fit the definition of a typical nonprofit organization. But to the extent that such groups are successful in actually producing and then marketing goods, they may well re-orient themselves into for-profit enterprises.
- *Wats* and similar religious institutions which have traditionally provided a host of both sacramental and charitable services fit this core definition. However, purely sacramental organizations, existing on an ad hoc basis and performing religious ceremonies only on specific occasions, clearly fall outside the nonprofit sector.
- Labor unions and trade associations may be technically outside the sector. The core definition excludes these organizational types, but in Thailand they operate both for the benefit of their own members (for example in seeking higher wages) and for the public at large. Cooperatives, however, should generally be excluded.
- Organizations such as sports clubs are legally registered as nonprofits, but in reality operate on a for-profit basis. The investment necessary to operate these clubs has led many to charge high membership and service fees. In most cases, the owners make a profit while members receive services in turn. In fact, the only reason they originally registered as nonprofits was because the government required such registration for all organizations involved in any type of economic activity that was not strictly a private enterprise.

Conclusion

With the exception of Buddhist institutions, nonprofit organizations in Thailand have been viewed with deep suspicion by the State, especially during times of military dictatorship. Today, this suspicion shows signs of abating. First, the fear of Communism is declining in the light of recent international developments. Second, Thailand's own rapid economic and social development is generating a widening gap in income distribution, which the State is finding it difficult, if not impossible, to shoulder by itself. While various indicators reveal economic and social improvement at the macroeconomic level, serious discrepancies remain at the microeconomic level. The State increasingly recognizes that the nonprofit sector can play an important role in the resolution of this problem, particularly at the grass-roots level.

Notes

1 *Sangha* is a Buddhist order of monks administered by a hierarchical system with the Supreme Patriarch at its head.
2 Hakka, like Cantonese, is the name of both a local non-Mandarin Chinese language or dialect and of the community (many of them emigrants to South-East Asia and elsewhere) that speak it.
3 Other ethnic minority groups in the country have not been as successful economically or socially. Minorities in rural areas are still very much marginalized and unorganized, mainly because of their scattered residence patterns.
4 The Department of Public Welfare came to be under the Ministry of Labor and Social Welfare after the new Ministry was established in 1993.

References

Dhiravegin, Likhit (1985), "Nationalism and the State in Thailand," in *Minorities in Buddhist Polities: Sri Lanka, Burma and Thailand.* Workshop organized by the International Centre for Ethnic Studies, Sri Lanka, with the cooperation of the Thai Studies Program, Chulalongkorn University and the United Nations University. Bangkok: June 25–28.
Khumthaweeporn, Chatchai (1990), "Christianity in Thailand," in *Belief and Religion in Thai Society.* Bangkok: Sukhothai Thammathirat University.

Muntarbhorn, Vitit (1991), "Occidental philosophy, oriental philology: law and organized private philanthropy in Thailand," in *Philanthropy and the Dynamics of Change in East and Southeast Asia*, ed. by Barnett F. Baron. Occasional Papers of the East Asian Institute, Columbia University. New York: Columbia University.

Salamon, Lester M. and Helmut K. Anheier (1992), "In search of the non-profit sector I: the question of definitions." *Voluntas*, 3(2):125–151. (See also Chapter 3 in this volume.)

Skinner, G. William (1957), "Chinese assimilation and Thai politics." *The Journal of Asian Studies*, XVI, 237–250.

Skroebanek, Siriporn (1983), "Feminist movement in Thailand (1855–1932)." *Satrithat*, 1(3) (August–October).

Suthasasna, Arong (1985), "The Muslims in Thai polity," in *Minorities in Buddhist Polities: Sri Lanka, Burma and Thailand*. Workshop organized by the International Centre for Ethnic Studies, Sri Lanka, with the cooperation of the Thai Studies Program, Chulalongkorn University and the United Nations University. Bangkok: June 25–28.

Part IV

DEFINING THE NONPROFIT
SECTOR IN POST-SOCIALIST
SOCIETIES

The following chapter on Hungary reports on the role the non-profit sector plays in post-Socialist societies. Although significant variations among post-Socialist countries exist, the Hungarian case is instructive for the larger processes and developments that have been, and are, taking place across the countries of this region. Their rich philanthropic traditions, and their relatively well-developed systems of private nonprofit institutions in the nineteenth and early twentieth centuries, were disrupted by war and the subsequent establishment of Communist regimes. Only after the mid-1980s did the countries of Central and Eastern Europe move toward a true multi-sector society, when cautious reforms opened up the first opportunities for the establishment of private institutions. There are, of course, exceptions like Poland, where Catholic Church institutions enjoyed at least some degree of autonomy from the government. Overall, however, before 1989, so-called "social organizations," i.e., nationalized and government-controlled institutions, took on some of the roles nonprofit organizations assume in democratic market economies. Examples include the Red Cross and youth groups, as well as professional and scholarly associations. Overall, however, these organizations were incorporated into the State apparatus, and enjoyed little independence.

This situation changed in the late 1980s, first gradually, and then dramatically, when foundations and associations began to be explicitly recognized by the law. Between 1987 and 1990 association and foundation laws were passed in Hungary, Poland, East Germany, and other countries. Since then, the nonprofit sector in the countries of Central and Eastern Europe has undergone rapid, sometimes explosive, development, and passed through periods of significant legal and administrative changes. These changes reflect an environment where the role of nonprofit organizations is still being formed, alongside similar processes affecting public and for-profit institutions. In a way, the legal and institutional order of post-Socialist countries remained in flux for an initial period; and only recently has the overall legal and policy environment for nonprofit organizations begun to consolidate.

Chapter 17

HUNGARY

Éva Kuti[1]

Introduction

This chapter discusses the definition of the nonprofit sector in Hungary within the context of the economic and political transformations that are taking place in this country. Until quite recently, the institutional set-up of the economy, the polity, even the society were very different from those of Western European countries. The sudden political changes of the late 1980s are now being followed by far-reaching institutional changes in Hungary's economy and society. After having been a "one-sector economy" (Marschall, 1990) for more than 40 years, the Hungarian economy is now restructuring. The withdrawal and redefinition of the State, as well as the development of the business and nonprofit sectors, have gathered momentum in recent years. The situation, however, remains somewhat fluid, full of uncertainties, and with considerable ambiguities about the role and status of public and private organizations.

Therefore, an overview of the different types of nonprofit organizations cannot be more than a snapshot of what is very much an emerging nonprofit sector. Legal, economic, and fiscal regulations as well as definitions are much less established in Hungary than in the United States or in Western European countries. For example, tax laws affecting the nonprofit sector have undergone several significant changes within a short period of time, and new and more comprehensive legislation is in preparation. As can be expected, such frequent modifications significantly influence the nonprofit sector, its size, composition, and structure. In order to understand the present situation and the directions of current changes, as well as the important distinction between foundations and associations, it is necessary to take a closer look at the historical development of the Hungarian nonprofit sector.

Historical background

Despite the centralization of the economy and society under State socialism between 1947 and 1989, foundations and voluntary associations have a long tradition in Hungary that reaches back well into the thirteenth century. In contrast to most other European countries, however, religious institutions were not the dominating force in the initial development of the Hungarian nonprofit sector. The Hungarian monarchy saw its power threatened by the feudal lords and the Catholic Church alike. Challenged by nobility as well as clergy, the monarchy turned to the citizens of the "free royal cities" for support. Consequently, to win and maintain such support, the monarchy granted citizens numerous civic rights and privileges.[2]

These privileges to the citizens in the "free royal cities" helped the development of a citizenry that was willing and able to create social institutions outside the arena of the Catholic Church. For instance, in 1309, in Pozsony, then among the largest towns in Hungary, citizens attempted to seize the ownership of a local hospital from a monastic order (Hahn, 1960:11). The secular hospitals and alms houses in the cities of the fourteenth and fifteenth centuries were mostly financed by private donations, bequests, and contributions by guilds. These early examples of nonprofit organizations in Hungary employed very few staff and were mostly run by volunteers.

Church foundations were usually created by bequests. Secular foundations independent of the Catholic hierarchy began to appear in the sixteenth century. A first law regulating foundations was enacted in 1723. This law gave the King the right to control the activities and the financial accounts of the foundations (Kecskés, 1988:111). Later, this control became the task and responsibility of the central, regional, and local governments.

Cooperation between private foundations and public institutions emerged at an early stage in the development of educational, cultural, and health services in Hungary. Moreover, in the seventeenth century, several cities mandated affluent citizens to bequeath some money or property to public hospitals. Some cities (Modor in 1664; Kőszeg in 1699) declared void testaments of wealthy citizens that failed to include donations to public welfare institutions (Hahn, 1960:16). On the other hand, when the Jesuit order was dissolved in 1773 the government did not nationalize its properties. Instead, an Education Fund was established which worked as an independent public law foundation (Karácsonyi, 1985:319–322). Similarly, when the largest Catholic university was secularized, it did not become a public institution; rather, it became a self-governing public law foundation.

The city of Pest pioneered early examples of what became a common arrangement between public and private institutions in the second half of the nineteenth century. In 1842, public and private contributions co-financed the establishment of an orphanage. The building was provided by the local government (municipality), whereas the operating costs were covered by private donations (Balázs, 1991:85). Foundations contributed to the financing of public welfare institutions in various ways: there were "foundation beds" in many public hospitals, and "foundation places" in many public schools, universities, orphanages, and shelters. Other foundations were set up to provide social services from buildings donated by the government. This general pattern of cooperation between foundations and local governments functioned rather well, and remained in effect until the Second World War.

In contrast to foundations, the relationships between associations and governments were less harmonious. While private foundations contributed to the solution of social problems at local levels, voluntary associations were seen as "emissaries" of the Enlightenment in general, and as advocates for greater political rights. Not surprisingly, secret agents' reports are among the most important sources of information on Hungarian voluntary associations during the last decades of the eighteenth century (Benda, 1957:155–157).

During this period Hungary was a part of the Habsburg Empire. Acceptance of political legitimacy of the Viennese Court, however, remained low among Hungarian citizens and aristocracy alike. The emphasis on agriculture at the expense of industrial and urban development made Hungary an ideal export market for

Austria's industry, which, in turn, resulted in serious distortions in Hungary's economic development. In this context, and with other institutional means lacking, the Hungarian associations became a vehicle for aspirations to political, economic, and cultural independence from Austria and its autocratic regime.

Consequently, almost all associations were abolished after the failed revolution of 1848–1849. In contrast, the endowments of the politically more "neutral" foundations were not confiscated; thus they could continue to deliver services. Between 1848 and 1867, the period called "the age of despotism and absolutism" by Hungarian historians, no voluntary association or group was tolerated by the Austrian governors. Even the Hungarian Academy of Sciences was prohibited from meeting until 1858. Attempts to create the "Transylvanian Museum Society," one of the first associations to be established in that period, were described in a contemporary report as "a triumphant struggle with the three-head dragon of centralization, Germanization, and bureaucracy" (Kovalcsik, 1986(2):68).

The development of a voluntary sector accelerated again only after the "Compromise of 1867" between Hungary and the Habsburg Court. The "Compromise" granted Hungary far-reaching independence from the Austrian Crown with the exception of financial, military, and foreign affairs. A Decree of 1873 regulated voluntary associations (Dobrovits, 1936:8-11). In 1912, regulations required voluntary associations to seek the approval of the Ministry of Internal Affairs for incorporation (Szabó, 1989:5). The same ministry also assumed the right to limit and even to ban voluntary associations if their activities were found detrimental to the State. This regulation remained in force until 1945.

Despite these strict conditions, almost all social, professional, religious, and age-related groups formed voluntary organizations. Even the worker and peasant movements and other political groups suspicious of the authorities found ways to create voluntary associations that the State could somehow "tolerate." Many associations proclaimed social and cultural aims. In some cases they served as a disguise for banned political parties, but in most cases they were a simple expression of civil society and the greater cultural variation of urban Hungary. While governments and Churches tried to gain some influence over voluntary associations, neither could dominate the voluntary sector as a whole.

At that time, voluntary associations were important in cultural and political fields. In contrast, their service-providing role was much less important. This is partly explained by the central role of the State in assuming responsibility for service provision. Its tradition dates back to the nineteenth century.[3] On the other hand, before the Second World War, Hungary remained a rural, traditional society. It is therefore not surprising to find informal systems of health care and other personal social services more important and larger when compared to those in Western Europe. Particularly in rural areas, people in need received informal assistance from neighbors and family members, pre-empting the need for charitable organizations. Consequently, charities represented only 6 percent of all voluntary associations (*Magyar Statisztikai Évkönyvek*, 1934 and 1938), and provided services primarily to the poor in urban areas.

Nevertheless, voluntary organizations played an important role in Hungary before 1945. According to a 1932 survey (*Magyar Statisztikai Évkönyv*, 1934:70–73), the 14,365 voluntary associations had nearly 3 million members among a total population of approximately 8.7 million. Some voluntary groups began to establish peak associations and federations in order to improve their advocacy work and to increase the scope of their activity.

The Second World War and the subsequent Communist takeover cut short the development of the Hungarian nonprofit sector. The Second World War affected the nonprofit sector in several ways. Voluntary associations suffered from a shortage of skilled staff and managers due to war losses. The holocaust reduced the Jewish population, whose charitable donations had been particularly important for the support of voluntary associations. In the course of the Nazi occupation, some voluntary associations became paramilitary organizations or part of the Nazi movement itself. These organizations were dissolved by government decree at the end of the war (Szabó, 1989:5).

In addition, the abolition of other voluntary associations was a much slower, though more painful process (Kovalcsik, 1986, 3:10–31). Rooted in Leninist ideology, the new Communist regime considered individuals as part of a potentially hostile, "bourgeois" mass that needed to be re-educated and re-oriented as socialists. Inherent in that concept was a fear that social movements might fall outside Party control. In order to counteract this fear, foundations were liquidated, and voluntary associations banned in the 1950s. What remained of the nonprofit sector was nationalized and moved under State control. The institutional effect of this far-reaching reorganization of the third sector was the establishment of "social organizations" such as the Hungarian Red Cross, the Adult Education Society, the Peace Council, and the Patriotic Front. Financed almost exclusively from State budgets, they worked in close cooperation with the various organizations of the Communist party.

The 1956 revolution revealed how deep a cleavage had developed between State and society. The failure of the uprising taught lessons to both sides. The Communist party, government, and the Kremlin understood that crude oppression was not the appropriate way of governing Hungary. The population learned that open revolt would most likely fail, and began to adopt more latent and subtle ways of resisting. These strategies created a curious atmosphere of distrust. The government worried about innocent-looking amateur theater groups, youth clubs, intellectual circles, or folk dance halls, yet it did not dare to ban these voluntary organizations – it only persecuted them.

In the 1960s and 1970s, governmental attitudes and legislations *vis-à-vis* voluntary associations were somewhat contradictory. While the State gradually loosened its strict control of voluntary associations, legal regulations became more strict and demanding. A 1970 government decree stated that even preparations to establish voluntary associations should be reported to the proper authorities. A 1981 decree authorized government bodies to ban such preparations for political reasons (Szabó, 1989:6). Nevertheless, it was characteristic of the political situation of the 1980s that the authorities rarely prohibited the creation of voluntary associations, nor did they very often attempt to do so, even though they had the legal means available to them.

In the 1980s, some of the newly emerging nonprofit organizations were substitutes for political parties. The highly political nature of these nonprofit organizations was obvious to the State and the population alike. For instance, one of the most important charities, the Fund for Poverty Relief, was the cradle for the Liberal Party, which later become the second largest political party of Hungary. Until 1989, however, political reform of any kind seemed almost impossible. Since then changes of the utmost importance have occurred, including the legalization of political parties, and the introduction of a market economy.

The nonprofit sector has experienced significant growth since 1989. According to official registers and tax records, both the number of nonprofit organizations and the amount of per capita donations have quadrupled; the number of private donors has doubled. This growth is partly explained by a deep distrust of central government and its institutions. It is not unusual for public opinion polls to report that respondents find the new government as untrustworthy as former ones. There seems to be a general preference to "work around" government in an attempt to control economic, political, and social processes as directly as possible. Nonprofit organizations seem appropriate vehicles for this.

The recent development of the Hungarian nonprofit sector has been very impressive. In the last three years, many different kinds of nonprofit organizations have been established, ranging from large grantmaking and operating foundations to small member associations and local groups. By the spring of 1992, the number of nonprofit organizations had already surpassed the pre-Second World War figure: in January 1995 about 40,000 nonprofit organizations existed among a total population of approximately 10 million.

Major types of nonprofit organizations

Three major types of nonprofit organizations exist in Hungary: social organizations, voluntary associations, and foundations. We will discuss each in turn.

Social organizations

State socialism, once established, either banned or nationalized nonprofit organizations. The nationalized, government-controlled institutions were called social organizations. This type of organization included Churches, trade unions, peace organizations, the Red Cross, minority associations, chambers of commerce, unions among agricultural, industrial, and trade cooperatives, youth organizations, women's organizations, international friendship societies, and quasi-political organizations.

Social organizations were part of the State-socialist ideology and its politics. Not surprisingly, perhaps, some religious teachings by Church organizations were not significantly different from the ideology suggested by Communist youth organizations; the Red Cross raised contributions only for allied developing countries; and leaders of unions and chambers were named by political authorities and paid by the State. The political dependence of these organizations was due to the general political situation, which forced both leaders and members of social organizations to follow the party line. Legally, however, the social organizations were relatively independent, and they were not, at least formally, part of government. They delivered some services, organized important events, and carried out some advocacy activities. That is why social organizations like the Communist youth organizations or the Patriotic Front became temporary shelters for opposition movements, until authorities realized the "danger" and "took the necessary measures."[4]

The status of the social organizations has been changing significantly since 1989. According to the Hungarian Civil Code, the legal regulation of voluntary associations now extends to social organizations, as applicable. There are also some special laws on social organizations which partly come from earlier periods, such as laws affecting the Red Cross and the Chambers of Commerce.[5] The current period is difficult for most social organizations. They are looking for a new identity, and are trying to find a new place and role under the changed conditions. In adapting, they are pursuing three common types of strategies.

First, some follow a strategy of depoliticization whereby they try to strengthen their role as service-providers while deemphasizing their political past. This strategy has been successfully adopted by the Red Cross and the Adult Education Society, because unsatisfied demand for their services made the process of depoliticization easier. While clients and new authorities blame them for their past, their language schools or shelters for refugees are desperately needed.

The second strategy was to establish renewed cooperation with the government. This was clearly the intention of the Churches in giving full ideological support to the government in an attempt to overwrite past behaviors. The renewed ties between government and Churches became evident in a coordinated criticism of Hungarian Radio and Television (HRT). While the government wanted to dispose of the HRT leadership for not following the "official political line," the actual charges were brought forward by the Churches.

The third strategy is the opposite of the second: servile supporters of the former regime find their reincarnation as bellicose advocacy organizations. This political sleight of hand has just been shown by the trade unions and employers' organizations.

The use of the term "social organizations" has also changed. The pejorative negative connotation of the word seems to have weakened somewhat, and the term is used more and more frequently to refer to non-profit-oriented organizations which are neither voluntary associations nor foundations. Consequently, most of these organizations can be considered part of the Hungarian non-profit sector today. From this point of view, their present role is more relevant than their legacy as dependent organizations of State socialist governments.

Voluntary associations

Though the borderline between association and social organization can be subtle, the term "association" is mainly used for describing organizations that are voluntary in the classical, Tocquevillian sense of the word. This does not imply that many voluntary organizations were untouched by the State socialist system. In fact, many "politically neutral" voluntary associations like voluntary fire brigades, sports clubs, or fishermen's and hunters' associations were tolerated and sometimes even supported by the government once the tensions of Stalinism eased in the late 1960s and 1970s. While their actual independence from Party and State might have been questionable at that time, they have now adapted to the changed situation and are no longer different from their counterparts that were established in the 1980s.

The emergence of voluntary associations outside the arena of close state control was one of the first signs of pluralism in Hungarian society (Harangi, 1986). Voluntary associations are defined in Article 31 of the Civil Code as autonomous organizations formed voluntarily for a purpose decided by their members and stated in their founding charter. Unlike foundations, voluntary associations are constituted by formal membership.

The new Association Law of 1989 (Law II/1989) guarantees the right of association. Associations need no government approval to be established. The association may have any purpose members see fit, with the exception of purposes explicitly prohibited by law, such as racism or violence. The legal requirements for the establishment of registered voluntary associations are as follows:

- a minimum of ten members must jointly declare the establishment of the organization;
- a charter and set of bylaws must state the purpose and basic setup and operation of the organization;
- officers must be elected; and
- the association and its officers must be registered in a court.[6]

Foundations

Foundations form a rapidly developing part of the Hungarian nonprofit sector. One-third, or 14,000, of all nonprofit organizations are foundations. All were established quite recently, because foundations were not legally recognized until 1987. They were banned from 1948 until 1978; and from 1978 to 1987, only private endowments without legal personality, and managed by public institutions, could be established. Since 1987 foundations exist as a legal form, although the permission of the relevant public authorities continued to be necessary for the establishment of a foundation until 1990. In that year, Law I/1990 stipulated that private and legal persons can set up foundations for a stated public cause without any government approval.

Conditions for the establishment of foundations are as follows (Civil Code, Article 74):

- stated public cause and purpose;
- founding statute, charter, and bylaws;
- proof that the endowment is sufficient in relation to the stated goals of the foundation;
- registration in a court.[7]

In the founding statute, the founder, or group of founders, sets out the rules and regulations for the governance of the foundation. A trustee, usually an existing or a newly created organization, can be named by the founder in the founding statute. If the founder makes no such arrangement, the court names the trustee of the foundation. If the trustee's activity does not comply with the foundation's purpose, the founder – or, if applicable, the court – can appoint another trustee.

The foundation is to be dissolved if its purpose, as provided for in the founding charter, has been achieved; the time-period for which the foundation was established has expired; or if a special condition is met as specified in the founding statute. The foundation can also be dissolved by the court at the state attorney's request if its purpose can no longer be fulfilled; its registration would now be declined because of interim legal changes; or its trustees do not comply with the foundation's aim and the founder fails to take remedial action. The endowment of dissolved foundations must be used to support similar foundations according to the *cy-près* rule, unless the foundation's charter includes specific instructions otherwise.

Changes in tax legislation

Until 1992, the tax treatment of nonprofit organizations used to be regulated by several, only loosely connected, legal instruments: a government decree issued in 1989 (16/1989), a law on taxation enacted in 1990 (Law XCI/1990), and the annual tax legislation passed by the Hungarian Parliament. These last could have changed the rules of taxation, but they did not.

Tax regulation guaranteed many privileges and exemptions to foundations. In contrast to U.S. tax law, the Hungarian tax treatment of foundations was more favorable than that of voluntary associations and social organizations. Business activities were not restricted, and business incomes were tax-exempt provided they were applied toward the charitable purpose of the foundation. Registered foundations were automatically eligible for tax deductibility.[8]

In case of other nonprofit organizations, only voluntary associations engaged in scientific and technical research, culture, environmental protection, sports, health care, social help, child care, and youth welfare were exempt from corporate income tax, provided profits were spent on charitable purposes. The tax-deductibility of membership fees and donations to voluntary associations was not guaranteed by law, but it could be (and sometimes was) approved by government authorities.

The highly favorable tax status for foundations was changed by the 1992 tax laws (Law LXXXVI/1991 and Law LXXXVII/1991). Registration no longer guarantees that foundations are eligible for either tax exemption or tax deductibility. Their business income will now be tax-exempt only if it does not exceed 10 percent of total income or HUF 10 million per year.

Registered foundations can apply to the Tax Authority for the tax deductibility of donations. This tax-deductible status will be awarded if:

- foundations are engaged in preventive medicine; health care; scientific or technical research; environmental protection; protection of cultural heritage; education; sport; religion; public security; or the care of the elderly, the poor, national or ethnic minorities, refugees, or Hungarian minorities in foreign countries; and
- donors receive neither direct nor indirect compensation for their donations.

The 1994 tax laws limited again the tax deductibility of donations. The limit for the tax-deductible donations of both private persons and companies will be 50 percent of the tax they actually paid in the previous year.

The tax regulation of voluntary associations has also changed. The tax treatment of business income is the same as for foundations. Donations to voluntary associations are still not tax-deductible, unless approved by the Tax Authority on a case-by-case basis.

Proposed changes in civil code

In the fall of 1992, the Ministry of Justice suggested the introduction of new legal types of nonprofit organizations, such as the service-providing nonprofit company, public law foundation, and public law association, into the Civil Code. Moreover, the new legislation has prohibited all other types of nonprofits from engaging in business activities. The modified Civil Code would be complemented by new legislation prepared by the Ministry of Finances to regulate the nonprofit sector financially.

The first draft of the law modifying the Civil Code provoked much debate and was challenged by nonprofit umbrella organizations, the Ministry of Finances, and other ministries. They interpreted this legal initiative by the Ministry of Justice as an attempt to recentralize government. The threat of government control challenged the newly established advocacy organizations to develop coalitions and common strategies. They managed to propose an alternative law, which was then partly accepted by the Ministry of Justice.

This second draft of the Civil Code was a compromise. It did not suggest major changes in the present regulation of private foundations in voluntary associations, nor did it prohibit them from engaging in business activities. It no longer proposed that service-providing nonprofit companies could be established only if government authorities grant special permission. On the other hand, the *cy-près* principle and the restrictions on the political campaigning activities of nonprofits suggested by the alternative law proposal were strongly debated.[9]

Problems of transition

The transition from State socialism to a "three-sector economy" is complex. The initial period of "enthusiastic" decentralization, denationalization, and depoliticization of the economy was followed by inflation, unemployment, and a shortage of skilled managers. Economic problems are compounded by an underdeveloped civil society. The overcentralized, overnationalized Hungarian political and economic system left little room for civil society and the development of public–private systems of cooperation and integration (Hankiss, 1979:94–137). The legitimacy of the public sector was low, as was the degree of citizen participation. Acts in defiance of the State were considered heroic, and deceiving the authorities and evading laws were seen as acts of bravery. This attitude helped preserve autonomy and a potential for political change, but its continuation in the transitional phase causes serious concern.

As stated above, the legal and economic regulation of foundations was very liberal until recently. This was partly a quasi-instinctive reaction to the previous ban, and partly the result of a deliberate decision (Sárközi, 1990:58). The reasoning behind this decision was that the recovery and development of the Hungarian nonprofit sector must be supported by regulation encouraging as many private initiatives as possible. Accordingly, the legal and tax treatment of the formerly banned foundations became more favorable than that of the other nonprofit institutions which had already enjoyed some limited existence before the political changes.

The tax incentives and otherwise high corporate tax rates made foundations a very attractive institutional form in Hungary. For lack of a consistent nonprofit regulation, even service-providing nonprofit organizations – which would be considered as public charities in the United States or voluntary associations in other countries – tended to choose the foundation form. Consequently, many different kinds of institutions carry the label "foundation" in Hungary.

Some foundations are practically for-profit organizations, and may be simply set up for tax evasion. This kind of abuse is especially frequent among corporate foundations. A large proportion of corporate foundations have been set up in order to support the employees or former employees of the founder. While some may contribute to the alleviation of commonly recognized social problems (especially the economic problems of retired people and large families), their "grants" represent little more than tax-exempt incomes for employees and managers alike.[10] The tax authorities are not in a position to enforce current tax laws.

In other cases, foundations were set up to diminish inequalities created by the State socialist system. There are many cultural, recreational, health, social, and community services in Hungary which are available free of charge to some citizens, but not others – especially lower-income groups and the rural population (Manchin and Szelényi, 1986). When these groups invested in a public works project – for instance, a sewage pipe, a pollution control network, a language school, or a cable television network – they expected their contribution to be tax-deductible. Since tax-deductibility could only be realized through foundations, they had to establish such organizations. Obviously, these are not foundations in the classical sense of the word, but member-serving nonprofit organizations. According to the new tax law their status of tax-deductibility should be withdrawn; however, the Tax Authority has not decided on its implementation.

Another problem is represented by public hospitals, clinics, universities, and colleges, which have all set up foundations for fundraising and business activities. Some schools and cultural institutions have also created foundations for the same reasons. These foundations are legally independent, but they are different from grantmaking private foundations, and similar to the fund-raising departments of health, educational, and cultural institutions in the United States. Public institutions in Hungary engage in fundraising and business activities to counteract the effects of budget cuts and declining public subsidies. They must look for additional resources in order to survive. Yet as public organizations they cannot offer tax-deductibility for potential donors. Thus, they create foundations to carry out fundraising and business activities.

The emergence of this type of foundation is indicative for the redefinition and reallocation of public and private roles in Hungary, not only in terms of funding, but also in the sense of service-delivery. For example, some of the former public institutions have already been transformed into foundations. This is the case for grantmaking government bodies and research institutes. Others like libraries, museums, and universities are being transformed from public institutions into public law foundations.

The use of the nonprofit form by the government in providing social services has a long tradition in Hungary, and goes back to the strong German legal influence on Hungary's Roman law system prior to the Second World War. In accordance with German public and civil law, public law foundations took on many social, educational, and cultural activities. Recent developments, however, make the establishment of public law foundations difficult. While foundations distributing government funds have been established, their founders are mostly government bodies, including ministries, and government-controlled social organizations financed from the State budget. Moreover, they often do not own the properties or funds donated to the new foundations.

Such donations represented a peculiar form of privatization. Some politicians created these "government foundations" solely to preserve their status. They became chairmen and board members of these new foundations, and thus were able to decide how to distribute public funds. These foundations were financially more or less dependent on the State budget, but legally they belonged to the private sector. The introduction of the legal form of public law foundation into the Civil Code was a reaction to this problem.

No doubt, one possible avenue of denationalization is to donate parts of State property to nonprofit organizations. The Hungarian government has taken some steps in this direction. Some buildings vacated by the Soviet Army were donated to voluntary organizations engaged in social care. The Association of Hungarian Arts managed to persuade the government to set up a foundation to support the arts. Its endowment consists of the State-owned shares of some joint-stock companies producing applied art objects, and some other properties offering studios and recreational facilities. Similar foundations have been created for supporting the Hungarian book industry, movie industry, and art cinemas.

Despite such examples, the general role that can be played by the nonprofit organizations in the denationalization and deregulation process remains unclear. While the overwhelming State control of the Hungarian economy and society has proved to be harmful in the past, this does not imply that nonprofit organizations can do without any public control of the use of public funds or property. In principle, nonprofit organizations work under public oversight, but for the time being this control is only partially guaranteed by the legal system and only partially supported by general social attitudes among the population.

The new tax regulation of the nonprofit sector shows that both government and legislative bodies seem to realize the problem and are beginning to make efforts to solve it. The fact that new regulations increase the tax authority's responsibility can be interpreted as a step toward the American model. But in contrast, another measure, the incorporation of the public law foundation as a legal form in the Civil Code, was a step in the opposite direction, toward the German system.

The government is planning to develop a comprehensive system of rules and regulations for the whole nonprofit sector. The importance of the sector is becoming more and more recognized, as indicated by direct State support, which has almost tripled over the past three years. According to a decision by Parliament, nonprofit organizations providing basic social, health, and cultural services have a right to the same per capita subsidies as public institutions.

This state support to the nonprofit sector is of vital importance because income levels remain low in Hungary, which limits any significant further growth in the share of private donations. The Parliament's decision accomplished a breakthrough: service-providing nonprofit organizations have become emancipated. This does not necessarily suggest that large numbers of nonprofit schools, hospitals, clinics, and nursing homes will emerge in a short time (the lack of capital represents a serious obstacle to such a development); but it is highly possible that nonprofit organizations may play a more important role in the future.

Defining the nonprofit sector

How well does the structural–operational definition suggested by Salamon and Anheier (1992) apply to the Hungarian situation? We will examine the applicability of each of the five criteria that make up the definition.

Formal, i.e., the organization must have some formal character. This criterion will not cause any difficulty in Hungary. Although there are some researchers who argue that theoretically there is no significant difference between informal groups and formal voluntary organizations, the formal character of the nonprofit organizations is generally accepted. Traditionally, groups without a legal charter are not regarded as organizations by the population.

Private, i.e., the organizations are formally part of the private sector and not institutionally part of government. In principle, this requirement is also met by the majority of Hungarian nonprofit organizations. Except for very few newly created public law foundations and associations, they are all registered under private law as private organizations. In practice, the situation is much more complicated. There are formerly State-controlled organizations which now play opposing roles; foundations created by the former government with boards in which the present government is not represented at all; organizations which were established by the former opposition now in government; foundations set up by State enterprises which have now been privatized, etc. Despite this confusing variety, we can state that Hungarian nonprofit organizations are generally more closely connected to the government than usual in the United States or in Western Europe. Some of the more opaque cases that now populate the Hungarian nonprofit landscape will probably disappear in the course of social and political consolidation.

Self-governing, i.e., the organizations must have their own internal decision-making structures and procedures. This criterion must be met (at least formally) by every Hungarian nonprofit institution, even though some of the modifications expressed in the case of the stipulation "private" would apply here too.

Non-profit-distributing, i.e., the organizations do not distribute profits to their owners and members. The non-distribution constraint is imposed on all Hungarian nonprofit organizations by the laws regulating their activities. Nevertheless, there are some fraudulent foundations which are explicitly set up to serve their founders' interests. It is almost impossible to identify such cases systematically. Abuse of nonprofit status is likely to be more frequent in the newly emerging and quickly changing Hungarian nonprofit sector than in that of other countries.

Voluntary, i.e., the organizations must have some meaningful degree of voluntary citizen involvement. There is no problem with this requirement. Quite a few nonprofit organizations use volunteers; membership is voluntary, as are donations; and almost all nonprofit organizations, including even public law foundations, have non-compensated voluntary boards.

In short, the structural–operational definition is, for the most part, applicable to the Hungarian nonprofit sector. This does not mean that the Hungarian third sector is similar to the American and West European nonprofit sectors. Its development was far from organic. Some of its fields and institutions could not develop at all before the political changes, either because the provision of some welfare services (e.g., health care education, social care) was considered to be a state monopoly, or because their establishment was simply forbidden (e.g., foundations). This distorted development resulted in an unusual structure of the nonprofit sector (with thousands of cultural and recreational organizations, sports clubs, and voluntary fire brigades, and very few service-providing nonprofits). Quick as they were, the recent changes could not completely restructure the nonprofit sector; the traces of the past decades are still clearly visible.

Conclusion

The changes brought about by the last five years have been profound enough to create the first contours of a future framework for the development of a three-sector economy. Needless to say, the division of labor between the three sectors has neither been fully worked out nor firmly established yet. All three sectors are searching for their political, economic, and social roles. There is much discussion about the new division of labor (and power) among government, local authorities, public institutions, employers' and employees' associations, trade unions, corporations, and voluntary nonprofit organizations.

The borderlines between the economic sectors are necessarily fluid and shifting under these conditions. Both the potential for, and the probability of, abuse and misuse of the nonprofit forms are great. Legal and economic regulations will incontestably need further modifications in the near future. The development of the nonprofit sector will be influenced by more general political and economic developments. Its fate cannot be more certain than the fate of the whole Hungarian economy. Development plans and ideas are equally fluid and open to external suggestions and influences.

In both theory and practice, the official and everyday definitions of the Hungarian nonprofit sector are influenced by the pre-war traditions, the State-socialist experience, and the American and Western European models. These various impacts have produced a complex mix of ideologies, terminologies, organizational forms, and regulations. Most government officials and nonprofit leaders agree that a comprehensive regulation of the nonprofit sector is necessary. The first proposal for such a regulation has already been prepared by the Ministry of Finances, but has become the target of a great deal of criticism. The final version of this regulation may be decisive for the choice of the model to be followed.

Hungary is a civil law country; its legal experts are close to the German legal tradition of codification and abstraction in designing comprehensive bodies of law. In contrast, American economic theories and policies are very popular among Hungarian economists, especially among experts dealing with financial and fiscal problems. The simultaneous preparation of two very different regulatory systems in two ministries has been quite revealing. While the Ministry of Justice was working on the inclusion of the legal form of the public law foundation in the Civil Code, the Ministry of Finances prepared the tax law which gave the Tax Authority the right to decide on the tax-deductibility status of foundations. The present situation is far from clear, but developments of the immediate past seem to suggest that the impact of the American model on Hungarian nonprofit regulation (and consequently on nonprofit definition) might be quite important.

Notes

1 Support by OTKA, the Hungarian National Scientific Research Fund, the Lukács Foundation, the Ministry of Culture, and the Ministry of Welfare is gratefully acknowledged.

2 As an early example of this struggle between throne and Church, we can cite the 1279 conflict between the Pope and King László IV. The King asked the citizens of Buda not to let the Pope's legate enter the city (Karácsonyi, 1985:34–35).

3 A law enacted in 1868 required all villages to establish public schools unless Church-run primary schools already operated in the same place (*Magyarország története tíz kötetben*, 1979(3):877–885). Another law passed by the Parliament in 1876 required towns and villages with more than 6000 inhabitants to employ at least one medical doctor. These doctors had to provide the poor with medical services free of charge. The voluntary health insurance societies for industrial workers were replaced by a public health insurance system in 1891 (Hahn, 1960:50–54, 73–77).

4 For instance, in the late 1980s, a leading scholarly publication, *"Medvetánc"* or "Bear-dance," could only be published because the Communist youth organization of Budapest University assumed legal responsibility for the journal. Moreover, as mentioned above, first meetings of the founders of one of the present political parties were organized under the political umbrella of the Patriotic Front.

5 These special laws and government decrees are Decree 25/1955 on the Red Cross, Decree 11/1985 on the Hungarian Chamber of Commerce, Law XXXIII/1989 on the political parties, and Law IV/1990 on the Churches.

6 The establishment of a voluntary association must be followed by an application for registration in the county or capital court. Registration cannot be refused if founders have fulfilled all the requirements of law. Application for registration must contain the articles of the association and the minutes of the statutory meeting.

7 Foundations must be registered in the county or capital court. Registration cannot be refused if founders meet the legal requirements. The foundation's legal personality is granted by the act of registration.

8 Founders or donors can decide whether to contribute a taxed amount

or to deduct their donations from their taxable income. This choice is important for payments from foundations, since payment is exempt from personal income tax if the contribution was a taxed amount, except payments to founders, joining members, or employees. Payments from foundations established before 1 January, 1988 are also tax-exempt.

9 This new version of the bill was passed by the Parliament in November 1993.

10 It is quite common for such foundations to cover the costs of recreational activities and foreign holidays, or to contribute to the education of staff and their family members.

References

Balázs, Magdolna (1991), "Az alapítványi élet indulása Magyar országon" [The beginnings of foundation development in Hungary]. *Esély*, 1: 82–91.

Benda, Kálmán (1957), *A magyar jakobinusok* [The Hungarian Jacobins]. Budapest: Bibliotheca Kiado.

Dobrovits, Sándor (1936), "Budapest egyesületei" [Voluntary associations in Budapest]. *Statisztikai Közlemények*, 74: 166.

Hahn, Géza (1960), *A magyar egészségügy története* [The history of health services in Hungary]. Budapest: Medicina.

Hankiss, Elemér (1979), *Társadalmi csapdák* [Social pitfalls]. Budapest: Magvető.

Harangi, László (1986), *Az öntevékeny szervezetek szerepe Magyarországon* [The role of voluntary organizations in Hungary]. Budapest: Művelődéskutató Intézet.

Karácsonyi, János (1985), *Magyarország egyháztörténete főbb vonásaiban 970–től 1900–ig* [The main events of the history of Churches in Hungary from 970 till 1900]. Budapest: Könyvértékesítő Vállalat.

Kecskés, László (1988), "Az alapítványi jog fejlődése" [The development of the legal regulation of foundations]. *Magyar Jog*, 2: 104–116.

Kovalcsik, József (1986), *A kultúra csarnokai I-III. kötet* [The homes of culture, Vols 1–3]. Budapest: Művelődéskutató Intézet.

Magyar Statisztikai Évkönyv [Hungarian Statistical Yearbook] (1934). Budapest: Központi Statisztikai Hivatal.

Magyar Statisztikai Évkönyv [Hungarian Statistical Yearbook] (1938). Budapest: Központi Statisztikai Hivatal.

Magyarország története tíz kötetben [The history of Hungary in ten volumes], (1979), III kötet [vol. 3]. Budapest: Akadémiai.

Manchin, R. and Szelényi, I. (1986), "Gazdasági és jóléti redisztibúció az államszocializmusban" [Economic and welfare redistribution under State Socialism]. *Medvetánc*, 3–4: 69–111.

Marschall, Miklós (1900), "The Non-profit Sector in a Centrally Planned Economy," in *The Third Sector: Comparative Studies of Non-profit Organizations*, edited by Helmut K. Anheier and Wolfgang Seibel. New York: De Gruyter.

Salamon, Lester, M. and Helmut K. Anheier (1992), "In search of the non-profit sector I: the question of definitions." *Voluntas*, 3(2):125–151. (See also Chapter 3 in this volume.)

Sárkőzi, Tamás (1990), "Az alapítványok jogi szabályozása Magyarországon" [The legal regulation of foundations in Hungary], in *Alapítványi Almanach, Magyarországi Alapitványok Szővetsége*. Budapest: Selyemgombolyító Rt.

Szabó, Lajos (1989), *A megújuló egyesűletek műkődésének szabályai* [Legal rules for the reviving of voluntary associations]. Budapest: Agrárinformációs vállalat.

Part V

CONCLUSION

Chapter 18

CONCLUSION

Lester M. Salamon and Helmut K. Anheier

Several conclusions flow from this Cook's Tour of the world of nonprofit organizations in 13 countries. In the first place, it should be clear from the preceding country chapters that few countries other than the United States, and perhaps the United Kingdom, have a coherent notion of an identifiable nonprofit sector. Rather, what exists is a wild assortment of institutional types that varies greatly in basic composition from place to place. The notions "nonprofit" or "voluntary" are highly culture-bound and dependent on different legal systems, particularly fiscal and corporate law. What is more, countries differ in the way they group some of these organizations into larger sets or "sectors" of one sort or another. Thus, in the German case, *Vereine* form the *Vereinswesen*, or associational sector, and foundations the foundation sector. In the United Kingdom, we find the voluntary sector, in Italy *associazionismo*, and in Sweden the *ideell* sector. In France, the associations and foundations that fit the core definition we presented in Chapter 3 are grouped together with mutual insurance organizations, savings banks and cooperatives into a broader notion referred to as the *économie sociale* sector. In Italy, the so-called social cooperatives and related self-help initiatives would also be included. By contrast, the dominant concept in the developing countries, that of NGOs, embraces a far narrower range of institutions than that reflected in our core definition. Under these circumstances, efforts to make cross-national comparisons using local definitions of this sector are destined to be seriously misleading at best.

In the second place, however, in each of the countries we were able to identify large numbers of entities that fit comfortably within the concept captured in our structural–operational definition. Examples are the German *Verein* and *Stiftung*, the French *association* and *fondation*, the *ideell förening* in Sweden, the *kōeki hōjin* in Japan, the *voluntariato* in Italy, and the nongovernmental organizations in developing countries. This means that while a common notion of a nonprofit sector has not developed across the countries we examined, we are nonetheless finding nonprofit institutions and organizations that are quite similar to each other.

This suggests that the conceptual tangle about the nonprofit sector does not rule out the possibility of meaningful comparative analysis. Even though no single concept of a "nonprofit sector" exists across the countries we studied, and even though local terminologies amount to a confusing picture, there are nonetheless striking similarities in the types of institutions that do exist outside the confines of the State and the market. The great similarity in the definition and treatment of associations among European countries is perhaps the best example of such commonalities. Such similarities point to what we see as one of the most important implications that follows from our work on definitions: if we move away from the *institutional notion of nonprofit sectors* toward an *operational definition of nonprofit organizations*, we indeed do come up with meaningful sets of organizations that can be compared across countries. The structural–operational definition intends to do just that: by identifying a set of organizations that are formal, private, nonbusiness, self-governing, and at least partly voluntary, the definition effectively creates a "nonprofit sector," understood as a set of organizations sharing common characteristics. For empirical purposes, we can then use the standard tools of national income accounting, social indicators research, and other social science methods to measure the size, scope, and structure of the nonprofit sector so defined cross-nationally.

This approach has one major drawback, however. What we carve out as the nonprofit sector in Sweden, the United Kingdom, France, Hungary, Thailand, or India, may not necessarily fit local terminology, nor correspond neatly to any sector notions held at the national level. This means that while we can identify nonprofit *organizations* according to the structural–operational definition, and while we can carry out meaningful measurements on them, we may not find institutional equivalences at the *sectoral* level. *In*

other words, seen from a comparative perspective, we may find nonprof-
it organizations, but not necessarily meaningful national notions of a
nonprofit sector. Thus, by introducing the concept of the nonprofit
sector, as identified by the structural–operational definition, we
are, in part, inventing the very object we want to study.

Does this strategy represent a serious handicap for the cross-
national study of nonprofit organizations? Given the complex and
confusing terminological nature of the topic at hand, we think not.
In fact, particularly in comparative research, such a strategy is
quite common, and, methodologically speaking, an accepted way
to cut through dense and imprecise conceptual dilemmas. Indeed,
the establishment and development of other fields in the social sciences took similar routes by following such an "operational
approach." National income accounting (United Nations, 1993),
organizational and institutional studies (Powell and DiMaggio,
1991) social and economic indicator research (Luxemburg Income
Study, 1990), and even the comparative study of democracy (Linz
and Stepan, 1978) are all examples of areas where cross-national
research efforts took off without prior agreement on substantive
definitions of what constitutes an economy, an organization, a
democracy – or the public good, for that matter.

Searching for underlying factors

What is important about the kind of operational definition developed here is not only that it allows us to depict a set of institutions
that share certain important features across national boundaries,
and to measure their presence or absence, but that it provides the
common denominator, yardstick, or reference point that allows us
to begin to address some of the central theoretical or analytical
issues in this field. What accounts, for example, for the presence or
absence of a more or less distinct nonprofit sector in different
societies? What differences exist in the size, scope, and structure of
this set of organizations from place to place, and what factors
underlie these differences and similarities? How does the nonprofit sector relate to the State or the business sector? And how is
this set of institutions likely to evolve in the years ahead?

Quite clearly, it is impossible to answer these questions fully
here. In fact, they will be more properly treated in subsequent

publications that follow from this project, both at the level of individual country reports, and as part of a fuller comparative analysis (see Salamon and Anheier, 1996 [forthcoming]). But it may be possible to suggest at least some potentially fruitful lines of thought for future exploration. In particular, while the character and role of the nonprofit sector in any country is ultimately shaped by the entire pattern of social, economic, and political development of that country,[1] at least four more specific factors also seem to play a significant role: first, the legal structure that exists; second, the level of development; third, the degree of centralization in political and social terms; and finally, the pattern of government policy towards the nonprofit sector. Let us examine each of these in turn.

Legal system

The legal system in place in a country can significantly affect the organizational universe that exists by making it easier or more difficult to establish certain kinds of institutions. The fact that a nonprofit sector seems to have a more vibrant and coherent existence in the U.K. and the U.S. than on the European continent or in Japan may be traceable at least in part to this factor.

What differentiates these two sets of societies is the presence of a common law legal system in the U.K. and the U.S., as opposed to a civil law system in France, Germany, Italy, Sweden, Hungary, and Japan. In civil law countries, the rights and obligations of individuals and organizations are explicitly spelled out in codified laws. If a particular type of institution is not explicitly provided for in the law in such countries, it does not have a legal right to exist. What is more, the State in such countries is assumed to act for the public, or common, good and is covered by public law. For an organization to function in a public capacity in such societies, it must therefore be given this right by a public institution. This can be done by creating a "public law corporation," i.e., a quasi-private organization that nevertheless functions within the bounds of public law; by designating certain private institutions as "public utilities;" or by specifying certain permissible activities the performance of which qualifies a private organization as a public-benefit entity.

In common law countries, by contrast, private institutions can claim the privilege of operating in the public interest as a matter of right. Instead of carefully codified laws on what constitutes a permissible private action for the public good, common law countries have built up much more ambivalent systems of case law that define what the evolving sense of the community means by the public good. The result is a somewhat more open field for the formation of nonprofit organizations claiming public-benefit status.

To be sure, the differences between common law and civil law legal systems have narrowed in recent decades and are often overwhelmed by other factors. Yet this factor still casts its own distinctive shadow on the type of nonprofit regime that exists.

Level of development

A second crucial factor that seems to affect the shape and character of the nonprofit sector in a society is the level of development it has achieved. "Development" is, of course, an ambiguous concept, embracing a wide assortment of possible dimensions. For our purposes here, however, several key features of development seem particularly important. The first is the degree of social differentiation that economic growth brings with it. As economic growth proceeds, the number and scope of social roles increases substantially, creating new and varied bases for social organization. Instead of a vast peasantry and a small landed élite, new occupations and professions emerge and hence new bases for forming organizations. The greater the degree of differentiation of social roles, therefore, the more highly defined the nonprofit sector is likely to be.

Of special importance in this regard is a second factor often associated with economic development: the rise of urban commercial and industrial élites and of middle-class professionals. In a real sense, the full creation of nonprofit organizations is the work of such elements, even though parts of the nonprofit sector, particularly foundations and cultural and educational institutions, have often reflected the preferences of other social strata as well (DiMaggio, 1987; Karl and Katz, 1987). While it may be an overstatement to assert that "no middle-class, no nonprofit sector," this equation has a certain degree of historical validity (Moore, 1967). At the very least, middle-class professionals have played a prominent role in the emergence of nonprofit sector organizations ever since the industrial revolution, and they are taking on similar functions in much of the developing world and in Eastern Europe. This point finds confirmation in the contrast between the relatively well-developed nonprofit sectors in Brazil and India and those in countries such as Ghana and perhaps Egypt.

Finally, development is important to the emergence of the nonprofit sector because of its implications for communications. Organizations live on communications much as armies march on their bellies. As economic development opens new communications links, rural peasants and the urban poor gain new sources of information not tied to traditional powers-that-be. In the process, they become available for new forms of mobilization and organization. Even middle-class professionals require effective communications to develop organizationally. The invention of the fax and other high-speed communications technology has thus been credited with contributing in important measure to the rapid democratization of Central and Eastern Europe in the latter 1980s, and with the spread of democratic regimes elsewhere in the world as well (Huntington, 1991). It can fairly be credited with the growth of nonprofit organizations in addition (Salamon, 1994).

These features may help to explain some of the peculiar characteristics of the nonprofit sector in the developing countries noted earlier – the politicization of even the most mainstream business and professional associations as new social forces take advantage of the nonprofit form to exert their influence, the importance of grass-roots NGOs functioning as agents of social change and not simply vendors of particular services, and the general sense of tension between the nonprofit sector and the State as new *modi vivendi* are worked out between rising and established social and economic groups.

Degree of centralization

A third factor affecting the structure of the nonprofit sector in different countries seems to be the degree of centralization the citizens are willing (or required) to tolerate in the country's basic political and institutional structures. Generally speaking, the more centralized the structure, the less room for a coherent nonprofit sector. By contrast, the less centralized the structure, the greater the opportunity for the operation of extensive nonprofit organizations. Thus, Germany, which has a federal administrative structure, has traditionally had a significant nonprofit sector, whereas France, a more centralized government, has had a much more limited nonprofit sphere historically. Since the early 1980s, the French government has moved toward greater decentralization, and the country's nonprofit sector has expanded accordingly. Similarly, India's less centralized political system seems to have permitted the rise of a vibrant nonprofit sector, whereas the sector in more centralized Egypt is more limited in both scale and scope.

What shapes the degree of centralization that exists in a particular society is, of course, quite complex. The presence historically of landed élites able to resist the control of a powerful monarch is one such consideration, as reflected in the history of England. So, too, is the presence of distinct ethnic or religious groups determined to maintain their own ways of life within an overall national structure, which characterizes the situation in India, the United States, and to a lesser extent, Germany. Similarly, the degree of centralization is affected by the relationship that exists between political authorities and religious ones. Where Church and State are essentially one, the opportunities for third-sector development are generally limited. Where a sharp separation exists between Church and State, the social space left open for the flowering of a third sector is much more extensive. Thus, the historically close relationship between State and Church in Italy has probably played a role in limiting the development of a coherent nonprofit sector in that country, while the sharp separation has helped to foster third-sector growth in the United States. Similarly, the rise of liberation theology and the break between at least segments of the Catholic Church and the State in Brazil in recent years has helped to stimulate the emergence of a nonprofit sphere in that country.

Governmental policy

A fourth factor affecting the scope and structure of the nonprofit sector in particular places is the posture that government takes toward this set of organizations. Indeed no other single factor may be as crucial to the viability of the nonprofit sector as this one. In part we have examined this factor already in discussing the nature of national legal systems and the degree of administrative centralization. But government's impact on the nonprofit sector has other

dimensions as well. One of these is the overall posture of governing élites toward alternative centers of organized action. Where
such élites are defensive and jealous of other potential power centers, they will either limit the scope of nonprofit organizations and
the incentives for voluntary action, or seek to use such institutions
as instruments for expanding their own influence and control.
Either way, the scope of independent nonprofit action will be
sharply circumscribed. This is the case in many developing countries, where democratic political traditions are still imperfectly
established and élites consequently reluctant to open the way for
truly independent nonprofit action. Elsewhere again, however,
nonprofit development has been circumscribed by hostile or suspicious government attitudes. What is more, such attitudes have
not always sprung from anti-democratic sentiments. On the contrary, they have often been motivated by a desire to promote
democratic control. This was the case in France, for example,
where concerns about the anti-democratic power of guilds and the
Church led to severe restrictions on associations for more than one
hundred years following the French Revolution. Similar tensions
between a popularly elected State and a rigid Church apparatus
led to restrictions on Church-related nonprofit organizations in
late nineteenth and early twentieth-century Italy.

As important as the overall posture taken by governing élites to
alternative centers of organized power is the extent to which the
State turns to such organizations to assist in the delivery of State-
financed services. Such supportive relationships between the
voluntary sector and the State have a long history in the United
States, but expanded greatly during the Great Society era of the
1960s. In the process, they prompted a tremendous surge in nonprofit sector growth (Salamon, 1995). Similarly, the German principle of "subsidiarity" has led to a mammoth pattern of
government support for the nonprofit sector in that country.[2]
More recently, dissatisfaction with exclusive reliance on the State
has led governments in Italy and France to turn to nonprofit organizations to assist in the provision of social welfare services. The
result has been a significant expansion of the nonprofit sector in
both of these countries.

While state support contributes to the growth of the nonprofit
sector, however, it also contributes to conceptual confusion in this
field. For many observers, the receipt of public funds transforms

voluntary organizations into agents of the State, destroying, or at least severely circumscribing, their independence. As we have seen, the U.N. System of National Accounts even treats nonprofit organizations receiving most of their income from government as part of the State for economic accounting purposes. While we have rejected this usage here, and while the empirical evidence does not support this position to the extent critics claim, the concerns nevertheless have some validity.

Conclusion

To be sure, no one of the four factors cited here will determine the contours of the nonprofit sector in a country by itself. What is important is the interaction among them. Thus the presence of a common law tradition is no guarantee of an open posture toward the formation of nonprofit organizations if the level of development and the historic structure of governmental authority work against it. This is evident, for example, in the case of Ghana, which has a common law legal code, but until recently had a political structure hostile to the formation of an independent nonprofit sphere. By contrast, nonprofit organizations have made much headway in Germany despite its civil law system thanks to a tradition of decentralization and the hold of the Catholic doctrine of "subsidiarity," which places a premium on solving problems through private institutions first and permits reliance on government only as a last resort.

While far from a complete "theory" of organizational patterns, the four factors identified here – type of legal system, level of development, degree of centralization, and posture of the State – provide at least a framework for identifying differences and similarities in the character and structure of the nonprofit sector in different locales and a vocabulary for clarifying certain fundamental differences.

Using these four basic dimensions it will be possible to describe more precisely some of the differences and similarities in societies that are relevant to the character and structure of the nonprofit sector. Thus, for example, the United States and the United Kingdom are both developed countries that share a common law tradition, both of which are features generally congenial to the development of the nonprofit sector. But in terms of the degree of centralization, England evolved a far more centralized political and institutional structure than the United States, and this has limited the space available for the development of the nonprofit sector.

Similarly, both Germany and Japan are civil law countries. While this creates a potential for tight limitation of the nonprofit sector, this limitation has materialized much more heavily in Japan than in Germany. One plausible reason for this is the much higher degree of political centralization in Japan, reflecting the homogeneity of the society and the power of the centralizing regimes that took power at the end of the feudal era. In Germany, by contrast, the survival of a tradition of federalism from feudal days, and the principle of subsidiarity borrowed from Catholic doctrine, have helped to preserve a much larger space for the development of nonprofit institutions.

Concepts are the building-blocks of theories. Unfortunately, the field of comparative research on nonprofit organizations and sectors has long suffered from a weakness in its conceptual foundations. This has made it very difficult to move closer toward the ultimate objective of research: the development of better and more comprehensive theories that can explain significant differences among nonprofit organizations and sectors across a broad spectrum of countries. The present volume on conceptual issues has sought to provide a useful, if small, step toward this goal by providing some of the conceptual building-blocks needed for this effort. While much remains to be done, both conceptually and empirically, before we will be able to formulate sound theories in this field, we hope that the preceding chapters have contributed to this endeavor in a constructive way.

Notes

1 See Anheier and Seibel (1990) on this point, particularly pp. 380–385.
2 For a comparative analysis of the U.S. and German systems of government subsidization of nonprofit organizations, see Salamon and Anheier, 1994.

References

Anheier, Helmut K. and Wolfgang Seibel (eds) (1990), *The Third Sector: Comparative Studies of Nonprofit Organizations*. Berlin/New York: De Gruyter.

DiMaggio, Paul (1987), "Nonprofit organizations in the production and distribution of culture," *in The Nonprofit Sector: A Research Handbook*, ed. W.W. Powell, pp. 195–220. New Haven: Yale University Press.

Huntington, Samuel (1991), *The Third Wave: Democratization in the Late Twentieth Century*. Norman, OK: Oklahoma University Press.

Karl, Barry and Stanley Katz (1987), "The American public foundation and the public sphere, 1890–1930." *Minerva*, 19:236–270.

Linz, Juan J. and Alfred Stepan (1987), *The Breakdown of Democratic Regimes*. Baltimore: Johns Hopkins University Press.

Luxemborg Income Study (LIS) (1990), *Poverty, Inequality, and Income Distribution in Comparative Perspective*. New York: Harvester Wheatsheaf.

Moore, Barrington (1967), *The Social Origins of Dictatorship and Democracy*. Boston: Beacon.

Powell, Walter W. and Paul DiMaggio (1991), *The New Institutionalism in Organizational Analysis*. Chicago: Chicago University Press, 1991.

Salamon, Lester M. (1994), "The rise of the nonprofit sector." *Foreign Affairs*, 73(4):109–122.

Salamon, Lester M. (1995), *Partners in Public Service*. Baltimore: Johns Hopkins University Press.

Salamon, Lester M. and Helmut K. Anheier (1994), "Private sector involvement in the delivery of social welfare services: mixed models from OECD countries." *LEED Notebook*, no. 19 (OECD/GD(94)69). Paris: OECD.

Salamon, Lester M. and Helmut K. Anheier (1996), *The Global Nonprofit Sector: A Comparative Analysis*. Manchester: Manchester University Press, forthcoming.

United Nations (1993), *System of National Accounts, 1993* (E.94.XVII.4, ST/ESA/STAT/SER.F/2/Rev. 4). New York: United Nations.

INDEX

Note: Page references in **bold** refer to tables; page references in *italic* refer to figures.